Rome

"All you've got to do is decide to go
and the hardest part is over.

So go!"

TONY WHEELER, COFOUNDER – LONELY PLANET

Contents

(left) **Italian gelato p33**
Rome has some of the world's finest ice-cream shops.

(above) **Pantheon p72** Tourists surround Rome's best-preserved ancient monument.

(right) **Roman Forum p57** Partial view of the ruins from Palatino.

Villa Borghese & Northern Rome p176

Vatican City, Borgo & Prati p116

Tridente, Trevi & the Quirinale p96

Centro Storico p70

Monti, Esquilino & San Lorenzo p136

Ancient Rome p50

Trastevere & Gianicolo p152

San Giovanni & Testaccio p166

Southern Rome p187

Welcome to Rome

A heady mix of haunting ruins, awe-inspiring art and vibrant street life, Italy's hot-blooded capital is one of the world's most romantic and inspiring cities.

Historical Legacies

The result of 3000 years of ad hoc urban development, Rome's cityscape is an exhilarating spectacle. Ancient icons such as the Colosseum, Roman Forum and Pantheon recall the city's golden age as *caput mundi* (capital of the world), while its many monumental basilicas testify to its historical role as seat of the Catholic Church. Lording it over the skyline, St Peter's Basilica is the Vatican's epic showpiece church, a towering masterpiece of Renaissance architecture. Elsewhere, ornate piazzas and showy fountains add a baroque flourish to the city's captivating streets.

Artistic Riches

Few cities can rival Rome's astonishing artistic heritage. Throughout history, the city has starred in the great upheavals of Western art, drawing the top artists of the day and inspiring them to push the boundaries of creative achievement. The result is a city awash with priceless treasures. Ancient statues adorn world-class museums; Byzantine mosaics and Renaissance frescoes dazzle in the city's art-rich churches; baroque facades flank medieval piazzas. Walk around the centre and you'll come across masterpieces by the giants of Western art – sculptures by Michelangelo, canvases by Caravaggio, Raphael frescoes and fountains by Bernini.

Living the Life

A trip to Rome is as much about lapping up the dolce vita lifestyle as gorging on art and culture. Idling around picturesque streets, whiling away hours at streetside cafes, people-watching on pretty piazzas – these are all an integral part of the Roman experience. The tempo rises as the heat of the day gives way to the evening cool and the fashionably dressed *aperitivo* (pre-dinner drinks) crowd descends on the city's bars and cafes. Restaurants and trattorias hum with activity and cheerful hordes mill around popular haunts before heading off to cocktail bars and late-night clubs.

Roman Feasting

Eating out is one of Rome's great pleasures and the combination of romantic alfresco settings and superlative food is a guarantee of good times. For contemporary fine dining and five-star wine there are any number of refined restaurants, but for a truly Roman meal head to a boisterous pizzeria or convivial neighbourhood trattoria. These are where the locals go to dine with friends and indulge their passion for thin, crispy pizzas, humble pastas, and cool white wines from the nearby Castelli Romani hills. Then to finish off, what about a gelato followed by a shot of world-beating coffee?

Why I Love Rome

By Duncan Garwood, Writer

As much as its great monuments – the Colosseum, St Peter's Basilica, the Pantheon – what I love about Rome are its details: the cobbled lanes and hidden corners, the vivid colours, the aroma of freshly ground coffee wafting out of its cafes. Rome's streets and piazzas are an endless source of entertainment and, as a history buff, I get a real kick when I think of all the legendary events that have taken place here. Rome is also a fabulous place to eat well and there's little I love more than a long lunch at a favourite trattoria.

For more about our writers, see p320

Top: The interior of the Pantheon (p72)

Rome's
Top 10

Colosseum *(p52)*

1 No photograph can prepare you for the thrill of seeing the Colosseum for the first time. More than any other monument, this iconic amphitheatre symbolises the power and drama of ancient Rome, and still today it's an electrifying sight. Its muscular form has survived in remarkably good shape and it doesn't take a huge leap of the imagination to picture it in its pomp, its steeply stacked stands full of frenzied spectators as armoured gladiators slug it out on the arena below.

⊙ *Ancient Rome*

Museo e Galleria Borghese *(p178)*

2 The greatest gallery you've never heard of, the Museo e Galleria Borghese houses some of Rome's most spectacular works of art. You'll need to book ahead, but it's a small price to pay for the chance to see a series of sensational baroque sculptures by Gian Lorenzo Bernini, as well as a celebrated statue by Canova and paintings by the likes of Caravaggio, Raphael and Titian. And when you've finished, the surrounding Villa Borghese park is the perfect place to digest what you've just seen. *DAVID* BY GIAN LORENZO BERNINI

⊙ *Villa Borghese & Northern Rome*

Vatican Museums (p122)

3 Rome boasts many artistic highlights, but few are as overpowering as Michelangelo's frescoes in the Sistine Chapel. A kaleidoscopic barrage of colours and images, they come as the grand finale of the Vatican Museums, Rome's largest and most popular art museum. Inside the vast complex, kilometre upon kilometre of corridors are lined with classical sculptures, paintings and tapestries as they lead inexorably towards the Raphael Rooms, a suite of four rooms brilliantly frescoed by Raphael, and, beyond that, the Sistine Chapel.

⊙ Vatican City, Borgo & Prati

St Peter's Basilica (p118)

4 You don't have to be a believer to be bowled over by St Peter's Basilica, Rome's largest and most spectacular church. Everything about the place is astonishing, from the sweeping piazza that announces it, to the grandiose facade and opulent interior. Topping everything is Michelangelo's extraordinary dome, a mould-breaking masterpiece of Renaissance architecture and one of Rome's landmark sights. This is a building that was designed to awe, and even in a city of churches like Rome it stands head and shoulders above everything else. THE DOME (P120), DESIGNED BY MICHELANGELO

⊙ Vatican City, Borgo & Prati

Pantheon (p72)

5 The best preserved of Rome's ancient monuments, the Pantheon is a truly extraordinary building. Its huge columned portico and thick-set walls impress, but it's only when you get inside that you get the full measure of the place. It's vast, and you'll feel very small as you look up at the record-breaking dome soaring above your head. Adding to the effect are the shafts of light that stream in through the central *oculus* (the circular opening at the dome's apex), illuminating the royal tombs set into the circular marble-clad walls.

⊙ Centro Storico

Roman Forum *(p57)*

6 To walk through the tumbledown remnants of the Roman Forum is to retrace the footsteps of the great figures of Roman history – people like Julius Caesar, Augustus and Pompey. And while the ruins can be confusing, it remains a stirring experience to stand at the heart of what was once the heart of the Roman Empire. Nearby, the Palatino (Palatine Hill) is where it all began: where Romulus supposedly killed Remus and founded the city in 753 BC, and where the ancient Roman emperors lived in unimaginable luxury.

👁 *Ancient Rome*

Via Appia Antica *(p189)*

7 The first great superhighway of the Roman world, Via Appia Antica is a gorgeous place to be on a clear, sunny morning. Running through lush green fields and strewn with piles of greying ruins, it's the very picture of pastoral Italian beauty. But the bucolic scenery belies its bloody past. It was here that Spartacus and 6000 of his slave army were crucified, and it was here that the ancients came to bury their dead: well-to-do Romans in elaborate mausoleums, the early Christians in the catacombs.

👁 *Southern Rome*

Capitoline Museums
(p61)

8 In ancient times, Campidoglio (the Capitoline Hill) was home to Rome's two most important temples. Nowadays, the main reason to make the short, steep climb to the top is to admire the views over the Roman Forum and visit the Capitoline Museums on Piazza del Campidoglio, itself one of Rome's most beautiful squares. The world's oldest public museums, these harbour some fantastic classical statuary, including the celebrated *Lupa Capitolina* (Capitoline Wolf), an icon of early Etruscan art, and some really wonderful paintings.

PIAZZA DEL CAMPIDOGLIO (P65)

⊙ *Ancient Rome*

Trevi Fountain *(p100)*

9 A stop at Rome's largest and most famous fountain is a traditional rite of passage for visitors to Rome. Every day crowds gather to toss coins into the fountain's water to ensure that one day they'll return to the Eternal City. The fountain, designed by Nicola Salvi in the 18th century, is a gloriously over-the-top rococo affair depicting wild horses, mythical figures and cascading rock falls. After a recent restoration, it's looking particularly splendid, and is most spellbinding when illuminated after dark.

⊙ *Tridente, Trevi & the Quirinale*

Piazza Navona *(p74)*

10 Rome's monumental piazzas each have their own distinct chatacter: there's the awe-inspiring majesty of St Peter's Square or the market clamour of Campo de' Fiori. But for sheer jaw-dropping beauty, nowhere can beat Piazza Navona. Set atop an ancient Roman arena in the heart of the historic centre, the piazza is the very picture of elegant baroque styling with its three ornamental fountains, domed church and handsome *palazzi* (mansions). Adding to the spectacle are the ringside cafes and the ever-present street artists.

⊙ *Centro Storico*

What's New

Chiesa di Santa Maria Antiqua

Once described as the Sistine Chapel of the early Middle Ages, the Chiesa di Santa Maria Antiqua recently re-opened after years of restoration. Its interior features stunning frescoes and one of the oldest icons in existence. (p60)

The Cloud

Contemporary architecture buffs can now have a field day exploring the city's brand new congress centre, aka La Nuvola (Cloud), designed by Massimiliano Fuksas in the Orwellian EUR district. (p196)

Fendi

Rome's home-grown haute-couture fashion house continues to turn heads with the opening of boutique hotel Fendi Private Suites (p213) and uber-chic rooftop bar Zuma (p111) in the Palazzo Fendi, plus a contemporary art exhibition space at the Palazzo della Civiltà Italiana (p196), its stylish headquarters in EUR.

Sbanco

The latest venture of Stefano Callegari, the founder of hit takeaway chain Trapizzino, trendy Sbanco serves some of the best soft-base pizzas in town, wonderfully accompanied by craft beer. (p172)

Roscioli Caffè

The name Roscioli is always a guarantee of good things. Its deli and bakery set the standards and the recently opened Roscioli Caffè fits the bill perfectly with smooth coffee and artfully crafted pastries. (p90)

Speakeasies

From Spirito (p148), reminiscent of 1920s Prohibition-era New York and hidden in a sandwich shop in Pigneto, to hard-to-find Keyhole (p161) in a Trastevere back street, underground speakeasies serving superbly mixed craft cocktails are Rome's hottest drinking trend right now.

Testaccio Food Stalls

Testaccio's covered market is an increasingly hot foodie hang-out. The latest food stall to open there is Cups, a takeaway backed by top city chef Cristina Bowerman, serving soups and sauces in cardboard cups. (p173)

Anticafé Roma

Modelled on a French cafe, Anticafé Roma is a kind of hybrid cafe–work space–living room where you pay for the time you spend there, not what you consume. There are sofas, board games, mellow tunes and free wi-fi. (p174)

Gentrification of Piazza Vittorio Emanuele

A twinset of brilliant new openings are kick-starting gentrification of the piazza: super-chic Generator Hostel (p214) with a roof terrace to die for, and fashionable Gatsby Café (p148), in a vintage hat shop.

Marta Ray

Ladies on the lookout for fashionable yet practical shoes are well served at Marta Ray, a lovely shop on Via dei Coronari specialising in ballet flats in a range of rainbow colours. (p91)

For more recommendations and reviews, see **lonelyplanet. com/italy/rome**

Need to Know

For more information, see Survival Guide (p259)

Currency

euro (€)

Language

Italian

Visas

Not required by EU citizens. Not required by nationals of Australia, Canada, New Zealand and the USA for stays of up to 90 days.

Money

ATMs are widespread. Major credit cards are widely accepted but some smaller shops, trattorias and hotels might not take them.

Mobile Phones

Local SIM cards can be used in European, Australian and un-locked US phones. Other phones must be set to roaming.

Time

Western European Time (GMT/UTC plus one hour)

Tourist Information

Turismo Roma (www.turismo roma.it/?lang=en; 🎔) Rome's official tourist website has comprehensive information about sights, accommodation, and city transport, as well as itineraries and up-to-date listings.

Daily Costs

Budget: Less than €110

➡ Dorm bed: €20–35

➡ Double room in a budget hotel: €60–130

➡ Pizza plus beer: €15

Midrange: €110–250

➡ Double room in a hotel: €110–200

➡ Local restaurant meal: €25–45

➡ Admission to museum: €5–16

➡ Roma Pass, a 72-hour card covering museum entry and public transport: €38.50

Top End: More than €250

➡ Double room in a four- or five-star hotel: €200–450

➡ Top restaurant dinner: €45–150

➡ Opera ticket €17–150

➡ City-centre taxi ride €10–15

➡ Auditorium concert tickets €25–90

Advance Planning

Two months before Book high-season accommodation.

One month before Check for concerts at www.auditorium. com and www.operaroma.it.

One to two weeks before Reserve tables at A-list restaurants; sort tickets for the pope's weekly audience at St Peter's; book a visit to Palazzo Farnese.

Few days before Book tickets for the Museo e Galleria Borghese (compulsory) and for the Vatican Museums and Colosseum (advisable to avoid queues).

Useful Websites

➡ **Turismo Roma** (www. turismoroma.it) Rome's official tourist website with inspirational and practical information.

➡ **060608** (www.060608.it) Great for practical details on sights, transport, up-coming events and more.

➡ **Coopculture** (www. coopculture.it) Information and ticket booking for Rome's monuments.

➡ **Vatican Museums** (www. museivaticani.va) Book tickets and guided tours to the museums and other Vatican sites.

➡ **Tavole Romane** (www. tavoleromane.it) Italian-language site covering the city's food scene.

WHEN TO GO

Spring (April to June) and autumn (September and October) are the best times – the weather's good and there are many festivals and outdoor events on.

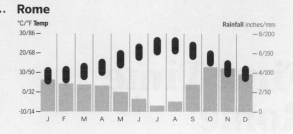

Rome

Arriving in Rome

Leonardo da Vinci (Fiumicino) Airport Leonardo Express trains to Stazione Termini 6.23am to 11.23pm, €14; slower FL1 trains to Trastevere, Ostiense and Tiburtina stations 5.57am to 10.42pm, €8; buses to Stazione Termini 6.05am to 12.30am, €6; private transfers from €22 per person; taxis €48 (fixed fare to within the Aurelian walls).

Ciampino Airport Buses to Stazione Termini 4am to 11.15pm, €5; private transfers €25 per person; taxis €30 (fixed fare to within the Aurelian walls).

Stazione Termini Airport buses and trains, and international trains, arrive at Stazione Termini. From here, continue by bus, metro or taxi.

For much more on **arrival** see p260

Getting Around

Public Transport includes buses, trams, metro and a suburban train network. The main hub is Stazione Termini. Tickets, which come in various forms, are valid for all forms of transport. Children under 10 years travel free.

➡ **Metro** The metro is quicker than surface transport but the network is limited. There are two main lines, A (orange) and B (blue), which cross at Stazione Termini. Trains run between 5.30am and 11.30pm (to 1.30am on Fridays and Saturdays).

➡ **Buses** Most routes pass through Stazione Termini. Buses run from approximately 5.30am until midnight, with limited services throughout the night.

➡ **Foot** Walking is the best way of getting around the *centro storico* (historic centre).

For much more on **getting around** see p262

Sleeping

Rome is expensive and busy; book ahead to secure the best deal. Accommodation ranges from palatial five-star hotels to hostels, B&Bs, *pensioni* and private rooms. Hostels are the cheapest, with dorm beds and private rooms: around Stazione Termini several budget hotels also offer 'dorm beds', meaning you can book a bed in a shared double, triple or quad hotel room. B&Bs and hotels cover every style and price range.

Useful Websites

➡ **Cross Pollinate** (www.cross-pollinate.com) Personally vetted rooms and apartments by the team behind Rome's super-efficient and stylish Beehive (p214) hostel.

➡ **Bed & Breakfast Association of Rome** (www.b-b.rm.it) B&Bs and short-term apartment rentals.

➡ **Bed & Breakfast Italia** (www.bbitalia.it) Rome's longest-established B&B network.

For much more on **sleeping** see p208

ORGANISED TOURS

Taking a guided tour is an excellent way of seeing a lot in a short time or investigating a sight in depth. Both the Colosseum and Vatican Museums offer official guided tours, but for a more personalised service consider a private guide or independent small-group tour (whereby you'll cut out the queue for tickets, skip the line to get in and occasionally gain access to parts of a building not usually open to the public).

First Time Rome

For more information, see Survival Guide (p259)

Checklist

➡ Check your passport is valid

➡ Organise travel insurance

➡ Inform your credit-/debit-card company of your travels

➡ Check that you can use your mobile phone

➡ Book accommodation and tickets for sights like the Vatican Museums, Colosseum, Museo e Galleria Borghese

➡ If coming at Christmas or Easter, check details of services at St Peter's Basilica and other churches

What to Pack

➡ Trainers or comfy walking shoes – cobbled streets can be murder on the feet

➡ Smart-casual evening clothes – Romans dress up to go out

➡ Purse with strap – petty theft can be a problem

➡ Water bottle – refill it at drinking water fountains

➡ Electrical adapter and phone charger

Top Tips for Your Trip

➡ Don't try to cover everything. Focus on a few sights/areas and leave the rest for next time.

➡ Rome's historic centre is made for leisurely strolling, so allow time for mapless wandering. Half the fun of Rome is discovering what's around the corner.

➡ When choosing where to eat, never judge a place by its appearance. Some of the best meals are had in modest-looking trattorias.

➡ To deal with the summer heat, adjust to the local rhythm: go out in the morning, rest after lunch and head out again in the late afternoon.

What to Wear

Appearances matter in Rome. That said, you'll need to dress comfortably because you'll be walking a lot. Suitable wear for men is generally trousers (pants) and shirts or polo shirts, and for women, skirts, trousers or dresses. Shorts, T-shirts and sandals are fine in summer but bear in mind that strict dress codes are enforced at St Peter's Basilica and the Vatican Museums. For evening wear, smart casual is the norm. A light sweater or waterproof jacket is useful in spring and autumn.

Be Forewarned

➡ Rome is a safe city but petty theft can be a problem and pickpockets are active in touristy areas and on crowded public transport. Use common sense and watch your valuables.

➡ In case of theft or loss, always report the incident to the police within 24 hours and ask for a statement.

➡ Expect queues at major sights such as the Colosseum, St Peter's Basilica and Vatican Museums. Pre-booking tickets costs extra but cuts waiting.

➡ August is Italy's main holiday period. Romans desert the city in droves and many shops and eateries close for a week or two around 15 August.

Money

Bancomat (ATMs) are common, but be aware of transaction fees. If an ATM rejects your card, try another before assuming the problem is with your card. Save money by drinking coffee standing at the bar rather than taking a seat. Also carry a water bottle and fill it at Rome's many fountains (nicknamed *nasoni*, meaning 'big noses'). Many museums are free on the first Sunday of the month, while the Vatican Museums are free on the last Sunday of the month.

For more information, see p269.

Taxes & Refunds

A 22% value-added tax known as IVA (Imposta sul Valore Aggiunta) is included in the price of most goods and services. Tax-free shopping is available at some shops.

All stays in the city are subject to an accommodation tax (p209) – the exact sum depends on the length of your sojourn and type of accommodation.

Tipping

Romans are not big tippers, but the following is a rough guide:

➜ **Taxis** Optional, but most people round up to the nearest euro.

➜ **Restaurants** Service *(servizio)* is generally included; if it's not, a euro or two is fine in pizzerias, no more than 10% in restaurants.

➜ **Bars** Not necessary, although many people leave small change if drinking at the bar.

➜ **Hotels** Tip porters about €5 at A-list hotels.

Language

You can get by with English, but you'll improve your experience no end by mastering a few basic words and expressions in Italian. This is particularly true in restaurants where menus don't always have English translations and some places rely on waiters to explain what's on. For more on language, see p273.

1 What's the local speciality?
Qual'è la specialità di questa regione?
kwa·le la spe·cha·lee·ta dee kwes·ta re·jo·ne

A bit like the rivalry between medieval Italian city-states, these days the country's regions compete in speciality foods and wines.

2 Which combined tickets do you have?
Quali biglietti cumulativi avete?
kwa·lee bee·lye·tee koo·moo·la·tee·vee a·ve·te

Make the most of your euro by getting combined tickets to various sights; they are available in all major Italian cities.

3 Where can I buy discount designer items?
C'è un outlet in zona? che oon owt·let in zo·na

Discount fashion outlets are big business in major cities – get bargain-priced seconds, samples and cast-offs for *la bella figura*.

4 I'm here with my husband/boyfriend.
Sono qui con il mio marito/ragazzo.
so·no kwee kon eel mee·o ma·ree·to/ra·ga·tso

Solo women travellers may receive unwanted attention in some parts of Italy; if ignoring fails have a polite rejection ready.

5 Let's meet at 6pm for pre-dinner drinks.
Ci vediamo alle sei per un aperitivo.
chee ve·dya·mo a·le say per oon a·pe·ree·tee·vo

At dusk, watch the main piazza get crowded with people sipping colourful cocktails and snacking the evening away: join your new friends for this authentic Italian ritual!

Etiquette

Italy is quite a formal society and the niceties of social interaction are observed.

➜ **Greetings** Greet people in bars, shops, trattorias etc with a *buongiorno* (good morning) or *buonasera* (good evening).

➜ **Asking for help** Say *mi scusi* (excuse me) to attract attention; use *permesso* (permission) to pass someone in a crowded space.

➜ **Dress** Cover up when visiting churches and go smart when eating out.

Roma Pass

This useful pass is available online, from tourist information points or from participating museums.

➜ **72 hours** (€38.50) Provides free admission to two museums or sites, as well as reduced entry to extra sites, unlimited city transport, and discounted entry to other exhibitions and events.

➜ **48 hours** (€28) Gives free admission to one museum or site, and then as per the 72-hour pass.

Top Itineraries

Day One

Ancient Rome (p50)

 Start the day at the **Colosseum**, Rome's huge gladiatorial arena – try to get there early to avoid the queues. Then head down to the **Palatino** to poke around crumbling ruins and admire sweeping views. From the Palatino, follow on to the **Roman Forum**, an evocative area of tumbledown temples, sprouting columns and ruined basilicas.

> **Lunch** Sample regional specialities at Terre e Domus (p67).

Ancient Rome (p50)

 After lunch climb up to **Piazza del Campidoglio** and the **Capitoline Museums**, where you'll find some sensational ancient sculpture. Done there, enjoy great views from the **Vittoriano** before pushing on to the *centro storico* (historic centre) to explore its labyrinthine medieval streets and headline sights such as the **Pantheon** and **Piazza Navona**.

> **Dinner** Dine on quality wood-fired pizza at Emma Pizzeria (p86).

Centro Storico (p70)

 After dinner get a taste of dolce vita bar life. Depending on what you're after, you could hang out with the beautiful people at chic **Etablì** near Piazza Navona, chat over coffee at **Caffè Sant'Eustachio**, or sup cocktails at the **Gin Corner**.

Day Two

Vatican City, Borgo & Prati (p116)

 On day two, hit the Vatican. First up are the **Vatican Museums**. Once you've blown your mind on the Sistine Chapel and its other myriad masterpieces, complete your tour at **St Peter's Basilica**. If you have the energy, climb its Michelangelo-designed dome for fantastic views over **St Peter's Square**. But if the queues are bad or you're suffering art overload, stop first for an early lunch.

> **Lunch** Savour Rome's best sliced pizza at Pizzarium (p132).

Tridente, Trevi & the Quirinale (p116)

 Recharged, jump on the metro and head back over the river to check out **Piazza di Spagna**. Plan your moves while sitting on the **Spanish Steps**, then push on to the **Trevi Fountain** where tradition dictates you throw a coin into the water to ensure your return to Rome. Next, head up the hill to catch the sunset on **Piazza del Quirinale** in front of the presidential palace, **Palazzo del Quirinale**.

> **Dinner** Dine on creative cuisine at fashionable Pianostrada (p86).

Centro Storico (p70)

 Spend the evening in the buzzing area around **Campo de' Fiori**. **Barnum Cafe** is a top place for cocktails and laid-back tunes or hit **Open Baladin** for a welcome taste of craft beer.

St Peter's Square (p130) and St Peter's Basilica (p118)

Day Three

Villa Borghese & Northern Rome (p176)

 Day three starts with a trip to the **Museo e Galleria Borghese** – don't forget to book – to marvel at amazing baroque sculpture. Afterwards, stroll through **Villa Borghese** down to **La Galleria Nazionale** for an injection of modern art.

 Lunch Fill up on the bargain buffet at the Osteria Flaminio (p184).

Tridente, Trevi & the Quirinale (p96)

In the afternoon, check what's going on at Rome's modernist cultural centre, the **Auditorium Parco della Musica**, before heading back to **Piazza del Popolo**. Just off the piazza, the **Basilica di Santa Maria del Popolo** is a magnificent repository of art. Next, dedicate some time to browsing the flagship stores and designer boutiques in the upscale streets off Via del Corso.

Dinner Enjoy innovation at Glass Hostaria (p160), or tradition at Da Enzo (p158).

Trastevere & Gianicolo (p152)

Over the river, the picture-perfect Trastevere neighbourhood bursts with life in the evening as locals and tourists flock to its many eateries and bars. Get into the mood with a glass of Tuscan red and regional snacks at **La Prosciutteria** before hitting the hard stuff at **Pimms' Good**.

Day Four

Southern Rome (p187)

 On day four it's time to venture out to **Via Appia Antica**. The main attractions here are the catacombs, and it's a wonderfully creepy sensation to duck down into these sinister pitch-black tunnels. Back above ground, you'll find the remains of an ancient racetrack at the nearby **Villa di Massenzio**.

 Lunch Eat on the Appia, at Qui Nun se More Mai. (p197)

Monti, Esquilino & San Lorenzo (p136)

Once you've eaten, head north to Stazione Termini and the nearby **Museo Nazionale Romano: Palazzo Massimo alle Terme**, a superb museum full of classical sculpture and stunning mosaics. Then, drop by the monumental **Basilica di Santa Maria Maggiore**, famous for its mosaics, and the **Basilica di San Pietro in Vincoli**, home to Michelangelo's muscular Moses sculpture. Finish up with some shopping in the fashionable boutiques of the charming **Monti** district.

Dinner Dine on marvellous Umbrian cuisine at L'Asino d'Oro (p145).

Monti, Esquilino & San Lorenzo (p136)

Stay put in Monti, where there's plenty of late-night action. Take your pick of wine bar or cafe to see out the day. **La Bottega del Caffè** is an ever-popular hang-out.

If You Like...

Museums & Galleries

Vatican Museums This vast museum complex's historic collection of classical art culminates in the Sistine Chapel. (p122)

Museo e Galleria Borghese Boasts the best baroque sculpture in town and some seriously good Old Masters. (p178)

Museo Nazionale Romano: Palazzo Massimo alle Terme Fabulous Roman frescoes and wall mosaics headline at this overlooked gem. (p138)

Capitoline Museums The world's oldest public museums are a must for anyone interested in ancient sculpture. (p61)

Galleria Doria Pamphilj This lavish private gallery is full of major works by big-name Italian and Flemish artists. (p82)

Galleria Nazionale d'Arte Antica: Palazzo Barberini A baroque palace laden with paintings by giants such as Caravaggio, Raphael and Hans Holbein. (p105)

Museo Nazionale Etrusco di Villa Giulia A lovely museum housing a wonderful collection of Etruscan art and artefacts. (p182)

Roman Relics

Colosseum Rome's great gladiatorial amphitheatre encapsulates all the blood and thunder of ancient Rome. (p52)

Pantheon With its revolutionary design, this awe-inspiring temple has served as an architectural blueprint for millennia. (p72)

Chiesa della Trinità dei Monti (p102) looms over the Spanish Steps (p98).

BRIAN KINNEY/SHUTTERSTOCK ©

Palatino Ancient emperors lived on the Palatino, the oldest and most exclusive part of imperial Rome. (p54)

Terme di Caracalla The hulking remains of this baths complex hint at the colossal scale of the ancient city. (p169)

Roman Forum This was ancient Rome's bustling centre full of temples, basilicas, shops and streets. (p57)

Domus Aurea Nero's sprawling Golden House was extravagant even by ancient Roman standards. (p140)

Via Appia Antica March down Rome's oldest road, built in the 4th century BC, en route to the catacombs. (p189)

Church Art

Sistine Chapel Michelangelo's frescoes are among the world's most famous works of art. (p126)

St Peter's Basilica Marvel at Michelangelo's *Pietà* and many other celebrated masterpieces. (p118)

Chiesa di San Luigi dei Francesi An ornate baroque church boasting a trio of Caravaggio paintings. (p76)

Basilica di Santa Maria del Popolo Works by Caravaggio, Raphael and Bernini adorn this magnificent Renaissance church. (p99)

Basilica di San Pietro in Vincoli Face up to Michelangelo's muscular *Moses* scuplture. (p140)

Basilica di Santa Maria in Trastevere An ancient basilica celebrated for its golden apse mosaics. (p154)

Basilica di Santa Prassede An off-the-radar gem with some of the city's finest Byzantine mosaics. (p140)

Going Underground

Basilica di San Clemente Descend into the bowels of this multilayered basilica to discover a pagan temple and 1st-century house. (p170)

Vatican Grottoes Extending beneath St Peter's Basilica, these underground chambers contain the tombs of several popes. (p121)

Catacombs Via Appia Antica is riddled with catacombs where the early Christians buried their dead. (p190)

Palazzo Valentini A multimedia display brings excavated ruins to life beneath a stately 16th-century mansion. (p104)

Case Romane Poke around the houses where two Roman martyrs lived before they were executed. (p170)

Tomb of St Peter Guided tours take you beneath St Peter's Basilica to what many claim is St Peter's tomb. (p121)

Street Life

Trastevere Students, tourists, locals, diners, drinkers, junkies and street-hawkers mingle on Trastevere's vivacious streets. (p156)

Spanish Steps Find a space and settle back to watch the ever-changing spectacle on the square below. (p98)

Piazza Navona This beautiful baroque arena provides the stage for a colourful cast of street artists, performers, waiters and tourists. (p74)

Pigneto With its noisy market and vibrant bar scene, this hip district is always lively. (148)

For more top Rome spots, see the following:
➡ Eating (p28)
➡ Drinking & Nightlife (p36)
➡ Entertainment (p40)
➡ Shopping (p44)

PLAN YOUR TRIP IF YOU LIKE...

Campo de' Fiori Market-stall holders holler at each other during the day and student drinkers strut their stuff by night. (p77)

Porta Portese Market Crowds take to the streets each Sunday to explore the stalls at Rome's weekly flea market. (p163)

Sweeping Views

Vittoriano Not recommended for vertigo sufferers, the summit of this marble monolith towers over the rest of Rome. (p66)

Gianicolo Hill Rising above Trastevere, the Gianicolo Hill affords sweeping panoramas over Rome's rooftops. (p157)

Orti Farnesiani A viewing terrace in the Palatino's medieval gardens commands grandstand views over the Roman Forum. (p55)

St Peter's Basilica Climb the dome and you're rewarded with huge 360-degree views. (p118)

Parco Savello Bask in memorable sunset views from this romantic garden on the Aventino hill. (p171)

Castel Sant'Angelo Rome spreads out before you from the panoramic terrace of this operatic castle. (p130)

Month By Month

January

As New Year celebrations fade, the winter cold digs in. It's a quiet time of year but the winter sales are a welcome diversion.

🛍 Shopping Sales

Running from early January, typically the first Saturday of the month, to mid-February, the winter fashion sales offer savings of between 20% and 50%.

February

Rome's winter quiet is shattered by high-spirited carnival celebrations and weekend invasions by cheerful rugby fans in town for the annual Six Nations rugby tournament.

✨ Carnevale Romano

Rome goes to town for carnival, with horse shows, costumed parades, street performers, fireworks and kids in fancy dress. Action is centred on Piazza del Popolo, Via del Corso, Piazza di Spagna and Piazza Navona.

March

The onset of spring brings blooming flowers, rising temperatures and unpredictable rainfall. Unless Easter falls in late March, the city is fairly subdued and low-season prices still apply.

🏃 Maratona di Roma

Sightseeing becomes sport at Rome's annual marathon, held in late March or early April. The 42km route starts and finishes near the Colosseum, taking in many of the city's big sights. Details online at www.maratonadiroma.it.

April

April is a great month in Rome, with lovely, sunny weather, fervent Easter celebrations, azaleas on the Spanish Steps

and Rome's birthday festivities. Expect high-season prices.

✨ Easter

Easter is a big deal in Rome. On Good Friday the pope leads a candlelit procession around the Colosseum, and there are other smaller parades around the city. At noon on Easter Sunday the Pope blesses the crowds in St Peter's Square.

◉ Mostra delle Azalee

From mid-April to early May, the Spanish Steps are decorated with hundreds of vases of blooming, brightly coloured azaleas.

✨ Natale di Roma

Rome celebrates its birthday on 21 April with music, historical re-creations and fireworks. Events are held at Via dei Fori Imperiali and the city's ancient sites.

May

May is a busy, high-season month. The weather's perfect – usually warm enough to eat outside – and the city is looking gorgeous with blue skies and spring flowers.

☆ Primo Maggio

Thousands of fans troop to Piazza di San Giovanni in Laterano for Rome's free May Day rock concert. It's a mostly Italian affair with big-name local performers, but you might catch the occasional foreign guest star.

June

Summer has arrived and with it hot weather and the Italian school holidays. The city's festival season breaks into full stride with many outdoor events.

☆ Lungo il Tevere

Nightly crowds converge on the river Tiber for this popular summer-long event. Stalls, clubs, bars, restaurants, cinemas, even dance floors line the river bank as Rome's nightlife goes alfresco.

☆ Roma Incontra il Mondo

From late June to mid-September Villa Ada is transformed into a colourful multi-ethnic village for this annual event. There's a laid-back party vibe and an excellent program of gigs ranging from reggae to jazz and world music.

🎎 Festa dei Santi Pietro e Paolo

On 29 June Rome celebrates its two patron saints, Peter and Paul, with flower displays on St Peter's Square, fireworks at Castel Sant'Angelo and festivities near the Basilica di San Paolo Fuori-le-Mura.

July

Hot summer temperatures make sightseeing a

physical endeavour, but come the cool of evening, the city's streets burst into life as locals come out to enjoy festivities.

🎎 Festa de' Noantri

Trastevere celebrates its roots with a raucous street party in the last two weeks of the month. Events kick off with a religious procession and continue with much eating, drinking, dancing and praying.

August

Rome melts in the heat as locals flee the city for their summer hols. Many businesses shut down around 15 August but hoteliers offer discounts and there are loads of summer events to enjoy.

🎎 Festa della Madonna della Neve

On 5 August rose petals are showered on celebrants in the Basilica di Santa Maria Maggiore to commemorate a miraculous 4th-century snowfall.

October

Autumn is a good time to visit – the warm weather is holding, Romaeuropa ensures plenty of cultural action and, with the schools back, there are far fewer tourists around.

☆ Romaeuropa

Established international performers join emerging stars at Rome's premier dance and drama festival. Events, staged across town from late September through to early December, range from avant-garde dance performances to

installations, multimedia shows and recitals.

☆ Festa del Cinema di Roma

Held at the Auditorium Parco della Musica in late October, Rome's film festival rolls out the red carpet for Hollywood hotshots and bigwigs from Italian cinema. Consult the program on its website.

November

Although the wettest month, November has its compensations – low-season prices, excellent jazz concerts and no queues outside the big sights.

☆ Roma Jazz Festival

For jazz fans, the Auditorium Parco della Musica is the place to be in November as performers from around the world play to appreciative audiences during the three-week Roma Jazz Festival. See www.romajazz festival.it for further details.

December

The build-up to Christmas feels festive, as the city twinkles in anticipation. Every church displays its own *presepe* (nativity scene), from intricate small tableaux to life-size extravaganzas.

🎎 Piazza Navona Christmas Fair

Rome's most beautiful baroque square becomes a big, brash marketplace as brightly lit market stalls set up shop, selling everything from nativity scenes to stuffed toys and teeth-cracking *torrone* (nougat).

With Kids

Despite a reputation as a highbrow cultural destination, Rome has a lot to offer kids. Child-specific sights might be thin on the ground but if you know where to go there's plenty to keep the little 'uns occupied and parents happy.

Enjoying some gelato

History for Kids

Colosseum

Everyone wants to see the Colosseum (p52) and it doesn't disappoint, especially if accompanied by tales of bloodthirsty gladiators and hungry lions. For maximum effect prep your kids beforehand with a Rome-based film.

Catacombs

Spook your teens with a trip to the catacombs on Via Appia Antica (p189). These creepy tunnels, full of tombs and ancient burial chambers, are fascinating, but not suitable for children under about seven years old.

Palazzo Valentini

Parents and older kids will enjoy the multimedia tour of Roman excavations beneath Palazzo Valentini (p104).

Museums for Kids

Explora

Near Piazza del Popolo, Explora – Museo dei Bambini di Roma (p182) is a hands-on museum for kids under 12, with interactive displays and a free play park.

Museo delle Cere

Go face to face with popes, rock stars and footy players at Rome's cheesy wax museum, the **Museo delle Cere** (Wax Museum; Map p300, D8; ☎06 679 64 82; www.museo dellecereroma.com; Piazza dei Santissimi Apostoli 67; adult/reduced €9/4.50; ☉9am-9pm summer, to 8pm winter; ☐Via IV Novembre).

Museo delle Mura

Walk along a stretch of the Aurelian Wall at the Museo delle Mura (p194), a small museum housed in one of Rome's ancient city gates.

Hands-On Activities

Trevi Fountain

Join the crowds and throw a coin into the Trevi Fountain (p100). And if the kids ask, you can tell them that about €3000 is thrown in on an average day.

Bocca della Verità

Put your hand in the Mouth of Truth (p67), but don't tell a fib or the Bocca may just bite your hand off. According to legend, that is.

Food for Kids

Pizza

Pizza *al taglio* (sliced pizza) is a godsend for parents. It's cheap (about €1 buys two small slices of pizza *bianca* – with salt and olive oil), easy to get hold of (there are hundreds of takeaways around town), and works wonders on flagging spirits.

Gelato

Ice cream is another *manna* from heaven, served in *coppette* (tubs) or *coni* (cones). Child-friendly flavours include *fragola* (strawberry), *cioccolato* (chocolate), and *bacio* (with hazelnuts).

Park Adventures

When the time comes to let the kids off the leash, head to Villa Borghese (p181), the most central of Rome's main parks. There's plenty of space to run around in – though it's not absolutely car-free – and you can

hire family bikes. Other handy parks are Villa Celimontana (p171) and Villa Torlonia (p183).

Animal Spotting

Animal Sculptures

Try to spot as many animal sculptures as you can. There are hundreds around town, including an elephant (outside the Chiesa di Santa Maria Sopra Minerva), lions (at the foot of the Cordonata staircase), bees (on Bernini's fountain just off Piazza Barberini), horses, eagles and, of course, Rome's trademark wolf in the Capitoline Museums (p61).

Cats

Cats have had the run of Rome's streets for centuries. These days they like to hang out in the ancient ruins on the Largo di Torre Argentina (p75).

Zoo

After all those churches and museums, the **Bioparco** (Map p316, E5; ☑06 360 82 11; www.bioparco.it; Viale del Giardino Zoologico 1; adult/reduced €16/13; ⊗9.30am-6pm summer, to 5pm winter; ⛴Bioparco) in Villa Borghese offers some light relief.

Family Day Trips

Ostia Antica

Many of Rome's ancient sites can be boring for children but Ostia Antica (p200) is different. Here your kids can run along the ancient town's streets, among shops, and all over its impressive amphitheatre.

Tivoli

Kids will enjoy exploring the gardens at Villa d'Este (p202) with their water-spouting fountains and grim-faced gargoyles. Nearby, the extensive ruins of Villa Adriana (p201) provide ample opportunity for hide and seek.

Like a Local

Gregarious and convivial, Romans enjoy their city. They love hanging out in its piazzas and speeding around the streets in small cars; they like to dress up and they adore going out. They know theirs is a beautiful city, but they're not jealous and everyone is welcome.

Drink Like a Local

Coffee

Prendere un caffè (having a coffee) is one of the great rituals of Roman life. As a rule, locals will stop at a bar for a coffee in the morning before work, and then again after lunch. To fit in with the crowd, ask for *un caffè* (the term *espresso* is rarely used) and drink standing at the bar. Also, never order a cappuccino after lunch.

For a taste of Rome's finest, head to Caffè Sant'Eustachio (p88) in the historic centre or Sciascia Caffè (p133) in Prati.

Aperitivo

Early evening means *aperitivo* (pre-dinner drinks) in many of Rome's fashionable bars. Hotspots include Gatsby Café (p148), a chic new cafe-bar on Piazza Vittorio Emanuele II, and Momart (p185), a popular bar off Via Nomentana. For a classic Roman drink, try a Negroni.

Cool Neighbourhoods

Trastevere

A picturesque district full of bars, cafes and trattorias, Trastevere has long been a foreigners' favourite. But Romans love it too, and amid the tourist bustle you'll find some characteristic city haunts.

Ostiense

With its disused factories, authentic trattorias and university campus, Ostiense is home to hot clubs and hip bars, as well as several cultural gems.

Pigneto

Pigneto, a former working-class district southeast of Termini, is one of the capital's coolest neighbourhoods, a bar-heavy pocket frequented by bohemians, fun-seekers and trendsetting urbanites.

Testaccio

Down by the Tiber, once-proletarian Testaccio is a local foodie hotspot with its market stalls, traditional Roman trattorias and ever-popular Pizzeria Da Remo (p173).

Evening Passeggiata

The *passeggiata* (traditional evening stroll) is a quintessential Roman experience. It's particularly colourful at weekends when families, friends and lovers take to the streets to strut up and down, slurp on gelato and window-shop.

To partake in the spectacle, head to Via del Corso around 6pm. Alternatively, park yourself on the Spanish Steps and watch the theatrics unfold beneath you on Piazza di Spagna (p98).

Football at the Stadio Olimpico

Football is a Roman passion, with support divided between the two local teams: Roma and Lazio. Both play their home games at the Stadio Olimpico (p186), Rome's impressive Olympic stadium. If you go to a game, make sure you get it right – Roma play in red and yellow and their supporters stand in the Curva Sud (South Stand); Lazio play in sky blue and their fans fill the Curva Nord (North Stand).

For Free

Rome is an expensive city, but you don't have to break the bank to enjoy it. A surprising number of its big sights are free and it costs nothing to stroll the historic streets, piazzas and parks, busking in their extraordinary beauty.

Need to Know

Transport
Holders of the Roma Pass (p17) are entitled to free public transport.

Wi-Fi
Free wi-fi is available in many hostels, hotels, bars and cafes.

Tours
To take a free tour check out www. newromefreetour.com.

Art & Museums

Churches
Feast on fine art in the city's churches. They're all free and many contain priceless treasures by big-name artists such as Michelangelo, Raphael, Bernini and Caravaggio. Major art churches include St Peter's Basilica (p118), Basilica di San Pietro in Vincoli (p140), Chiesa di San Luigi dei Francesi (p76), and Basilica di Santa Maria del Popolo (p99).

Vatican Museums
Home to the Sistine Chapel and kilometres of awesome art, the Vatican Museums (p122) are free on the last Sunday of the month.

State Museums
Eight of Rome's municipal museums are free, including **Museo Carlo Bilotti** (Map p316, D6; ☏06 06 08; www.museocarlobilotti. it; Viale Fiorello La Guardia; ⊙10am-4pm Tue-Fri, 10am-7pm Sat & Sun winter, 1-7pm Tue-Fri, 10am-7pm Sat & Sun summer; ⌕Via Pinciana) and **Museo Barracco di Scultura Antica** (Map p296, D6; www.museobarracco.it; Corso Vittorio Emanuele II 166; admission free; ⊙10am-4pm Tue-Sun winter, 1-7pm Tue-Sun summer; ⌕Corso Vittorio Emanuele II) FREE. All state-run museums are *gratis* on the first Sunday of the month.

Monuments

Pantheon
A pagan temple turned church, the Pantheon (p72) is a staggering work of architecture and an astonishing sight with its cavernous interior and soaring dome.

Trevi Fountain
You don't have to spend a penny to admire the Trevi Fountain (p100), although most people throw a coin in to ensure they'll return to Rome.

Bocca della Verità
According to legend, if you tell a lie at the Bocca della Verità (p67; Mouth of Truth), it'll bite your hand off.

Piazzas & Parks

Piazzas
Hanging out and people-watching on Rome's piazzas is a signature Roman experience. Top spots include Piazza Navona (p74), Campo de' Fiori (p77), Piazza di Spagna (p98), and Piazza del Popolo (p101).

Parks
It doesn't cost a thing to enjoy Rome's parks. The most famous is Villa Borghese (p181) but also worth searching out are Villa Torlonia (p183), Villa Celimontana (p171), Gianicolo Hill (p157), and Via Appia Antica (p189).

Fresh vegetables and Italian pasta on display

 **Eating**

This is a city that lives to eat. Food feeds the Roman soul, and a social occasion would be nothing without it. Cooking with local, seasonal ingredients has been the norm for millennia. Over recent decades the restaurant scene has become increasingly sophisticated, but the city's traditional no-frills trattorias still provide some of Rome's most memorable gastronomic experiences.

Roman Cuisine

Like most Italian cuisines, the *cucina romana* (Roman cooking) was born of careful use of local ingredients – making use of the cheaper cuts of meat, like *guanciale* (pig's cheek), and greens that could be gathered wild from the fields.

There are a few classic Roman dishes that almost every trattoria and restaurant in Rome serves. These carb-laden comfort foods are seemingly simple, yet notoriously difficult to prepare well. Iconic Roman dishes include carbonara (pasta with pig's cheek, egg and salty *pecorino romano*, a type of sheep's milk cheese), *alla gricia* (with pig's cheek and onions), *amatriciana* (invented when a chef from Amatrice added tomatoes to *alla gricia*) and *cacio e pepe* (with *pecorino romano* cheese and black pepper). As wonderful and deeply gratifying as these timeless dishes are the centuries-old dining traditions that have been meticulously preserved alongside them: many trattorias in Rome, as tradition demands, only cook up gnocchi (dumplings) on Thursdays, *baccalà* with *ceci* (salted cod with chickpeas) on Fridays, and tripe on Saturdays.

DINING IN ROME

The number of special-occasion, fine-dining restaurants is ever rising in Rome. Five chefs in Rome were awarded their first Michelin star in 2017, while chef Riccardo di Giacinto at All'Oro (p185) raised the gastronomic bar by moving premises and incorporating a gorgeous, 14-room boutique hotel into his new foodie empire. At Palazzo Manfredi, enviably across the street from the Colosseum, chef Giuseppe Di Iorio continues to create buzz at Michelin-starred Aroma (p173), as does Francesco Apreda at Imàgo (p109) – views from both addresses are as sensational as the mind-blowing cuisine. Favouring a modern Roman cuisine, these top chefs look to traditional Roman dishes or ingredients for inspiration and play with unexpected flavours and combinations to create a highly creative, gastronomic dining experience.

All-day dining is increasingly popular, with a few notable all-things-to-all-people restaurants including Baccano (p110), Porto Fluviale (p197) and the multistorey mall Eataly (p197), which has restaurants to suit almost every mood, from a hankering for *fritti* (fried things) to fine dining. Dazzling new food mall Mercato Centrale (p145) at Stazione Termini, meanwhile, brings many of the city's finest culinary artisans under one roof, including master pizza-maker Gabriele Bonci of Pizzarium (p132) fame.

Gourmet fast food also thrives as Roman traditions are turned on their head to inspire highly creative and gourmet quick-eats at wildly popular addresses like Supplizio (p85), serving posh *supplì* (fried rice balls), Trapizzino (p173), with the doughy, cone-shaped *trapizzino* ('sandwich'), Pasta Chef (p144), for quality pasta to go, and Zia Rosetta (p143) with gourmet mini *panini* (sandwiches).

In Testaccio's covered market, Michelin-starred female chef Cristina Bowerman – one of the few Italian female chefs to have a Michelin star for her restaurant Glass Hostaria (p160) in Trastevere – is now wooing local foodies with cardboard cups of gourmet soups and savoury dishes at Cups (p173). The celebrity chef's latest venture, **Romeo e Giulietta** – a vast restaurant, pizzeria, bakery, deli and cocktail bar rolled into one, opened in March 2017 on Piazza dell'Emporio in Testaccio – only further underlines her commitment to making haute cuisine accessible to all.

PLAN YOUR TRIP EATING

NEED TO KNOW

Prices

The pricing here refers to the average cost of a meal that includes *primo* (first course), *secondo* (second course) and *dolce* (dessert), plus a glass of wine. Don't be surprised to see *pane e coperto* (bread and cover charge; €1 to €5 per person) added to your bill.

€ less than €25

€€ €25–€45

€€€ more than €45

Opening Hours

➤ Most restaurants open noon to 3pm and 7.30pm to 11pm, usually closing one day per week (often Sunday or Monday).

➤ In August most eateries close for at least a week; some close for the entire month. Ring first to check that everyone hasn't gone to the beach.

Etiquette

➤ Dress up to dine out.

➤ Bite through hanging spaghetti – no slurping it up please.

➤ Pasta is eaten with a fork (no spoon).

➤ It's OK to eat pizza with your hands.

➤ In Italian homes, *fare la scarpetta* (make a little shoe) with your bread to wipe plates clean.

➤ If invited to someone's home, traditional gifts are a tray of *dolci* (sweets) from a *pasticceria* (pastry shop), a bottle of wine or flowers.

Tipping

Although service is included, leave a tip: anything from 5% in a pizzeria to 10% in a more upmarket place. At least round up the bill.

Health food is another big craze, pioneered by players like Green & Go (p144) and Aromaticus (p143), which is inside a plant shop to boot.

For the sweet toothed, *pasticcerie* (pastry shops) are also being reinvented as places of chic artistry, with Pasticceria De Bellis (p85) the vanguard of this trend. In the *centro storico* Tiramisù Zum (p85) only serves the classic Italian dessert, in every imaginable

FASTING & FEASTING

The classic way to celebrate any feast day in Italy is to precede it with a day of eating *magro* (lean) to prepare for the overindulgence to come. On Vigilia (Christmas Eve), for example, tradition dictates that you eat little during the day and have a fish-based dinner as a prelude to the excesses of the 25th.

Most festivals have some kind of food involved, but many of them have no other excuse than food. These are called *sagre* (feasting festivals) and are usually celebrations of local specialities such as hazelnuts, wine and sausages.

flavour. In fashionable Monti, a knowing crowd hobnobs over exquisite tiramisu miniatures and one-bite pralines at Grezzo (p144), a chocolate boutique where everything is raw, organic and gluten-free.

NEIGHBOURHOOD SPECIALITIES

Most entrenched in culinary tradition is the Jewish Ghetto area, with its hearty Roman-Jewish cuisine. Deep-frying is a staple of *cucina ebraico-romanesca* (Roman-Jewish cooking), which developed between the 16th and 19th centuries when the Jews were confined to the city's ghetto. To add flavour to their limited ingredients – those spurned by the rich, such as courgette (zucchini) flowers – they began to fry everything from mozzarella to *baccalà* (salted cod). Particularly addictive are the locally grown artichokes, which are flattened out to form a kind of flower shape and then deep-fried to a golden crisp and salted to become *carciofo alla giudia* (Jewish-style artichokes). By contrast, *carciofo alla romana* (Roman-style artichokes) are stuffed with parsley, mint and garlic, then braised in an aromatic mix of broth and white wine until soft.

For the heart (and liver and brains) of the *cucina romana,* head to Testaccio, a traditional working-class district clustered around the city's former slaughterhouse. In the past, butchers who worked in the city abattoir were often paid in cheap cuts of meat as well as money. The Roman staple *coda alla vaccinara* translates as 'oxtail cooked butcher's style'. This is cooked for hours to create a rich sauce with tender slivers of meat. A famous Roman dish that's not for the faint-hearted is pasta with *pajata,* made with the entrails of young veal calves,

considered a delicacy since they contain the mother's congealed milk. If you see the word *coratella* in a dish, it means you'll be eating *lights* (lungs), kidneys and hearts.

Seasonal Calendar

As is the case all over Italy, Romans eat according to what's in season. Fresh, often sun-ripened ingredients zing with flavour, and the best food is *zero-chilometri* – the less distance it has had to travel, the better.

SPRING

➡ Spring is prime time for lamb, usually roasted with potatoes – *agnello al forno con patate.* Sometimes it's described as *abbacchio* (Roman dialect for lamb) *scottadito* ('hot enough to burn fingers').

➡ March is the best month for *carciofo alla giudia* (Jewish-style artichokes), when the big round artichokes from Cerveteri appear on the table (smaller varieties are from Sardinia), but you can continue eating this delicious dish until June.

➡ May and June are favourable fishing months, and thus good for cuttlefish and octopus, as well as other seafood.

➡ Grass-green *fave* (broad beans) are eaten after a meal (especially on 1 May), accompanied by some salty *pecorino* cheese.

➡ The lighter green, fluted *zucchine romanesche* (Roman courgette) appear on market stalls, usually with the flowers still attached – these orange petals, deep-fried, are a delectable feature of Roman cooking.

SUMMER

➡ *Tonno* (tuna) comes fresh from the seas around Sardinia; *linguine ai frutti di mare* and *risotto alla pescatora* are good light summer dishes.

➡ Summertime is *melanzane* (aubergine or eggplant) time: tuck into them grilled as antipasti or fried and layered with rich tomato sauce in *melanzane alla parmagiana.* It's also time for leafy greens, and Rome even has its own lettuce, the sturdy, flavourful *lattuga romana.*

➡ Tomatoes are at their full-bodied finest, and seductive heaps of *pesche* (peaches), *albicocche* (apricots), *fichi* (figs) and *meloni* (melons) dominate market stalls.

AUTUMN

➡ *Alla cacciatora* (hunter-style) dishes are sourced from Lazio's hills, with meats such as *cinghiale* (boar) and *lepre* (hare).

➡ Fish is also good in autumn; you could try fried

Eating by Neighbourhood

Villa Borghese & Northern Rome
Park cafes and smart,
fashionable restaurants (p184)

Vatican City, Borgo & Prati
Sophisticated restaurants,
delicious takeaways,
heavenly gelaterie (p131)

Tridente, Trevi & the Quirinale
Classy neighbourhood
eateries, great gelaterie
and upmarket cafes (p105)

Centro Storico
Romantic hideaways,
old-school trattorias,
top pizzerias (p82)

Monti, Esquilino & San Lorenzo
Ethnic eats, cool bars,
boho restaurants (p143)

Trastevere & Gianicolo
Touristy but terrific
trattorias, gelaterie, bars
and pizzerias (p158)

Ancient Rome
Hidden gems among
the tourist traps (p67)

San Giovanni & Testaccio
Traditional Roman cuisine
and top street food (p172)

Southern Rome
Trendsetting foodie venues in
ex-industrial Ostiense district (p196)

0 ——— 1 km
0 ——— 0.5 miles

---

fish from Fiumicino, such as *triglia* (red mullet),
or mixed small fish, such as *alici* (anchovies).

➡ Autumn equals mushrooms – the meaty
porcini, *galletti* and *ovuli*. Heaping the markets
are *broccoletti* (also called *broccolini*), a cross
between broccoli and asparagus, *uva* (grapes),
pere (pears) and nuts.

WINTER

➡ Winter is the ideal time to eat cockle-warming
dishes with *ceci* (chickpeas) and vegetable-rich
minestrone, as well as herb-roasted *porchetta di
Ariccia* (pork from Ariccia).

➡ *Puntarelle* ('little points' – Catalonian
chicory), found only in Lazio, is a delicious,
faintly bitter winter green.

➡ Markets are piled high with *broccolo
romanesco* (Roman broccoli), *aranci* (oranges)
and *mandarini* (mandarins).

➡ In February, look out for *frappé* (strips of fried
dough sprinkled with sugar), eaten at carnival
time.

When to Eat

For *colazione* (breakfast), most Romans
head to a bar for a cappuccino and *cornetto*
(croissant).

The main meal of the day is *pranzo*
(lunch), eaten at about 1.30pm. Many shops
and businesses close for one to three hours
every afternoon to accommodate the meal
and siesta that follows. On Sundays *pranzo*
is particularly important.

Many restaurants offer 'brunch' at weekends, but this isn't the breakfast-lunch
combination featuring pancakes and eggs
that English and American visitors might
expect. Brunch in Rome tends to mean a
buffet, available from around noon to 3pm.

Aperitivo is a buffet of snacks to accompany evening drinks, usually from around
6pm till 9pm, and costing around €10 for a
drink and unlimited platefuls.

Cena (dinner), eaten any time from
about 8.30pm, is usually simple, although

this is changing as fewer people make it home for the big lunchtime feast.

A full Italian meal consists of an *antipasto* (starter), a *primo piatto* (first course), a *secondo piatto* (second course) with an *insalata* (salad) or *contorno* (vegetable side dish), *dolci* (sweet), fruit, coffee and *digestivo* (liqueur). When eating out, however, you can do as most Romans do, and mix and match: order, say, a *primo* followed by an *insalata* or *contorno*.

Where to Eat

Take your pick according to your mood and your pocket, from the frenetic energy of a Roman pizzeria to the warm familiarity of a third-generation-run, centuries-old trattoria, from chic bars laden with a sumptuous *apertivi* banquets to modern bistros and gastronomic dines where both presentation and flavours are works of art.

ENOTECHE

Romans rarely drink without eating, and you can eat well at many *enoteche,* wine bars that usually serve snacks (such as cheeses or cold meats, bruschette and *crostini*) and hot dishes. Some, such as Palatium (p109) or Casa Bleve (p85), offer full-scale dining.

TRATTORIAS, OSTERIAS & RESTAURANTS

Traditionally, trattorias were family-run places that offered a basic, affordable local menu, while *osterie* usually specialised in one dish and *vino della casa* (house wine). There are still lots of these around. *Ristoranti* offer more choices and smarter service, and are more expensive.

PIZZERIAS

Remarkably, pizza was only introduced to Rome post-WWII, by southern immigrants. It caught on. Every Roman's favourite casual (and cheap) meal is the gloriously simple pizza, with Rome's signature wafer-thin bases, covered in fresh, bubbling toppings, slapped down on tables by waiters on a mission. Pizzerias often only open in the evening, as their wood-fired ovens take a while to get going.

Most Romans will precede their pizza with a starter of bruschetta or *fritti* (mixed fried foods, such as zucchini flowers, potato, olives etc) and wash it all down with beer – only craft beer in the case of the city's trendiest new pizzerias. Pizza menus are traditionally divided into *pizza rosso* ('red' pizza meaning with tomato sauce) and *pizza bianco* ('white' pizza with no tomato sauce, traditionally simply sprinkled with rosemary, salt and olive oil, but available with a variety of optional toppings today). Some places in Rome – including trendy new Sbanco (p172) by Stefano Callegari of Trapizzino (p173) fame – serve pizza with a thicker, fluffier base, more Neapolitan in style.

For a snack on the run, Rome's pizza *al taglio* (by the slice) places are hard to beat, with toppings loaded atop thin, crispy, light-as-air, slow-risen bread that verge on the divine. There's been an increase of more gourmet pizza places in the last decade, their king being Gabriele Bonci's Pizzarium (p132), close to the Vatican and inside Mercato Centrale (p145).

FAST FOOD

Fast food is a long-standing Roman tradition, with plenty of street-food favourites.

ROMAN FOOD BLOGS

Katie Parla (http://katieparla.com) On-the-pulse restaurant reviews and culinary insights by food-and-beverage journalist Katie, a Rome-based, New Jersey native and author of the highly recommended *Tasting Rome* (2017).

Eizabeth Minchilli in Rome (www.elizabethminchilliinrome.com) Reliable dining recommendations by the author of *Eating Rome,* an American food writer at home in Italy.

Gillian's Lists (www.gillianslists.com) Rome-based blogger with a penchant for beaches, coffee and cocktails.

Heart Rome (www.heartrome.com) Food and lifestyle in the eternal city seen through the smart eyes of Australian Maria Pasquale.

An American in Rome (http://anamericaninrome.com) Bar and restaurant reviews by freelance writer Natalie Kennedy who arrived in Rome, fresh from California, in 2010.

A *tavola calda* (hot table) offers cheap, pre-prepared pasta, meat and vegetable dishes, while a *rosticceria* sells mainly cooked meats. Neither is best for a romantic meal, but they're often very tasty.

Another favourite on the run are *arancini,* fried risotto balls that have fillings such as mozzarella and ham. These originate from Sicily, but are much loved in Rome too, where they're known as *supplì.*

GELATERIE

Eating gelato is as much a part of Roman life as morning coffee – try it and you'll understand why. The city has some of the world's finest ice-cream shops, which use only the finest seasonal ingredients, sourced from the finest locations. In these artisan gelaterie you won't find a strawberry flavour in winter, for example, and pistachios are from Bronte, almonds from Avola, and so on. It's all come a long way since Nero snacked on snow mixed with fruit pulp and honey. A rule of thumb is to check the colour of the pistachio flavour: ochre-green means 'good', bright-green means 'bad'. In the height of summer Romans love to eat *grattachecca* (literally 'scratched ice'), with kiosks selling crushed ice topped with fruit and syrup along the riverside open from May to September. It's a great way to cool down.

Most places open from around 8am to 1am, with shorter hours in winter. Prices range from around €2 to €3.50 for a *cona* (cone) or *coppetta* (tub or cup).

DELIS & MARKETS

Rome's well-stocked delis and fresh-produce markets are a fabulous feature of the city's foodscape. Most neighbourhoods have a few local delis and their own daily food market. For deli supplies and wine, shop at *alimentari,* which generally open 7am to 1.30pm and 5pm to 8pm daily except Thursday afternoon and Sunday (during the summer months they will often close on Saturday afternoon instead of Thursday). Markets operate from around 7am to 1.30pm, Monday to Saturday. There are also some excellent farmers' markets, mostly taking place at the weekends.

Rome's most famous markets:

➡ **Mercato di Campo de' Fiori** (p85) The most picturesque, but also the most expensive. Prices are graded according to the shopper's accent.

➡ **Nuovo Mercato Esquilino** (p151) Cheap and the best place to find exotic herbs and spices.

➡ **Piazza dell' Unità** (Map p304) Near the Vatican, perfect for stocking up for a picnic.

➡ **Mercato di Piazza San Cosimato** (p160) Trastevere's neighbourhood market, at least a century old and still the biz for fresh, locally sourced foodstuffs.

➡ **Nuovo Mercato di Testaccio** (p175) A purpose-built covered market hall crammed with enticing stalls, including many serving gourmet 'fast food' to go.

Vegetarian, Vegan & Gluten-Free Dining

Vegetarians eat exceedingly well in Rome, with a wide choice of bountiful antipasti, pasta dishes, *insalate, contorni* (side dishes) and pizzas. Some high-end restaurants such as Imàgo (p109) even serve a vegetarian menu, and slowly but surely, exclusively vegetarian and/or vegan eateries and cafes are cropping up: try Babette (p106) and Il Margutta (p106) near the Spanish Steps, or Vitaminas 24 (p148) in edgy Pigneto.

Be mindful of hidden ingredients not mentioned on the menu – for example, steer clear of anything that's been stuffed (like courgette flowers, often spiced up with anchovies) or check that it's *senza carne o pesce* (without meat or fish). To many Italians, vegetarian means you don't eat red meat.

Vegans are in for a tougher time. Cheese is used universally, so you must specify that you want something *senza formaggio* (without cheese). Also remember that *pasta fresca,* which may also turn up in soups, is made with eggs. The safest bet is to self-cater or try a dedicated vegetarian restaurant, which will always have some vegan options.

Most restaurants offer gluten-free options, as there is a good awareness of celiac disease here: one of the city's top restaurants, Aroma (p173), has a four-course, gluten-free menu (€115). Just say *Io sono celiaco* or *senza glutine* when you sit down, and usually the waiters will be able to recommend suitable dishes.

Lonely Planet's Top Choices

Pianostrada (p86) Urban bistro chic in the *centro storico*.

Panella (p145) The ultimate budget-dine ticket, any time of day.

Sbanco (p172) The hottest pizzeria of the moment with a buzzy, warehouse-vibe.

Pizzarium (p132) Scissor-cut chunks of pizza to go from Rome's master pizza maker.

La Ciambella (p83) Hybrid restaurant-bar by the Panethon.

Best by Budget

€

Pizzarium (p132) Top-of-the-range *pizza al taglio* (pizza by the slice).

Panella (p145) Heavenly bakery serving fresh-baked food all day on a flowery, sun-flooded terrace.

Pasta Chef (p144) Fast-food pasta joint in the pretty heart of Monti.

Mordi e Vai (p173) Food stall serving classic Roman fast food.

€€

Pianostrada (p86) Creative modern cuisine and a fashionable bistro vibe.

L'Asino d'Oro (p145) Umbrian creative cuisine at reasonable prices (especially lunch).

La Ciambella (p83) Relaxed all-day eatery in the shadow of the Pantheon.

Tram Tram (p147) Wildly popular *osteria* (tavern) mixing Roman classic with Sicilian seafood in student-filled San Lorenzo.

Litro (p160) Creative Roman kitchen in unknown Monteverde with organic produce and Rome's best biodynamic wines.

€€€

Metamorfosi (p185) Roy Caceres' stupendously good Michelin-starred cooking.

Salumeria Roscioli (p86) Gourmet Italian food at a vaunted deli-restaurant.

Enoteca La Torre (p132) Michelin-starred glamour in the Fendi sisters' Villa Laetitia.

Antonello Colonna Open (p146) Michelin-starred, 'New Roman' dining beneath a dazzling all-glass roof.

Best by Cuisine

Traditional Roman

Flavio al Velavevodetto (p173) Classic *cucina romana*, served in huge portions.

Da Felice (p173) In the heartland of Roman cuisine, and sticking to a traditional weekly timetable.

Armando al Pantheon (p83) Family-run trattoria offering hearty Roman cuisine in the shadow of the Pantheon.

Da Enzo (p158) Hugely popular Trastevere address, known for quality sourced ingredients.

Da Augusto (p159) Dreamy summertime dining and fabulous mamma-style cooking on one of Trastevere's prettiest piazzas.

Modern Roman

Glass Hostaria (p160) Innovative cuisine by celebrity female chef Cristina Bowerman in her contemporary Trastevere, Michelin-starred restaurant.

Antonello Colonna Open (p146) Antonello Colonna's glass-roofed restaurant offers creative takes on Roman classics.

Renato e Luisa (p86) Always-packed trattoria that takes classic Roman cooking and mixes it up.

Ristorante L'Arcangelo (p132) Updated takes on classic Roman dishes at this Prati hotspot.

Pianostrada (p86) Uber fashionable, bistro-and-bar dining on funky Roman-inspired plates to share or scoff alone.

Regional

Colline Emiliane (p110) Sensational home cooking from Emilia-Romagna.

Seacook (p197) Chic seafood fresh from Salento in southern Italy.

Trattoria Monti (p146) Top-notch traditional cooking from the Marches, including heavenly fried things.

Terre e Domus (p67) All ingredients are sourced from the surrounding Lazio region.

La Prosciutteria (p159) Made-to-measure *taglieri* (wooden chopping boards) and *panini* loaded with Tuscan cold cuts, cheeses, fruit and veg at this Florentine salami shop.

Cotto Crudo (p131) Pick up a *panino* with the best ham and cheese from Emilia-Romagna.

Best Pizzerias

Sbanco (p172) Creative pizzas and craft beer served in casual bar-like setting.

Emma Pizzeria (p86) Smart outfit dishing up excellent wood-fired pizzas in the historic centre.

Pizzeria Da Remo (p173) Spartan but stunning: the frenetic Roman pizzeria experience in Testaccio.

Panattoni (p158) Streetside tables and fabulous pizza haul in the hoards to Trastevere's *'l'obitorio'* (the morgue).

Alle Carette (p143) Top-notch *baccalà* (salted cod) and down-to-earth pizza, super-thin and swiftly cooked on Monti's prettiest car-free street.

Best Local Dining

Pizzeria Da Remo (p173) The full neighbourhood Roman pizza experience, with lightning-fast waiters serving paper-thin pizzas.

Da Felice (p173) Traditional local cooking in Testaccio, the heartland of Roman cuisine.

Antico Forno Urbani (p86) Queue up with the locals for *pizza al taglio* in the Ghetto.

Da Teo (p158) Reservations essentials at this hugely popular trattoria with terrace seating on a pretty Trastevere piazza.

Pizza Ostiense (p197) Fabulous thin-crust pizza in Rome's ex-industrial, hip neighbourhood of Ostiense.

Hostaria Romana (p109) Buzzing trattoria dining footsteps from the Trevi Fountain.

Best See & Be Seen

Said (p147) Hipster all-rounder in a 1920s chocolate factory in San Lorenzo.

Dal Bolognese (p107) Moneyed, moghuls and models mingle just off Piazza del Popolo.

Il Sorpasso (p132) Cool vintage-styled bar restaurant, haunt of Prati's fashionable crowd.

Temakinho (p144) Hip, Brazilian-sushi hybrid in Monti mixing powerful caipirinhas.

Best for Ambience

Aroma (p173) The Michelin-starred rooftop restaurant of the Palazzo Manfredi hotel has 'marry-me' views over the Colosseum.

La Veranda (p131) A location in Paolo Sorrentino's *The Great*

Beauty; dine beneath 15th-century Pinturicchio frescoes.

Antonello Colonna Open (p146) Restaurant on a mezzanine under a soaring glass ceiling in the Palazzo degli Esposizioni.

Casa Bleve (p85) Gracious colonnaded wine bar with a stained-glass ceiling.

Caffetteria Chiostro del Bramante (p83) Hidden cafe overlooking Bramante's graceful Renaissance cloister.

Best Gelaterie

Fatamorgana (p131) Rome's finest artisanal flavours, now in multiple central locations.

Gelateria del Teatro (p84) Around 40 choices of delicious ice cream, all made on site.

Gelateria Dei Gracchi (p106) A taste of heaven in several locations across Rome.

Fior di Luna (p160) Great artisan ice cream In Trastevere.

Neve di Latte (p185) Classic flavours served near the MAXXI art museum.

Best Pizza by the Slice

Pizzarium (p132) Pizza slices created by the master, Gabriele Bonci.

Forno Roscioli (p85) Thin and crispy, this is some of the best *pizza rossa* (with tomato and oregano) in Rome, if not the world.

Forno di Campo de' Fiori (p85) Food-of-the-gods *pizza rossa* and *bianca* (with olive oil and rosemary).

Antico Forno Urbani (p86) A kosher bakery in the Ghetto with incredible *pizza bianca*.

Best Food Shops

Eataly (p197) Mall-sized, state-of-the-art food emporium, with produce from all over Italy, and multiple restaurants.

Salumeria Roscioli (p92) The rich scents of fine Italian produce, cured meats and cheeses intermingle in this superlative deli.

Antica Caciara Trasteverina (p163) Century-old deli with fresh ricotta, to-die-for *ricotta infornata* (oven-baked ricotta), wheels of Lazio's celebrated, black-waxed *pecorino romano* DOP and aromatic garlands of *guanciale* (pig's jowl).

Volpetti (p175) This super-stocked deli is a treasure trove of gourmet delicacies and helpful staff.

Confetteria Moriondo & Gariglio (p93) Revel in magical chocolate creation at this historic confectioners.

Grezzo (p144) Raw chocolate in every guise.

Best Pastry Shops

Pasticceria De Dellis (p85) Work-of-art cakes, pastries and *dolci* at this chic *pasticceria*.

Biscottificio Innocenti (p163) Classic old-school Trastevere bakery, with piled-high biscuits such as *brutti ma buoni* (ugly but good).

I Dolci di Nonna Vincenza (p85) Heavenly Sicilian pastries.

Andreotti (p197) Poem-worthy treats from buttery *crostate* (tarts) to the piles of golden *sfogliatelle romane* (ricotta-filled pastries).

Pasticceria Gruè (p185) Modern *pasticceria*-cum-cafe with artfully crafted cakes and pastries.

Alfresco drinking and dining

Drinking & Nightlife

Often the best way to enjoy nightlife in Rome is to wander from restaurant to bar, getting happily lost down picturesque cobbled streets. There's simply no city with better backdrops for a drink: you can savour a Campari overlooking the Roman Forum or sample some artisanal beer while watching the light bounce off baroque fountains.

Rome After Dark

Night-owl Romans tend to eat late, then drink at bars before heading off to a club at around 1am. Like most cities, Rome is a collection of districts, each with its own character, which is often completely different after dark. The *centro storico* (historic centre) and Trastevere pull in a mix of locals and tourists as night falls. Ostiense and Testaccio are the grittier clubbing districts, with clusters of clubs in a couple of locations – Testaccio has a parade of crowd-pleasing clubs running over the hill of Monte Testaccio. There are also subtle political divisions. San Lorenzo and Pigneto, to the south of Rome, are popular with a left-leaning, alternative crowd, while areas to the north (such as Ponte Milvio and Parioli) attract a more right-wing, bourgeois mileu.

The *bella figura* (loosely translated as 'looking good') is important. The majority of locals spend evenings checking each other out, partaking in gelato, and not drinking too much. However, this is changing and certain areas – those popular with a younger crowd – can get rowdy with drunk teens and tourists (for example, Campo de' Fiori and parts of Trastevere).

Rome in Summer (& Winter)

From around mid-June to mid-September, many nightclubs and live-music venues close, some moving to EUR or the beaches at Fregene or Ostia. The area around the Isola Tiberina throngs with life nightly during the Lungo Il Tevere (p23), a summer festival along the riverbank, which sprouts bars, stalls and an open-air cinema.

Be aware that in winter, bars often close earlier in the evening, particularly in areas where the norm is to drink outside. That said, an increasing number of bars have heated pavement terraces in winter, ensuring year-round alfresco drinking.

Where to Drink

ENOTECHE

The *enoteca* (wine bar) was where the old boys from the neighbourhood used to drink rough local wine poured straight from the barrel. Times have changed: nowadays they tend to be sophisticated but still atmospheric places, offering Italian and international vintages, delicious cheeses and cold cuts.

BARS & PUBS

Bars range from regular Italian cafe-bars that have seemingly remained the same for centuries, to chic, carefully styled places made for esoteric cocktails – such as Co.So (p149) and Salotto 42 (p90) – and laid-back, perennially popular haunts – such as Freni e Frizioni (p161) – that have a longevity rarely seen in other cities. Pubs are also popular, with several long running Irish-style pubs filled with chattering Romans, and more pub-like bars opening on the back of the artisanal beer trend.

NIGHTCLUBS

Rome has a range of nightclubs, mostly in Ostiense and Testaccio, with music policies ranging from lounge and jazz to dancehall and hip-hop. Clubs tend to get busy after midnight, or even after 2am. Often admission is free, but drinks are expensive. Cocktails can cost from €10 to €20, but you can drink much more cheaply in the studenty clubs of San Lorenzo, Pigneto and the *centri sociali* (social centres).

CENTRI SOCIALI

Rome's flip side is a surprising alternative underbelly, centred on left-wing *centri sociali*: grungy squatter arts centres that host live music and contemporary-arts events. They offer Rome's most unusual, cheap and

alternative nightlife options. These include **Brancaleone** (☏339 5074012; www.branca leone.it; Via Levanna 11; ⊗hours vary, typically 10pm-late; ☒Via Nomentana) and **Esc Atelier** (Map p311; www.escatelier.net; Via dei Volsci 159; ⊗hours vary; ☒Via Tiburtina, ☒Via dei Reti).

What to Drink

LAZIO WINES

Lazio wines may not be household names, but it's well worth trying some local wines while you're here. Although whites dominate Lazio's production – 95% of the region's Denominazione di Origine Controllata (DOC; the second of Italy's four quality classifications) wines are white – there are a few notable reds as well. To sample Lazio wines, Palatium (p109) and Terre e Domus (p67) are the best places to go. For biodynamic vintages, head for Litro (p160) in Monteverdi.

CRAFT BEER

In recent years beer drinking has really taken off in Italy, and especially in Rome, with specialised bars and restaurants offering microbrewed beers. Local favourites include Birradamare in Fiumicino, Porto Fluviale (p197) in Ostiense, and Birra Del Borgo in Rieti (on the border between Lazio and

Abruzzo), which opened local beer haunts Bir & Fud (p162) and Open Baladin (p90). Local beers reflect the seasonality that's so important in Rome – for example, in winter look for beers made from chestnuts.

COCKTAILS, APERITIFS & DIGESTIVES

The cocktail scene in Rome has caught up fast and is thriving, with mixologists shaking some superb local creations such as the Carbonara sour at Co.So (p149), featuring vodka infused with pork fat in a homage to the classic Roman pasta sauce. It was fashionable speakeasy Jerry Thomas Project (p90), well-placed in the *centro storico*, who kickstarted the cocktail revolution in Rome, and some of the finest and funkiest cocktails remain underground in speakeasy bars like Keyhole (p161) in Trastevere and Spirito (p148), brilliantly at home in the back of a sandwich shop in Pigneto. Gin cocktails are the speciality of the Gin Corner (p90), at home in the Hotel Adranio, while other cocktail hot spots, like Barnum Cafe (p90) or Gatsby Café (p148), double as laid-back cafes by day.

Popular aperitifs are based on bitter alcoholic liqueurs, such as Campari Soda or Aperol spritz, which mixes Aperol with prosecco. Crodino is a herbal, medicinal-tasting nonalcoholic aperitif. Italians love to finish off a meal with a digestif. The best of these aren't shop bought, so if it's *fatta in casa* (made at home), give it a try.

COFFEE

For an espresso (a shot of strong black coffee), ask for *un caffè;* if you want it with a drop of hot or cold milk, order *un caffè macchiato* ('stained' coffee) *caldo/freddo*. Long black coffee (as in a watered-down version) is known as *caffè lungo* (an espresso with more water) or *caffè all'american* (a filter coffee). If you fancy a coffee but one more shot will catapult you through the ceiling, you can drink *orzo*, made from roasted barley but served like coffee.

Then, of course, there's the cappuccino (coffee with frothy milk, served warm rather than hot). If you want it without froth, ask for a *cappuccino senza schiuma;* if you want it hot, ask for it *ben caldo*. Italians drink cappuccino only during the morning and never after meals.

In summer, *cappuccino freddo* (iced coffee with milk, usually already sugared), *caffè freddo* (iced espresso) and *granita di caffè* (frozen coffee, usually with cream) top the charts.

A *caffè latte* is a milkier version of the cappuccino with less froth; a *latte macchiato* is even milkier (warmed milk 'stained' with a spot of coffee). A *caffè corretto* is an espresso 'corrected' with a dash of grappa or something similar.

There are two ways to drink coffee in a Roman bar-cafe: either standing at the bar, in which case you pay first at the till and then, with your receipt, order at the counter; or you can sit down at a table and enjoy waiter service. In the latter case you'll pay up to double what you'd pay at the bar. In both scenarios, a complimentary glass of tap water is invariably served with your coffee – if it isn't, don't be shy to ask for one.

Gay & Lesbian Rome

There is only a smattering of dedicated gay and lesbian clubs and bars in Rome, though many nightclubs host regular gay and lesbian nights. For local information, pick up a copy of the monthly magazine *AUT,* published by **Circolo Mario Mieli** (www.mariomieli.org). There's also info at **AZ Gay** (www.azgay.it). Lesbians can find out more about the local scene at **Coordinamento Lesbiche Italiano** (www.clrbp.it).

Most gay venues (bars, clubs and saunas) require you to have an Arcigay (p268) membership card. These cost €15/8 per year/three months and are available from any venue that requires one.

Drinking & Nightlife by Neighbourhood

→ **Centro Storico** (p88) Bars and a few clubs, a mix of touristy and sophisticated.

→ **Trastevere** (p161) Everyone's favourite place for a *passeggiata* (evening stroll), with plenty of bars and cafes.

→ **Testaccio** (p174) With a cluster of mainstream clubs, this nightlife strip offers poptastic choice.

→ **Ostiense** (p197) Home to Rome's cooler nightclubs, housed in ex-industrial venues.

→ **San Lorenzo** (p149) Favoured by students, with a concentration of bars and alternative clubs.

→ **Pigneto** (p148) Bohemian ex-working-class district lined with bars and restaurants.

Lonely Planet's Top Choices

Gatsby Café (p148) Fantastic coffee, cocktails and uber-chic retro vibe in an upcycled 1950s hat shop.

Spirito (p148) Fashionable cocktail bar hidden, speakeasy-style, in the back of a Pigneto sandwich shop.

Sciascia Caffè (p133) Classy joint serving the unparalleled *caffè eccellente,* a velvety smooth espresso in a chocolate-lined cup.

Barnum Cafe (p90) Cool vintage armchairs to sink into by day and dressed-up cocktails by night.

Open Baladin (p90) Craft beer and pub vibe in the *centro storico.*

Best Cafes

La Casa del Caffè Tazza d'Oro (p88) With lovely burnished 1940s fittings, great coffee and, in summer, *granita.*

Sciascia Caffè (p133) Delicious coffee in an elegant interior.

Caffè Sant'Eustachio (p88) Historic cafe famous for its world-beating coffee.

La Casetta a Monti (p147) Uber-cute cafe behind a foliage-draped facade in Monti's cobbled heart.

Antico Caffè Greco (p111) Old-world elegance at Rome's oldest cafe (1760), by the Spanish Steps.

Best Enoteche

Il Sorì (p149) Gourmet wine bar and artisan *bottegha* (shop) with wine tastings and 'meet the producer' soirées.

Il Goccetto (p90) An old-school *vino e olio* (wine and oil) shop

makes for a great neighbour-hood wine bar.

Bibenda Wine Concept (p174) Modern wine bar with a good choice of regional Italian labels.

Litro (p160) A drinking-dining hybrid with savvy sommeliers and the finest selection of biodynamic wines in the city.

Ai Tre Scalini (p144) Buzzing *enoteca* that feels as convivial as a pub.

Best Aperitivo

Freni e Frizioni (p161) Perenially cool bar with lavish nightly buffet of snacks.

Doppiozeroo (p197) Popular Ostiense address with impressive buffet choice.

Momart (p185) Students and local professionals love the expansive array of pizza and other snacks.

Pimm's Good (p161) Pimms cocktails, generous complimentary nibbles and party-loving bar staff in Trastevere.

Zuma Bar (p111) When the urge for a posh cocktail on a designer rooftop beckons.

Best for Beer

Bar San Calisto (p161) Linger over cheep beer on Trastevere's loveliest pavement terrace.

Ma Che Siete Venuti a Fà (p162) Pint-sized bar crammed with real-ale choices.

Open Baladin (p90) More than 40 beers on tap and up to 100 bottled brews.

Be.re (p133) Craft beer flows at this modern Vatican newcomer.

Birra Più (p149) Pigneto hub, with a great range of craft beers on tap.

BrewDog Roma (p69) Hit the beer and stumble out to Colosseum views.

Best Alternative

Rivendita Libri, Cioccolata e Vino (p161) Cream-topped shots served in chocolate shot glasses (bags of fun) in Trastevere – the place to be after 10pm.

Lanificio 159 (p186) Cool underground venue hosts live gigs and club nights.

Yeah! Pigneto (p149) Pigneto bar with live gigs and DJs in Rome's most boho district.

Anticafé Roma (p174) Laid-back spot where you pay for your time not what you drink.

Best Clubs

Circolo Illuminati (p197) Wildly popular Ostiense club on the international DJ club circuit, with an underground vibe and star-topped courtyard garden.

Vinile (p198) Food, music, dancing and party happenings on the southern fringe of Ostiense.

Vicious Club (p149) Uber-trendy club and cocktail bar near Termini station.

Goa (p198) Rome's serious superclub, at home in a former motorbike repair shop in industrial-styled Ostiense.

Best Gay Venues

Coming Out (p175) A friendly gay bar near the Colosseum, open all day, with gigs, drag shows and karaoke later on.

L'Alibi (p175) Kitsch shows and house, techno and dance pumping up a mixed gay and straight crowd.

My Bar (p175) A mixed crowd by day, and gayer by night, in the shadow of the Colosseum.

Roma supporters at Stadio Olimpico (p186)

☆ Entertainment

Watching the world go by in Rome is often entertainment enough, but don't overlook the local arts and sports scene. As well as gigs and concerts in every genre, there are fantastic arts festivals, especially in summer, performances with Roman ruins as a backdrop, and football games that split the city asunder.

Music & Dance
CLASSICAL MUSIC

Music in Rome is not just about catching Rome's world-class **Orchestra dell'Accademia Nazionale di Santa Cecilia** (www.santacecilia.it) at the Auditorium Parco della Musica (p186). There are concerts by the Accademia Filarmonica Romana at Teatro Olimpico (p186); the **Auditorium Conciliazione** (Map p304; ✆06 6813 4748; www.auditorium conciliazione.it; Via della Conciliazione 4; ☐Piazza Pia), Rome's premier classical music venue before the newer auditorium was opened, is

still a force to be reckoned with; and the **Istituzione Universitaria dei Concerti** (IUC; Map p311; ✆06 361 00 51; www.concertiiuc.it; Piazzale Aldo Moro 5; ☐Via dell'Università), holds concerts in the Aula Magna of La Sapienza University.

Free classical concerts are held in many of Rome's churches, especially at Easter and around Christmas and New Year; look out for information at Rome's tourist kiosks. Rome's second-largest church after St Peter's, the Basilica di San Paolo Fuori le Mura (p195), hosts an important choral mass on 25 January and the hymn 'Te Deum' is sung at the Chiesa del Gesù (p80) on 31 December.

OPERA, BALLET & CONTEMPORARY DANCE

Rome's opera house, the Teatro dell'Opera di Roma (p150), is a magnificent, grandiose venue, lined in gilt and red, but productions can be a bit hit and miss. It's also home to Rome's official Corps de Ballet and has a ballet season running in tandem with its opera performances. Both ballet and opera move outdoors for the summer season at the ancient Roman baths, Terme di Caracalla (p175), which is an even more spectacular setting.

You can also see opera in various other outdoor locations; check listings or at the tourist information kiosks for details.

Rome's Auditorium Parco della Musica (p181) hosts classical and contemporary dance performances, as well as the Equilibrio Festival della Nuova Danza in February. The Auditorium Conciliazione is another good place to catch contemporary dance companies.

JAZZ, ROCK & POP

Besides the Auditorium Parco della Musica, large concerts also take place at Rome's sports stadiums, including Stadio Olimpico (p186) and the racetrack on the Appia Nuova, the Ippodromo La Capannelle.

The *centri sociali*, alternative arts centres set up in venues around Rome, are also good places to catch a gig, especially Brancaleone (p37) in northern Rome, with music policies encompassing hip-hop, electro, dubstep, reggae and dancehall.

Theatre

Rome has a thriving local theatre scene, with theatres including both traditional places and smaller experimental venues. Performances are usually in Italian.

Particularly wonderful are the summer festivals that make use of Rome's archaeological scenery. Performances take place in settings such as Villa Adriana in Tivoli, Ostia Antica's Roman theatre and the Teatro di Marcello (p80). In summer the **Miracle Players** (☑06 7039 3427; www.miracle players.org) perform classic English drama or historical comedy in English next to the Roman Forum and other open-air locations. Performances are usually free.

Outdoor Cinema

There are various atmospheric outdoor summer film festivals; check festival websites for progamme and ticketing details. The Isola del Cinema (p91) shows independent

PLAN YOUR TRIP ENTERTAINMENT

NEED TO KNOW

Tickets

Tickets for concerts, live music and theatrical performances are widely available across the city. Prices range enormously depending on the venue and artist. Hotels can often reserve tickets for guests, or you can contact the venue or organisation directly – check listings publications for booking details. Otherwise you can try the following:

➡ **Vivaticket** (www.vivaticket.it)
➡ **Orbis** (Map p312; ☑06 482 74 03)

Internet Resources

➡ **Comune di Roma** (www.060608.it)
➡ **Romeing** (www.romeing.it)
➡ **In Rome Now** (www.inromenow.com)
➡ **Tutto Teatro** (www.tuttoteatro.com)
➡ **Rome Opera Omnia** (www.roma operaomnia.com)
➡ **Eventful** (http://rome.eventful.com)

films in the romantic setting of the Isola Tiberina annually in July and August. This runs in conjunction with the riverside Lungo il Tevere (p23) festival.

Spectator Sports

FOOTBALL

In Rome you're either for A S Roma (*giallorossi* – yellow and reds) or Lazio (*biancazzuri* – white and blues), with both teams playing in Serie A (Italy's premier league). A striking new 52,500-seat stadium – a contemporary glass-and-steel structure inspired by the Colosseum – is planned for Roma at Tor di Valle in southwest Rome, due to be completed in time for the 2021–22 season. Both sets of supporters have an unfortunate controversial minority who have been known to cause trouble at matches.

September to May, there's a game at home for Roma or Lazio almost every weekend and a trip to Rome's football stadium, the Stadio Olimpico (p186), is an unforgettable experience. Note that ticket purchase regulations are strict. Tickets have to bear the holder's name and passport or ID number, and you must present a photo ID at the turnstiles when entering the stadium. Two tickets are permitted per purchase for Serie A, Coppa Italia and UEFA Champions

Terme di Caracalla (p169)

League games. Tickets cost from €17 to €250. You can buy them from www.listicket. it, at Lottomatica (lottery centres) or one of the A S Roma or Lazio stores around the city. To get to the stadium, take metro line A to Ottaviano–San Pietro, then bus 32.

BASKETBALL

Basketball is a popular spectator sport in Rome, though it inspires nothing like the fervour of football. Rome's team, **Virtus Roma** (www.virtusroma.it), plays throughout the winter months at the **Palalottomatica** (☑06 54 09 01; www.palalottomatica.it; Piazzale dello Sport 1; Ⓜ EUR Palasport) in EUR.

RUGBY UNION

Italy's rugby team, the Azzurri (the Blues), entered the Six Nations tournament in 2000 although success has been scarce. The team plays home international games at the Stadio Olimpico (p186).

TENNIS

Italy's premier tennis tournament, the **Internazionali BNL d'Italia** (www. internazionalibnlditalia.com) is one of the most important events on the European tennis circuit. Every May the world's top players meet on the clay courts at the monumental, Fascist-era Foro Italico (p186). Tickets can usually be bought at the Foro Italico each day of the tournament, except for the final days, which are sold out weeks in advance.

EQUESTRIAN EVENTS

Rome's top equestrian event is the Piazza di Siena showjumping competition (www. piazzadisiena.org), an international annual event held in May, gorgeously set in Villa Borghese.

Rome by Neighbourhood

➜ **Centro Storico** (p91) Great for concerts in churches or theatre (usually in Italian).

➜ **Trastevere & Gianicolo** (p162) A few blues and jazz live-music venues.

➜ **Monti, Esquilino & San Lorenzo** (p150) Several intimate live-music venues.

➜ **Villa Borghese & Northern Rome** (p186) Home to the great Auditorium Parco della Musica, as well as Rome's major sporting venues.

➜ **San Giovanni & Testaccio** (p198) Regular live gigs in the district's clubs.

A S ROMA VERSUS LAZIO

The Rome derby is one of the football season's highest-profile games. The rivalry between Roma and Lazio is fierce and little love is lost between the fans. If you go to the Stadio Olimpico, make sure you get it right – Roma fans (in deep red with a natty orange trim) flock to the Curva Sud (southern stand), while Lazio supporters (in light blue) stand in the Curva Nord (northern stand). If you want to sit on the fence, head to the Tribuna Tevere or Tribuna Monte Mario.

For more details on the clubs, check out www.asroma.it and www.sslazio.it (both in Italian).

Lonely Planet's Top Choices

Auditorium Parco della Musica (p186) An incredible venue hosting an eclectic, must-see program of music, art and more.

Terme di Caracalla (p169) Opera and ballet performed with the amazing backdrop of the ruined Roman Baths of Caracalla.

Teatro dell'Opera di Roma (p150) Rome's premier opera house.

Roma Incontra il Mondo (p23) Cool world music festival in the parklands of Villa Ada.

Caffè Letterario (p198) Entertaining post-industrial all-rounder, in a former garage in southern Rome: fantastic live music and intellectual lounge vibe.

Nuovo Cinema Palazzo (p150) Alternative film, theatre, live music and DJ sets in an old cinema.

Best Classical Venues

Auditorium Parco della Musica (p186) Great acoustics, top international classical musicians and multiple concert halls.

Teatro dell'Opera di Roma (p150) Great, red-velvet and gilt interior for Rome's opera and dance companies.

Terme di Caracalla (p175) Wonderful outdoor setting for summer opera and ballet.

Chiesa di Sant'Agnese in Agone (p74) Chamber music in a Baroque church overlooking Piazza Navona.

Best for Live Gigs

Nuovo Cinema Palazzo (p150) Exciting creative happenings in San Lorenzo's former Palace Cinema.

Blackmarket (p150) Bar filled with vintage sofas and armchairs, great for eclectic, mainly acoustic live music.

Caffè Letterario (p198) Live gigs in a post-industrial space of a former garage: designer looks, gallery, co-working space, stage and lounge bar.

Lanificio 159 (p186) Ex-wool factory hosting underground live gigs alongside club nights.

ConteStaccio (p175) Free live music on the Testaccio clubbing strip.

Best for Jazz

Alexanderplatz (p133) Rome's foremost jazz club, with a mix of international and local musicians.

Auditorium Parco della Musica (p186) Stages, among other things, the Roma Jazz Festival.

Charity Café (p150) Spindly tables and chairs, in an intimate space, hosting regular live gigs.

Big Mama (p162) An atmospheric Trastevere venue for jazz, blues, funk, soul and R&B.

Gregory's Jazz Club (p112) Popular with local musicians, a smooth venue close to the Spanish Steps.

Best Theatres

Scavi Archeologici di Ostia Antica (p200) Wonderful summer theatre in the ancient amphitheatre built by Agrippa.

Teatro Argentina (p91) Rome's premier theatre with a wide-ranging programme of plays, performances and concerts.

Teatro India (p91) The alternative home of the Teatro di Roma.

Best Sporting Venues

Foro Italico (p186) Magnificent Fascist-era sports complex.

Stadio Olimpico (p186) Rome's 70,000-seat football stadium, part of the Fascist-era Foro Italico.

Piazza di Siena (p181) Lovely racecourse in the heart of the Villa Borghese park.

Palazzetto dello Sport (p196) Circular stadium near to EUR in Southern Rome.

Best Festivals

Carnevale Romano (p22) Processions, costumes, parties and confetti – a blow-out before Lent celebrating the end of winter.

Roma Incontra il Mondo (p23) Glorious World music acts play close to the lake in Villa Ada.

Lungo il Tevere (p23) Open-air cinema and stalls line the Tiber riverbank and Tiberina island.

Romaeuropa (p23) Autumn celebration of theatre, opera and dance.

Festa de' Noantri (p23) Trastevere's raucous street party in July.

🛍 Shopping

Rome enthralls with a fabulous portfolio of specialist shops, independent boutiques and artisan workshops – guaranteed to please the most hedonist of shoppers. 'Retro' is among the Roman shopping scene's many unique qualities, with jewel-like boutiques, dusty picture-framing and basket-weaving workshops, historic department stores all oozing an impossibly chic, old-school glamour. Meander, explore backstreets, enjoy.

Fashion

Big-name designer boutiques gleam in the grid of streets between Piazza di Spagna and Via del Corso in Tridente. All the great names are here, as well as many lesser-known designers, all selling highly fashionable clothes, shoes and accessories. The immaculately clad designer-fashion spine is Via dei Condotti, but plenty of haute-couture boutiques also pepper Via Borgognona, Via della Borghese, Via della Vite and Via del Babuino.

Downsizing a euro or two, cheaper mid-range clothes shops line Via Frattuni, Via Nazionale, Via del Corso, Via dei Giubbonari and Via Cola di Rienzo, with some enticing small boutiques set amid the chains.

Best for cutting-edge designer boutiques and vintage clothes is Via del Governo Vecchio, running from a small square just off Piazza Navona towards the river. Other places for one-off boutiques are Via del Pellegrino and around Campo de' Fiori. Via del Boschetto, Via Urbana and Via dei Serpenti in the Monti area feature unique clothing boutiques, including a couple where you can get your clothes adjusted to fit, as well as jewellery makers. Monti's also a centre for vintage clothes shops, as well as a weekend vintage market, Mercato Monti Urban Market (p151).

Antiques

For antiques, Via dei Coronari, old-world Via Margutta, Via Giulia and Via dei Banchi Vecchi are the best places to look – quality is high, as are the prices.

Artisans

Rome's shopping scene has a surprising number of artists and artisans who create their goods on the spot in hidden workshops. There are several places in Tridente where you can get a bag, wallet or belt made to your specifications; in other shops you can commission lamps or embroidery.

Foodstuffs

Rome is deli heaven, of course. Also well worth a visit are Rome's many wonderful food markets – there's usually one in every district – where you can buy cheese, salami and other delicious stuff; note there are now various farmers' markets as well at weekends.

Rome by Neighbourhood

➜ **Centro Storico** (p91) Boutiques, one-off designers, antiques, vintage and jewellery, as well as some swoon-worthy delicatessens.

➜ **Tridente, Trevi & the Quirinale** (p112) From high-fashion designer stores around Via Condotti to affordable chains on busy Via del Corso.

➜ **Monti, Esquilino & San Lorenzo** (p151) Centre for independent fashion, homewares and vintage boutiques.

➜ **Trastevere & Gianicolo** (p162) Gifts and one-off shops in one of Rome's prettiest neighbourhoods.

➜ **San Giovanni & Testaccio** (p175) Browse a colourful food market and glorious delis.

➜ **Southern Rome** (p197) Home of mall-like food emporium Eataly.

Lonely Planet's Top Choices

Benheart (p162) Handmade shoes and jackets by one of Italy's savviest young talents.

Porta Portese Market (p163) Mammoth Sunday-morning flea market.

Confetteria Moriondo & Gariglio (p93) Historic chocolate shop selling handmade chocolates made from 19th-century recipes.

Re(f)use (p112) Ethical fashion accessories by Roman designer Ilaria Venturini Fendi.

Salumeria Roscioli (p92) Foodie heaven.

Best for Fashion

Tina Sondergaard (p151) Retro-inspired dresses, adjusted to fit.

Gente (p114) Emporium-style, multi-label boutique.

Manila Grace (p114) Essential homegrown label for dedicated followers of fashion.

Balenciaga (p114) Fashion shopping in a designer, 19th-century *palazzo* (mansion).

Best for Shoes

Marta Ray (p91) Women's ballerina flats in a rainbow of stylish colours.

Fausto Santini (p115) Rome's best-known shoe designer,

known for beguilingly simple, architectural shoe designs.

Rechicle (p133) Vintage fashion boutique: find that perfect pair of vintage heels.

Best Artisanal

Artisanal Cornucopia (p113) Chic concept store showcasing handmade, artisan pieces by Italian designers.

Ibiz – Artigianato in Cuoio (p92) Father-and-daughter team producing bags and sandals from butter-soft leathers.

Il Sellaio (p133) Beautifully crafted leather bags, belts and accessories.

Flumen Profumi (p113) Artisan fragrances with a 'made in Rome' couture label.

Best Homewares

Bialetti (p186) The place to go for cool Italian kitchenware.

Mercato Monti Urban Market (p151) Vintage homeware finds cram this weekend market.

c.u.c.i.n.a. (p115) Gastronomic gadgets to enhance your culinary life.

Best for Gifts

Federico Buccellati (p114) Handcrafted silverware by one of Italy's most prestigious silver- and goldsmiths.

Fabriano (p113) Desirable leather-bound diaries, quirky paper jewellery by local designers and products embossed with street maps of Rome.

I Colori di Dentro (p93) Take the Roman sun home with a painting by Maria Grazia Luffarelli.

Best for Food

Volpetti (p175) Bulging with delicious delicacies, and notably helpful staff.

Antica Caciara Trasteverina (p163) Wonderful, century-old deli in Trastevere.

Salumeria Roscioli (p86) Byword for foodie excellence.

Biscottificio Innocenti (p163) Enchanting, old-world biscuit shop in a Trastevere backstreet.

Eataly (p197) Mall-scale food shop, filled with products from all over Italy.

Best for Books

Almost Corner Bookshop (p163) Superbly stocked, English language bookshop.

Feltrinelli International (p151) Limited but excellent range of latest releases in various languages.

Libreria l'Argonauta (p186) Travel literature specialist.

Explore Rome

ROME'S
TOP SIGHTS

Neighbourhoods at a Glance

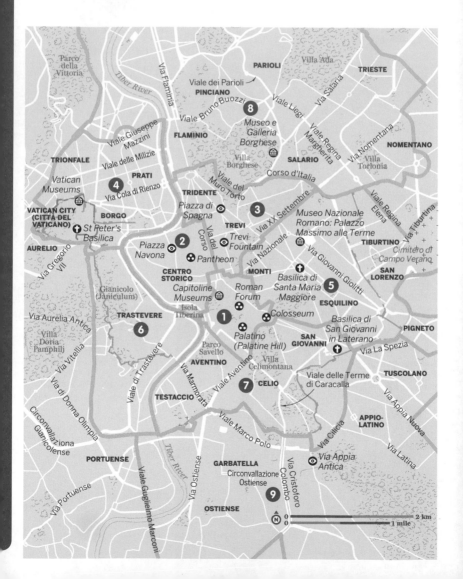

➊ Ancient Rome p50

In a city of extraordinary beauty, Rome's ancient heart stands out. It's here you'll find the great icons of the city's past: the Colosseum; the Palatino; the forums; and the Campidoglio, the historic home of the Capitoline Museums. Touristy by day, it's quiet at night with few after-hours attractions.

➋ Centro Storico p70

A tightly packed tangle of animated piazzas and cobbled alleys, the historic centre is the Rome many come to find. The Pantheon and Piazza Navona are the star turns, but you'll also find a whole host of monuments, museums, boutiques, cafes and restaurants, stylish bars and art-laden churches.

➌ Tridente, Trevi & the Quirinale p96

With the dazzling Trevi Fountain and Spanish Steps among its A-lister sights, this central part of Rome is glamorous and tourist-busy. Designer boutiques and swish hotels grace the web of streets in Tridente, while the Trevi Fountain area swarms with overpriced eateries. Lording over it all, the presidential Palazzo del Quirinale exudes sober authority.

➍ Vatican City, Borgo & Prati p116

The Vatican, the world's smallest sovereign state, sits over the river from the historic centre. With the domed bulk of St Peter's Basilica at its centre, the Vatican boasts some of Italy's most revered artworks, as well as batteries of overpriced restaurants and souvenir shops. Nearby, the landmark Castel Sant'Angelo looms over the Borgo district and upscale Prati offers excellent accommodation and shopping.

➎ Monti, Esquilino & San Lorenzo p136

Centred on transport hub Stazione Termini, this large area can seem busy and overwhelming, but hidden among its traffic-noisy streets are some beautiful churches, Rome's best unsung art museum at Palazzo Massimo alle Terme, and any number of trendy bars and restaurants in the fashionable Monti, student-loved San Lorenzo and bohemian Pigneto districts.

➏ Trastevere & Gianicolo p152

With its old-world cobbled lanes and boho vibe, ever-trendy Trastevere is one of Rome's most vivacious neighbourhoods. Outrageously photogenic and pleasurably car-free, its labyrinth of backstreet lanes heaves after dark as crowds swarm to its fashionable restaurants and bars. Rising up behind, Gianicolo Hill offers a breath of fresh air and a superb view of Rome.

➐ San Giovanni & Testaccio p166

Encompassing two of Rome's seven hills, this sweeping, multifaceted area offers everything from medieval churches and ancient ruins to colourful markets and popular clubs. Its best-known drawcards are the Basilica di San Giovanni in Laterano and Terme di Caracalla. Down by the river, Testaccio is a trendy district known for its nose-to-tail Roman cuisine and thumping nightlife.

➑ Villa Borghese & Northern Rome p176

This moneyed area encompasses Rome's most famous park (Villa Borghese) and its most expensive residential district (Parioli). Concert-goers head to the Auditorium Parco della Musica, while art-lovers can choose between MAXXI, the Museo Nazionale Etrusco di Villa Giulia or the Museo e Galleria Borghese.

➒ Southern Rome p187

Boasting a wealth of diversions, this huge area extends to Rome's southern limits. Find glorious ancient ruins along the cobbled Via Appia Antica, explore post-industrial Ostiense and its edgy street art, dining and nightlife, or head to EUR, an Orwellian quarter of wide boulevards and linear buildings.

Ancient Rome

COLOSSEUM & PALATINO | THE FORUMS & AROUND

Neighbourhood Top Five

❶ Colosseum (p52) Getting your first glimpse of Rome's iconic amphitheatre. The 2000-year-old stadium is both an architectural masterpiece and a stark reminder of the brutality of ancient times.

❷ Palatino (p54) Exploring the haunting ruins of the Palatine Hill, ancient Rome's legendary birthplace and, in imperial times, its most exclusive neighbourhood.

❸ Capitoline Museums (p61) Going face to face with centuries of awe-inspiring art at the world's oldest public museums.

❹ Roman Forum (p57) Discovering the basilicas, temples and triumphal arches of what was once the nerve centre of the vast Roman Empire.

❺ Vittoriano (p66) Surveying the city spread out beneath you from atop this colossal marble extravaganza.

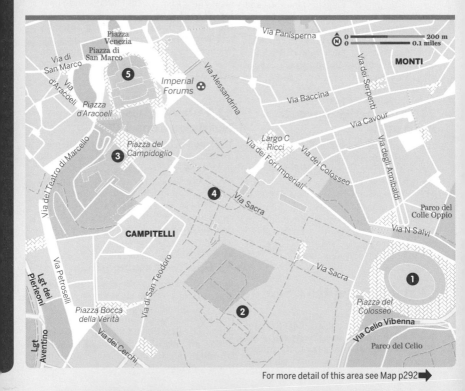

For more detail of this area see Map p292➡

Explore: Ancient Rome

Located to the south of the city centre, this area contains the great ruins of the ancient city, all within easy walking distance of each other. The sites start to get crowded mid-morning and throng with tourists until mid- to late afternoon.

The area has two focal points: the Colosseum (p52) to the southeast, and the Campidoglio (Capitoline Hill) to the northwest. In between lie the forums: the Roman Forum (p57) to the left of Via dei Fori Imperiali as you walk up from the Colosseum, the Imperial Forums (p64) to the right. Rising above the Roman Forum is the Palatino (p54), and behind that the grassy expanse of the Circo Massimo (p64). To the northwest of the Circo, you'll find the Bocca della Verità (p67) and a couple of early Roman temples in an area that used to be ancient Rome's cattle market (Forum Boarium).

To explore Ancient Rome, the obvious starting point is the Colosseum, which is easily accessible by metro. From there you could go directly up to the Roman Forum, but if you go first to the Palatino (the Colosseum ticket covers the Palatino and Roman Forum), you'll get some wonderful views over the forums. Once you're done in the Roman Forum head up to Piazza del Campidoglio (p65) and the Capitoline Museums (p61). Nearby, the mammoth white Vittoriano (p66) is hard to miss.

Local Life

➜**Exhibitions** While tourists clamber all over the Vittoriano, locals head inside to catch an art exhibition at the Complesso del Vittoriano (p66). Accessible from the Forum side of the monument, the gallery hosts an eclectic program of temporary shows.

➜**Celebrations** Join Romans to celebrate the city's birthday, Natale di Roma, on 21 April. The program varies each year but events are generally held around Via dei Fori Imperiali, the Campidoglio (p65) and the Circo Massimo (p64).

➜**Via Crucis** Easter is a big deal in Rome. On Good Friday crowds gather at the Colosseum (p52) to witness the pope lead the traditional Via Crucis procession, an event that is broadcast around the world.

Getting There & Away

➜**Bus** In the northwest of the neighbourhood Piazza Venezia is an important hub. Many services stop in or near here, including bus 40, 64, 87, 170, 916 and H.

➜**Metro** Metro line B has stations at the Colosseum (Colosseo) and Circo Massimo. If taking the metro at Termini, follow signs for Line B 'direzione Laurentina'.

Lonely Planet's Top Tip

The big sights in this part of Rome are among the city's most visited. To avoid the worst of the crowds try to visit early morning or in the late afternoon, when it's cooler and the light is much better for taking photos. Also, be sure to wear comfy shoes as the ancient Roman cobblestones are murder on the feet and you'll be doing plenty of walking.

ANCIENT ROME

Best Places to Eat

➜ Terre e Domus (p67)

➜ Ristorante Roof Garden Circus (p67)

➜ San Teo (p67)

For reviews, see p67.

Best Places to Drink

➜ 0,75 (p69)

➜ Cavour 313 (p69)

➜ Terrazza Caffarelli (p69)

➜ BrewDog Roma (p69)

For reviews, see p69.

Best Lookouts

➜ Vittoriano (p66)

➜ Orti Farnesiani, Palatino (p54)

➜ Tabularium, Capitoline Museums (p61)

➜ Mercati di Traiano Museo dei Fori Imperiali (p65)

For reviews, see p64.

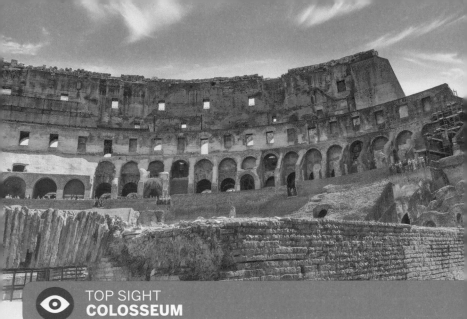

TOP SIGHT
COLOSSEUM

An awesome, spine-tingling sight, the Colosseum is the most thrilling of Rome's ancient monuments. It was here that gladiators met in mortal combat and condemned prisoners fought off wild beasts in front of baying, bloodthirsty crowds. Two thousand years on and it's one of Italy's top tourist attractions, drawing more than six million visitors a year.

The emperor Vespasian (r AD 69–79) originally commissioned the amphitheatre in AD 72 in the grounds of Nero's vast Domus Aurea complex. He never lived to see it finished, though, and it was completed by his son and successor Titus (r 79–81) in AD 80. To mark its inauguration, Titus held games that lasted 100 days and nights, during which some 5000 animals were slaughtered. Trajan (r 98–117) later topped this, holding a marathon 117-day killing spree involving 9000 gladiators and 10,000 animals.

The 50,000-seat arena was Rome's first, and greatest, permanent amphitheatre. For some five centuries it was used to stage lavish, crowd-pleasing spectacles to mark important anniversaries or military victories. Gladiatorial combat was eventually outlawed in the 5th century but wild animal shows continued until the mid-6th century.

Following the fall of the Roman Empire, the Colosseum was largely abandoned. It was used as a fortress by the powerful Frangipani family in the 12th century and later plundered of its precious building materials. Travertine and marble stripped from the Colosseum were used to decorate a number of Rome's notable buildings, including Palazzo Venezia, Palazzo Barberini and Palazzo Cancelleria.

More recently, pollution and vibrations caused by traffic and the metro have taken a toll. To help counter this, it was recently given a major clean-up, the first in its 2000-year history, as part of a €25-million restoration project sponsored by the luxury shoemaker Tod's.

DON'T MISS

➡ The stands
➡ The arena
➡ The hypogeum

PRACTICALITIES

➡ Colosseo
➡ Map p292, G6
➡ ☎ 06 3996 7700
➡ www.coopculture.it
➡ Piazza del Colosseo
➡ adult/reduced incl Roman Forum & Palatino €12/7.50
➡ ⏱ 8.30am-1hr before sunset
➡ Ⓜ Colosseo

The Exterior

The outer walls have three levels of arches, framed by Ionic, Doric and Corinthian columns. These were originally covered in travertine, and marble statues filled the niches on the 2nd and 3rd storeys. The upper level, punctuated with windows and slender Corinthian pilasters, had supports for 240 masts that held the awning over the arena, shielding the spectators from sun and rain. The 80 entrance arches, known as *vomitoria*, allowed the spectators to enter and be seated in a matter of minutes.

The Arena

The stadium originally had a wooden floor covered in sand – *harena* in Latin, hence the word 'arena' – to prevent combatants from slipping and to soak up spilt blood. From the floor, trapdoors led down to the hypogeum, a subterranean complex of corridors, cages and lifts beneath the arena floor.

The Seating

The *cavea*, for spectator seating, was divided into three tiers: magistrates and senior officials sat in the lowest tier, wealthy citizens in the middle and the plebs in the highest tier. Women (except for vestal virgins) were relegated to the cheapest sections at the top. And as in modern stadiums, tickets were numbered and spectators were assigned a precise seat in a specific sector – in 2015, restorers uncovered traces of red numerals on the arches, indicating how the sectors were numbered.

The podium, a broad terrace in front of the seats, was reserved for the emperor, senators and VIPs.

Hypogeum

The hypogeum served as the stadium's backstage area. It was here that stage sets were prepared and combatants, both human and animal, would gather before show time. 'Gladiators entered the hypogeum through an underground corridor which led directly in from the nearby Ludus Magnus (gladiator school)', explains the Colosseum's Technical Director, Barbara Nazzaro.

A second gallery, the so-called *Passaggio di Commodo* (Passage of Commodus), was reserved for the emperor, allowing him to avoid the crowds as he entered the stadium.

To hoist people, animals and scenery up to the arena, the hypogeum had a sophisticated network of 80 winch-operated lifts, all controlled by a single pulley system.

THE NAME

The arena was originally known as the Flavian Amphitheatre (Anfiteatro di Flavio) in honour of Vespasian's family name, and although it was Rome's most fearsome arena, it wasn't the biggest – the Circo Massimo could hold up to 250,000 people. The name Colosseum, when introduced in the Middle Ages, wasn't a reference to its size but to the Colosso di Nerone, a giant statue of Nero that stood nearby.

Games staged at the Colosseum usually involved gladiators fighting wild animals or each other. But contrary to Hollywood folklore, bouts rarely ended in death as the games' sponsor was required to pay compensation to a gladiator's owner if the gladiator died in action.

GUIDED TOURS

The hypogeum, along with the top tier, can be visited on a guided tour. This must be booked in advance and costs €9 plus the normal Colosseum ticket.

TOP SIGHT
PALATINO

Sandwiched between the Roman Forum and the Circo Massimo, the Palatino (Palatine Hill) is an atmospheric area of towering pine trees, majestic ruins and memorable views. It was here that Romulus supposedly founded the city in 753 BC and Rome's emperors lived in unabashed luxury.

Roman myth holds that Romulus founded Rome on the Palatino after he'd killed his twin Remus in a fit of anger. Archaeological evidence clearly can't prove this, but it has dated human habitation on the hill to the 8th century BC.

As the most central of Rome's seven hills, and because it was close to the Roman Forum, the Palatino was ancient Rome's most exclusive neighbourhood. The emperor Augustus lived here all his life and successive emperors built increasingly opulent palaces. But after Rome's fall, it fell into disrepair and in the Middle Ages churches and castles were built over the ruins. Later, wealthy Renaissance families established gardens on the hill.

Most of the Palatino as it appears today is covered by the ruins of Emperor Domitian's vast complex, which served as the main imperial palace for 300 years. Divided into the Domus Flavia, Domus Augustana, and a *stadio* (stadium), it was built in the 1st century AD.

DON'T MISS

➡ Stadio
➡ Domus Augustana
➡ Orti Farnesiani

PRACTICALITIES

➡ Palatine Hill
➡ Map p292, E7
➡ ☑06 3996 7700
➡ www.coopculture.it
➡ Via di San Gregorio 30, Piazza di Santa Maria Nova
➡ adult/reduced incl Colosseum & Roman Forum €12/7.50
➡ ⊘8.30am-1hr before sunset
➡ ⓜColosseo

Stadio

On entering the Palatino from Via di San Gregorio, head uphill until you come to the first recognisable construction, the **stadio**. This sunken area, which was part of the main imperial palace, was used by the emperor for private games. A path to the side of the stadio leads to the towering remains of a complex built by Septimius Severus, comprising **Terme di Settimio Severo**, a baths complex, and **Domus Severiana**, a palace, where, if they're open, you can visit the **Arcate Severiane** (Severian Arches; ⊘8.30am-4pm Tue, Thu & Fri), a series of arches built to facilitate further development.

Domus Augustana & Domus Flavia

Next to the *stadio* are the ruins of the **Domus Augustana** (Emperor's Residence; pictured left), the emperor's private quarters in the imperial palace. This was built on two levels, with rooms leading off a *peristilio* (peristyle or porticoed courtyard) on each floor. You can't get down to the lower level, but from above you can see the basin of a big, square fountain and beyond it rooms that would originally have been paved in coloured marble.

North of the Museo Palatino is the **Domus Flavia**, the public part of the palace. This was centred on a grand columned peristyle – the grassy area with the base of an octagonal fountain – off which the main halls led: the emperor's audience chamber *(aula Regia)*; a *basilica* where the emperor judged legal disputes; and the *triclinium*, a large banqueting hall.

Museo Palatino

The grey building next to the Domus houses the **Museo Palatino**, a small museum dedicated to the history of the area. Archaeological artefacts on show include a beautiful 1st-century bronze, the *Erma di Canefora*, and a celebrated 3rd-century graffito depicting a man with a donkey's head being crucified.

Casa di Livia & Casa di Augusto

Among the best-preserved buildings on the Palatino is the **Casa di Livia** (incl Casa di Augusto visit/guided tour €4/9; ⊘visits 12.45pm daily, pre-booking necessary), northwest of the Domus Flavia. Home to Augustus' wife Livia, it was built around an atrium leading onto frescoed reception rooms. Nearby, the **Casa di Augusto** (incl Casa di Livia visit/guided tour €4/9; ⊘visits 12.45pm daily, reservations necessary), Augustus' private residence, features some superb frescoes in vivid reds, yellows and blues.

Criptoportico Neroniano

Northeast of the Casa di Livia lies the **Criptoportico Neroniano** a 130m tunnel where Caligula was thought to have been murdered, and which Nero later used to connect his Domus Aurea with the Palatino. It's now occasionally used to stage temporary exhibitions.

Orti Farnesiani

Covering the **Domus Tiberiana** (Tiberius' palace) in the northwest corner of the Palatino, the **Orti Farnesiani** is one of Europe's earliest botanical gardens. Named after Cardinal Alessandro Farnese, who had it laid out in the mid-16th century, it commands breathtaking views over the Roman Forum.

ROMULUS & REMUS

Rome's mythical founders were supposedly brought up on the Palatino by a shepherd, Faustulus, after a wolf had saved them from death. Their shelter, the 8th-century-BC **Capanne Romulee** (Romulean Huts), is situated near the Casa di Augusto. In 2007 the discovery of a mosaic-covered cave 15m beneath the Domus Augustana reignited interest in the legend. According to some scholars, this was the Lupercale, the cave believed by ancient Romans to be where Romulus and Remus were suckled by a wolf.

There are no great eating options in the immediate vicinity so consider bringing a picnic. The best spot is the Vigna Barberini (Barberini Vineyard), a grassy area off the path down to the Roman Forum.

PALACE

The Palatino's imperial connection has worked its way into the English language. The word 'palace' is, in fact, a derivation of the hill's Latin name, *Palatium*.

PALATINO (PALATINE HILL)

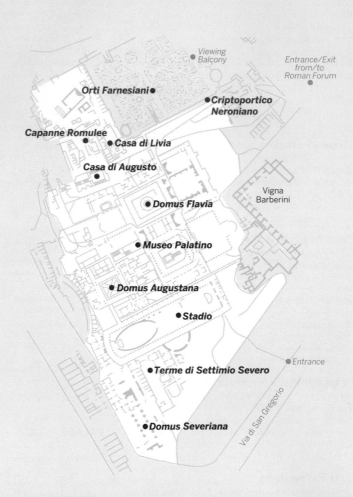

Viewing
Balcony

Entrance/Exit
from/to
Roman Forum

Orti Farnesiani ●

●**Criptoportico
Neroniano**

Capanne Romulee
●

● **Casa di Livia**

Casa di Augusto
●

Vigna
Barberini

● **Domus Flavia**

● **Museo Palatino**

● **Domus Augustana**

● **Stadio**

● Entrance

● **Terme di Settimio Severo**

Via di San Gregorio

● **Domus Severiana**

The Roman Forum was ancient Rome's showpiece centre, a grandiose district of temples, basilicas and vibrant public spaces. Nowadays, it's a collection of impressive, if sketchily labelled, ruins that can leave you drained and confused. But if you can get your imagination going, there's something wonderfully compelling about walking in the footsteps of Julius Caesar and other legendary figures of Roman history.

Originally an Etruscan burial ground, the Forum was first developed in the 7th century BC, growing over time to become the social, political and commercial hub of the Roman empire. Like many of ancient Rome's great urban developments, it fell into disrepair after the fall of the Roman Empire. In the Middle Ages it was known as the Campo Vaccino ('Cow Field') and extensively plundered for its stone and marble. The area was systematically excavated in the 18th and 19th centuries, and excavations continue to this day.

Via Sacra Towards Campidoglio

Entering from Largo della Salara Vecchia – you can also enter from the Palatino or via an entrance near the Arco di Tito – you'll see the **Tempio di Antonino e Faustina** (pictured above) ahead to your left. Erected in AD 141, this was transformed into a church in the 8th century, the **Chiesa di San Lorenzo in Miranda**. To your right, the 179 BC **Basilica Fulvia Aemilia** was a 100m-long public hall with a two-storey porticoed facade.

At the end of the path, you'll come to **Via Sacra**, the Forum's main thoroughfare, and the **Tempio di Giulio Cesare**.

DON'T MISS

- → Curia
- → Arco di Settimio Severo
- → Tempio di Saturno
- → Chiesa di Santa Maria Antiqua
- → Casa delle Vestali
- → Basilica di Massenzio
- → Arco di Tito

PRACTICALITIES

- → Foro Romano
- → Map p292, D5
- → ☎ 06 3996 7700
- → www.coopculture.it
- → Largo della Salara Vecchia, Piazza di Santa Maria Nova
- → adult/reduced incl Colosseum & Palatino €12/7.50
- → ☾ 8.30am-1hr before sunset
- → 🚌 Via dei Fori Imperiali

Roman Forum

A HISTORICAL TOUR

In ancient times, a forum was a market place, civic centre and religious complex all rolled into one, and the greatest of all was the Roman Forum (Foro Romano). Situated between the Palatino (Palatine Hill), ancient Rome's most exclusive neighbourhood, and the Campidoglio (Capitoline Hill), it was the city's busy, bustling centre. On any given day it teemed with activity. Senators debated affairs of state in the **❶ Curia**, shoppers thronged the squares and traffic-free streets and crowds gathered under the **❷ Colonna di Foca** to listen to politicians holding forth from the **❷ Rostrum**. Elsewhere, lawyers worked the courts in basilicas including the **❸ Basilica di Massenzio**, while the Vestal Virgins quietly went about their business in the **❹ Casa delle Vestali**.

Special occasions were also celebrated in the Forum: religious holidays were marked with ceremonies at temples such as **❺ Tempio di Saturno** and **❻ Tempio di Castore e Polluce**, and military victories were honoured with dramatic processions up Via Sacra and the building of monumental arches like **❼ Arco di Settimio Severo** and **❽ Arco di Tito**.

The ruins you see today are impressive but they can be confusing without a clear picture of what the Forum once looked like. This spread shows the Forum in its heyday, complete with temples, civic buildings and towering monuments to heroes of the Roman Empire.

TOP TIPS

➡ Get grandstand views of the Forum from the Palatino and Campidoglio.

➡ Visit first thing in the morning or late afternoon; crowds are worst between 11am and 2pm.

➡ In summer it gets hot in the Forum and there's little shade, so take a hat and plenty of water.

Colonna di Foca & Rostri

The free-standing, 13.5m-high Column of Phocus is the Forum's youngest monument, dating to AD 608. Behind it, the Rostri provided a suitably grandiose platform for pontificating public speakers.

Campidoglio (Capitoline Hill)

ADMISSION

Although valid for two days, admission tickets only allow for one entry into the Forum, Colosseum and Palatino.

Tempio di Saturno

Ancient Rome's Fort Knox, the Temple of Saturn was the city treasury. In Caesar's day it housed 13 tonnes of gold, 114 tonnes of silver and 30 million sestertii worth of silver coins.

IASCIC/SHUTTERSTOCK©

VIACHESLAV LOPATIN/SHUTTERSTOCK ©

Tempio di Castore e Polluce

Only three columns of the Temple of Castor and Pollux remain. The temple was dedicated to the Heavenly Twins after they supposedly led the Romans to victory over the Latin League in 496 BC.

Arco di Settimio Severo
One of the Forum's signature monuments, this imposing triumphal arch commemorates the military victories of Septimius Severus. Relief panels depict his campaigns against the Parthians.

Curia
This big barn-like building was the official seat of the Roman Senate. Most of what you see is a reconstruction, but the interior marble floor dates to the 3rd-century reign of Diocletian.

①

⑦

②

Basilica di Massenzio
Marvel at the scale of this vast 4th-century basilica. In its original form the central hall was divided into enormous naves; now only part of the northern nave survives.

Via Sacra

JULIUS CAESAR
Julius Caesar was cremated on the site where the Tempio di Giulio Cesare now stands.

③

⑥

Tempio di Giulio Cesare

④

⑧

Arco di Tito
Said to be the inspiration for the Arc de Triomphe in Paris, the well-preserved Arch of Titus was built by the emperor Domitian to honour his elder brother Titus.

Casa delle Vestali
White statues line the grassy atrium of what was once the luxurious 50-room home of the Vestal Virgins. The virgins played an important role in Roman religion, serving the goddess Vesta.

THE VESTAL VIRGINS

Despite privilege and public acclaim, life as a vestal virgin was no bed of roses. Every year, six physically perfect patrician girls aged between six and 10 were chosen by lottery to serve Vesta, goddess of hearth and household. Once selected, they faced a 30-year period of chaste servitude at the Tempio di Vesta. Their main duty was to ensure the temple's sacred fire never went out. If it did, the priestess responsible would be flogged. If a priestess were to lose her virginity, she risked being buried alive as the offending man was flogged to death.

The Forum's main drag, Via Sacra was the principal route of the Roman Triumph. This official victory parade, originally awarded by the Senate to a victorious general but later reserved for emperors, was a huge spectacle involving a procession from the *Porta Triumphalis* (Triumphal Gate) through the Forum to the Temple of Jupiter Capitolinus on the Capitoline Hill.

Built by Augustus in 29 BC, this marks the spot where Julius Caesar was cremated. Heading right up Via Sacra brings you to the **Curia**, the original seat of the Roman Senate. This barn-like construction was rebuilt on various occasions and what you see today is a 1937 reconstruction of how it looked in the reign of Diocletian (r 284–305).

In front of the Curia, and hidden by scaffolding, is the **Lapis Niger**, a large piece of black marble that's said to cover the tomb of Romulus.

At the end of Via Sacra, the 23m-high **Arco di Settimio Severo** (Arch of Septimius Severus) is dedicated to the eponymous emperor and his sons, Caracalla and Geta. Close by are the remains of the **Rostri** (Rostra), an elaborate podium where Shakespeare had Mark Antony make his famous 'Friends, Romans, countrymen...' speech. Facing this, the **Colonna di Foca** (Column of Phocus) rises above what was once the Forum's main square, **Piazza del Foro**.

The eight granite columns that rise behind the Colonna are all that survive of the **Tempio di Saturno** (Temple of Saturn), an important temple that doubled as the state treasury. Behind it are (from north to south): the ruins of the **Tempio della Concordia** (Temple of Concord), the **Tempio di Vespasiano** (Temple of Vespasian and Titus) and the **Portico degli Dei Consenti**.

Basilica Giulia & Chiesa di Santa Maria Antiqua

From the path that runs parallel to Via Sacra, you'll pass the stubby ruins of the **Basilica Giulia**, which was begun by Caesar and finished by Augustus. At the end of the basilica, three columns remain from the 5th-century BC **Tempio di Castore e Polluce** (Temple of Castor and Pollux). Nearby, the 6th-century **Chiesa di Santa Maria Antiqua** (⊘currently closed) is the oldest Christian monument in the Forum.

Via Sacra Towards the Colosseum

Returning to Via Sacra you'll come to the **Casa delle Vestali** (House of the Vestal Virgins), home of the virgins who tended the flame in the adjoining **Tempio di Vesta**.

Further on, past the **Tempio di Romolo** (Temple of Romulus), is the **Basilica di Massenzio** (Basilica di Costantino), the largest building on the Forum. Started by the Emperor Maxentius and finished by Constantine in 315, it originally measured approximately 100m by 65m.

Beyond the basilica, the **Arco di Tito** (Arch of Titus) was built in AD 81 to celebrate Vespasian and Titus' victories against rebels in Jerusalem.

TOP SIGHT
CAPITOLINE MUSEUMS

Housed in two stately *palazzi* (mansion) on Piazza del Campidoglio, the Capitoline Museums are the world's oldest public museums. Their origins date to 1471, when Pope Sixtus IV donated a number of bronze statues to the city, forming the nucleus of what is now one of Italy's finest collections of classical sculpture. There's also a formidable picture gallery with works by many big-name Italian artists.

The entrance to the museums is in **Palazzo dei Conservatori** (pictured above), where you'll find the original core of the sculptural collection on the 1st floor, and the Pinacoteca (picture gallery) on the 2nd storey.

Before you head up to start on the sculpture collection proper, take a moment to admire the marble body parts littered around the ground-floor **courtyard**. The mammoth head, hand, and feet all belonged to a 12m-high statue of Constantine that once stood in the Basilica di Massenzio in the Roman Forum.

Palazzo dei Conservatori

Of the permanent sculpture collection on the 1st floor, the Etruscan *Lupa Capitolina* (Capitoline Wolf) is the most famous piece. Standing in the **Sala della Lupa**, this 5th-century-BC bronze wolf stands over her suckling wards, Romulus and Remus, who were added to the composition in 1471.

Other crowd-pleasers include the *Spinario*, a delicate 1st-century-BC bronze of a boy removing a thorn from his foot in the **Sala dei Trionfi**, and Gian Lorenzo Bernini's *Medusa* bust in the **Sala delle Oche**.

DON'T MISS

→ *Lupa Capitolina*
→ *Spinario*
→ *La Buona Ventura*
→ *Galata Morente*
→ *Venere Capitolina*

PRACTICALITIES

→ Musei Capitolini
→ Map p292, B4
→ ☏ 06 06 08
→ www.museicapitolini.org
→ Piazza del Campidoglio 1
→ adult/reduced €11.50/9.50
→ ⏱ 9.30am-7.30pm, last admission 6.30pm
→ 🚍 Piazza Venezia

TREATY OF ROME

With frescoes depicting episodes from ancient Roman history and two papal statues – one of Urban VIII by Bernini and one of Innocent X by Algardi – the **Sala degli Orazi e Curiazi** provided the grand setting for one of modern Europe's key events. On 25 March 1957 the leaders of Italy, France, West Germany, Belgium, Holland and Luxembourg gathered here to sign the Treaty of Rome and establish the European Economic Community, the precursor of the European Union.

Stop by the Terrazza Caffarelli (p69) on the 2nd floor of Palazzo dei Conservatori for coffee and memorable views.

THE CONSERVATORI

Palazzo dei Conservatori takes its name from the *Conservatori* (elected magistrates) who used to hold their public hearings in the *palazzo* in the mid-15th century.

Also on this floor, in the modern **Esedra di Marco Aurelio** wing, is an imposing bronze **equestrian statue** of the emperor Marcus Aurelius – the original of the copy that stands in the piazza outside. Here you can also see the foundations of the Temple of Jupiter, one of the ancient city's most important temples that once stood on the Capitoline Hill.

Pinacoteca

The 2nd floor of Palazzo dei Conservatori is given over to the Pinacoteca, the museum's picture gallery. Dating to 1749, the collection is arranged chronologically with works from the Middle Ages through to the 18th century.

Each room harbours masterpieces, but two stand out: **Sala Pietro da Cortona**, which features Pietro da Cortona's famous depiction of the *Ratto delle sabine* (Rape of the Sabine Women; 1630), and **Sala di Santa Petronilla**, named after Guercino's huge canvas *Seppellimento di Santa Petronilla* (The Burial of St Petronilla; 1621–23). This airy hall boasts a number of important canvases, including two by Caravaggio: *La Buona Ventura* (The Fortune Teller; 1595), which shows a gypsy pretending to read a young man's hand while stealing his ring, and *San Giovanni Battista* (John the Baptist; 1602), an unusual nude depiction of the New Testament saint.

Tabularium

A tunnel links Palazzo dei Conservatori to Palazzo Nuovo on the other side of the square via the **Tabularium**, ancient Rome's central archive, beneath **Palazzo Senatorio**. The tunnel is lined with panels and inscriptions from ancient tombs, but more inspiring are the views over the Roman Forum from the brick-lined Tabularium.

Palazzo Nuovo

Palazzo Nuovo is crammed to its elegant 17th-century rafters with classical Roman sculpture.

From the lobby, where the curly-bearded **Mars** glares ferociously at everyone who passes by, stairs lead up to the main galleries where you'll find some real showstoppers. Chief among them is the *Galata Morente* (Dying Gaul) in the **Sala del Gladiatore**. This sublime piece, actually a Roman copy of a 3rd-century-BC Greek original, movingly captures the quiet, resigned anguish of a dying Gaul warrior.

Next door, the **Sala del Fauno** takes its name from the red marble statue of a faun.

Another superb figurative piece is the sensual yet demure portrayal of the *Venere Capitolina* (Capitoline Venus) in the **Gabinetto della Venere**, off the main corridor, and also worth a look are the busts of philosophers, poets and orators in the **Sala dei Filosofi**.

CAPITOLINE MUSEUMS

GROUND FLOOR

Palazzo Nuovo

Mars•

Cordonata

Piazza del Campidoglio

Palazzo Senatorio & Tabularium

Main Entrance

Courtyard

•Head of Constantine

stairs

Palazzo dei Conservatori

FIRST FLOOR

Palazzo Nuovo

Gabinetto della Venere

stairs

Sala del Gladiatore

Venere Capitolina•

Faun•

Salone

Galata Morente

Sala dei Filosofi

Sala del Fauno

Palazzo dei Conservatori

Sala dei Trionfi

Spinario

Sala degli Orazi e Curiazi

Sala della Lupa

Lupa•

•Lupa Capitolina

Sala delle Oche

•Medusa

Esedra di Marco Aurelio

Equestrian Statue of Marcus Aurelius

•Foundations of Temple of Jupiter

SECOND FLOOR
Palazzo dei Conservatori

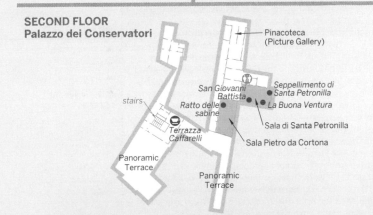

Pinacoteca (Picture Gallery)

San Giovanni Battista

Seppellimento di Santa Petronilla

stairs

Ratto delle sabine

•La Buona Ventura

Terrazza Caffarelli

Sala di Santa Petronilla

Sala Pietro da Cortona

Panoramic Terrace

Panoramic Terrace

◉ SIGHTS

◉ Colosseum & Palatino

COLOSSEUM RUINS
See p52.

PALATINO ARCHAEOLOGICAL SITE
See p54.

ARCO DI COSTANTINO MONUMENT
Map p292 (Via di San Gregorio; ⓂColosseo)
On the western side of the Colosseum, this
monumental triple arch was built in AD 315
to celebrate the emperor Constantine's victory over his rival Maxentius at the Battle
of the Milvian Bridge (AD 312). Rising to a
height of 25m, it's the largest of Rome's sur-
viving triumphal arches.

CIRCO MASSIMO HISTORIC SITE
Map p292 (Circus Maximus; ☑06 06 08; Piazza
di Porta Capena; adult/reduced €5/4; ⊘archaeo-
logical area 10am-4pm Sat & Sun, by reservation
only Tue-Fri; ⓂCirco Massimo) Now a huge
basin of dusty grass, Circo Massimo was
ancient Rome's largest chariot racetrack, a

250,000-seater capable of holding up to a
quarter of the city's population. The 600m
track circled a wooden dividing island with
ornate lap indicators and Egyptian obelisks.

At its southern end, a small segment of
the original stadium was recently opened
to the public after six years of restoration.

◉ The Forums & Around

ROMAN FORUM ARCHAEOLOGICAL SITE
See p57.

**BASILICA DEI SS COSMA
E DAMIANO** BASILICA
Map p292 (☑06 692 04 41; www.cosmadamiano.
com; Via dei Fori Imperiali 1; presepe €1; ⊘10am-
1pm & 3-6pm; ⓆVia dei Fori Imperiali) Backing
onto the Roman Forum, this 6th-century
basilica incorporates parts of the **Foro di
Vespasiano** and **Tempio di Romolo**, visible
at the end of the nave. The real reason to visit, though, is to admire the church's vibrant
6th-century apse mosaics, depicting Peter
and Paul presenting saints Cosma, Damiano, Theodorus and Pope Felix IV to Christ.

◉ TOP SIGHT
IMPERIAL FORUMS

The sprawl of ruins over the road from the Roman
Forum are known collectively as the Imperial Forums.
Constructed between 42 BC and AD 112, they were
mostly buried in 1933 when Mussolini bulldozed Via
dei Fori Imperiali through the area. Excavations have
since unearthed much of them, but visits are limited to
the **Mercati di Traiano** (Trajan's Markets), accessible
through the **Museo dei Fori Imperiali** (p65).

Little that is recognisable remains of the **Foro di
Traiano** (Trajan's Forum), except for some pillars from
the **Basilica Ulpia** and the **Colonna Traiana** (Trajan's
Column), whose minutely detailed reliefs depict Trajan's
military victories over the Dacians (from modern-day
Romania). To the southeast, three columns rise from the
Foro di Augusto (Augustus' Forum). The 30m-high wall
behind the forum was built to protect it from the fires
that frequently swept down from the nearby Suburra
slums. The **Foro di Nerva** (Nerva's Forum) is now largely
buried, although part of a temple to Minerva still stands.
Originally, it would have connected the Foro di Augusto
to the 1st-century **Foro di Vespasiano** (Vespasian's Forum). Over the road, three columns are the most visible
remains of the **Foro di Cesare** (Caesar's Forum).

DON'T MISS...

➜ Mercati di Traiano
➜ Colonna Traiana
➜ Basilica Ulpia

PRACTICALITIES

➜ Fori Imperiali
➜ Map p292, D2
➜ Via dei Fori Imperiali
➜ ⓆVia dei Fori
Imperiali

ℹ POSING CENTURIONS

Although they've been officially banned, you might find costumed centurions offering to pose for a photo with you outside the Colosseum, Roman Forum and Vittoriano. They're not doing this for love and will expect payment. There's no set rate but €5 is more than enough – and that's €5 in total, not per person. Also be very wary of handing your phone/camera to them as they might refuse to give it back until you pay up.

Also worth a look is the 18th-century Neapolitan **presepe** (nativity scene) in a room off the salmon-pink 17th-century cloister.

★MERCATI DI TRAIANO MUSEO
DEI FORI IMPERIALI   MUSEUM
Map p292 (☎06 06 08; www.mercatiditraiano.it; Via IV Novembre 94; adult/reduced €11.50/9.50; ☺9.30am-7.30pm, last admission 6.30pm; ☑Via IV Novembre) This striking museum brings to life the **Mercati di Traiano**, emperor Trajan's great 2nd-century complex, while also providing a fascinating introduction to the Imperial Forums (p64) with multimedia displays, explanatory panels and a smattering of archaeological artefacts.

Sculptures, friezes and the occasional bust are set out in rooms opening onto what was once the Great Hall. But more than the exhibits, the real highlight here is the chance to explore the echoing ruins of the vast complex. The three-storey hemicycle was originally thought to have housed markets and shops – hence its name – but historians now believe it was largely used to house the forum's administrative offices.

Rising above the markets is the **Torre delle Milizie** (Militia Tower; Map p292; ☑Via IV Novembre), a 13th-century red-brick tower.

CARCERE MAMERTINO   HISTORIC SITE
Map p292 (Carcer Tullianum; ☎06 6989 6375; www.operaromanapellegrinaggi.org; Clivo Argentario 1; adult/reduced €10/5; ☺8.30am-4.30pm; ☑Via dei Fori Imperiali) Hidden beneath the 16th-century Chiesa di San Giuseppe dei Falegnami, the Mamertine Prison was ancient Rome's maximum-security jail. St Peter did time here and while imprisoned, supposedly created a miraculous stream of water to baptise his jailers.

On its bare stone walls, you can make out traces of medieval frescoes depicting Jesus, the Virgin Mary and Sts Peter and Paul.

Visits take in a small street-level museum, a two-room affair with artefacts excavated on the site, while tablets provide graphic 3D illustration of how the complex developed over time.

From the museum, stairs lead down to the prison below, which is set on two levels: the 7th-century BC *carcere* (prison) proper with its frescoed walls, and beneath that a dungeon known as the Tullianum. This chilling stone cell is where enemies of the state were thrown and left to die.

⊙ Campidoglio

Rising above the Roman Forum, the Campidoglio (Capitoline Hill) was one of the seven hills on which Rome was founded. At its summit were Rome's two most important temples: one dedicated to Jupiter Capitolinus (a descendant of Jupiter, the Roman equivalent of Zeus) and one to the goddess Juno Moneta (which housed Rome's mint). These days, the hill wields political clout as home of Rome's city hall (Palazzo Senatorio).

CAPITOLINE MUSEUMS   MUSEUM
See p61.

PIAZZA DEL CAMPIDOGLIO   PIAZZA
Map p292 (☑Piazza Venezia) This hilltop piazza, designed by Michelangelo in 1538, is one of Rome's most beautiful squares.

UNDERGROUND ARTS CENTRE

The sheer depth of Rome's archaeological legacy came to light in 2012, when archaeologists unearthed a 900-seat *athenaeum* (arts centre) 5m below Piazza Venezia. Dating to the 2nd-century reign of Hadrian, the **Auditoria di Adriano** consists of three 13m-high arched halls where spectators would have relaxed on terraced marble seating to be entertained by poets and philosophers.

The discovery came during tunnelling work on a new metro line, illustrating the difficulties that engineers face as they inch through the city's treasure-laden undersoil.

The complex is off-limits to visitors.

There are several approaches but the most dramatic is via the graceful **Cordonata** (Map p292; Piazza d'Aracoeli) staircase up from Piazza d'Aracoeli.

The piazza is flanked by **Palazzo Nuovo** and **Palazzo dei Conservatori**, together home to the Capitoline Museums, and **Palazzo Senatorio**, the seat of Rome city council. In the centre is a copy of an **equestrian statue** of Marcus Aurelius.

The original, which dates to the 2nd century AD, is in the Capitoline Museums.

CHIESA DI SANTA MARIA IN ARACOELI   CHURCH

Map p292 (Scala dell'Arce Capitolina; ⊙9am-6.30pm summer, to 5.30pm winter; ⬚Piazza Venezia) Atop the steep 14th-century Aracoeli staircase, this 6th-century Romanesque church marks the highest point of the Campidoglio. Its rich interior boasts several treasures including a wooden gilt ceiling, an impressive Cosmatesque floor and a series of 15th-century Pinturicchio frescoes illustrating the life of St Bernadine of Siena. Its main claim to fame, though, is a wooden baby Jesus that's thought to have healing powers.

In fact, the Jesus doll – in the Cappella del S Bambino to the left of the main altar – is a copy. The original, which was supposedly made of wood from the garden of Gethsemane, was pinched in 1994 and has never been recovered.

The church sits on the site of the Roman temple to Juno Moneta and has long had an association with the nativity. According to legend, it was here that the Tiburtine Sybil told Augustus of the coming birth of Christ.

◉ Piazza Venezia

VITTORIANO   MONUMENT

Map p292 (Victor Emmanuel Monument; Piazza Venezia; ⊙9.30am-5.30pm summer, to 4.30pm winter; ⬚Piazza Venezia) FREE Love it or loathe it, as many Romans do, you can't ignore the Vittoriano (aka the Altare della Patria, Altar of the Fatherland), the massive mountain of white marble that towers over Piazza Venezia. Begun in 1885 to honour Italy's first king, Victor Emmanuel II – who's immortalised in its vast equestrian statue – it incorporates the **Museo Centrale del Risorgimento** (Map p292; ☎06 679 35 98; www.risorgimento.it; Vittoriano, Piazza Venezia; adult/reduced €5/2.50; ⊙9.30am-6.30pm; ⬚Piazza Venezia), a small museum documenting Italian unification, and the **Tomb of the Unknown Soldier**.

For Rome's best 360-degree views, take the **Roma dal Cielo** (Map p292; Vittoriano, Piazza Venezia; adult/reduced €7/3.50; ⊙9.30am-7.30pm, last admission 7pm; ⬚Piazza Venezia) lift to the top.

Housed in the monument's eastern wing is the **Complesso del Vittoriano** (Map p292; ☎06 871 51 11; www.ilvittoriano.com; Via di San

---

❶ NAVIGATING THE ANCIENT SITES

As fascinating as Rome's ancient ruins are, they are not well labelled and it can be hard to know where to go and what to look at.

Entrances

The Roman Forum and Palatino effectively form a single unified site. They're covered by the same ticket (along with the Colosseum) and once you've entered it, you can walk freely between the two areas. There are four entrances:

➡ Largo della Salara Vecchia for the Roman Forum.

➡ By the Carcere Mamertino for the Roman Forum.

➡ Via di San Gregorio 30 for the Palatino.

➡ Piazza di Santa Maria Nova (near the Arco di Tito) for both – go left for the Palatino or straight ahead for the Forum.

Specialist Guides

Electa publishes a number of specialist guidebooks to Rome's archaeological sites, including the *Colosseum* (€5); the *Foro, Palatine and Colosseum* (€10); the *Archaeological Guide to Rome* (€12.90); *The Appian Way* (€15); and *The Baths of Caracalla* (€8). All are available at the Colosseum bookshop.

THE MOUTH OF TRUTH

A bearded face carved into a giant marble disc, the **Bocca della Verità** (Mouth of Truth; Map p292; Piazza Bocca della Verità 18; ☉9.30am-5.50pm; ☐Piazza Bocca della Verità) is one of Rome's most popular curiosities. Legend has it that if you put your hand in the mouth and tell a lie, the Bocca will slam shut and bite your hand off.

The mouth, which was originally part of a fountain, or possibly an ancient manhole cover, now lives in the portico of the Chiesa di Santa Maria in Cosmedin, a handsome medieval church.

Pietro in Carcere; variable; ☉9.30am-7.30pm Mon-Thu, to 10pm Fri & Sat, to 8.30pm Sun; ☐Via dei Fori Imperiali), a gallery space that regularly hosts major art exhibitions.

ROMAN INSULA
RUINS

Map p292 (☎06 06 08; Piazza d'Aracoeli; adult/reduced €4/3; ☉guided tours by reservation only; ☐Piazza Venezia) At the foot of the Campidoglio, next to the Aracoeli staircase, you can see the ruins of a 2nd-century apartment block (*insula*). The ground floor is thought to have served as a tavern, with four upper storeys given over to housing.

To visit you'll have to reserve in advance, but you can get a pretty good idea of the cramped, squalid conditions many ancients lived in just by looking in from the street.

PALAZZO VENEZIA
HISTORIC BUILDING

Map p292 (Piazza Venezia; ☐Piazza Venezia) Built between 1455 and 1464, this was the first of Rome's great Renaissance palaces. For centuries it served as the embassy of the Venetian Republic – hence its name – but it's most readily associated with Mussolini, who installed his office here in 1929, and famously made speeches from the balcony. Nowadays, it's home to the tranquil **Museo Nazionale del Palazzo Venezia** (Map p292; ☎06 6999 4283; www.museopalazzo venezia.beniculturali.it; Via del Plebiscito 118; adult/reduced €5/2.50; ☉8.30am-7.30pm Tue-Sun; ☐Piazza Venezia) and its eclectic collection of Byzantine and early Renaissance paintings, ceramics, bronze figures, weaponry and armour.

BASILICA DI SAN MARCO
BASILICA

Map p292 (Piazza di San Marco 48; ☉10am-1pm Tue-Sun & 4-6pm Tue-Fri, 4-8pm Sat & Sun; ☐Piazza Venezia) The early-4th-century Basilica di San Marco stands over the house where St Mark the Evangelist is said to have stayed while in Rome. Its main attraction is the golden 9th-century apse mosaic showing Christ flanked by several saints and Pope Gregory IV.

 ## EATING

SAN TEO
PASTICCERIA, CAFE €

Map p292 (Via di San Teodoro 88; snacks & pastries €1-4.50; ☉7am-8pm; ☐Via dei Cerchi) With *dolci* (sweets) laid out like jewels and an array of artfully crafted tarts and pastries, this *pasticceria*-cum-cafe puts on a great display. Leave the crowds at the Bocca della Verità and sneak off to indulge your sweet tooth with macarons, marrons glacés and creamy *cannoli*. Savoury snacks are also available.

TERRE E DOMUS
LAZIO CUISINE €€

Map p292 (☎06 6994 0273; Via Foro Traiano 82-4; meals €30; ☉9am-midnight Mon & Wed-Sat, 10am-midnight Sun; ☐Via dei Fori Imperiali) This modern white-and-glass restaurant is the best option in the touristy Forum area. With minimal decor and large windows overlooking the Colonna di Traiano, it's a relaxed spot to sit down to traditional local staples, all made with ingredients sourced from the surrounding Lazio region, and a glass or two of regional wine.

RISTORANTE ROOF GARDEN CIRCUS
RISTORANTE €€€

Map p292 (☎06 678 78 16; www.fortyseven hotel.com; Via Petroselli 47, Hotel Forty Seven; meals €60; ☉noon-10.30pm; ☐Via Petroselli) The rooftop of the Forty Seven hotel sets the romantic stage for chef Giacomo Tasca's seasonal menu of classic Roman dishes and contemporary Mediterranean cuisine. With the Aventino hill rising in the background, you can tuck into stalwarts such as spaghetti *ajo e ojo* (with garlic and olive oil) or opt for something richer like fillet of beef with zucchini, peppermint and roasted peppers.

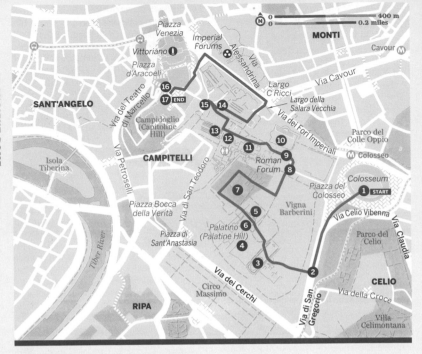

◈ Neighbourhood Walk
Explore the Ruins

START COLOSSEUM
END CAPITOLINE MUSEUMS
LENGTH 1.5KM; FOUR HOURS

Start at the ❶ **Colosseum** (p52), the great gladiatorial arena that more than any other monument encapsulates the drama of the ancient city. From there, follow Via di San Gregorio along to the ❷ **Palatino** (p54), 1st-century Rome's most sought-after neighbourhood where the emperor lived alongside the cream of imperial society. The ruins here are confusing, but their scale gives some sense of the luxury in which the ancient VIPs liked to live.

Beyond the ❸ **stadio**, you can still make out parts of the ❹ **Domus Augustana**, the emperor's private palace quarters, and the ❺ **Domus Flavia**, where he would hold official audiences. Take time to pop into the ❻ **Museo Palatino**, before heading up to the ❼ **Orti Farnesiani**. These gardens weren't part of the ancient city but give good views over the Roman Forum. Next, stroll down to the Forum entering near the

❽ **Arco di Tito**, one of the site's great triumphal arches. Beyond this, pick up ❾ **Via Sacra**, the Forum's main drag. Follow this down, passing the hulking ❿ **Basilica di Massenzio**, and after 100m or so you'll come to the ⓫ **Casa delle Vestali**, where the legendary Vestal Virgins lived tending to their duties and guarding their virtue. Beyond the three columns of the ⓬ **Tempio di Castore e Polluce**, you'll see a flattened area littered with column bases and brick stumps. This is the ⓭ **Basilica Giulia**, where lawyers and magistrates worked in the crowded law courts. Meanwhile, senators debated matters of state in the ⓮ **Curia**, over on the other side of the Forum. Nearby, the ⓯ **Arco di Settimio Severo** stands testament to the military victories of the emperor Septimius Severus. From the Arco double back down Via Sacra and exit the Forum onto Via dei Fori Imperiali. Work your way up to ⓰ **Piazza del Campidoglio** (p65) to round things off in style at the ⓱ **Capitoline Museums** (p61).

🍷 DRINKING &
⚓ NIGHTLIFE

BREWDOG ROMA CRAFT BEER

Map p292 (☎392 9308655; www.brewdog.com/bars/worldwide/roma; Via delle Terme di Tito 80; ☉noon-1am Sun-Thu, to 2am Fri & Sat; Ⓜ Colosseo) This new bar by Scottish brewery BrewDog has proved a hit with Rome's craft-beer lovers since opening in the shadow of the Colosseum in late 2015. With a stripped-down grey-and-brick look, and up to 20 brews on tap, it's a fine spot to kick back after a day on the sights.

TERRAZZA CAFFARELLI CAFE

Map p292 (Caffetteria dei Musei Capitolini; ☎06 6919 0564; Piazzale Caffarelli 4; ☉9.30am-7pm; 🚌Piazza Venezia) The Capitoline Museums' stylish terrace cafe is a memorable place to relax over a drink or light lunch (*panini,* salads, pastas) and swoon over magical views of the city's domes and rooftops. Although it is part of the museum complex, you don't need a ticket to come here as it has an independent entrance on Piazzale Caffarelli.

0,75 BAR

Map p292 (☎06 687 57 06; www.075roma.com; Via dei Cerchi 65; ☉11am-2am; 🛜; 🚌Via dei Cerchi) This welcoming bar overlooking the Circo Massimo is good for a lingering evening drink, an *aperitivo* or casual meal (mains €6 to €16.50). It's a friendly place with a laid-back vibe, an international crowd, attractive wood-beam look, and cool tunes.

PICNIC PROVISIONS

Trawling through Ancient Rome's extensive ruins can be hungry work. But rather than stopping off for an overpriced bite in a touristy restaurant, search out **Alimentari Pannella Carmela** (Via dei Fienili 61; panini €2-4.80; ☉8.30am-2.30pm Mon-Sat & 5-8pm Mon-Fri; 🚌Via Petroselli) for a fresh, cheap *panino*. A small, workaday food store concealed behind a curtain of creeping ivy, it's a lunchtime favourite supplying hungry workers with fresh, made-to-order *panini*, pizza slices, salads, and marinated vegetables.

CAVOUR 313 WINE BAR

Map p292 (☎06 678 54 96; www.cavour313.it; Via Cavour 313; ☉12.30-3.15pm daily & 6-11.30pm Mon-Thu, 6pm-midnight Fri & Sat, 7-11pm Sun, closed Aug; Ⓜ Cavour) Close to the Forum, Cavour 313 is a historic wine bar, a snug, wood-panelled retreat frequented by everyone from tourists to actors and politicians. It serves a selection of salads, cold cuts and cheeses (€9 to €12), but the headline act here is the wine. And with more than 1000 labels to choose from, you're sure to find something to please your palate.

Centro Storico

PANTHEON & AROUND | PIAZZA NAVONA & AROUND | CAMPO DE' FIORI & AROUND | JEWISH GHETTO |
ISOLA TIBERINA | PIAZZA COLONNA & AROUND

Neighbourhood Top Five

1 Pantheon (p72) Stepping into this ancient temple and feeling the same sense of awe that the ancients must have felt 2000 years ago.

2 Piazza Navona (p74) Marvelling at the beauty of this textbook baroque piazza with its flamboyant fountains and elegant domedchurch.

3 Galleria Doria Pamphilj (p82) Having the scion of the aristocratic Doria Pamphilj dynasty talk you through his family art collection at this fabulous private gallery.

4 Chiesa di San Luigi dei Francesi (p76) Clocking three Caravaggio masterpieces at this historic church, one of Rome's many baroque treasures.

5 Jewish Ghetto (p79) Escaping the crowds in the shadowy backstreets before getting to grips with the area's traditional Roman-Jewish cooking.

For more detail of this area see Map p296 and p298 ➡

Explore: Centro Storico

Rome's *centro storico* (historic centre) is made for leisurely strolling, and although you could spend weeks exploring its every corner, you can cover most of the main sights in two or three days. Many people enter the area by bus, getting off at Largo di Torre Argentina (p75), from where it's a short walk up to the Pantheon (p72) and beyond that to Rome's political nerve-centre Piazza Colonna (p81). Nearby, on Via del Corso, the Galleria Doria Pamphilj (p82) houses one of the capital's finest private art collections. To the west of the Pantheon, bohemian boutiques, cool bars and popular pizzerias in the narrow lanes around Piazza Navona (p74), itself one of Rome's great must-see sights, are a magnet for tourists and hip Romans.

On the other side of Corso Vittorio Emanuele II, the main thoroughfare through the area, all roads lead to Campo de' Fiori (p77), home of a colourful daily market and hectic late-night drinking scene. From 'il Campo' you can shop your way down to the medieval Jewish Ghetto (p79), an atmospheric neighbourhood of romantic corners, hidden piazzas and kosher eateries.

Local Life

→**Backstreet eating** The restaurants on Piazza Navona and near the Pantheon on Piazza Rotonda attract a touristy crowd. Locals tend to head to eateries in the quieter back streets, such as Dal Cavalier Gino (p87).

→**Shopping** As much as visitors, Romans love wandering the *centro storico*, browsing its many shops and artisans' studios. For a taster, head to Via del Governo Vecchio (p77), a charming strip lined with arty boutiques and vintage clothing shops.

→**Wine bars** You can't get more Roman than a glass of wine in a traditional *enoteca* (wine bar). These are something of a dying breed, but you can still find them, and places like Il Goccetto (p90) fit the bill to a tee.

Getting There & Away

→**Bus** The best way to access the *centro storico*. A whole fleet serves the area from Termini, including numbers 40 and 64, which both stop at Largo di Torre Argentina and continue down Corso Vittorio Emanuele II. From Via del Tritone near Barberini metro station, bus 492 runs to Corso del Rinascimento for Piazza Navona.

→**Metro** There are no metro stations in the neighbourhood but it's within walking distance of Barberini, Spagna and Flaminio stations, all on line A.

→**Tram** Number 8 runs from Piazza Venezia to Trastevere by way of Via Arenula.

Lonely Planet's Top Tip

The *centro storico* is an expensive part of town but there are ways of making your money go further. You can see masterpieces by the likes of Michelangelo, Raphael, Caravaggio and Bernini for nothing by visiting the area's churches, all of which are free to enter.

✕ Best Places to Eat

→ Pianostrada (p86)

→ La Ciambella (p83)

→ Emma Pizzeria (p86)

→ Forno Roscioli (p85)

→ Armando al Pantheon (p83)

→ Casa Coppelle (p83)

For reviews, see p82.

☐ Best Places to Drink

→ Barnum Cafe (p90)

→ Open Baladin (p90)

→ Caffè Sant'Eustachio (p88)

→ La Casa del Caffè Tazza d'Oro (p88)

→ Roscioli Caffè (p90)

For reviews, see p88.

◉ Best Art Churches

→ Chiesa di San Luigi dei Francesi (p76)

→ Chiesa del Gesù (p80)

→ Chiesa di Sant'Ignazio di Loyola (p82)

→ Basilica di Santa Maria Sopra Minerva (p75)

→ Basilica di Sant'Agostino (p76)

→ Chiesa Nuova (p77)

For reviews, see p75. ▶

TOP SIGHT
PANTHEON

A striking 2000-year-old temple, now a church, the Pantheon is Rome's best-preserved ancient monument and one of the most influential buildings in the Western world. Its greying, pockmarked exterior might look its age, but inside it's a different story, and it's a unique and exhilarating experience to pass through its vast bronze doors and gaze up at the largest unreinforced concrete dome ever built.

DON'T MISS

➡ The entrance doors
➡ The dome
➡ Raphael's tomb

PRACTICALITIES

➡ Map p296, F4
➡ www.pantheonroma.com
➡ Piazza della Rotonda
➡ admission free
➡ ⊙8.30am-7.15pm Mon-Sat, 9am-5.45pm Sun
➡ 🚇Largo di Torre Argentina

History

In its current form the Pantheon dates to around AD 125. The original temple, built by Marcus Agrippa in 27 BC, burnt down in AD 80, and although it was rebuilt by Domitian, it was struck by lightning and destroyed for a second time in AD 110. The emperor Hadrian had it reconstructed between AD 118 and 125, and it's his version you see today.

Hadrian's temple was dedicated to the classical gods – hence the name Pantheon, a derivation of the Greek words *pan* (all) and *theos* (god) – but in 608 it was consecrated as a Christian church after the Byzantine emperor Phocus donated it to Pope Boniface IV. It was dedicated to the Virgin Mary and all the martyrs and took on the name by which it is still officially known, the Basilica di Santa Maria ad Martyres.

Thanks to this consecration, it was spared the worst of the medieval plundering that reduced many of Rome's ancient buildings to near dereliction. But it didn't escape entirely unscathed – its gilded-bronze roof tiles were removed and, in the 17th century, Pope Urban VIII had the portico's bronze ceiling melted down to make 80 canons for Castel Sant'Angelo and to provide Bernini with bronze for the baldachin at St Peter's Basilica.

During the Renaissance, the building was much admired – Brunelleschi used it as inspiration for his cupola in Florence and Michelangelo studied it before designing the dome at St Peter's Basilica – and it became an important burial chamber. Today, you'll find the tomb of the artist Raphael here alongside those of kings Vittorio Emanuele II and Umberto I.

Exterior

Originally, the Pantheon was on a raised podium, its entrance facing onto a rectangular porticoed piazza. Nowadays, the dark-grey pitted exterior faces onto busy, cafe-lined Piazza della Rotonda. And while its facade is somewhat the worse for wear, it's still an imposing sight. The monumental entrance **portico** consists of 16 Corinthian columns, each 11.8m high and each made from a single block of Egyptian granite, supporting a triangular **pediment**. Behind the columns, two 20-tonne bronze doors – 16th-century restorations of the original portal – give onto the central rotunda.

Little remains of the ancient decor, although rivets and holes in the brickwork indicate where marble-veneer panels were once placed.

Interior

Although impressive from outside, it's only when you get inside that you can really appreciate the Pantheon's full size. With light streaming in through the **oculus** (the 8.7m-diameter hole in the centre of the dome), the cylindrical marble-clad interior seems vast, an effect that was deliberately designed to cut worshippers down to size in the face of the gods.

Opposite the entrance is the church's main **altar**, over which hangs a 7th-century icon of the *Madonna col Bambino* (Madonna and Child). To the left (as you look in from the entrance) is the tomb of Raphael, marked by Lorenzetto's 1520 sculpture of the *Madonna del Sasso* (Madonna of the Rock). Neighbouring it are the tombs of King Umberto I and Margherita of Savoy. Over on the opposite side of the rotunda is the tomb of King Vittorio Emanuele II.

The Dome

The Pantheon's dome (pictured left), considered the Romans' most important architectural achievement, was the largest dome in the world until the 15th century when Brunelleschi beat it with his Florentine cupola. Its harmonious appearance is due to a precisely calibrated symmetry – its diameter is exactly equal to the building's interior height of 43.4m. At its centre, the oculus, which symbolically connected the temple with the gods, plays a vital structural role by absorbing and redistributing the dome's huge tensile forces.

Radiating out from the oculus are five rows of 28 coffers (indented panels). These were originally ornamented but more importantly served to reduce the cupola's immense weight.

THE INSCRIPTION

For centuries the Latin inscription over the entrance led historians to believe that the current temple was Marcus Agrippa's original. Certainly, the wording suggests this, reading: 'M.AGRIPPA.L.F.COS. TERTIUM.FECIT' or 'Marcus Agrippa, son of Lucius, in his third consulate built this'. However, excavations in the 19th-century revealed traces of an earlier temple and scholars realised that Hadrian had simply placed Agrippa's original inscription over his new temple.

The stripping of the Pantheon's bronze by the Barberini pope Urban VIII gave rise to the saying, still in use today: 'What the barbarians didn't do, the Barberini did'.

PENTECOST AT THE PANTHEON

Each Pentecost, tens of thousands of red petals are rained down on the Pantheon through the oculus. This centuries-old tradition represents the Holy Spirit descending to earth.

TOP SIGHT
PIAZZA NAVONA

With its showy fountains, graceful baroque *palazzi* and pavement cafes, Piazza Navona is central Rome's elegant showcase square. Long a hub of local life, it hosted Rome's main market for close on 300 years, and today attracts a colourful daily circus of street artists, hawkers, tourists and pigeons.

DON'T MISS
....
→ Fontana dei Quattro Fiumi
→ Chiesa di Sant'Agnese in Agone
→ Palazzo Pamphilj

PRACTICALITIES
....
→ Map p296, E4
→ ▢Corso del Rinascimento

Stadio di Domiziano

Like many of the city's landmarks, the piazza sits over an ancient monument, in this case the 1st-century-AD **Stadio di Domiziano** (Domitian's Stadium; Map p296; ☑06 4568 6100; www.stadiodomiziano.com; Via di Tor Sanguigna 3; adult/reduced €8/6; ☺10am-7pm Sun-Fri, to 8pm Sat). This 30,000-seat stadium, whose subterranean remains can be accessed from Via di Tor Sanguigna, used to host athletic meets – hence, the name Navona, a corruption of the Greek word *agon,* meaning public games. Inevitably, though, it fell into disrepair and it wasn't until the 15th century that the crumbling arena was paved over and Rome's central market was transferred here from the Campidoglio.

Fountains

The piazza's grand centrepiece is Gian Lorenzo Bernini's **Fontana dei Quattro Fiumi** (Fountain of the Four Rivers). Completed in 1651, this flamboyant fountain features a tapering Egyptian obelisk and muscular personifications of the rivers Nile, Ganges, Danube and Plate, representing the four continents of the then-known world. Legend has it that the Nile figure is shielding his eyes from the nearby Chiesa di Sant'Agnese in Agone designed by Bernini's bitter rival, Francesco Borromini. In truth, Bernini completed his fountain two years before his contemporary started work on the church's facade and the gesture simply indicated that the source of the Nile was unknown at the time.

The **Fontana del Moro**, at the southern end of the square, was designed by Giacomo della Porta in 1576. Bernini added the Moor in the mid-17th century, but the surrounding Tritons are 19th-century copies.

At the northern end of the piazza, the 19th-century **Fontana del Nettuno** depicts Neptune fighting with a sea monster, surrounded by sea nymphs.

Chiesa di Sant'Agnese in Agone

With its theatrical facade and rich, domed interior, the **Chiesa di Sant'Agnese in Agone** (www.santagneseinagone.org; concerts €13; ☺9.30am-12.30pm & 3.30-7pm Tue-Sat, 9am-1pm & 4-8pm Sun) is typical of Francesco Borromini's baroque style. The church, which hosts an annual season of chamber-music concerts, is said to stand on the spot where the martyr Agnes performed a miracle before being killed. According to legend, she was stripped naked by her executioners, but her hair miraculously grew to cover her body and preserve her modesty.

Palazzo Pamphilj

Commissioned by Giovanni Battista Pamphilj to celebrate his election as Pope Innocent X, this elegant baroque **palazzo** (http://roma.itamaraty.gov.br/it; ☺by reservation only) was built between 1644 and 1650 by Borromini and Girolamo Rainaldi. Inside, there are some impressive frescoes by Pietro da Cortona but the building, which has been the Brazilian Embassy since 1920, can only be visited on a prebooked guided tour.

⊙ SIGHTS

Bound by the River Tiber and Via del Corso, the *centro storico* is made for aimless wandering. Even without trying you'll come across some of Rome's great sights: the Pantheon, Piazza Navona and Campo de' Fiori, as well as a host of monuments, museums and churches. To the south, the lively Ghetto has been home to Rome's Jewish community since the 2nd century BC.

⊙ Pantheon & Around

PANTHEON   CHURCH
See p72.

BASILICA DI SANTA MARIA
SOPRA MINERVA   BASILICA
Map p296 (www.santamariasopraminerva.it; Piazza della Minerva 42; ☺6.40am-7pm Mon-Fri, 6.40am-12.30pm & 3.30-7pm Sat, 8am-12.30pm & 3.30-7pm Sun; ⓠLargo di Torre Argentina) Built on the site of three pagan temples, including one dedicated to the goddess Minerva, the Dominican Basilica di Santa Maria Sopra Minerva is Rome's only Gothic church. However, little remains of the original 13th-century structure and these days the main drawcard is a minor Michelangelo sculpture and the magisterial, art-rich interior.

Inside, to the right of the altar in the **Cappella Carafa** (also called the Cappella della Annunciazione), you'll find some superb 15th-century frescoes by Filipino Lippi and the majestic tomb of Pope Paul IV.

Left of the high altar is one of Michelangelo's lesser-known sculptures, *Cristo Risorto* (Christ Bearing the Cross; 1520), depicting Jesus carrying a cross while wearing some jarring bronze drapery. This wasn't part of the original composition and was added after the Council of Trent (1545–63) to preserve Christ's modesty.

An altarpiece of the *Madonna and Child* in the second chapel in the northern transept is attributed to Fra Angelico, the Dominican friar and painter, who is also buried in the church.

The body of St Catherine of Siena, minus her head (which is in Siena), lies under the high altar, and the tombs of two Medici popes, Leo X and Clement VII, are in the apse.

PIÈ DI MARMO   MONUMENT
Map p296 (Via di Santo Stefano del Cacco; ⓠVia del Corso) The Piè di Marmo is one of the Romans' favourite monuments. This giant marble foot started life on a statue in a 1st-century temple dedicated to the Egyptian gods Isis and Serapis. Some 1600 years later it cropped up on the street that now bears its name, Via del Piè di Marmo. It was moved to its current position on Via di Santo Stefano del Cacco in 1878 to clear a path for King Vittorio Emanuele II's funeral procession to the Pantheon.

LARGO DI TORRE ARGENTINA   PIAZZA
Map p296 (ⓠLargo di Torre Argentina) A busy transport hub, Largo di Torre Argentina is set around the sunken **Area Sacra** (Map p296), and the remains of four Republican-era temples, all built between the 2nd and 4th centuries BC. These ruins, which are among the oldest in the city, are reckoned to be where Julius Caesar was murdered in 44 BC, and while out of bounds to humans, they are today home to a thriving stray cat population and a volunteer-run **cat sanctuary** (Map p296; www.romancats.com; ☺noon-6pm daily).

On the piazza's western flank stands Teatro Argentina (p91), Rome's premier theatre.

MUSEO NAZIONALE
ROMANO: CRYPTA BALBI   MUSEUM
Map p296 (☏06 3996 7700; www.coopculture.it; Via delle Botteghe Oscure 31; adult/reduced €7/3.50; ☺9am-7.45pm Tue-Sun; ⓠVia delle Botteghe Oscure) The least known of the Museo Nazionale Romano's four museums, the Crypta Balbi sits over the ruins of several medieval buildings, themselves set atop the

---

ELEFANTINO

Just south of the Pantheon, the **Elefantino** (Map p296; Piazza della Minerva; ⓠLargo di Torre Argentina) is a curious and much-loved statue of a puzzled-looking elephant carrying a 6th-century-BC Egyptian obelisk. Commissioned by Pope Alexander VII and completed in 1667, the elephant, symbolising strength and wisdom, was sculpted by Ercole Ferrata to a design by Gian Lorenzo Bernini. The obelisk was taken from the nearby Basilica di Santa Maria Sopra Minerva.

Teatro di Balbo (13 BC). Archaeological finds illustrate the urban development of the surrounding area, while the museum's underground excavations, which can currently be visited only by guided tour, provide an interesting insight into Rome's multi-layered past.

⊙ Piazza Navona & Around

PIAZZA NAVONA   PIAZZA
See p74.

BASILICA DI SANT'AGOSTINO   BASILICA
Map p296 (Piazza di Sant'Agostino 80; ⊘7.30am-noon & 4-7.30pm; ⑨Corso del Rinascimento) The plain white facade of this early Renaissance church, built in the 15th century and renovated in the late 1700s, gives no indication of the impressive art inside. The most famous work is Caravaggio's *Madonna dei Pellegrini* (Madonna of the Pilgrims), in the first chapel on the left, but you'll also find a fresco by Raphael and a much-venerated sculpture by Jacopo Sansovino.

The *Madonna del Parto* (Madonna of Childbirth), Sansovino's 1521 statue of the Virgin Mary with baby Jesus, is a favourite with expectant mums who traditionally pray to it for a safe pregnancy. The Madonna also stars in Caravaggio's *Madonna dei Pellegrini,* which caused uproar when it was unveiled in 1604 with its depiction of Mary's two devoted pilgrims as filthy, badly dressed beggars.

Painting almost a century before, Raphael provoked no such scandal with his fresco of Isaiah, visible on the third pillar on the left side of the nave.

VIA DEI CORONARI   AREA
Map p296 (⑨Corso del Rinascimento) This cobbled Renaissance street lined with antique shops, designer bakeries, boutiques and costume jewellers is a lovely place for a stroll. It follows the course of the ancient Roman road that connected Piazza Colonna with the Tiber, but owes its name to the medieval *coronari* (rosary-bead sellers) who used to hang out here, hawking their wares to pilgrims as they passed en route to St Peter's Basilica.

TOP SIGHT
CHIESA DI SAN LUIGI DEI FRANCESI

Home to Rome's French community since 1589, this opulent baroque church features a celebrated trio of Caravaggio paintings: *Vocazione di San Matteo* (Calling of St Matthew), *Martiro di San Matteo* (Martyrdom of St Matthew) and *San Matteo e l'angelo* (St Matthew and the Angel), known collectively as the St Matthew cycle.

These three canvases, housed in the Cappella Contarelli to the left of the main altar, are among the earliest of Caravaggio's religious works, painted between 1600 and 1602, but they are inescapably his, featuring a down-to-earth realism and the stunning use of chiaroscuro. Caravaggio's refusal to adhere to the artistic conventions of the day and glorify his religious subjects often landed him in hot water, and his first version of *San Matteo e l'angelo,* which depicted St Matthew as a bald, bare-legged peasant, was originally rejected by his outraged patron, Cardinal Matteo Contarelli.

Before you leave the church, take a moment to enjoy Domenichino's faded 17th-century frescoes of St Cecilia in the second chapel on the right. St Cecilia is also depicted in the altarpiece by Guido Reni, which is a copy of a work by Raphael.

DON'T MISS...

➡ *Vocazione di San Matteo*

➡ *Martiro di San Matteo*

➡ *San Matteo e l'angelo*

➡ Domenichino's St Cecilia frescoes

PRACTICALITIES

➡ Map p296, E4

➡ Piazza di San Luigi dei Francesi 5

➡ ⊘9.30am-12.45pm & 2.30-6.30pm Mon-Fri, 9.30am-12.15pm & 2.30-6.45pm Sat, 11.30am-12.45pm & 2.30-6.45pm Sun

➡ ⑨Corso del Rinascimento

CHIESA DI SANTA MARIA DELLA PACE & CHIOSTRO DEL BRAMANTE
CHURCH, GALLERY

Map p296 (www.chiostrodelbramante.it; Via Arco della Pace 5; exhibitions adult/reduced €13/11; ☺church 9am-11.45pm Mon, Wed & Sat, cloister 10am-8pm Mon-Fri, to 9pm Sat & Sun; 🚌Corso del Rinascimento) Tucked away in the back streets behind Piazza Navona, this small baroque church boasts a columned semicircular facade by Pietro da Cortona and a celebrated Raphael fresco, *Sibille* (Sibyls; c 1515) – look up to the right as you enter.

Next door, the **Chiostro del Bramante** (Bramante Cloister) is a masterpiece of High Renaissance architectural styling that is now used to stage art exhibitions and cultural events.

The cloister, which you can visit freely by popping up to the 1st-floor cafe (p83), was originally part of the same monastery complex as the adjoining church. Its sober, geometric lines and perfectly proportioned spaces provide a marked counterpoint to the church's undulating facade, beautifully encapsulating the Renaissance aesthetic that Bramante did so much to promote.

PASQUINO
STATUE

Map p296 (Piazza Pasquino; 🚌Corso Vittorio Emanuele II) This unassuming sculpture is Rome's most famous 'talking statue'. During the 16th century, when there were no safe outlets for dissent, a Vatican tailor named Pasquino began sticking notes to the statue with satirical verses lampooning the church and aristocracy. Soon others joined in and, as the trend spread, talking statues popped up all over town.

The sculpture is now off-limits to disgruntled Romans but there's a convenient board next to it where people still leave messages, traditionally known as *pasquinade*.

VIA DEL GOVERNO VECCHIO
AREA

Map p296 (🚌Corso Vittorio Emanuele II) Striking off west from Piazza Pasquino, Via del Governo Vecchio is an atmospheric cobbled lane full of fashion boutiques, lively eateries and vintage clothes shops. The road, once part of the papal processional route between the Basilica di San Giovanni in Laterano and St Peter's, acquired its name (Old Government St) in 1755 when the pontifical government relocated from Palazzo Nardini at No 39 to Palazzo Madama.

The Renaissance architect Bramante is thought to have lived at No 123.

MUSEO DI ROMA
MUSEUM

Map p296 (🚮06 0608; www.museodiroma.it; Piazza di San Pantaleo 10 & Piazza Navona 2; adult/reduced €8.50/6.50, temporary exhibitions extra; ☺10am-7pm Tue-Sun; 🚌Corso Vittorio Emanuele II) The baroque Palazzo Braschi houses the Museo di Roma's eclectic collection of paintings, photographs, etchings, clothes and furniture, charting the history of Rome from the Middle Ages to the early 20th century. But just as striking as the collection is the 17th-century *palazzo* itself, with its courtyard, monumental baroque staircase, and frescoed halls.

CHIESA NUOVA
CHURCH

Map p296 (Chiesa di Santa Maria in Vallicella; Piazza della Chiesa Nuova; ☺7.30am-7pm; 🚌Corso Vittorio Emanuele II) Hardly new as its name would suggest, this imposing landmark church boasts a distinguished 17th-century facade and a vast baroque interior. Of particular note are the superb ceiling frescoes by Pietro da Cortona and a trio of paintings by Peter Paul Rubens.

Built in 1575 as part of a complex to house Filippo Neri's Oratorian order, it was originally a large plain church in accordance with Neri's wishes. But when Neri died in 1595 the artists moved in – Rubens painted over the high altar, and Pietro da Cortona decorated the dome, tribune and nave. Neri was canonised in 1622 and is buried in a chapel to the left of the altar.

Next to the church is Borromini's **Oratorio dei Filippini**, and behind it the **Torre dell'Orologio** (Map p296; Piazza dell'Orologio; 🚌Corso Vittorio Emanuele II), a clock tower built to decorate the adjacent convent.

❂ Campo de' Fiori & Around

CAMPO DE' FIORI
PIAZZA

Map p296 (🚌Corso Vittorio Emanuele II) Noisy, colourful 'Il Campo' is a major focus of Roman life: by day it hosts one of Rome's best-known markets, while at night it morphs into a raucous open-air pub as drinkers spill out from its many bars and eateries. For centuries the square was the site of public executions, and it was here that philosopher Giordano Bruno was burned for heresy in 1600. The spot is marked by a sinister statue of the hooded monk, which was created by Ettore Ferrari in 1889.

The piazza's poetic name (Field of Flowers) is a reference to the open meadow that stood here before the square was laid out in the mid-15th century.

PALAZZO FARNESE
HISTORIC BUILDING

Map p296 (www.inventerrome.com; Piazza Farnese; €9; ⊙guided tours 3pm, 4pm & 5pm Mon, Wed & Fri; ⬚Corso Vittorio Emanuele II) Home of the French Embassy, this formidable Renaissance *palazzo,* one of Rome's finest, was started in 1514 by Antonio da Sangallo the Younger, continued by Michelangelo and finished by Giacomo della Porta. Inside, it boasts a series of frescoes by Annibale and Agostino Carracci that are said by some to rival Michelangelo's in the Sistine Chapel. The highlight, painted between 1597 and 1608, is the monumental ceiling fresco *Amori degli Dei* (The Loves of the Gods) in the Galleria dei Carracci.

Visits to the *palazzo* are by 45-minute guided tour only (in English, French and Italian), for which you'll need to book at least a week in advance – see the website for details. Photo ID is required for entry and children under 10 are not admitted.

The twin fountains in the square outside are enormous granite baths taken from the Terme di Caracalla.

PALAZZO SPADA
HISTORIC BUILDING

Map p298 (Palazzo Capodiferro; ☑06 683 2409; http://galleriaspada.beniculturali.it; Piazza Capo di Ferro 13; adult/reduced €5/2.50; ⊙8.30am-7.30pm Wed-Mon; ⬚Corso Vittorio Emanuele II) With its stuccoed ornamental facade and handsome courtyard, this grand *palazzo* is a fine example of 16th-century Mannerist architecture. Upstairs, a small four-room gallery houses the Spada family art collection with works by Andrea del Sarto, Guido Reni, Guercino and Titian, while downstairs Francesco Borromini's famous optical illusion, aka the *Prospettiva* (Perspective), continues to confound visitors.

VIA GIULIA
AREA

Map p296 (⬚Via Giulia) Designed by Bramante in 1508 as part of a big urban development program ordered by Pope Julius II, Via Giulia is one of Rome's most charming streets, a picturesque strip of churches, colourful Renaissance *palazzi* and potted orange trees.

TOP SIGHT **MUSEO NAZIONALE ROMANO: PALAZZO ALTEMPS**

Just north of Piazza Navona, Palazzo Altemps is a beautiful late-15th-century *palazzo,* housing the best of the Museo Nazionale Romano's formidable collection of classical sculpture. Many pieces come from the celebrated Ludovisi collection, amassed by Cardinal Ludovico Ludovisi in the 17th century.

Prize exhibits include the beautiful 5th-century-BC *Trono Ludovisi* (Ludovisi Throne), a carved marble block whose central relief shows a naked Venus (Aphrodite) being modestly plucked from the sea. In the neighbouring room, the *Ares Ludovisi,* a 2nd-century-BC representation of a young, clean-shaven Mars, owes its right foot to a Gian Lorenzo Bernini restoration in 1622.

Another affecting work is the sculptural group *Galata Suicida* (Gaul's Suicide), a melodramatic depiction of a Gaul knifing himself to death over a dead woman.

The building itself provides an elegant backdrop with a grand central courtyard and frescoed rooms. These include the **Sala delle Prospettive Dipinte**, which was painted with landscapes and hunting scenes for Cardinal Altemps, the rich nephew of Pope Pius IV (r 1560–65) who bought the *palazzo* in the late 16th century.

The museum also houses the Museo Nazional Romano's Egyptian collection.

DON'T MISS...

➡ *Trono Ludovisi*

➡ *Ares Ludovisi*

➡ *Galata Suicida*

➡ Sala delle Prospettive Dipinte

PRACTICALITIES

➡ Map p296, E3

➡ ☑06 3996 7700

➡ www.coopculture.it

➡ Piazza Sant'Apollinare 44

➡ adult/reduced €7/3.50

➡ ⊙9am-7.45pm Tue-Sun

➡ ⬚Corso del Rinascimento

At its southern end, the 17th-century **Fontana del Mascherone** (Map p298; ⌨Lungotevere dei Tebaldi) features the face of a man seemingly surprised by water spewing from his mouth. Just beyond it, and spanning the road, is the **Arco Farnese** (Map p296), an overhead arch designed by Michelangelo as part of an unfinished project to connect Palazzo Farnese with Villa Farnesina on the opposite side of the Tiber.

Continuing north, on the left, down Via di Sant'Eligio, is the lovely Raphael-designed **Chiesa di Sant'Eligio degli Orefici** (Map p296; ✆06 686 8260; Via di Sant'Eligio 8a; ◷by reservation only 9am-1pm Mon-Fri; ⌨Lungotevere dei Tebaldi).

BASILICA DI SAN GIOVANNI BATTISTA DEI FIORENTINI   BASILICA

Map p296 (Piazza dell'Oro 2; ◷7.30am-noon & 5-7pm; ⌨Ponte Vittorio Emanuele II) The last resting place of Francesco Borromini and Carlo Maderno, this graceful 16th-century church was commissioned by Pope Leo X as a showcase for Florentine artistic talent. Jacopo Sansovino won a competition for its design, which was then executed by Antonio Sangallo the Younger and Giacomo della Porta. Carlo Maderno completed the elongated cupola in 1614, while the travertine facade was added by Alessandro Galilei in the mid-18th century.

PALAZZO DELLA CANCELLERIA   HISTORIC BUILDING

Map p296 (Piazza della Cancelleria; exhibition adult/reduced €9/7; ◷exhibition 9.30am-7.30pm; ⌨Corso Vittorio Emanuele II) As impressive an example of Renaissance architecture as you'll find in Rome, this huge *palazzo* was built for Cardinal Raffaele Riario between 1483 and 1513. It was later acquired by the Vatican and became the seat of the Papal Chancellery. It is still Vatican property and nowadays houses various Church offices, including the Roman Rota, the Holy See's highest ecclesiastical court.

The *palazzo* also provides the grand setting for an exhibition dedicated to machines designed by Leonardo da Vinci. But if that doesn't appeal, it's worth nipping through to the courtyard to take a peek at Bramante's glorious double loggia.

Incorporated into the *palazzo,* the 4th-century **Basilica di San Lorenzo in Damaso** (Map p296; ◷7.30am-noon & 4.30-7.30pm Mon-

ARCO DEGLI ACETARI

For one of Rome's most picture-perfect scenes head to the **Arco degli Acetari** (Vinegar-Makers' Arch; Map p296; Via del Pellegrino 19; ◷6.30am-11pm; ⌨Corso Vittorio Emanuele II), a dark archway just off Campo de' Fiori. The arch in itself isn't especially memorable, but if you duck under it you'll emerge onto a tiny medieval square enclosed by rusty orange houses and full of colourful cascading plants. Cats and bicycles litter the cobbles, while overhead washing hangs off pretty flower-lined balconies.

Sat, 8.30am-1pm & 5-8pm Sun) is one of Rome's oldest churches.

CHIESA DI SANT'ANDREA DELLA VALLE   CHURCH

Map p296 (Piazza Vidoni 6; ◷7.30am-7.45pm; ⌨Corso Vittorio Emanuele II) A must for opera fans, this towering 17th-century church is where Giacomo Puccini set the first act of *Tosca*. Its most obvious feature is Carlo Maderno's soaring dome, the highest in Rome after St Peter's, but its cavernous baroque interior reveals a wonderful series of frescoes by Matteo Preti and Domenichino, and, in the dome, Lanfranco's heady depiction of heaven, *Gloria del Paradiso* (Glory of Paradise; 1625–28).

⊙ Jewish Ghetto

Centred on lively Via Portico d'Ottavia, the **Jewish Ghetto** (Map p298; ⌨Lungotevere de' Cenci) is an atmospheric area studded with artisans' studios, vintage clothing shops, kosher bakeries and popular trattorias.

Rome's Jewish community dates back to the 2nd century BC, making it one of the oldest in Europe. The first Jews came to the city as business envoys but many later arrived as slaves following the Roman wars in Judaea and Titus' defeat of Jerusalem in AD 70. Confinement to the Ghetto came in 1555 when Pope Paul IV ushered in a period of official intolerance that lasted, on and off, until the 20th century. Ironically, though, confinement meant that Jewish cultural and religious identity survived intact.

TOP SIGHT
CHIESA DEL GESÙ

An imposing example of Counter-Reformation architecture, this landmark *chiesa* is Rome's most important Jesuit church. Consecrated in 1584, it's fronted by a harmonious and much-copied facade by Giacomo della Porta. But more than the masonry, the star turn is the lavish interior and its astounding ceiling fresco, the *Trionfo del Nome di Gesù* (Triumph of the Name of Jesus; 1679) by Giovanni Battista Gaulli. The artist, better known as Il Baciccia, also created much of the stucco decoration and the cupola frescoes.

In the northern transept, the Cappella di Sant'Ignazio houses the tomb of Ignatius Loyola, the Spanish soldier who founded the Jesuits in 1540. The altar-tomb, designed by baroque maestro Andrea Pozzo, is a sumptuous marble-and-bronze affair with lapis lazuli–encrusted columns and, on top, a lapis lazuli globe representing the Trinity. On either side are sculptures whose titles neatly encapsulate the Jesuit ethos: to the left, *Fede che vince l'Idolatria* (Faith Defeats Idolatry); and on the right, *Religione che flagella l'Eresia* (Religion Lashing Heresy).

The Spanish saint lived in the church from 1544 until his death in 1556 and you can visit his private rooms to the right of the main church.

DON'T MISS...

→ The *Trionfo del Nome di Gesù* fresco
→ Cappella di Sant'Ignazio

PRACTICALITIES

→ Map p296
→ ☑06 69 7001
→ www.chiesadelgesu.org
→ Piazza del Gesù
→ ⊘7am-12.30pm & 4-7.45pm, St Ignatius rooms 4-6pm Mon-Sat, 10am-noon Sun
→ ▣Largo di Torre Argentina

MUSEO EBRAICO DI ROMA
SYNAGOGUE, MUSEUM

Map p298 (Jewish Museum of Rome; ☑06 6840 0661; www.museoebraico.roma.it; Via Catalana; adult/reduced €11/5; ⊘10am-5.15pm Sun-Thu, 10am-3.15pm Fri summer, 10am-4.15pm Sun-Thu, 9am-1.15pm Fri winter; ▣Lungotevere de' Cenci) The historical, cultural and artistic heritage of Rome's Jewish community is chronicled in this small but engrossing museum. Housed in the city's early-20th-century synagogue, Europe's second largest, it displays parchments, precious fabrics, marble carvings, and a collection of 17th- and 18th-century silverware. Documents and photos attest to life in the Ghetto and the hardships suffered by the city's Jewish people during WWII. Admission also includes a guided tour of the main synagogue.

To learn more about the Jewish Ghetto, the museum runs hour-long tours (adult/reduced €8/5), bookable at the ticket office.

FONTANA DELLE TARTARUGHE
FOUNTAIN

Map p298 (Piazza Mattei; ▣Via Arenula) This playful, much-loved fountain features four boys gently hoisting tortoises up into a bowl of water. Created by Giacomo della Porta and Taddeo Landini in the late 16th century, it's the subject of a popular local legend, according to which it was created in a single night.

PORTICO D'OTTAVIA
RUINS

Map p298 (Via Portica d'Ottavia 29; ⊘9am-7pm summer, to 6pm winter; ▣Lungotevere de' Cenci) The Portico d'Ottavia is the oldest quadriporto (four-sided porch) in Rome. The dilapidated columns and fragmented pediment once formed part of a vast rectangular portico, supported by 300 columns and extending for 132m by 119m. Much of what you see today is from a 3rd-century restoration of the portico Augustus built in 23 BC on the site of the Portico di Metella (146 BC). Named after the emperor's sister, Octavia, it housed Rome's fish market from the Middle Ages until the late 19th century.

Behind the portico, and currently covered in scaffolding, is the 8th-century Chiesa di Sant'Angelo.

TEATRO DI MARCELLO
HISTORIC BUILDING

Map p298 (Theatre of Marcellus; Via del Teatro di Marcello; ▣Via del Teatro di Marcello) To the east of Rome's Jewish Ghetto, the Teatro di Marcello is the star turn of the dusty Area dcl Teatro di Marcello. A 20,000-seat mini-Colosseum, the theatre was planned by Julius Caesar and completed in 11 BC by Augustus who named it after a favourite nephew, Marcellus. In the 16th century, a *palazzo*, which now contains several exclusive apartments, was built on top of the original structure.

BASILICA DI SAN NICOLA
IN CARCERE
BASILICA

Map p298 (Via del Teatro di Marcello 46; excavations €3; ☉10am-7pm, excavations 10am-6pm Mon-Fri, to 5pm Sat & Sun; 🚇Via del Teatro di Marcello) This innocuous-looking 11th-century church harbours some fascinating Roman excavations. Beneath the main church you can poke around the claustrophobic foundations of three Republican-era temples and the remnants of an Etruscan vegetable market. The temples, which were used as a prison in medieval times – hence *carcere* (prison) in the church's name – were incorporated into the church's structure as witnessed by the marble columns in the basilica's side.

Visits are by guided tour only and led by experts from the Sotterranei di Roma association.

◉ Isola Tiberina

One of the world's smallest inhabited islands, boat-shaped Isola Tiberina (Tiber Island) has been associated with healing since the 3rd century BC, when the Romans built a temple to the god of medicine Asclepius (aka Aesculapius) here. And still today people come to be cured, though they now head to the island's hospital, the Ospedale Fatebenefratelli.

The island is connected to the mainland by two bridges: the 62 BC **Ponte Fabricio**, Rome's oldest standing bridge, which links with the Jewish Ghetto, and **Ponte Cestio**, which runs over to Trastevere.

Visible to the south are the remains of the Pons Aemilius – aka the **Ponte Rotto** (Broken Bridge; Map p292) – ancient Rome's first stone bridge, which was all but swept away in a 1598 flood.

CHIESA DI SAN BARTOLOMEO
CHURCH

Map p298 (Piazza di San Bartolomeo all'Isola 22, Isola Tiberina; ☉9.30am-1.30pm & 3.30-5.30pm Mon-Sat, 9.30am-1pm Sun; 🚇Lungotevere dei Pierleoni) Built on the ruins of the Roman temple to Aesculapius, the Graeco-Roman god of medicine, the Isola Tiberina's 10th-century church is an interesting hybrid of architectural styles. The facade and the richly frescoed ceiling are baroque; the bell tower is 12th-century Romanesque; and the 28 columns that divide the interior date to ancient times.

◉ Piazza Colonna & Around

PIAZZA COLONNA
PIAZZA

Map p296 (🚇Via del Corso) Together with the adjacent Piazza di Montecitorio, this stylish piazza is Rome's political nerve centre. On its northern flank, the 16th-century **Palazzo Chigi** (Map p296; www.governo.it; Piazza Colonna 370; ☉guided visits 9am-noon Sat, twice monthly Sep-Jun, bookings required) FREE has been the official residence of Italy's prime minister since 1961. In the centre, the 30m-high **Colonna di Marco Aurelio** (Map p296) was completed in AD 193 to honour Marcus Aurelius' military victories.

The column's vivid reliefs depict scenes from battles against the Germanic tribes (169–173) and, further up, the Sarmatians (174–176). In 1589 Marcus was replaced on the top of the column with a bronze statue of St Paul.

PALAZZO DI
MONTECITORIO
HISTORIC BUILDING

Map p296 (📞800 012955; www.camera.it; Piazza di Montecitorio; ☉guided visits 10.30am-3.30pm 1st Sun of the month; 🚇Via del Corso) FREE Home to Italy's Chamber of Deputies, this baroque *palazzo* was built by Bernini in 1653, expanded by Carlo Fontana in the late 17th century, and given an art nouveau facelift in 1918. Visits take in the mansion's lavish reception rooms and the main chamber where the 630 deputies debate beneath a beautiful Liberty-style skyline.

The **obelisk** (Map p296) outside was brought from Heliopolis in Egypt by Augustus to celebrate victory over Cleopatra and Mark Antony in 30 BC.

PIAZZA DI PIETRA
PIAZZA

Map p296 (🚇Via del Corso) This charming piazza, surrounded by popular bars and cafes, is overlooked by 11 huge Corinthian columns, all that's left of the 2nd-century **Tempio di Adriano** (Map p296). The temple formerly housed Rome's stock exchange and is now used to host conferences and business events.

TOP SIGHT
GALLERIA DORIA PAMPHILJ

Hidden behind the grey exterior of Palazzo Doria Pamphilj, this gallery boasts one of Rome's richest private art collections, with works by Raphael, Tintoretto, Titian, Caravaggio, Bernini and Velázquez.

Palazzo Doria Pamphilj dates to the mid-15th century, but its current look was largely the work of its owners, the Doria Pamphilj family, who acquired it in the 18th century. The Pamphilj's golden age, during which the family collection was started, came during the papacy of one of their own, Innocent X (r 1644–55).

Masterpieces abound, but look out for Titian's *Salomè con la testa del Battista* (Salome with the Head of John the Baptist) and two early Caravaggios: *Riposo durante la fuga in Egitto* (Rest During the Flight into Egypt) and *Maddalene Penitente* (Penitent Magdalen). Also of note is Alessandro Algardi's bust of Donna Olimpia and the *Battaglia nel porto di Napoli* (Battle in the Bay of Naples), one of the few paintings in Rome by Pieter Bruegel the Elder.

The collection's undisputed star, though, is Velázquez' portrait of Pope Innocent X, who grumbled that the depiction was 'too real'. For a comparison, check out Bernini's sculptural interpretation of the same subject.

DON'T MISS

➡ *Salomè con la testa del Battista*

➡ *Riposo durante la fuga in Egitto*

➡ *Ritratto di papa Innocenzo X*

➡ *Battaglia nel porto di Napoli*

PRACTICALITIES

➡ Map p296, H5

➡ ☎06 679 73 23

➡ www.doriapamphilj.it

➡ Via del Corso 305

➡ adult/reduced €12/8

➡ ⏱9am-7pm, last entry 6pm

➡ 🚌Via del Corso

CHIESA DI SANT'IGNAZIO DI LOYOLA   CHURCH
Map p296 (www.santignazio.gesuiti.it; Piazza di Sant'Ignazio; ⏱7.30am-7pm Mon-Sat, 9am-7pm Sun; 🚌Via del Corso) Flanking a delightful rococo piazza, this important Jesuit church boasts a Carlo Maderno facade and two celebrated *trompe l'œil* frescoes by Andrea Pozzo (1642–1709). One cleverly depicts a fake dome, while the other, on the nave ceiling, shows St Ignatius Loyola being welcomed into paradise by Christ and the Madonna.

For the best views of this dizzying work, stand on the small yellow spot on the nave floor and look up – alternatively, use the conveniently positioned floor mirror. Thanks to Pozzo's virtuoso use of perspective, a mass of figures, led by St Ignatius, appears to float heavenwards past a series of soaring columns and arches.

A second marble disk marks the best place to admire the dome, actually a flat canvas, which was painted in 1685.

The church, which was built by the Jesuit architect Orazio Grassi in 1626, flanks **Piazza di Sant'Ignazio** (Map p296; 🚌Via del Corso), an exquisite square laid out in 1727

to resemble a stage set. Note the exits into 'the wings' at the northern end and how the undulating surfaces create the illusion of a larger space.

 EATING

Around Piazza Navona, Campo de' Fiori and the Pantheon you'll find all manner of eateries, including some of the capital's best restaurants, alongside hundreds of overpriced tourist traps. The atmospheric Ghetto is famous for its Roman-Jewish cuisine.

🍴 Pantheon & Around

PIZZA ZAZÀ   PIZZA €
Map p296 (☎06 6880 1357; www.pizzazaza.it; Piazza Sant'Eustachio 49; pizza slice around €3; ⏱10am-11pm; 🚌Corso del Rinascimento) Handily sandwiched between Piazza Navona and the Pantheon, this bright and breezy takeaway dishes up tasty slices of low-cal pizza, made with carefully sourced organic ingredients. Order to go or grab an outside table and watch the world pass by as you munch.

★LA CIAMBELLA   ITALIAN €€
Map p296 (☑06 683 2930; www.la-ciambella.it;
Via dell'Arco della Ciambella 20; meals €35-45;
☻bar 7.30am-midnight, wine bar & restaurant
noon-11pm Tue-Sun; ▣Largo di Torre Argentina)
Central but largely undiscovered by the
tourist hordes, this friendly wine-bar-cum-
restaurant beats much of the neighbourhood competition. Its spacious, light-filled
interior is set over the ruins of the Terme di
Agrippa, visible through transparent floor
panels, and its kitchen sends out some excellent food, from tartares and chickpea pancakes to slow-cooked beef and traditional
Roman pastas.

ARMANDO AL PANTHEON   ROMAN €€
Map p296 (☑06 6880 3034; www.armando
alpantheon.it; Salita dei Crescenzi 31; meals €40;
☻12.30-3pm Mon-Sat & 7-11pm Mon-Fri; ▣Largo
di Torre Argentina) With its cosy wooden interi-
or and unwavering dedication to old-school
Roman cuisine, Armando al Pantheon is a
regular go-to for local foodies. It's been on
the go for more than 50 years and has served
its fair share of celebs, but it hasn't let fame
go to its head and it remains as popular as
ever. Reservations essential.

GINGER   ITALIAN €€
Map p296 (☑06 6830 8559; www.gingersaporie
salute.com; Piazza Sant'Eustachio 54; meals €30;
☻8am-midnight; ▣Corso del Rinascimento)
Boasting a white, casually contemporary
interior and alfresco seating on a characteristic piazza, this is one of Rome's new breed
of all-day eateries. It serves everything from
coffee and fresh fruit juices to gourmet
panini and a full restaurant menu featuring the likes of tonnarelli con polpa (square
spaghetti with octopus) and a killer chocolate orange cake.

OSTERIA DEL SOSTEGNO   TRATTORIA €€
Map p296 (☑06 679 38 42; www.ilsostegno.it; Via
delle Colonnelle 5; meals €40; ☻12.30-3.30pm &
7.30-11.30pm, closed Sun dinner & Mon; ▣Largo
di Torre Argentina) Follow the green neon arrow to the end of a narrow alley and you'll
find this well-kept secret. It's an intimate
place and a long-standing favourite of journalists and politicians who sneak off here to
dine on old-school staples such as tagliolini
con funghi porcini (flat ribbon with porcini mushrooms) and pollo alla cacciatora
(chicken in a white wine sauce).

CASA COPPELLE   RISTORANTE €€€
Map p296 (☑06 6889 1707; www.casacoppelle.it;
Piazza delle Coppelle 49; meals €65, tasting menu
€85; ☻noon-3.30pm & 6.30-11.30pm; ▣Corso
del Rinascimento) Boasting an enviable setting
near the Pantheon and a plush, theatrical
look – think velvet drapes, black lacquer tables and bookshelves – Casa Coppelle sets a
romantic stage for high end Roman-French
cuisine. Gallic trademarks like snails and
onion soup feature alongside updated Roman favourites such as pasta amatriciana
(with tomato sauce and pancetta) and cacio
e pepe (pecorino and black pepper), here reinvented as a risotto with prawns.

GREEN T   CHINESE €€€
Map p296 (☑06 679 8628; www.green-tea.it; Via
del Piè di Marmo 28; lunch menus €9.50-17, meals
€45-50; ☻12.30-3pm & 7.30-midnight Mon-Sat;
▣Via del Corso) With five rooms decorated
in antique oriental style, this four-floor
feng shui–designed restaurant flies the flag
for quality Chinese food in Rome. Expect
spicy Sechuan dishes, dim sum, wok-tossed
vegetables and a selection of fine teas. Save
money at lunch by opting for one of the daily
fixed-price menus.

✗ Piazza Navona & Around

CAFFETTERIA CHIOSTRO
DEL BRAMANTE   CAFE €
Map p296 (☑06 6880 9036; www.chiostro
delbramante.it; Via Arco della Pace 5; meals €15-
25; ☻10am-8pm Mon-Fri, to 9pm Sat & Sun; ☎;
▣Corso del Rinascimento) Many of Rome's galleries and museums have in-house cafes but
few are as beautifully located as the Caffetteria Chiostro del Bramante on the 1st floor
of Bramante's elegant Renaissance cloister.
With outdoor tables overlooking the central
courtyard and an all-day menu offering everything from cakes and coffee to baguettes,
risottos and Caesar salads, it's a great spot
for a break.

BAGUETTERIA DEL FICO   SANDWICHES €
Map p296 (☑06 9604 5541; www.facebook.
com/baguetteriadelfico; Via della Fossa 12; panini
€5.50-9; ☻10am-2am; ▣Corso del Risorgimento)
An upmarket baguette bar ideal for a midday bite or late snack. Choose your bread,
then select from the rich array of fillings –
cured hams, pungent cheeses, marinated
vegetables, salads, homemade sauces.

CENTRO STORICO GELATO STOPS

Gelateria del Teatro (Map p296; ☑06 4547 4880; www.gelateriadelteatro.it; Via dei Coronari 65; gelato €2.50-5; ⊙10.30am-8pm winter, 10am-10.30pm summer; ⊠Via Zanardelli) All the ice cream served at this excellent gelateria is prepared on-site – look through the window and you'll see how. There are about 40 flavours to choose from, all made from thoughtfully sourced ingredients such as hazelnuts from the Langhe region of Piedmont and pistachios from Bronte in Sicily.

Venchi (Map p296; ☑06 6992 5423; www.venchi.com; Via degli Orfani 87; gelato €2.50-5; ⊙10.30am-11pm Sun-Thu, to midnight Fri & Sat summer, 10am-10pm Sun-Thu, to 11pm Fri & Sat winter; ⊠Via del Corso) Forget fancy flavours and gelato experiments, Venchi is all about the unadulterated enjoyment of chocolate. The wall shelves and counter displays feature myriad beautifully packaged delicacies, from pralines to chilli chocolate bars, as well as an assortment of decadent choc-based ice creams.

Giolitti (Map p296; ☑06 699 1243; www.giolitti.it; Via degli Uffici del Vicario 40; gelato €2.50-4.50; ⊙7am-1am; ⊠Via del Corso) Rome's most celebrated gelateria started as a dairy in 1900 and still keeps the tourists happy with its creamy flavours. Gregory Peck and Audrey Hepburn swung by in *Roman Holiday* and, more recently, Barack Obama's daughters stopped off while pops was at a G8 event. The marron glacé was supposedly a favourite of Pope John Paul II.

ALFREDO E ADA
TRATTORIA €€

Map p296 (☑06 687 8842; Via dei Banchi Nuovi 14; meals €25-30; ⊙noon-3pm & 7-10pm Tue-Sat; ⊠Corso Vittorio Emanuele II) For an authentic trattoria experience, search out this much-loved local eatery. It's distinctly no-frills with simple wooden tables, paper napkins and homey clutter, but there's a warm, friendly atmosphere and the traditional Roman food is filling and flavoursome.

RETROBOTTEGA
RISTORANTE €€

Map p296 (☑06 68136310; www.retro-bottega.com; Via della Stelletta 4; meals €35; ⊙noon-midnight Tue-Sun; ⊠Corso del Rinascimento) Something of a departure for Rome, Retrobottega is an advocate of the casual dining experience. Here you'll be setting your own place and sitting at high bar-style tables or a counter overlooking the open kitchen. The food, in keeping with the young, modern vibe, is creative and artfully presented.

VIVI BISTROT
BISTRO €€

Map p296 (☑06 683 3779; www.vivibistrot.com; Palazzo Braschi, Piazza Navona 2; meals €25-30; ⊙10am-midnight Tue-Sun; ⊠Corso del Rinascimento) Rustic decor goes hand in hand with baroque elegance at this handsome bistro on the ground floor of Palazzo Braschi. With its country wood tables, dried flowers and a menu that ranges from salads and pastas to curries, cakes and scones, it's a great spot to escape the hurly-burly outside.

LA CAMPANA
TRATTORIA €€

Map p296 (☑06 687 5273; www.ristorantelacampana.com; Vicolo della Campana 18; meals €35-40; ⊙12.30-3pm & 7.30-11pm Tue-Sun; ⊠Via di Monte Brianzo) Caravaggio, Goethe and Federico Fellini are among the luminaries who have dined at what is said to be Rome's oldest trattoria, dating back to around 1518. Nowadays, local families crowd its soberly attired interior to dine on fresh fish and traditional Roman dishes in a warm, relaxed atmosphere. Bookings recommended.

LILLI
ROMAN €€

Map p296 (☑06 686 1916; www.trattorialilli.it; Via di Tor di Nona 23; meals €25-30; ⊙12.30-3pm & 7.30-11pm, closed Sun dinner & Mon; ⊠Lungotevere Tor di Nona) Few tourists make it to this long-standing neighbourhood trattoria on a cobbled cul-de-sac a five-minute walk from Piazza Navona. But it still gets busy as local diners pile in to its dated interior to enjoy comforting favourites such as spaghetti carbonara and boiled beef with green sauce.

LA FOCACCIA
PIZZA €€

Map p296 (☑06 6880 3312; Via della Pace 11; pizzas €7-9, meals €25-30; ⊙11pm-midnight; ⊠Corso del Rinascimento) This unassuming pizzeria near the Chiostro del Bramante is an excellent choice if you're after a simple meal in a warm, cheerful setting. In summer, the outside tables are the ones to go for, but come here in winter and you'll find the surprisingly large interior full of happy diners.

Kick off with a *supplì* (rice croquette) before launching into the main event, Neapolitan-style wood-fired pizza.

DA FRANCESCO
TRATTORIA, PIZZA €€

Map p296 (☑06 686 40 09; www.dafrancesco. it; Piazza del Fico 29; pizzas €7-14, meals €30-35; ⊗noon-3.30pm & 7pm-12.30am; ☐Corso Vittorio Emanuele II) Dining at this quintessential Roman pizzeria-cum-trattoria is all about the buzzing atmosphere and cheerful, noisy vibe. With a small interior and tables spilling out onto the pretty piazza outside, it serves Roman-style thin-crust pizzas and a full menu of daily pastas and meaty stalwarts. Get here early or expect to wait.

CASA BLEVE
RISTORANTE €€€

Map p296 (☑06 686 59 70; www.casableve.it; Via del Teatro Valle 48-49; meals €55-70; ⊗12.30-3pm & 7.30-11pm Mon-Sat; ☐Largo di Torre Argentina) Ideal for a special occasion dinner, this palatial restaurant-wine-bar dazzles with its column-lined dining hall and stained-glass roof. Its wine list, one of the best in town, accompanies a refined menu of creative antipasti, seasonal pastas and classic main courses.

✕ Campo de' Fiori & Around

★FORNO ROSCIOLI
PIZZA, BAKERY €

Map p296 (☑06 686 4045; www.anticoforno roscioli.it; Via dei Chiavari 34; pizza slices from €2, snacks €2; ⊗6am-8pm Mon-Sat, 9am-7pm Sun; ☐Via Arenula) This is one of Rome's top bakeries, much loved by lunching locals who crowd here for luscious sliced pizza, prize pastries and hunger-sating *supplì* (risotto balls). The *pizza margherita* is superb, if messy to eat, and there's also a counter serving hot pastas and vegetable side dishes.

TIRAMISÙ ZUM
DESSERTS €

Map p296 (☑06 6830 7836; www.facebook.com/ zumroma; Piazza del Teatro di Pompeo 20; desserts €2.50-6; ⊗11am-11.30pm Sun-Thu, to 1am Fri & Sat; ☐Corso Vittorio Emanuele II) The ideal spot for a mid afternoon pick-me-up, this fab dessert bar specialises in tiramisu, that magnificent marriage of mascarpone and liqueur-soaked ladyfinger biscuits. Choose between the classic version with its cocoa powdering or one of several tempting variations with pistachio nuts, blackberries and raspberries, and Amarena cherries.

I DOLCI DI NONNA VINCENZA
PASTRIES, CAFE €

Map p298 (www.dolcinonnavincenza.it; Via Arco del Monte 98a; pastries from €2.50; ⊗7.30am-8.30pm Mon-Sat, 8am-8.30pm Sun; ☐Via Arenula) Bringing the flavours of Sicily to Rome, this pastry shop is a real joy. Browse the traditional cakes and tempting *dolci* (sweet pastries) in the old wooden dressers, before adjourning to the adjacent bar to tear into the heavenly selection of creamy, flaky, puffy pastries and ricotta-stuffed *cannoli*.

FORNO DI CAMPO DE' FIORI
PIZZA, BAKERY €

Map p296 (www.fornocampodefiori.com; Campo de' Fiori 22; pizza slices around €3; ⊗7.30am-2.30pm & 4.45-8pm Mon-Sat, closed Sat dinner Jul & Aug; ☐Corso Vittorio Emanuele II) This buzzing bakery on Campo de' Fiori, divided into two adjacent shops, does a roaring trade in *panini* and delicious fresh-from-the-oven *pizza al taglio* (pizza by the slice). Aficionados swear by the *pizza bianca* ('white' pizza with olive oil, rosemary and salt), but the *panini* and *pizza rossa* ('red' pizza, with olive oil, tomato and oregano) taste plenty good too.

SUPPLIZIO
FAST FOOD €

Map p296 (☑06 8987 1920; www.facebook.com/ supplizioroma; Via dei Banchi Vecchi 143; supplì €3-7; ⊗noon-8pm Mon-Thu, noon-3.30pm & 6.30-10.30pm Fri & Sat; ☐Corso Vittorio Emanuele II) Rome's favourite snack, the *supplì* (a fried croquette filled with rice, tomato sauce and mozzarella), gets a gourmet makeover at this elegant street food joint. Sit back on the vintage leather sofa and dig into a crispy classic or push the boat out and try something different, maybe a little fish number stuffed with fresh anchovies, cheese, bread and raisins.

PASTICCERIA DE BELLIS
PASTRIES €

Map p296 (☑06 686 1480; www.pasticceria debellis.com; Piazza del Paradiso 56-57; pastries €4.50-12, burgers €6-9; ⊗9am-8pm; ☐Corso Vittorio Emanuele II) The beautifully crafted cakes, pastries and *dolci* made at this chic *pasticceria* are miniature works of art. Curated in every detail, they look and taste magnificent, from traditional breakfast *cornetti* (croissants) to *cannoli*, mono-portions of cheesecake and a selection of sumptuous burgers.

MERCATO DI CAMPO DE' FIORI
MARKET €

Map p296 (⊗7am-2pm Mon-Sat; ☐Corso Vittorio Emanuele II) The most picturesque – but also the most expensive – of Rome's neighbourhood markets. Each weekday morning, local shoppers mix with tourists and visitors amid the colourful stalls of seasonal fruit and veg that take over this historic piazza.

★PIANOSTRADA RISTORANTE €€

Map p298 (☑06 8957 2296; Via delle Zoccolette 22; meals €40; ☉1-4pm & 7pm-midnight Tue-Fri, 10am-midnight Sat & Sun; ☐Via Arenula) Hatched in foodie Trastevere but now across the river in a mellow white space with vintage furnishings and glorious summer courtyard, this bistro is a fashionable must. Reserve ahead, or settle for a stool at the bar and enjoy big bold views of the kitchen at work. Cuisine is refreshingly creative, seasonal and veg-packed, including gourmet open sandwiches and sensational homemade focaccia as well as full-blown mains.

★EMMA PIZZERIA PIZZA €€

Map p296 (☑06 6476 0475; www.emmapizzeria. com; Via Monte della Farina 28-29; pizzas €8-18, mains €35; ☉12.30-3pm & 7-11.30pm; ☐Via Arenula) Tucked in behind the Chiesa di San Carlo ai Catinari, this smart, modern pizzeria is a top spot for a cracking pizza and smooth craft beer (or a wine from its pretty extensive list). It's a stylish setup with outdoor seating and a spacious, art-clad interior, and a menu that lists seasonal, wood-fired pizzas alongside classic Roman pastas and mains.

DITIRAMBO TRATTORIA €€

Map p296 (☑06 687 1626; www.ristorantediti rambo.it; Piazza della Cancelleria 72; meals €35-40; ☉12.45-3.15pm & 7-11pm, closed Mon lunch; ☐Corso Vittorio Emanuele II) Since opening in 1996, Ditirambo continues to win diners over with its informal trattoria vibe and seasonal, organic cuisine. Dishes cover many bases, ranging from old-school favourites to thoughtful vegetarian offerings and more exotic fare such as a *millefoglie* of sea bream and crunchy artichokes. Book ahead.

RENATO E LUISA LAZIO CUISINE €€

Map p296 (☑06 686 9660; www.renatoeluisa.it; Via dei Barbieri 25; meals €45; ☉8pm-12.30am Tue-Sun; ☐Largo di Torre Argentina) Highly rated locally, this small backstreet trattoria is often packed. Chef Renato's menu features updated Roman classics that are modern and seasonal but also undeniably local, such as his signature *cacio e pepe e fiori di zucca* (pasta with pecorino cheese, black pepper and courgette flowers).

AR GALLETTO ROMAN, OSTERIA €€

Map p296 (☑06 686 17 14; www.ristorante argallettoroma.com; Piazza Farnese 102; meals €35-40; ☉12.30-3.30pm & 7.30-11.30pm; ☐Corso Vittorio Emanuele II) Overlooking Piazza Farnese, one of Rome's loveliest squares, this long-running restaurant impresses with its friendly service, authentic Roman pastas and seafood mains.

GRAPPOLO D'ORO ITALIAN €€

Map p296 (☑06 689 7080; www.hosteriagrappolo doro.it; Piazza della Cancelleria 80; tasting menu €28, meals €35; ☉12.30-3.30pm & 6.30-11.15pm, closed Wed lunch; ☐Corso Vittorio Emanuele II) This informal eatery stands out among the many lacklustre options around Campo de' Fiori. The emphasis is on seasonal regional cuisine with the occasional twist, so look out for aubergine and ricotta starters, homemade *tagliolini* (flat spaghetti) with pecorino, pancetta and black pepper, and beef cheeks braised in Chianti.

SALUMERIA ROSCIOLI DELI, RISTORANTE €€€

Map p298 (☑06 687 5287; www.salumeriaroscioli. com; Via dei Giubbonari 21; meals €55; ☉12.30-4pm & 7pm-midnight Mon-Sat; ☐Via Arenula) The name Roscioli has long been a byword for foodie excellence in Rome, and this luxurious deli-restaurant is the place to experience it. Tables are set alongside the deli counter, laden with mouth-watering Italian and foreign delicacies, and in a small bottle-lined space behind it. The sophisticated food is top notch and there are some truly outstanding wines to go with it.

✖ Jewish Ghetto

ANTICO FORNO URBANI PIZZA, BAKERY €

Map p298 (Piazza Costaguti 31; pizza slices from €1.50; ☉7.40am-2.30pm & 5-7.45pm Mon-Fri, 8.30am-1.30pm Sat, 9.30am-1pm Sun; ☐Via Arenula) A popular kosher bakery, this Ghetto institution makes some of the best pizza *bianca* in town, as well as freshly baked bread, biscuits and focaccias. It gets very busy but once you catch a whiff of the yeasty odours wafting off the counter, it's nearly impossible to resist the temptation for a quick pit stop.

BOCCIONE BAKERY €

Map p298 (☑06 687 8637; Via del Portico d'Ottavia 1; ☉7am-7.30pm Sun-Thu, to 3pm Fri; ☐Via Arenula) This tiny, unsigned shop is the Ghetto's most famous bakery, where locals come to

KOSHER ROME

If you want to eat kosher in Rome head to Via del Portico d'Ottavia, the main strip through the **Jewish Ghetto** (p79). Lined with trattorias and restaurants specialising in Roman-Jewish cuisine, it's a lively hangout, especially on hot summer nights when diners crowd the many sidewalk tables. For a taste of typical Ghetto cooking, try **Nonna Betta** (Map p298; ☑06 6880 6263; www.nonnabetta.it; Via del Portico d'Ottavia 16; meals €30-35; ☉11am-11pm Wed-Mon; ☐Via Arenula), a small tunnel of a trattoria serving traditional kosher food and local staples such as *carciofi alla guidia* (crisp fried artichokes). Further down the road, the unmarked **Cremeria Romana** (Map p298; www.cremeriaromana.com; Via del Portico d'Ottavia 1b; gelato €3; ☉9am-6pm Mon-Fri & Sun, closed Fri dinner & Sat, longer hours summer; ☐Via Arenula) has a small selection of tasty kosher gelato.

buy their special occasion *dolci* (cakes and pastries). It's authentically no-frills, and the burnished cakes, tarts and biscuits are bursting with fruit, sultanas and ricotta.

BEPPE E I SUOI FORMAGGI CHEESE €€
Map p298 (☑06 6819 2210; www.beppeeisuoi formaggi.it; Via Santa Maria del Pianto 9-11; meals €30-40; ☉9-10.30pm Mon-Sat; ☐Via Arenula) It's all in the name – Beppe and his cheeses. Serving cheese throughout the day, this small restaurant, attached to a well-stocked deli selling *formaggi* of all shapes and smells, is a mecca for aficionados. Breakfast on ricotta and honey, lunch on robiola, and end the day with a dinner of warmed camembert.

LA TAVERNA DEGLI AMICI RISTORANTE €€
Map p298 (☑06 6992 0637; www.latavernadegli amici.net; Piazza Margana 37; meals €40; ☉12.30-3pm & 7.30-11.30pm, closed Sun dinner & Mon; ☐Piazza Venezia) With its wood-beamed ceilings, rustic decor and setting on a tranquil medieval piazza, La Taverna sets a handsome stage for traditional Roman fare, fresh seafood and homemade desserts.

PIPERNO RISTORANTE €€€
Map p298 (☑06 6880 6629; www.ristorante piperno.it; Via Monte de' Cenci 9; meals €45-55; ☉12.45-2.20pm & 7.45-10.20pm, closed Sun dinner & Mon; ☐Via Arenula) This historic Ghetto restaurant, complete with a formal, slightly stilted look, is a top spot at which to get to grips with traditional Jewish-Roman cooking and local offal dishes. Signature hits include deep-fried *filetti di baccalà* (cod fillets) and *animelle di agnello con carciofi* (lamb sweetbreads with artichokes). To finish off, try the *palle di Nonno fritte* (fried ricotta balls). Booking is recommended.

✖ Isola Tiberina

SORA LELLA ROMAN €€€
Map p298 (☑06 686 1601; www.trattoriasoralella. com; Via Ponte Quattro Capi 16, Isola Tiberina; tasting menus €45-50, meals €50; ☉12.30-3pm & 7.30-11pm Wed-Tue; ☐Lungotevere dei Cenci) This long-standing family-run restaurant enjoys a memorable setting in a tower on the Tiber's tiny island. Named after a much-loved actress (the owner's mum), it serves a classic Roman menu spiced up with the occasional fish dish. There are also homemade desserts and several tasting menus, including one for vegetarians – something of a rarity in meat-loving Rome.

✖ Piazza Colonna & Around

CIAO CHECCA FAST FOOD €
Map p296 (www.ciaochecca.com; Piazza di Firenze 25-26; meals €10-15; ☉9.30am-10.30pm; ☐Via di Monte Brianzo) 🍴 From create-your-own cooked breakfasts to gluten-free pastas, cheeseburgers or earthy chickpea soups, this upscale fast-food joint is the answer to most eating needs. Expect crowds and recyclable cartons of seasonally inspired dishes to eat in or takeaway.

DAL CAVALIER GINO TRATTORIA €€
Map p296 (☑06 687 3434; Vicolo Rosini 4; meals €35; ☉1-3.45pm & 8-11pm Mon-Sat; ☐Via del Corso) Close to parliament, Gino's is a hidden backstreet trattoria perennially packed with journalists, politicians, locals and tourists. Join the crowd for well-executed staples such as *tagliolini alla gricia* (flat spaghetti with lardons of cured pork) and *coniglio al*

vino bianco (rabbit in a white wine sauce), all served under gaudily painted murals.

OSTERIA DELL'INGEGNO   ITALIAN €€
Map p296 (☑06 678 06 62; www.osteriadellin gegno.com; Piazza di Pietra 45; meals €30-45; ☺10am-1am; ☐Via del Corso) An all-day res-taurant wine-bar with a colourful, art-filled interior, a casual, inclusive vibe, and a prime location on a charming central pi-azza. The daily menu hits all the right notes with a selection of seasonal pastas, creative mains and homemade desserts, while the 200-strong wine list boasts some interesting Italian labels.

MATRICIANELLA   TRATTORIA €€
Map p296 (☑06 683 2100; www.matricianella. it; Via del Leone 4; meals €35-40; ☺12.30-3pm & 7.30-11pm Mon-Sat; ☐Via del Corso) With its gingham tablecloths, chintzy murals and fading prints, Matricianella is an archetypal trattoria, much loved for its traditional Ro-man cuisine. Its loyal locals keep coming back for evergreen crowd-pleasers such as artichoke *alla giudia* (fried, Jewish style), and more challenging dishes like *animelle d'abbacchio* (grilled lamb's sweetbreads).

ENOTECA AL
PARLAMENTO ACHILLI   GASTRONOMY €€€
Map p296 (☑06 8676 1422; www.enotecal parlamento.com; Via dei Prefetti 15; meals from €90, tasting menus €110-130; ☺12.30-2.30pm & 7.30-10.30pm; ☐Via del Corso) Housed in one of the capital's historic wine shops, chef Mas-simo Viglietti's Michelin-starred restaurant marries a classic setting with creatively combined dishes and deconstructions of classic Roman staples. Typical of this style is his 'Idea of Gricia', made with *cacio e pepe* (pecorino and black pepper) ravioli and a consommè of *guanciale* (cured pig's cheek).

🍷 DRINKING & NIGHTLIFE

Nightlife in the *centro storico* is centred on two main areas: the lanes around Piazza Navona, with a number of elegant bars catering to the hip beautiful people; and the rowdier area around Campo de' Fiori, where the crowd is younger and the drinking heavier. The area around the Pantheon is the place to go for coffee, with two of the city's most celebrated cafes nearby.

📍 Pantheon & Around

CAFFÈ SANT'EUSTACHIO   COFFEE
Map p296 (www.santeustachioilcaffe.it; Piazza Sant'Eustachio 82; ☺8.30am-1am Sun-Thu, to 1.30am Fri, to 2am Sat; ☐Corso del Rinascimen-to) This small, unassuming cafe, generally three deep at the bar, is reckoned by many to serve the best coffee in town. To make it, the bartenders sneakily beat the first drops of an espresso with several teaspoons of sugar to create a frothy paste to which they add the rest of the coffee.

LA CASA DEL CAFFÈ TAZZA D'ORO COFFEE
Map p296 (☑06 678 9792; www.tazzadoro coffeeshop.com; Via degli Orfani 84-86; ☺7am-8pm Mon-Sat, 10.30am-7.30pm Sun; ☐Via del Cor-so) A busy, stand-up affair with burnished 1940s fittings, this is one of Rome's best coffee houses. Its espresso hits the mark nicely and there's a range of delicious coffee concoctions, including a cooling *granita di caffè*, a crushed-ice coffee drink served with whipped cream. There's also a small shop and, outside, a coffee *bancomat* for those out-of-hours caffeine emergencies.

📍 Piazza Navona & Around

ETABLÌ   WINE BAR, CAFE
Map p296 (☑06 9761 6694; www.etabli.it; Vicolo delle Vacche 9a; ☺cafe 7.30am-6pm, wine bar 6pm-1am; 🛜; ☐Corso del Rinascimento) Housed in a 16th-century *palazzo,* Etablì is a rustic-chic lounge-bar-restaurant where you can drop by for a morning coffee, have a light lunch or chat over an *aperitivo.* It's laid-back and good-looking, with original French-inspired country decor – leather armchairs, rough wooden tables and a crackling fire-place. It also serves full restaurant dinners (€45) and hosts occasional live music.

CIRCUS   BAR
Map p296 (☑06 9761 9258; www.circusroma. it; Via della Vetrina 15; ☺10am-2am; 🛜; ☐Corso del Rinascimento) A great little bar tucked around the corner from Piazza Navona. It's a laid-back place – think sofas, TV switched on, newspapers to read – popular with a young international crowd who come here to catch up with friends and hang out over a leisurely drink. The atmosphere heats up in the evening, when cocktails and shots take over from tea and cappuccino.

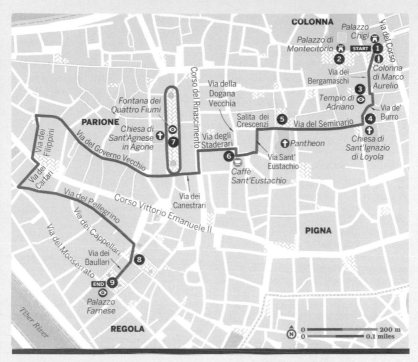

Neighbourhood Walk
Centro Storico Piazzas

START PIAZZA COLONNA
END PIAZZA FARNESE
LENGTH 1.5KM; 3½ HOURS

Start in **1 Piazza Colonna** (p81), an elegant square dominated by the 30m-high Colonna di Marco Aurelio and flanked by Palazzo Chigi, the official residence of the Italian prime minister. Next door, and facing onto **2 Piazza di Montecitorio**, is the equally impressive seat of Italy's Chamber of Deputies, Palazzo di Montecitorio. From Piazza Colonna follow Via dei Bergamaschi down to **3 Piazza di Pietra** (p81), a refined rectangular space overlooked by the columned facade of the 2nd-century Tempio di Adriano. Continue past the pillars down Via de' Burro to **4 Piazza di Sant'Ignazio**, a small stagy rococo piazza whose resident church boasts some magnificent *trompe l'œil* ceiling frescoes by Andrea Pozzo. From here, it's a short walk along Via del Seminario to **5 Piazza della Rotonda**, where the Pantheon needs no introduction.

Leaving the Pantheon, head up Salita dei Crescenzi and go left along Via Sant'Eustachio to **6 Piazza Sant'Eustachio**. On this small square, busy Caffè Sant'Eustachio is reckoned by many to serve the best coffee in town. Suitably recharged, follow Via degli Staderari to Corso del Rinascimento, drop a quick left followed by a short right and you'll find yourself emerging onto **7 Piazza Navona** (p74). Here, among the street artists, tourists and pigeons, you can compare the two giants of Roman baroque – Gian Lorenzo Bernini, creator of the Fontana dei Quattro Fiumi, and Francesco Borromini, author of the Chiesa di Sant'Agnese in Agone.

Exit the piazza and follow Via del Governo Vecchio. At the end, turn left down Via dei Filippini to Corso Vittorio Emanuele II, the thoroughfare that bisects the historic centre. Cross over and follow Via dei Cartari down to Via del Pellegrino. Follow on to **8 Campo de' Fiori** (p77), a colourful, chaotic market square, and beyond that, the more sober **9 Piazza Farnese** overshadowed by the Renaissance Palazzo Farnese.

GIN CORNER
COCKTAIL BAR

Map p296 (☑06 6880 2452; www.facebook.com/thegincorner; Via Pallacorda 2, Hotel Adriano; ◷6pm-midnight; ⛴Via di Monte Brianzo) Forget fine wines and craft beers, this chic bar in the Hotel Adriano is all about the undistilled enjoyment of gin. Here the making of a simple gin and tonic is raised to an art form – the menu lists more than 10 varieties – and martinis are beautifully executed. You can also get cocktails made from other spirits if gin isn't your thing.

🍸 Campo de' Fiori & Around

★ OPEN BALADIN
BAR

Map p298 (☑06 683 8989; www.openbaladin roma.it; Via degli Specchi 6; ◷noon-2am; 🛜; ⛴Via Arenula) For some years, this cool, modern pub near Campo de' Fiori has been a leading light in Rome's craft beer scene, and with more than 40 beers on tap and up to 100 bottled brews, many from Italian artisanal microbreweries, it's still a top place for a pint.

★ BARNUM CAFE
CAFE

Map p296 (☑06 6476 0483; www.barnumcafe. com; Via del Pellegrino 87; ◷9am-10pm Mon, to 2am Tue-Sat; 🛜; ⛴Corso Vittorio Emanuele II) A laid-back *Friends*-style cafe, evergreen Barnum is the sort of place you could quickly get used to. With its shabby-chic vintage furniture and white bare-brick walls, it's a relaxed spot for a breakfast cappuccino, a light lunch or a late afternoon drink. Come evening, a coolly dressed-down crowd sips seriously good cocktails.

ROSCIOLI CAFFÈ
CAFE

Map p298 (☑06 8916 5330; www.rosciolicaffe. com; Piazza Benedetto Cairoli 16; ◷7am-11pm Mon-Sat, 8am-6pm Sun; ⛴Via Arenula) The Roscioli name is a sure bet for good food and drink in this town: the family runs one of Rome's most celebrated delis (p86) and a hugely popular bakery (p85), and this cafe doesn't disappoint either. The coffee is wonderfully luxurious, and the artfully crafted pastries, petits fours and *panini* taste as good as they look.

JERRY THOMAS PROJECT
COCKTAIL BAR

Map p296 (☑370 114 6287; www.thejerrythomas project.it; Vicolo Cellini 30; ◷10pm-4am Tue-Sat; ⛴Corso Vittorio Emanuele II) A self-styled speakeasy with a 1920s look and a password

to get in – check the website and call to book – this hidden bar has led the way in Rome's recent love affair with cocktails. Its master mixologists know their stuff and the retro decor gives the place a real Prohibition-era feel. Note there's a €5 'membership' fee.

L'ANGOLO DIVINO
WINE BAR

Map p296 (☑06 686 4413; www.angolodivino. it; Via dei Balestrari 12; ◷10.30am-3pm Tue-Sat, plus 5pm-1am daily; ⛴Corso Vittorio Emanuele II) A hop and a skip from Campo de' Fiori, this warm wine bar is an oasis of genteel calm, with a carefully curated wine list (mostly Italian but a few French and New World labels), a selection of regional Italian cheeses and cured meats, and a small daily menu of hot and cold dishes.

IL GOCCETTO
WINE BAR

Map p296 (www.facebook.com/Ilgoccetto; Via dei Banchi Vecchi 14; ◷11.30am-2.30pm Tue-Sat, plus 6.30pm-midnight Mon-Sat, closed mid-Aug; ⛴Corso Vittorio Emanuele II) This authentic, old-school *vino e olio* (wine and oil) shop has everything you could want in a neighbourhood wine bar: a colourful cast of regulars, a cosy, bottle-lined interior, a selection of cheeses and cold cuts, and a serious, 800-strong wine list.

ESCOSAZIO
JUICE BAR

Map p296 (☑06 6476 0784; www.escosazio. it; Via dei Banchi Vecchi 135; ◷8.30am-8pm Mon-Sat; ⛴Corso Vittorio Emanuele II) Rome is discovering juice bars right now and this friendly bolthole is a good bet for a refreshing smoothie or juice extract. Keep it simple with a freshly squeezed OJ, or spice things up with a *digestivo* made from orange, pineapple, fennel and ginger.

🍸 Piazza Colonna & Around

SALOTTO 42
BAR

Map p296 (☑06 678 5804; www.salotto42.space; Piazza di Pietra 42; ◷10.30am-2am; ⛴Via del Corso) On a picturesque piazza, facing the columns of the Temple of Hadrian, this is a glamorous lounge bar, complete with subdued lighting, vintage 1950s armchairs, Murano lamps and heavyweight design books. Come for the daily lunch buffet or to hang out with the 'see and be seen' crowd over one of its signature cocktails.

GRAN CAFFÈ LA CAFFETTIERA   CAFE

Map p296 (✆06 679 8147; www.grancaffela
caffettiera.com; Piazza di Pietra 65; ⊙7.30am-
10pm; ☒Via del Corso) This stately art-deco
cafe overlooking graceful Piazza di Pietra is
a polished performer. Star of the show are
its Neapolitan cakes, including that most
beloved of pastries, *sfogliatella* (a flaky pastry shell stuffed with ricotta and shards of
candied fruit).

☆ ENTERTAINMENT

ISOLA DEL CINEMA   OUTDOOR CINEMA

Map p298 (www.isoladelcinema.com; Isola Tiberina; tickets €6) From mid-June to September,
the Isola Tiberina sets the stage for a season
of outdoor cinema, featuring Italian and
international films, some shown in their
original language.

TEATRO ARGENTINA   THEATRE

Map p296 (✆06 68400 0311; www.teatrodiroma.
net; Largo di Torre Argentina 52; tickets €12-32;
☒Largo di Torre Argentina) Founded in 1732,
Rome's top theatre is one of the two official
homes of the Teatro di Roma – the other
is the **Teatro India** (Map p318; ✆06 68400
0311; www.teatrodiroma.net; Lungotevere Vittorio Gassman 1; Ⓜ Stazione Trastevere) in the
southern suburbs. Rossini's *Barber of Seville*
premiered in 1816, and these days the
theatre stages a wide-ranging program of
drama (mostly in Italian), high-profile dance
performances and classical music concerts.

🛍 SHOPPING

**The area west of Piazza Navona is riddled
with small shops and indie boutiques
selling everything from designer
fashions to vintage clothes, handcrafted accessories and collectable
antiques. Streets to target include Via
del Governo Vecchio and, to the north,
Via dei Coronari. Near Campo de' Fiori,
you'll find more one-off boutiques on
Via del Pellegrino and midrange clothing
stores on and around Via dei Giubbonari.**

🛍 Pantheon & Around

NAMASTÈY   TEA

Map p296 (✆06 6813 5660; www.namastey.it; Via
della Palombella 26; ⊙10.30am-7.30pm Tue-Sat,

11.30am-7.30pm Sun, closed Aug; ☒Largo di Torre
Argentina) After a visit to this charming shop,
you'll be reminded of it every time you have
a tea. Set up like an apothecary with ceiling-
high shelves and rows of jars, it stocks blends
from across the globe, as well as everything
you could ever need for your home tea ritual
– teapots, cups, infusers and filters.

LE ARTIGIANE   ARTS & CRAFTS

Map p296 (✆06 6830 9347; www.leartigiane.it;
Via di Torre Argentina 72; ⊙10am-7.30pm; ☒Lar-
go di Torre Argentina) A space for local artisans to showcase their wares, this eclectic
shop is part of an ongoing project to sustain
and promote Italy's artisanal traditions. It's
a browser's dream with an eclectic range
of handmade clothes, costume jewellery,
ceramics, design objects and lamps.

STILO FETTI   STATIONERY

Map p296 (✆06 678 9662; www.stilofetti.it; Via
degli Orfani 82; ⊙3.30-7.30pm Mon, 9am-7pm Tue-
Sat; ☒Via del Corso) Technology might have
largely done it for fountain pens but their
romance remains and this old-fashioned
family-run shop, on the go since 1893, has
a wonderful selection. All styles are covered
and you'll find many top brands, from Faber-
Castell to Mont Blanc and Montegrappa, the
luxury Italian pen-maker favoured by royalty and world leaders.

ALBERTA GLOVES   FASHION & ACCESSORIES

Map p296 (✆06 679 7318; Corso Vittorio Emanuele II 18; ⊙10am-7pm Mon-Sat; ☒Largo di Torre
Argentina) From elbow-length silk evening
gloves to tan-coloured driving mitts, this
tiny family-run shop has a handmade glove
for every possible occasion. Silk scarves
and woolly hats too. Reckon on about €40 to
€45 for a classic pair of leather gloves.

🛍 Piazza Navona & Around

MARTA RAY   SHOES

Map p296 (✆06 6880 2641; www.martaray.it; Via
dei Coronari 121; ⊙10am-8pm; ☒Via Zanardelli)
Women's ballet flats and elegant, everyday
bags, in rainbow colours and butter-soft
leather, are the hallmarks of the emerging
Marta Ray brand. At this store, one of three
in town, you'll find a selection of trademark
ballerinas and a colourful line in modern,
beautifully designed handbags.

CENTRO STORICO ENTERTAINMENT

SBU
CLOTHING

Map p296 (☑06 6880 2547; www.sbu.it; Via di San Pantaleo 68-69; ⊗10am-7.30pm Mon-Sat; 🚇Corso Vittorio Emanuele II) The flagship store of hip jeans label SBU, aka Strategic Business Unit, occupies a 19th-century workshop near Piazza Navona, complete with cast-iron columns and wooden racks. Alongside jeans, superbly cut from top-end Japanese denim, you can also pick up casual shirts, jackets, hats, sweaters and T-shirts.

OFFICINA PROFUMO FARMACEUTICA DI SANTA MARIA NOVELLA
PERFUMES, COSMETICS

Map p296 (☑06 687 9608; www.smnovella.com; Corso del Rinascimento 47; ⊗10am-7.30pm Mon-Sat; 🚇Corso del Rinascimento) A branch of one of Italy's oldest pharmacies stocks natural perfumes and cosmetics as well as herbal infusions, teas and potpourri, all shelved in wooden, glass-fronted cabinets under a flamboyant Murano chandelier. The original pharmacy was founded in Florence in 1612 by the Dominican monks of Santa Maria Novella, and today many of its cosmetics are still based on 17th-century herbal recipes.

NARDECCHIA
ART

Map p296 (☑06 686 9318; Via del Monserrato 106; ⊗10am-1pm & 4-7.30pm, closed Mon morning & Sun; 🚇Lungotevere dei Tebaldi) Famed for its antique prints, historic Nardecchia sells everything from 18th-century etchings by Giovanni Battista Piranesi to more affordable 19th-century panoramas of Rome. Expect to pay at least €150 for a small framed print.

LUNA & L'ALTRA
FASHION & ACCESSORIES

Map p296 (☑06 6880 4995; www.lunaelaltra.com; Piazza Pasquino 76; ⊗3.30-7.30pm Mon, 10am-7.30pm Tue-Sat; 🚇Corso Vittorio Emanuele II) An address for those with their finger on the pulse, this all-white fashion boutique is one of a number of independent stores on and around Via del Governo Vecchio. In its austere, gallery-like interior, clothes by designers Comme des Garçons, Issey Miyake and Yohji Yamamoto are exhibited in reverential style.

ALDO FEFÈ
ARTS & CRAFTS

Map p296 (☑06 6880 3585; Via della Stelletta 20b; ⊗8am-7.30pm Mon-Sat; 🚇Corso del Rinascimento) In his small workshop, master craftsman Aldo Fefè continues to bind books and produce beautifully hand-painted notebooks, albums, boxes and photo albums (from €18).

You can also buy Florentine wrapping paper and calligraphic pens here.

CASALI
ART

Map p296 (☑06 687 3705; Via dei Coronari 115; ⊗10am-1pm & 3-7.30pm Mon-Fri, 10am-1pm Sat; 🚇Via Zanardelli) On Via dei Coronari, a street renowned for its antique shops, Casali deals in original and reproduction etchings and prints, many delicately hand-coloured. The shop is small but the choice isn't, ranging from 16th-century botanical manuscripts to postcard prints of Rome.

PATRIZIA CORVAGLIA
JEWELLERY

Map p296 (☑06 4555 1441; www.patriziacorvaglia.it; Via dei Banchi Nuovi 45; ⊗11am-7.30pm Mon-Sat; 🚇Corso Vittorio Emanuele II) At her boutique in the former workshop of Renaissance goldsmith Benvenuti Cellini, Patrizia Corvaglia designs and handcrafts her own line of jewellery. Her abstract, sometimes baroque, creations feature precious silver and gold set with raw gemstones.

🏠 Campo de' Fiori & Around

★IBIZ – ARTIGIANATO IN CUOIO
FASHION & ACCESSORIES

Map p296 (☑06 6830 7297; www.ibizroma.it; Via dei Chiavari 39; ⊗9.30am-7.30pm Mon-Sat; 🚇Corso Vittorio Emanuele II) In her diminutive family workshop, Elisa Nepi and her team craft exquisite, soft-as-butter leather wallets, bags, belts and sandals, in simple but classy designs and myriad colours. You can pick up a belt for about €35, while for a bag you should bank on at least €110.

SALUMERIA ROSCIOLI
FOOD & DRINKS

Map p298 (☑06 687 5287; www.salumeriaroscioli.com; Via dei Giubbonari 21; ⊗8.30am-8.30pm Mon-Sat; 🚇Via Arenula) The rich scents of cured meats, cheeses, conserves, olive oil and balsamic vinegar intermingle at this top-class deli, one of Rome's finest. Alongside iconic Italian products, you'll also find a vast choice of wines and a range of French cheeses, Spanish hams and Scottish salmon.

You can also dine here at the deli's excellent in-house restaurant (p86).

JERRY THOMAS EMPORIUM
DRINKS

Map p296 (☑06 8697 0138; Vicolo Cellini 16; ⊗2-8pm Tue-Sat; 🚇Corso Vittorio Emanuele II) An offshoot of the cult Jerry Thomas Project (p90) speakeasy, this shop stocks a collector's dream of vermouth, spirits and liqueurs. Among the Italian and international labels, you'll find limited editions and artisanal blends made from historical recipes.

RACHELE
CHILDREN'S CLOTHING

Map p296 (329 648 1004; www.facebook.com/racheleart; Vicolo del Bollo 6; ⊘10.30am-2pm & 3.30-7.30pm Tue-Sat; Corso Vittorio Emanuele II) If your 12-year-old (or younger) needs a wardrobe update, you would do well to look up Rachele in her delightful shop just off Via del Pellegrino. With everything from hats and mitts to romper suits and jackets, all brightly coloured and all handmade, this sort of shop is a dying breed. Most items are around the €40 to €50 mark.

I COLORI DI DENTRO
ART

Map p296 (06 683 24 94; www.mgluffarelli.com; Via dei Banchi Vecchi 29; ⊘11am-6.45pm Mon-Sat; Corso Vittorio Emanuele II) Take home some Mediterranean sunshine. Artist Maria Grazia Luffarelli's paintings are a riotous celebration of Italian colours, with sunny yellow landscapes, blooming flowers, Roman cityscapes and comfortable-looking cats. You can buy original watercolours or prints, as well as postcards, T-shirts, notebooks and calendars.

MONDELLO OTTICA
FASHION & ACCESSORIES

Map p296 (06 686 1955; www.mondelloottica.it; Via del Pellegrino 98; ⊘10am-1.30pm & 4-7.30pm Tue-Sat; Corso Vittorio Emanuele II) Eyewear becomes art at this modish optician's on Via del Pellegrino. Known for its avant-garde window displays, often styled by contemporary artists, Mondello Ottica sells boldly coloured frames by leading designers such as Belgian brand Theo.

ATELIER PATRIZIA PIERONI
FASHION & ACCESSORIES

Map p296 (Arsenale Gallery; 06 6880 2424; www.patriziapieroni.it; Via del Pellegrino 172; ⊘3.30-7.30pm Mon, 10am-7.30pm Tue-Sat; Corso Vittorio Emanuele II) The atelier of celebrated Roman designer Patrizia Pieroni is a watchword for original, high-end women's fashion. The virgin white interior creates a clean, contemporary showcase for Patrizia's latest colourful creations, and exhibitions and cultural events are often hosted here.

🏠 Piazza Colonna & Around

★ CONFETTERIA MORIONDO & GARIGLIO
CHOCOLATE

Map p296 (06 699 0856; Via del Piè di Marmo 21-22; ⊘9am-7.30pm Mon-Sat; Via del Corso) Roman poet Trilussa was so smitten with this historic chocolate shop – established by the Torinese confectioners to the royal house of Savoy – that he was moved to mention it in verse. Decorated like an elegant tearoom, with crimson walls, tables and glass cabinets, it specialises in delicious handmade chocolates, many prepared according to original 19th-century recipes.

BARTOLUCCI
TOYS

Map p296 (www.bartolucci.com; Via dei Pastini 98; ⊘10am-10.30pm; Via del Corso) It's difficult to resist going into this magical toyshop where everything is carved out of wood. By the main entrance, a Pinocchio pedals his bike robotically, perhaps dreaming of the full-size motorbike parked nearby, while inside there are all manner of ticking clocks, rocking horses, planes and more Pinocchios than you're likely to see in your whole life.

MATERIE
JEWELLERY

Map p296 (06 679 3199; www.materieshop.com; Via del Gesù 73; ⊘10.30-7.30pm Mon-Sat; Via del Corso) A showcase for unique jewellery crafted from materials as diverse as silver, silicon, rubber, metal, plastic and stone. Each year owner Viviana Violo selects a new range of eclectic designs, all handmade by Italian and international jewellers, to sell at her small, tranquil shop. She also stocks a small selection of bags, scarves and other accessories.

LE TARTARUGHE
FASHION & ACCESSORIES

Map p296 (06 679 2240; www.letartarughe.eu; Via del Piè di Marmo 17; ⊘10am-7.30pm Tue-Sat, 4-7.30pm Mon; Via del Corso) Fashionable, versatile and elegant, Susanna Liso's catchy seasonal designs adorn this relaxed, white-walled boutique. Her clothes, often blended from raw silks, cashmere and fine merino wool, provide vibrant modern updates on classic styles. You'll also find a fine line in novelty accessories.

RICHARD I'ANSON / GETTY IMAGES ©

1. Fontana del Nettuno, Piazza Navona (p74) 2. Diners on Campo de' Fiori (p77) 3. St Peter's Square (p130)

Showtime on Rome's Piazzas

From the baroque splendour of Piazza Navona to the clamour of Campo de' Fiori and the majesty of St Peter's Square, Rome's showcase piazzas encapsulate much of the city's beauty, history and drama.

Piazza Navona

In the heart of the historic centre, Piazza Navona (p74) is the picture-perfect Roman square. Graceful baroque *palazzi* (mansions), flamboyant fountains, packed pavement cafes and costumed street artists set the scene for the daily invasion of camera-toting tourists.

St Peter's Square

The awe-inspiring approach to St Peter's Basilica, this monumental piazza (p130) is a masterpiece of 17th-century urban design. The work of Bernini, it's centred on a towering Egyptian obelisk and flanked by two grasping colonnaded arms.

Piazza del Popolo

Neoclassical Piazza del Popolo (p101) is a vast, sweeping spectacle. In centuries past, executions were held here; nowadays crowds gather for political rallies, outdoor concerts or just to hang out.

Piazza del Campidoglio

The centrepiece of the Campidoglio (Capitoline Hill), this Michelangelo-designed piazza (p65) is thought by many to be the city's most beautiful. Surrounded on three sides by *palazzi*, it's home to the Capitoline Museums.

Campo de' Fiori

Home to one of Rome's historic markets and a boozy bar scene, Campo de' Fiori (p77) buzzes with activity day and night.

Piazza di Spagna

In Rome's swank shopping district, Piazza di Spagna (p98) has long attracted footsore foreigners who come to sit on the Spanish Steps and watch the world go by.

Tridente, Trevi & the Quirinale

PIAZZA DEL POPOLO & AROUND | PIAZZA DI SPAGNA & AROUND | PIAZZA DI TREVI, QUIRINALE HILL & AROUND | PIAZZA BARBERINI & AROUND

Neighbourhood Top Five

1 Spanish Steps (p98) People-watching, selfie-snapping and daydreaming with a view down the glittering backbone of the Tridente shopping district, Via dei Condotti.

2 Basilica di Santa Maria del Popolo (p99) Gazing at Caravaggio masterpieces in this unsung artistic treasure trove.

3 Villa Medici (p103) Taking a guided tour of the formal gardens and astounding views ensnaring this magnificent villa.

4 Palazzo Barberini (p105) Revelling in architectural treasures, a glut of masterpieces and the breathtaking Cortona ceiling in this sumptuous baroque *palazzo* (mansion).

5 Shopping (p112) Browsing for ethical fashion, artisanal perfume, personalised marble plaques and dozens of other unique souvenirs on and around Via dei Condotti.

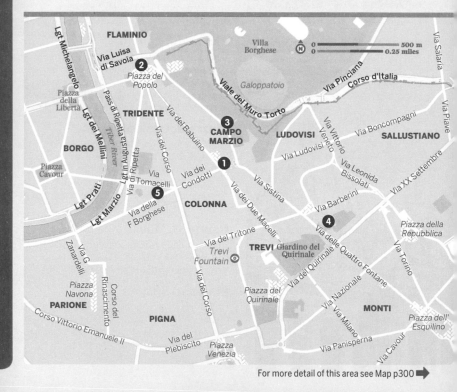

For more detail of this area see Map p300 ➡

Explore: Tridente, Trevi & the Quirinale

Tridente is Rome's most glamorous district, full of designer boutiques, fashionable bars and swish hotels. However, it's not just about shopping, dining and drinking. The area also contains the vast neoclassical showpiece, Piazza del Popolo (p101); the wonderfully frivolous Spanish Steps (p98); the grandiose Villa Medici (p103); the controversial Museo dell'Ara Pacis (p101); artists' street Via Margutta (p115); and several masterpiece-packed churches. To see all the sights here, factoring in some window-shopping, would take a day, and it's all easily walked – a short walk from the Centro Storico or Piazza Venezia – and easily accessed from the Spagna and Flaminio metro stations.

Alongside Tridente, the Roman hill of Quirinale is home to the extraordinary Trevi Fountain (p100) and the imposing Palazzo del Quirinale (p103), as well as important churches by the twin masters of Roman baroque, Bernini and Borromini. Other artistic hot spots in the area include the lavish Galleria Colonna (p102) and the fabulous Palazzo Barberini (p105) – to see all this at leisure you'll need several days. Busy during the day, both Tridente and the Quirinale are sleepy after dark.

Local Life

→**Ambling** Imagine yourself in *Roman Holiday* along the cobbled Via Margutta (p115), a car-free street studded with art galleries, and just a stone's throw from the Spanish Steps.

→**Escape the Trevi Fountain crowds** Find yourself wonderfully alone, admiring amphorae containing papal innards in Chiesa di Santissimi Vincenzo e Anastasio (p104) or fabulously feminine frescoes beneath art nouveau glass at Galleria Sciarra (p104).

→**Cheap eats** Follow the savvy student crowd to Pastificio (p107) for a pot of perfectly cooked pasta standing up, followed by a portion of equally perfect tiramisu to take away from famous Pompi (p107).

Getting There & Away

→**Metro** The Trevi and Quirinale areas are closest to the Barberini metro stop, while Spagna and Flaminio stations are perfectly placed for Tridente. All three stops are on line A.

→**Bus** Numerous buses run down to Piazza Barberini or along Via Veneto; many stop at the southern end of Via del Corso and on Via del Tritone, ideal for a foray into Tridente.

Lonely Planet's Top Tip

Plan your itinerary in advance to accommodate differing opening hours: Gallerie Colonna is only open Saturday morning, for example; during art exhibitions Scuderie al Quirinale has late-night opening (until 10.30pm) on Friday and Saturday; and many local churches close for two or three hours over lunch so are best visited in the morning or late afternoon.

Best Places to Eat

→ Imàgo (p109)
→ Colline Emiliane (p110)
→ Fiaschetteria Beltramme (p107)
→ Pastificio (p107)
→ Hostaria Romana (p109)
→ Il Margutta (p106)

For reviews, see p105. →

Best Places to Drink

→ Zuma Bar (p111)
→ Stravinkij Bar (p111)
→ Il Palazzetto (p111)
→ Antico Caffè Greco (p111)
→ Pepy's Bar (p112)
→ Caffè Ciampini (p112)

For reviews, see p111. →

Best Churches

→ Basilica di Santa Maria del Popolo (p99)
→ Chiesa di Sant'Andrea al Quirinale (p103)
→ Chiesa di San Carlino alle Quattro Fontane (p104)
→ Chiesa di Santa Maria della Vittoria (p105)
→ Chiesa di Santissimi Vincenzo e Anastasio (p104)

For reviews, see p101. →

TRIDENTE, TREVI & THE QUIRINALE

TOP SIGHT
PIAZZA DI SPAGNA & THE SPANISH STEPS

A magnet for visitors since the 18th century, the Spanish Steps (Scalinata della Trinità dei Monti) rising up from Piazza di Spagna provide a perfect people-watching perch: think hot spot for selfies, newly-wed couples posing for romantic photos etc. In the late 1700s the area was much loved by English visitors on the Grand Tour and was known to locals as the *ghetto de l'inglesi* (the English ghetto).

Piazza di Spagna was named after the Spanish Embassy to the Holy See, but the staircase – 135 gleaming steps designed by the Italian Francesco de Sanctis and built in 1725 with a legacy from the French – leads up to the hilltop French Chiesa della Trinità dei Monti. The dazzling sweep of stairs reopened in September 2016 after a €1.5 million clean-up job funded by luxury Italian jewellery house Bulgari.

At the foot of the steps, the fountain of a sinking boat, the **Barcaccia** (1627), is believed to be by Pietro Bernini, father of the more famous Gian Lorenzo. It's fed from an aqueduct, the ancient Roman Acqua Vergine, as are the fountains in Piazza del Popolo and the Trevi Fountain. Here there's not much pressure, so it's sunken as a clever piece of engineering. Bees and suns decorate the structure, symbols of the commissioning Barberini family. It was damaged in 2015 by Dutch football fans, and the Dutch subsequently offered to repair the damage.

To the southeast of the piazza, adjacent Piazza Mignanelli is dominated by the Colonna dell'Immacolata, built in 1857 to celebrate Pope Pius IX's declaration of the Immaculate Conception.

DON'T MISS

➡ City views from the top of the Spanish Steps

➡ Fontana della Barcaccia

➡ Chiesa della Trinità dei Monti

PRACTICALITIES

➡ Map p300, D4

➡ Ⓜ Spagna

TOP SIGHT
BASILICA DI SANTA MARIA DEL POPOLO

A magnificent repository of art, this is one of Rome's earliest and richest Renaissance churches, parts of which were designed by Bramante and Bernini. The lavish chapels, decorated by Caravaggio, Bernini, Raphael, Pinturicchio and others, were commissioned by local noble families.

History
The first chapel was built here in 1099, over the tombs of the Domiti family, to exorcise the ghost of Nero, who was secretly buried on this spot and whose malicious spirit was thought to haunt the area. There were subsequent overhauls, but the church's most important makeover came when Bramante renovated the presbytery and choir in the early 16th century and Pinturicchio added a series of frescoes. Also in the Bramante-designed apse are Rome's first stained-glass windows, crafted by Frenchman Guillaume de Marcillat in the early 16th century. The altar houses the 13th-century painting *Madonna del Popolo*. The church's most famous works, by Caravaggio, were added in 1601, and Bernini further reworked the church in the 17th century.

PRACTICALITIES

→ Map p300, A1

→ www.smariadelpopolo. com

→ Piazza del Popolo 12

→ ☉10.30am-12.30pm & 4-6.30pm Mon-Thu, 10.30am-6.30pm Fri & Sat, 4.30-6.30pm Sun

→ Ⓜ Flaminio

Chigi Chapel
Raphael designed the Cappella Chigi, dedicated to his patron, the enormously wealthy banker Agostino Chigi, but never lived to see it completed. Bernini finished the job for him more than 100 years later, contributing statues of Daniel and Habakkuk to the altarpiece, which was built by Sebastiano del Piombo. Only the floor mosaics were retained from Raphael's original design, including that of a kneeling skeleton, placed there to remind the living of the inevitable.'

Cerasi Chapel
The church's dazzling highlight is the Cappella Cerasi, to the left of the main altar, with its two facing works by Caravaggio: the *Conversion of Saul* (1601) and the *Crucifixion of St Peter* (1601), dramatically spotlit via the artist's use of light and shade. The former is the second version, as the first was rejected by the patron. The latter is frighteningly realistic: the artist has used perspective to emphasise the weight of the cross, and St Peter's facial expression as he is upturned is heartrendingly human. The central altarpiece painting is the *Assumption* (1590) by Annibale Carracci.

Della Rovere Chapel
The frescoes in the lunettes, depicting the stories of St Jerome (to whom the chapel is dedicated), and the Nativity with St Jerome above the altar in this chapel were painted by Pinturicchio in the 15th century, and glow with jewel-bright colours.

TOP SIGHT
TREVI FOUNTAIN

Rome's most famous fountain, the iconic Fontana di Trevi, is a baroque extravaganza, a foaming masterpiece that almost fills an entire piazza. This is where movie star Anita Ekberg cavorted in a ball gown in Fellini's classic *La Dolce Vita* (1960); apparently she wore waders under her iconic black dress.

The flamboyant baroque ensemble, 20m wide and 26m high, was designed by Nicola Salvi in 1732 and depicts sea-god Oceanus' chariot being led by Tritons with sea-horses – one wild, one docile – representing the moods of the sea.

The fountain water comes from the Aqua Virgo, an underground aqueduct that is over 2000 years old, was built by General Agrippa under Augustus and brings water from the Salone springs around 19km away. The name Trevi refers to the *tre vie* (three roads) that converge at the fountain.

To the eastern side of the fountain is a large round stone urn. The story goes that Salvi, during the construction of the fountain, was harassed by a barber, who had his shop to the east of the fountain and who was critical of the work in progress. Thus the sculptor added this urn in order to block the irritating critic.

The famous tradition (since the 1954 film *Three Coins in the Fountain)* is to toss a coin into the fountain, thus ensuring your return to Rome. Up to €3000 is thrown into the Trevi each day. This money is collected daily and goes to the Catholic charity Caritas.

Between 2013 and 2015, Fendi fashion house invested €2.18 million in the restoration of the now-gleaming baroque ensemble. And in 2017, to celebrate 90 years of fashion-house operation, Fendi staged a magical 'Legends and Fairy Tales' fashion show in the Trevi Fountain. Launching Fendi's autumn-winter haute-couture collection, catwalk models walked on water – or rather they strutted across a glass walkway constructed above the water – as the sun set over Piazza di Trevi.

DON'T MISS

➡ The contrasting sea-horses, or moods of the sea.

➡ Throwing a coin or three into the fountain.

➡ Papal innards in Chiesa di Santissimi Vincenzo e Anastasio.

PRACTICALITIES

➡ Fontana di Trevi

➡ Map p300, D6

➡ Piazza di Trevi

➡ Ⓜ Barberini

SIGHTS

Piazza del Popolo, the Spanish Steps, the Trevi Fountain, Rome's most fashionable district, Palazzo Barberini and a sprinkling of Caravaggios...this area is one of Rome's richest, in terms of cuisine, art and culture (as well as hard cash) and offers an embarrassment of treasures for visitors.

⊙ Piazza del Popolo & Around

BASILICA DI SANTA MARIA DEL POPOLO
BASILICA

See p99.

PINCIO HILL GARDENS
GARDENS

Map p300 (MFlaminio) Overlooking Piazza del Popolo, 19th-century Pincio Hill is named after the Pinci family, who owned this part of Rome in the 4th century. It's quite a climb up from the piazza, but at the top you're rewarded with lovely views over to St Peter's and the Gianicolo Hill. Alternatively, approach from the top of the Spanish Steps. From the gardens, strike out to explore Villa Borghese, Villa Medici (p103) or Chiesa della Trinità dei Monti (p102) at the top of the Spanish Steps.

MUSEO DELL'ARA PACIS
MUSEUM

Map p300 (✏06 06 08; www.arapacis.it; Lungotevere in Auga; adult/reduced €11/9; ⊗9.30am-7.30pm Mon-Sat; MFlaminio) The first modern construction in Rome's historic centre since WWII, Richard Meier's controversial and widely detested glass-and-marble pavilion houses the *Ara Pacis Augustae* (Altar of Peace), Augustus' great monument to peace. One of the most important works of ancient Roman sculpture, the vast marble altar – measuring 11.6m by 10.6m by 3.6m – was completed in 13 BC.

CASA DI GOETHE
MUSEUM

Map p300 (✏06 3265 0412; www.casadigoethe.it; Via del Corso 18; adult/reduced €5/3; ⊗10am-6pm Tue-Sun; MFlaminio) A gathering place for German intellectuals, the Via del Corso

---

TOP SIGHT
PIAZZA DEL POPOLO

For centuries the site of public executions (the last was in 1826), this piazza was once much less grand than today, with a public fountain, horse trough and washing cistern. It was laid out in 1538 to provide a more grandiose entrance to what was then Rome's main northern gateway. Via Flaminia connected the city with the north from here. The piazza has been remodelled several times since, most significantly by Giuseppe Valadier in 1823, who created the gaping ellipse we see today.

In the centre, the 36m-high **obelisk** was brought by Augustus from Heliopolis, in ancient Egypt, and originally stood in Circo Massimo. To the east is the viewpoint of the **Pincio Hill Gardens**. This is not one of Rome's original seven hills, as it lay outside the original city boundary; it was included within the city from the 3rd century.

Guarding the piazza's southern end are Carlo Rainaldi's twin 17th-century baroque churches, **Chiesa di Santa Maria dei Miracoli** (⊗6.45am-12.30pm & 4.30-7.30pm Mon-Sat, 8am-1.15pm & 4.30-7.45 Sun) and **Basilica di Santa Maria in Montesanto** (Chiesa degli Artisti; www.chiesadegliartisti.it; ⊗5.30-8pm Mon-Fri, 11am-1.30pm Sun), while on the northern flank is the **Porta del Popolo** created by Bernini to celebrate Queen Christina of Sweden's defection to Catholicism and subsequent arrival in Rome.

DON'T MISS...

➜ The obelisk
➜ The view from the Pincio Hill Gardens

PRACTICALITIES

➜ Map p300, A1
➜ MFlaminio

TOP SIGHT
GALLERIA COLONNA

This dazzlingly opulent gallery, the only part of Palazzo Colonna open to the public, houses the Colonna family's small but stunning private art collection. The polished yellow columns represent the 'Colonna' (which also means column) of the family name.

The purpose-built gallery (constructed by Antonio del Grande from 1654 to 1665) has six rooms crowned by fantastical ceiling frescoes, all dedicated to Marcantonio Colonna, the family's greatest ancestor, who defeated the Turks at the naval Battle of Lepanto in 1571. Works by Giovanni Coli and Filippo Gherardi in the Great Hall, Sebastiano Ricci in the Landscapes Room, and Giuseppe Bartolomeo Chiari in the Throne Room all commemorate his efforts.

Of the 16th- to 18th-century paintings on display, Annibale Carracci's *Mangiafagioli* (The Bean Eater) is generally considered the outstanding masterpiece. One wing includes the sumptuous Chapel Hall and the rich 17th-century Artemisia tapestries collection. Note also the cannonball lodged in the gallery's marble stairs, a vivid reminder of the 1849 siege of Rome.

Its terrace cafe is open from May to October.

DON'T MISS...

➡ Fantastic ceiling frescoes

➡ Annibale Carracci's *Mangiafagioli*

PRACTICALITIES

➡ Map p300, D8

➡ ☑06 678 43 50

➡ www.galleria colonna.it

➡ Via della Pilotta 17

➡ adult/reduced €12/10

➡ ◷9am-1.15pm Sat, closed Aug

➡ ◲Via IV Novembre

---

apartment where Johann Wolfgang von Goethe enjoyed a happy Italian sojourn (despite complaining of the noisy neighbours) from 1786 to 1788 is now a lovingly maintained small museum. Exhibits include fascinating Piranesi engravings of 18th-century Rome, as well as Goethe's sketches and letters, plus some lovely sketches of him by his friend Tischbein. With advance permission, ardent fans can use the library full of first editions.

◉ Piazza di Spagna & Around

PIAZZA DI SPAGNA & THE SPANISH STEPS
PIAZZA

See p98.

CHIESA DELLA TRINITÀ DEI MONTI
CHURCH

Map p300 (☑06 679 41 79; Piazza Trinità dei Monti 3; ◷7.30am-8pm Tue-Fri, 10am-5pm Sat & Sun; Ⓜ Spagna) Looming over the Spanish Steps, this landmark church was commissioned by King Louis XII of France and consecrated in 1585. Apart from the great views from outside, it has some wonderful frescoes by

Daniele da Volterra. His *Deposizione* (Deposition), in the second chapel on the left, is regarded as a masterpiece of mannerist painting.

KEATS-SHELLEY HOUSE
MUSEUM

Map p300 (☑06 678 42 35; www.keats-shelley-house.org; Piazza di Spagna 26; adult/reduced €5/4; ◷10am-1pm & 2-6pm Mon-Sat; Ⓜ Spagna) The Keats-Shelley House is where Romantic poet John Keats died of tuberculosis at the age of 25, in February 1821. Keats came to Rome in 1820 to try to improve his health in the Italian climate, and rented two rooms on the 3rd floor of a townhouse next to the Spanish Steps, with painter companion Joseph Severn (1793–1879). Watch a film on the 1st floor about the Romantics, then head upstairs to see where Keats and Severn lived and worked.

VIA DEI CONDOTTI
AREA

Map p300 (Ⓜ Spagna) High-rolling shoppers and window-dreamers take note, this is Rome's smartest shopping strip. At the eastern end, near Piazza di Spagna, Antico Caffè Greco (p111) was a favourite meeting point of 18th- and 19th-century writers.

Other top shopping streets in the area include Via Frattina, Via della Croce, Via delle Carrozze and Via del Babuino.

 VILLA MEDICI PALACE

Map p300 (☑06 676 13 11; www.villamedici.it; Viale Trinità dei Monti 1; 1½hr guided tour adult/reduced €12/6; ☺10am-7pm Tue-Sun; Ⓜ Spagna) This sumptuous Renaissance palace was built for Cardinal Ricci da Montepulciano in 1540, but Ferdinando dei Medici bought it in 1576. It remained in Medici hands until 1801, when Napoleon acquired it for the French Academy. Guided tours take in the wonderful landscaped gardens, cardinal's painted apartments, and incredible views over Rome – tours in English depart at noon. Note the pieces of ancient Roman sculpture from the Ara Pacis embedded in the villa's walls.

⊙ Piazza di Trevi, Quirinale Hill & Around

TREVI FOUNTAIN FOUNTAIN
See p100.

PIAZZA DEL QUIRINALE PIAZZA

Map p300 (Ⓜ Barberini) A wonderful spot to enjoy a glowing Roman sunset, this piazza, which is dominated by the imposing presidential palace of Palazzo del Quirinale (p103), marks the summit of Quirinal Hill. The central obelisk was moved here from the **Mausoleo di Augusto** (Map p300; Piazza Augo Imperatore; ☐ Piazza Augusto Imperatore) in 1786 and is flanked by 5.5m statues of Castor and Pollux reining in a couple of rearing horses. Catch the weekly changing of the (young and very fidgety) guards on Sunday at 6pm in summer, 4pm the rest of the year.

**CHIESA DI SANT'ANDREA
AL QUIRINALE** CHURCH

Map p300 (Via del Quirinale 29; ☺9am-noon & 3-6pm Tue-Sun; ☐ Via Nazionale) It's said that in his old age Bernini liked to come and enjoy the peace of this late 17th century church, regarded by many as one of his greatest. Faced with severe space limitations, he managed to produce a sense of grandeur by designing an elliptical floor plan with a series of chapels opening onto the central area.

◉ TOP SIGHT
PALAZZO DEL QUIRINALE

Overlooking the high-up Piazza del Quirinale is the imposing presidential palace, formerly the papal summer residence. The immense Palazzo del Quirinale served as the papal summer residence for almost three centuries, until the keys were begrudgingly handed over to Italy's new king in 1870. Since 1948 it has been home to the Presidente della Repubblica, Italy's head of state. Pope Gregory XIII (r 1572–85) originally chose the site and over the next 150 years the top architects of the day worked on it, including Bernini, Domenico Fontana and Carlo Maderno.

Shorter tours visit the sumptuous reception rooms, while the longer tour includes the interiors as well as the gardens and carriages. Catch the weekly changing of the guards outside the palace on Sunday at 6pm in summer, 4pm the rest of the year.

On the other side of the piazza, **Scuderie Papali al Quirinale** (Map p300; ☑06 3996 7500; www.scuderiequirinale.it; Via XXIV Maggio 16; adult/reduced €12/9.50; ☺10am-8pm Sun-Thu, to 10.30pm Fri & Sat; ☐ Via Nazionale), the palace's former stables, is now a magnificent space that hosts art exhibitions; recent shows have included Matisse and Frida Kahlo.

DON'T MISS...

➔ Longer guided tours that cover palace and gardens.

➔ Sunday concerts in the chapel designed by Carlo Maderno.

➔ Splendid exhibitions in Scuderie Papali, the former stables.

PRACTICALITIES

➔ Map p300, E7

➔ www.quirinale.it

➔ Piazza del Quirinale

➔ 1¼hr tour €1.50, 2½hr tour adult/reduced €10/5

➔ ☺9.30am-4pm Tue, Wed & Fri-Sun, closed Aug

➔ Ⓜ Barberini

TRIDENTE, TREVI & THE QUIRINALE SIGHTS

HIDDEN CURIOSITIES

When the camera-wielding Trevi Fountain crowd gets too much, nip up the church steps and into **Chiesa di Santissimi Vincenzo e Anastasio** (Map p300; www. santivincenzoeanastasio.it; Vicolo dei Modelli 73; ⊙9am-1pm & 4-8pm; MBarberini). Original-ly known as the 'Papal church' due to its proximity to the papal residence on Quirinal Hill, this 17th-century church overlooking Rome's most spectacular fountain safe-guards the hearts and internal organs of dozens of popes – preserved in amphorae in a tiny gated chapel to the right of the apse. This practice began under Pope Sixtus V (1585–90) and continued until the 20th century when Pope Pius X (1903–1914) de-cided it was not for him.

To admire another hidden treasure sans crowds, meander west from Trevi Foun-tain, along pedestrian Via delle Muratte, and duck a block south to **Galleria Sciarra** (Map p300; Via Marco Minghetti 9-10; ⊙9am-8pm Mon-Fri; MBarberini), a stunning interior courtyard with an art nouveau glass roof and vibrant frescoes depicting the late 19th-century aristocratic Roman woman in all her feminine guises: as wife, mother, musician and so on. Further frescoes evoke the female virtues of strength, patience, modesty, kindness etc. Hidden away inside 16th-century **Palazzo Sciarra Colonna di Carbognano** on Via Marco Minghetti, the frescoes and unusual glass roof date to 1890 when the courtyard was remodelled and spruced up by the wealthy Sciarra fam-ily. Spot the single man in the frescoes: late Romantic writer Gabriele d'Annunzio.

CHIESA DI SAN CARLINO ALLE QUATTRO FONTANE   CHURCH
Map p300 (Via del Quirinale 23; ⊙10am-1pm Mon-Sat, noon-1pm Sun; ⬚Via Nazionale) This tiny church is a masterpiece of Roman baroque. It was Borromini's first church, and the play of convex and concave surfaces and the dome illuminated by hidden windows clev-erly transform the small space into a place of light and beauty. The church, completed in 1641, stands at the intersection known as the **Quattro Fontane**, named after the late-16th-century fountains on its four corners, representing Fidelity, Strength and the riv-ers Arno and Tiber.

BASILICA DEI SANTI APOSTOLI   CHURCH
Map p300 (Piazza dei Santissimi Apostoli; ⊙7am-noon & 4-7pm; ⬚Via IV Novembre) This much-altered 6th-century church is dedicated to the apostles James and Philip, whose relics are in the crypt. Its most obvious attraction is the portico with its Renaissance arches and the two-tier facade topped by 13 towering figures. Inside, the flashy baroque interior was completed in 1714 by Carlo and Franc-esco Fontana. Highlights include the ceiling frescoes by Baciccia and Antonio Canova's grandiose tomb of Pope Clement XIV.

CITTÀ DELL'ACQUA   ARCHAEOLOGICAL SITE
Map p300 (https://vicuscaprarius.com; Vicolo del Puttarello 25; adult/reduced €3/1.50; ⊙11am-5.30pm Wed-Fri, to 7pm Sat & Sun; MBarber-ini) The little-known excavations of Vicus Caprarius (the name of the ancient street) include a Roman house and a Hadrian-era cistern that connected with the Aqua Virgo cistern. Eight metres deep, they lie just a few paces from the eternal hubbub of the Trevi Fountain – the spring waters that once fed these waterworks now gush forth from the fountain.

LE DOMUS ROMANE DI PALAZZO VALENTINI   ARCHAEOLOGICAL SITE
Map p300 (☑06 2276 1280; www.palazzovalentini. it; Via Foro Traiano 85; adult/reduced €12/8, advance booking fee €1.50; ⊙9.30am-6.30pm Wed-Mon; ♿; MBarberini) Underneath a grand mansion that's been the seat of the Province of Rome since 1873 lie the archaeo-logical remains of several lavish ancient Ro-man houses; the excavated fragments have been turned into a fascinating multimedia 'experience'. Tours are every 30 minutes, but alternate between Italian, English and French. Book ahead online or by phone, es-pecially during holiday periods.

Visits take you on a virtual tour of the dwellings, complete with sound effects, vividly projected frescoes and glimpses of ancient life as it might have been lived in the area around the buildings. It's genuinely thrilling and great for older kids.

⊙ Piazza Barberini & Around

PIAZZA BARBERINI
PIAZZA

Map p300 (MBarberini) More a traffic thoroughfare than a place to linger, this noisy square is named after the Barberini family, one of Rome's great dynastic clans. In the centre, the Bernini-designed **Fontana del Tritone** (Fountain of the Triton; Map p300) depicts the sea-god Triton blowing a stream of water from a conch while seated in a large scallop shell supported by four dolphins. Bernini also crafted the **Fontana delle Api** (Fountain of the Bees; Map p300) in the northeastern corner, again for the Barberini family, whose crest featured three bees in flight.

★PALAZZO BARBERINI
GALLERY

Map p300 (Galleria Nazionale d'Arte Antica; ☑06 481 45 91; www.barberinicorsini.org; Via delle Quattro Fontane 13; adult/reduced €5/2.50, incl Palazzo Corsini €10/5; ☻8.30am-7pm Tue-Sun; MBarberini) Commissioned to celebrate the Barberini family's rise to papal power, Palazzo Barberini is a sumptuous baroque palace that impresses even before you clap eyes on the breathtaking art. Many high-profile architects worked on it, including rivals Bernini and Borromini; the former contributed a large square staircase, the latter a helicoidal one. Amid the masterpieces, don't miss Pietro da Cortona's *Il Trionfo della Divina Provvidenza* (Triumph of Divine Providence; 1632–39), the most spectacular of the *palazzo* ceiling frescoes in the 1st-floor main salon.

Other must-sees include Hans Holbein's famous portrait of a pugnacious Henry VIII (c 1540); Filippo Lippi's luminous *Annunciazione e due devoti* (Annunciation with two Kneeling Donors); and Raphael's *La Fornarina* (The Baker's Girl), a portrait of his mistress, who worked in a bakery in Trastevere. Works by Caravaggio include *San Francesco d'Assisi in meditazione* (St Francis in Meditation), *Narciso* (Narcissus; 1571–1610) and the mesmerisingly horrific *Giuditta e Oloferne* (Judith Beheading Holophernes; c 1597–1600).

CONVENTO DEI CAPPUCCINI
MUSEUM

Map p300 (☑06 487 11 85; www.cappuccini viaveneto.it; Via Vittorio Veneto 27; adult/reduced €8.50/5; ☻9am-7pm; MBarberini) This church and convent complex safeguards what is possibly Rome's strangest sight: crypt chapels where everything from the picture frames to the light fittings is made of human bones. Between 1732 and 1775 resident Capuchin monks used the bones of 3700 of their departed brothers to create this macabre *memento mori* (reminder of death) – a 30m-long passageway ensnaring six crypts, each named after the type of bone used to decorate (skulls, shin bones, pelvises etc).

There's an arch crafted from hundreds of skulls, vertebrae used as fleurs-de-lis, and light fixtures made of femurs. The accompanying multimedia museum tells the story of the Capuchin order of monks, including a work attributed to Caravaggio: *St Francis in Meditation*. Don't miss the adjoining **Chiesa dei Cappuccini** (1626), accessible via the outside staircase.

CHIESA DI SANTA MARIA DELLA VITTORIA
CHURCH

Map p312 (☑06 4274 0571; Via XX Settembre 17; ☻8.30am-noon & 3.30-6pm; MRepubblica) This modest church is an unlikely setting for an extraordinary work of art – Bernini's extravagant and sexually charged *Santa Teresa trafitta dall'amore di Dio* (Ecstasy of St Teresa). This daring sculpture depicts Teresa, engulfed in the folds of a flowing cloak, floating in ecstasy on a cloud while a teasing angel pierces her repeatedly with a golden arrow.

GAGOSIAN GALLERY
GALLERY

Map p300 (☑06 420 86 498; www.gagosian.com; Via Francesco Crispi 16; ☻10.30am-7pm Tue-Sat; MBarberini) FREE Since it opened in 2007, the Rome branch of Larry Gagosian's contemporary art empire has hosted the big names of modern art: Cy Twombly, Damien Hirst and Lawrence Weiner, to name a few. The gallery is housed in an artfully converted 1920s bank, and was designed by Roman architect Firouz Galdo and Englishman Caruso St John.

✖ EATING

Classy eateries are sandwiched between fashion boutiques in this designer district, with kitchens covering the whole gambit of Roman cooking styles. In the Quirinale and Trevi Fountain area, take care selecting where to eat: avoid tourist restaurants with English menus, waiters touting for business on the street outside or (worst of all) plastic

plates of food showcased on a table on the street in front. But gems still sparkle among the stones, with some notable restaurants around the presidential palace and parliament.

✖ Piazza del Popolo & Around

FATAMORGANA CORSO
GELATERIA €

Map p300 (✆06 3265 2238; www.gelateria fatamorgana.com; Via Laurina 10; 2/3/4/5 scoops €2.50/3.50/4.50/5; ⊙noon-11pm; MFlaminio) The wonderful all-natural, gluten-free gelato served at Fatamorgana is arguably Rome's best artisanal ice cream. Innovative and classic tastes of heaven abound, including flavours such as pear and caramel, all made from the finest seasonal ingredients. There are several branches around town.

FOL
FAST FOOD €

Map p300 (✆06 8756 13 49; www.folpopcorn.com; Via di Ripetta 28; small/big cup €4/5; ⊙11am-10pm; MFlaminio) When traditional Roman street food tires, nip into this gourmet popcorn shop for a punnet of caramel, chocolate, pistachio or cappuccino popcorn. Wacky savoury flavours include margherita (aka pizza), bacon, chilli pepper and crema di formaggio (cream cheese).

GELATERIA DEI GRACCHI
GELATERIA €

Map p300 (✆06 322 47 27; www.gelateriadei gracchi.it; Via di Ripetta 261; cones & tubs €2.50-4.50; ⊙noon-8.10pm Sat-Wed, to midnight Thu & Fri; MFlaminio) Handily located just off Piazza del Popolo, this outpost of the venerable Gelataria dei Gracchi, by the Vatican, is known for its superb ice cream made from the best ingredients. Flavours are classic.

★IL MARGUTTA
VEGETARIAN €€

Map p300 (✆06 3265 0577; www.ilmargutta.bio; Via Margutta 118; lunch buffet weekdays/weekends €15/25, meals €15-40; ⊙8.30am-11.30pm; ✐; MSpagna, Flaminio) This chic art-gallery-bar-restaurant gets packed at lunchtime with Romans feasting on its good-value, eat-as-much-as-you-can buffet deal. Everything is organic, the evening menu tempting with creative dishes such as tofu with marinated ginger and smoked tubers, or grilled chicory with almond cream, almond cream and candied tangerine. Among the various tasting menus is a vegan option.

AL GRAN SASSO
TRATTORIA €€

Map p300 (✆06 321 48 83; www.algransasso. com; Via di Ripetta 32; meals €30-35; ⊙12.30-3.30pm & 7-11pm Sun-Fri Sep-Jul; MFlaminio) A top lunchtime spot, this is a classic, dyed-in-the-wool trattoria specialising in old-school country cooking. It's a relaxed place with a welcoming vibe, garish murals on the walls (strangely often a good sign) and tasty, value-for-money food. The fried dishes are excellent, or try one of the daily specials, chalked up on the board outside.

BUCA DI RIPETTA
ITALIAN €€

Map p300 (✆06 321 93 91; Via di Ripetta 36; meals €45; ⊙noon-3.30pm & 7-11pm; MFlaminio) Popular with actors and directors from the district, who know a good thing when they see it, this foodie destination offers robust Roman cuisine. Try the zuppa rustica con crostini do pane aromatizzati (country-style soup with rosemary-scented bread) or the matolino do latte al forno alle erbe con patate (baked suckling pork with potatoes) and you'll be fuelled either for more sightseeing or for a lie down.

BUCCONE
RISTORANTE, WINE BAR €€

Map p300 (✆06 361 21 54; Via di Ripetta 19; meals €30; ⊙9am-9.30pm Mon-Sat, 11am-6pm Sun; MFlaminio) Step in under the faded gilt-and-mirrored sign and you'll feel as though you've gone back in time. Once a coach house, then a tavern, this building became a wine shop in the 1960s, furnished with 19th-century antiques and lined with around a thousand Italian wines. It serves simple food such as mixed plates of cured meat and cheese, but on Saturday offers a proper hot cena (dinner).

BABETTE
ITALIAN €€€

Map p300 (✆06 321 15 59; www.babette ristorante.it; Via Margutta 1d; meals €50; ⊙1-3pm & 7-10.45pm Tue-Sun, closed Jan; ✐; MSpagna, Flaminio) Babette is run by two sisters who used to produce a fashion magazine, hence the effortlessly chic interior of exposed brick walls and vintage painted signs. Cuisine is a feast of Italian dishes with a creative French twist: tortiglioni with courgette, saffron and pistachio pesto, for example, followed by rabbit loin in juniper sauce, then torta Babette (a light-as-air lemon cheesecake).

Romans flock here at weekends for Babette's good-value lunch buffet (€28), which includes water, bread, dessert and coffee.

DAL BOLOGNESE

ITALIAN €€€

Map p300 (📞06 361 14 26; Piazza del Popolo 1; meals €70; ⏰12.45-3pm & 8.15-11pm Tue-Sun, closed Aug; Ⓜ️Flaminio) The moneyed and models mingle at this historically chic restaurant. Dine inside, surrounded by wood panelling and exotic flowers, or outside, people-watching with views over Piazza del Popolo. As the name suggests, Emilia-Romagna dishes are the name of the game; everything is good, but try the tortellini in soup, tagliatelle with ragú, or the damn fine fillet steak.

✖️ Piazza di Spagna & Around

⭐PASTIFICIO

FAST FOOD €

Map p300 (Via della Croce 8; pasta, wine & water €4; ⏰1-3pm Mon-Sat; Ⓜ️Spagna) A brilliant budget find, this old-fashioned pasta shop (1918), with a kitchen hatch, serves up two choices of pasta at lunchtime. It's fast food, Italian style – freshly cooked (if you time it right) pasta, with wine and water included. Grab a space to stand and eat between shelves packed with packets of dry pasta or take it away.

POMPI

DESSERTS €

Map p300 (www.barpompi.it; Via della Croce 82; tiramisu €4; ⏰10.30am-9.30pm; Ⓜ️Spagna) Rome's most famous vendor of tiramisu (which literally means 'pick me up') sells takeaway cartons of the deliciously yolky yet light-as-air dessert. As well as classic, it comes in pistachio, strawberry, hazelnut and banana-chocolate variations. Eat on the spot (standing) or buy frozen portions that will keep for a few hours until you're ready to tuck in at home.

VENCHI

GELATO €

Map p300 (📞06 6979 7790; www.venchi.com; Via della Croce 25-26; 2-/3-/4-scoop cone €3.50/4.50/5; ⏰10.30am-11pm Sun-Thu, to midnight Fri & Sat; Ⓜ️Spagna) Walk into this dazzling white-and-gold boutique with vaulted ceiling and frescoes and try not to stare gobsmacked at the entire back wall dripping in shiny dark chocolate – 350kg in all mixed with a spot of olive oil. Shop here for chocolates and gelato, crafted with pride by the Turin chocolate house since 1878. The chocolate, topped perhaps with whipped cream and/or hazelnuts, is predictably divine.

⭐FIASCHETTERIA BELTRAMME

TRATTORIA €€

Map p300 (📞06 6979 7200; Via della Croce 39; meals €40; ⏰12.15-3pm & 7.30-10.45pm; Ⓜ️Spagna) A super spot for authentic Roman dining near the Spanish Steps, Fiaschetteria (meaning 'wine-sellers') is a hole-in-the-wall, stuck-in-time place with a short menu. Fashionistas with appetites dig into traditional Roman dishes made using recipes unchanged since the 1930s when a waiter at the 19th-century wine bar (from 1886 to be precise) started serving food. Seeking the perfect carbonara? This is the address.

GINGER

BRASSERIE €€

Map p300 (📞06 9603 6390; www.ginger.roma.it; Via Borgognona 43; sandwiches €7-10, salads €9-14, meals €50; ⏰10am-11.30pm; Ⓜ️Spagna) 🌿 This buzzy white-tiled space is a fantastic all-day dining spot near the Spanish Steps. The focus is on organic 'slow food' dishes using seasonal Appellation d'Origine Protégée (AOP) ingredients, and all appetites are catered for with gourmet, French baguette-style sandwiches, steamed 'baskets', meal-sized salads and healthy mains like salmon with orange mayonnaise.

NINO

TUSCAN €€

Map p300 (📞06 679 56 76; www.ristorantenino. it; Via Borgognona 11; meals €45; ⏰12.30-3pm & 7.30-11pm Mon-Sat; Ⓜ️Spagna) With a look that has worked since it opened in 1934 (wrought-iron chandeliers, polished dark wood and white tablecloths), Nino is enduringly popular with the rich and famous. Waiters can be brusque if you're not on the A-list, but the food is quality hearty fare, including memorable steaks and Tuscan bean soup.

ANTICA ENOTECA

WINE BAR €€

Map p300 (📞06 679 08 96; www.facebook.com/ anticaenoteca; Via della Croce 76b; meals €35; ⏰noon-midnight; Ⓜ️Spagna) Locals and tourists alike have propped up the 19th-century wooden bar here since 1842 when this wine bar first opened its doors near the Spanish Steps. Summer ushers the action outside, while wintertime is around tables in a modern, tastefully distressed interior. Sample wines by the glass, nibble antipasti and order well-priced soul food such as soups, pasta, polenta and pizza.

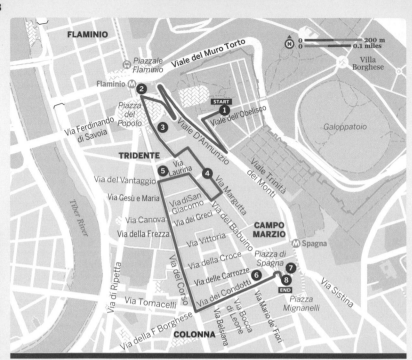

🏃 Neighbourhood Walk
Literary Footsteps

START PINCIO HILL GARDENS
END KEATS-SHELLEY HOUSE
LENGTH 1KM; TWO HOURS

This walk explores the literary haunts, both real and fictional, which speckle the Tridente district.

Begin your walk in ❶**Pincio Hill Gardens** (p101), where Henry James' Daisy Miller walked with Frederick Winterbourne. Then make your way downhill to Piazza del Popolo and visit the church of ❷**Santa Maria del Popolo** (p99). Dan Brown's *Angels & Demons* made use of this remarkable church in its convoluted plot.

From here it's merely a few steps to ❸**Hotel de Russie** (p213), favoured by the artistic avant-garde in the early 20th century. Jean Cocteau stayed here with Picasso, and wrote a letter home in which he described plucking oranges from outside his window.

Running parallel to Via del Babuino is ❹**Via Margutta** (p115). Famous for its artistic and cinematic connections, this picturesque cobbled street was where Truman Capote wrote his short story *Lola* about a raven who lived with him at his apartment. Fellini, Picasso, Stravinsky and Puccini all lived here at some point, and as did Gregory Peck's character in *Roman Holiday* (exteriors of his apartment were shot at No 51).

Next, make your way to Via del Corso, to see the ❺**Casa di Goethe** (p101) where Goethe had a whale of a time from 1786 to 1788. Head down Via del Corso then turn left up into Via dei Condotti, where William Thackeray stayed in 1854, stopping at ❻**Antico Caffè Greco** (p111), a former haunt of Casanova, Goethe, Keats, Byron and Shelley. Leaving here, you're almost at the ❼**Spanish Steps** (p98), which Dickens described in his *Pictures from Italy*. Byron stayed on Piazza di Spagna, at No 25, in 1817. Just south of the steps is the apartments where Keats died of tuberculosis, aged just 25. The ❽**Keats-Shelley House** (p102) is now a small museum devoted to the romantic poets.

OSTERIA MARGUTTA   OSTERIA €€

Map p300 (☑06 323 10 25; www.osteriamargutta.
it; Via Margutta 82; meals €50; ☺12.30-3pm &
7.30-11pm Tue-Sat, 12.30-3pm Sun, 7.30-11pm
Mon; Ⓜ Spagna) This vintage *osteria* (tavern),
around since 1965, oozes theatre: a rich interior mixes blue glass with rich reds and
fringed lampshades, while the flower- and
ivy-strewn street terrace is one of summertime's prettiest. Plaques on the chairs testify
to the famous thespians who've dined here
on its classic regional dishes. Top wine list
and occasional live jazz too.

**TRATTORIA OTELLO ALLA
CONCORDIA**   TRATTORIA €€

Map p300 (☑06 679 11 78; Via della Croce 81;
meals €35; ☺12.30-3pm & 7.30-11pm Mon-Sat;
Ⓜ Spagna) A vintage favourite with tourists
and locals alike, Otello is a haven of peace
near the Spanish Steps. Tucked back off the
road, summertime dining is in the beautiful
vine-covered courtyard of an 18th-century
palazzo. Cuisine is traditional Roman, with
all the pasta classics like carbonara and *ceci
e pepe* (cheese and pepper) on the menu.

★IMÀGO   ITALIAN €€€

Map p300 (☑06 6993 4726; www.imago
restaurant.com; Piazza della Trinità dei Monti
6, Hotel Hassler; tasting menus €120-150; ☺7-
10.30pm Feb-Dec; ☑; Ⓜ Spagna) Even in a city
of great views, the panoramas from the Hassler Hotel's Michelin-starred romantic rooftop restaurant are special, extending over a
sea of roofs to the great dome of St Peter's
Basilica; request the corner table. Complementing the views are the bold, mod-Italian
creations of culinary whizz, chef Francesco
Apreda.

PALATIUM   LAZIO €€€

Map p300 (☑06 6920 2132; http://enoteca
regionalepalatium.it; Via Frattina 94; meals €45-
50; ☺bar 11am-11pm, restaurant 12.30-3.30pm
& 7.30-10.30pm; ☑Via del Corso) A rich showcase of regional bounty, this contemporary
enoteca regionale serves excellent artisanal
cheeses and salami as well as classic Roman
staples such as *tonnarelli cacio e pepe* (thick
spaghetti with pecorino cheese and black
pepper). It also stocks an impressive array of
Lazio wines; try lesser-known drops such as
Aleatico.

✕ Piazza di Trevi, Quirinale Hill & Around

★BISTRO DEL QUIRINO   ITALIAN €

Map p300 (☑06 9887 8090; www.bistrotquirino.
com; Via delle Vergini 7; brunch €10, à la carte €25;
☺noon-3.30pm & 4pm-2am; ☑Via del Corso) For
unbeatable value near Trevi Fountain, reserve a table at this artsy bistro adjoining
Teatro Quirino. Theatre posters add bags of
colour to the spacious interior where a banquet of a 'brunch' buffet – fantastic salads,
antipasti, hot and cold dishes – is laid out for
knowing Romans to feast on.

From 4pm, the bistro morphs into a cafe –
until 6.30pm when the sacrosanct *aperitivo*
spread kicks in.

HOSTARIA ROMANA   TRATTORIA €€

Map p300 (☑06 474 52 84; www.hostariaromana.
it; Via del Boccaccio 1; meals €40; ☺12.30-3pm &
7.15-11pm Mon-Sat; Ⓜ Barberini) A highly recommended address for lunch or dinner near
Trevi Fountain, Hostaria Romana cooks up
meaty, traditional classics like grilled goat
chops, veal cutlets, roast suckling pig and
T-bone steaks to a mixed Roman and tourist crowd. Busy, bustling and noisy, this is
everything an Italian *trattoria* should be.
Sign your name on the graffiti-covered walls
before leaving.

VINERIA IL CHIANTI   TUSCAN €€

Map p300 (☑06 679 24 70; www.vineriailchianti.
com; Via del Lavatore 81-82a; meals €45; ☺10am-
1am; ☑Via del Tritone) With a name like Il Chianti, this pretty ivy-clad wine bar can only
be Tuscan. Cosy up inside its bottle-lined
interior or grab a table on the street terrace
and dig into superb Tuscan dishes like *stra-
cotto al Brunello* (beef braised in Brunello
wine) or handmade pasta laced with *lardo
di Colonnata* (aromatic pork fat aged in Car-
rara marble vats).

PICCOLO ARANCIO   TRATTORIA €€

Map p300 (☑06 678 61 39; www.piccoloarancio.
it; Vicolo Scanderbeg 112; meals €30; ☺noon-3pm
& 7pm-midnight Tue-Sun; ☑Via del Corso) In a
'hood riddled with tourist traps, this backstreet eatery – tucked inside a tiny salmon-
pink house next to the grandiose Palazzo
Scanderberg – stands out. Meals open with
a complimentary glass of chilled *prosecco*

TRIDENTE, TREVI & THE QUIRINALE EATING

TOP-NOTCH REGIONAL DINING

Sensational regional cuisine from Emilia-Romagna aside, what makes **Colline Emiliane** (Map p300; ☎06 481 75 38; www.collineemiliane.com; Via degli Avignonesi 22; meals €45; ⊗12.45-2.45pm & 7.30-10.45pm Tue-Sun, closed Sun dinner & Mon; ⓂBarberini) so outstanding is its family vibe and overwhelmingly warm service. Stronghold of the Latini family since the 1930s, son Luca today runs the show together with his mother Paola (dessert queen), aunt Anna (watch her making fresh pasta each morning in the glassed-off lab) and father Massimo.

The kitchen flies the flag for Emilia-Romagna, the well-fed Italian province that has blessed the world with Parmesan, balsamic vinegar, bolognese sauce and Parma ham. Winter ushers white truffles with eggs, pasta or gooey Fontina cheese onto the menu. Whatever you do, don't scrimp on *dolci* – Anna's warm caramelised hazelnut-and-walnut tart is out of this world.

and the kitchen mixes Roman classics with more interesting dishes like homemade *ravioli all'arancia* (ravioli filled with orange and ricotta), smoked swordfish and knuckle of veal. Tables spill onto the quaint cobbled street in summer.

BACCANO
BRASSERIE €€

Map p300 (☎06 6994 1166; www.baccanoroma.com; Via delle Muratte 23; meals €45; ⊗8.30am-2am; ⊡Via del Corso) Possibly one of the most elegant addresses near Trevi Fountain, this French-style brasserie has all-day dining in an interior of polished wood, potted palms, high ceilings and cosy booths. Its shellfish platters and cocktails are both sensational, and the kitchen is very international (think burgers, club sandwiches etc). In winter, cuddle up beneath a cherry-red and grey blanket on the smart pavement terrace.

LE TAMERICI
SEAFOOD €€€

Map p300 (☎06 6920 0700; www.facebook.com/letamerici; Vicolo Scavolino 79; meals around €50; ⊗12.30-3.30pm & 7-11.30pm Mon-Sat Sep-Jul; ⊡Via del Tritone) Exceptional seafood and wine is a winning epicurean combo at Le Tamerici, a cream-hued, elegant escape from the Trevi Fountain hubbub. Hidden away down an alleyway, it impresses with its wine list, range of *digestivi* and light-as-air homemade pasta dishes laced with seafood – all served in two intimate rooms with bleached-wood beamed ceilings.

AL MORO
ITALIAN €€€

Map p300 (☎06 678 34 96; www.ristorante almororoma.com; Vicolo delle Bollette 13; meals €60; ⊗12.30-3.30pm & 7.30-11.30pm Mon-Sat; ⊡Via del Corso) A pair of potted olive trees mark the entrance to this one-time Fellini haunt, a step back in time with its picture-

gallery dining rooms, Liberty wall lamps, cantankerous buttoned-up waiters and old-money regulars. Join faux royals for timeless classics like *trippa alla romana* (tripe), *cicoria al brodo* (chicory in broth) and veal liver with crusty sage and butter.

✖ Piazza Barberini & Around

CRISPI
HEALTH FOOD €

Map p300 (☎06 4201 4040; Via Francesco Crispi 80; meals €9.50; ⊗10.30am-7.30pm Mon-Fri; ⊗; ⓂBarberini) Homemade soups, quiches, wraps, salads, cookies and cakes jam-packed with natural goodness make for a super-powered lunch at this organic market and bistro, run by talented baker Flaminia and partner Matthew. Don't miss the creative fruit and veg juices (€6.50) and extract shots. Eat in, at bar stools around high tables between shelves of herbal teas, grains and pulses, or take away.

OFFICINA NATURALE
FAST FOOD €

Map p300 (☎06 8767 1200; www.officinanaturale.com; Via Barberini 59; paninis €3.50, pastas €7-10; ⊗7am-6pm Mon-Fri; ⊗; ⓂBarberini) Dubbing itself a cafe-gelateria-deli-bistrot, this spacious white-tiled eatery is particularly popular with lunching office workers. Menus are chalked up around the light-filled interior, listing *panini* and daily pastas alongside ice creams, smoothies and fruit salads. Eat in or takeaway.

FORNO CERULLI
PIZZA €

Map p300 (☎06 488 26 27; www.fornocerulli1937.it; Via di San Nicola da Tolentino 53; pizza from €3; ⊗8am-4pm Mon-Fri; ⓂBarberini) Blink and you might well miss this hidden-away *pizza al taglio* joint, much loved by local office workers for its artisan flavours. Grab a bar stool and munch on slices of delicious, freshly made pizza and *foccacia* cooked in a traditional wood-fired oven. Salads, pasta, breads, biscuits and cakes too, all to eat in or take away.

DRINKING & NIGHTLIFE

Piazza del Popolo & Around

STRAVINSKIJ BAR BAR

Map p300 (06 3288 8874; Via del Babuino 9, Hotel de Russie; 9am-1am; Flaminio) Can't afford to stay at the celeb-magnet Hotel de Russie (p213)? Then splash out on a drink at its swish bar. There are sofas inside, but best is a drink in the sunny courtyard, with sun-shaded tables overlooked by terraced gardens. Impossibly romantic in the best dolce vita style, it's perfect for a pricey cocktail or beer accompanied by appropriately posh bar snacks.

CAFFÈ RIPETTA CAFE

Map p300 (06 321 05 24; Via di Ripetta 72; 8.30am-11pm; Flaminio) Buzzing with a young buoyant, staunchly Roman crowd, this sassy corner cafe is a relaxed and easy spot for lapping up a bit of local dolce vita over a love-heart-topped cappuccino – inside at the all-white bar or on the street-smart pavement terrace, heated in winter. Pizza (€8.50 to €11) and *panini* (€4.50 to €6), too.

LOCARNO BAR BAR

Map p300 (www.hotellocarno.com; Via della Penna 22; 7pm-1am; Flaminio) Fashionistas and style gurus congregate at this rakish lounge bar for their 7pm *aperitivo* (pre-dinner drinks). Part of the art-deco Hotel Locarno (p212) near Piazza del Popolo, it's an inspiring spot for a sundowner with romantic corners, a shaded outdoor terrace, heavy cast-iron tables and a decadent Agatha Christie–era feel.

CANOVA BAR

Map p300 (06 361 22 31; http://lnx.canova piazzadelpopolo.it; Piazza del Popolo 16; 7.30am-12.30am; Flaminio) While left-wing authors Italo Calvino and Alberto Moravia used to drink at **Rosati** (Map p300; 06 322 58 59; www.barrosati.com; Piazza del Popolo 5; 7.30am-11.30pm; Flaminio) on the other side of the square, their right-wing counterparts came to Canova, in the biz since 1890. Piazza views from the buzzing street terrace (heated in winter) remain as good as ever, and come 6pm, there's a generous *aperitivi* spread to nibble on with a sundowner.

'GUSTO WINE BAR

Map p300 (06 322 62 73; www.gusto.it; Piazza Augo Imperatore 9; 12.30-3.30pm & 7pm-midnight; Via del Corso) All exposed-brickwork and industrial chic, this warehouse-style hybrid is an atmospheric place to lounge on the terrace sipping wine – of which there are more than 200 different labels to choose from. The complex includes an *osteria*, restaurant and design-driven kitchen shop selling Smeg toasters, cook books, rose-shaped muffin tins et al.

Piazza di Spagna & Around

★ZUMA BAR COCKTAIL BAR

Map p300 (06 9926 6622; www.zuma restaurant.com; Via della Fontanella di Borghese 48, Palazzo Fendi; 6pm-1am Sun-Thu, to 2am Fri & Sat; Via del Corso) Dress up for a drink on the rooftop terrace of Palazzo Fendi of fashion-house fame – few cocktail bars in Rome are as sleek, hip or achingly sophisticated as this. City rooftop views are predictably fabulous; cocktails mix exciting flavours like shiso with juniper berries, elderflower and *prosecco;* and DJ sets spin Zuma playlists at weekends.

★ANTICO CAFFÈ GRECO CAFE

Map p300 (06 679 17 00; Via dei Condotti 86; 9am-9pm; Spagna) Rome's oldest cafe, open since 1760, is still working the look with the utmost elegance: waiters in black tails and bow tie, waitresses in frilly white pinnies, scarlet flock walls and age-spotted gilt mirrors. Prices reflect this amazing heritage: pay €9 for a cappuccino sitting down or join locals for the same (€2.50) standing at the bar.

★IL PALAZZETTO CAFE, COCKTAIL BAR

Map p300 (06 6993 41000; Viccolo del Bottino 8; noon-8.30pm Tue-Sun, closed in rain; Spagna) No terrace proffers such a fine

TRIDENTE, TREVI & THE QUIRINALE DRINKING & NIGHTLIFE

view of the comings and goings on the Spanish Steps over an expertly shaken cocktail (€10 to €13). Ride the lift up from the discreet entrance on narrow Via dei Bottino or look for steps leading to the bar from the top of the steps. Given everything is alfresco, the bar is only open in warm, dry weather.

CAFFÈ CIAMPINI   CAFE

Map p300 (☏06 678 56 78; www.caffeciampini. com; Viale Trinità dei Monti; ◷8am-11pm Mar-Oct; ⓂSpagna) Hidden away a short walk from the top of the Spanish Steps towards the Pincio Hill Gardens, this graceful seasonal cafe has a vintage garden-party vibe, with green wooden latticework and orange trees framing its white-clothed tables. There are lovely views over the backstreets behind Spagna, and the *gelato* – particularly the *tartufo al cioccolato* (chocolate truffle) – is renowned. Serves food too.

BABINGTON'S TEA ROOMS   CAFE

Map p300 (☏06 678 08 46; www.babingtons.com; Piazza di Spagna 23; ◷10am-9.15pm; ⓂSpagna) Founded in 1893, at a time when tea could only be bought in pharmacies, Babington's Tea Rooms were opened by two English women with the intention of serving up a decent cuppa to the hordes of English tourists in Rome. Traditional cream teas, scones, muffins, fruity teacakes, dainty finger sandwiches, fried breakfasts and other English culinary treats remain its unique selling point.

CANOVA TADOLINI   CAFE, BAR

Map p300 (☏06 3211 0702; www.canovatadolini. com; Via del Babuino 150a/b; ◷8am-midnight; ⓂSpagna) In 1818 sculptor Canova signed a contract for this studio that agreed it would be forever preserved for sculpture. The place is still stuffed with statues and it's a unique experience to sit among the great maquettes and sip a cappuccino, beer or glass of wine over snacks, a cake or quick *panino*. Pay first at the till then head left to the bar.

📍 Piazza Barberini & Around

PEPY'S BAR   CAFE

Map p300 (☏06 4040 2364; www.pepysbar.it; Piazza Barberini 53; ◷7am-2am; ☏; ⓂBarberini) Play the Roman: sit at a bistro table on the narrow pavement terrace and watch the fountains gush and *motorini* whizz by on Piazza Barberini at this down-to-earth, neighbourhood cafe in Trevi. It is a perfect spot for a relaxed drink any time of day, and its all-day sandwiches – made with perfectly square, crustless white bread – are almost too beautiful to eat.

☆ ENTERTAINMENT

GREGORY'S JAZZ CLUB   JAZZ

Map p300 (☏06 679 63 86; www.gregorysjazz. com; Via Gregoriana 54d; obligatory drink €15-20; ◷8pm-2am Tue-Sun; ⓂBarberini, Spagna) If Gregory's were a tone of voice, it'd be husky: unwind over a whisky in the downstairs bar, then unwind some more on squashy sofas upstairs to slinky live jazz and swing, with quality local performers who also like to hang out here.

🛍 SHOPPING

Tridente is queen of Rome shopping. Main street Via del Corso and the streets surrounding it are lined cheek by jowl with beautiful boutiques selling everything from savvy street wear and haute-couture fashion to handmade paper stationery, artisan jewellery, perfume, homewares and food. Specialist streets include quaint Via Margutta for antiques; Via dei Condotti for designer fashion; and Via della Pugna for small, independent boutiques.

🛍 Piazza del Popolo & Around

★RE(F)USE   DESIGN

Map p296 (☏06 6813 6975; www.carmina campus.com; Via della Fontanelle di Borghese 40; ◷11am-7pm; ▣Via del Corso) Fascinating to browse, this clever boutique showcases unique Carmina Campus pieces – primarily bags and jewellery – made from upcycled objects and recycled fabrics. The brand is the love child of Rome-born designer Ilaria Venturini Fendi (of the Fendi family), a passionate advocate of ethical fashion, who crafts contemporary bracelets from beer and soft drink cans, and bold bags from recycled materials.

PREPARE TO BE PAMPERED

Kami Spa (Map p300; ☑06 4201 0039; www.kamispa.com; Via degli Avignonesi 11-12; massage €120-280; ⊙10am-10pm; Ⓜ Barberini) A luxurious spa not far from the Trevi Fountain, this is a soothing place to recharge your batteries. Think hot stone massages, Balinese palm massages, massages with Moroccan rose petal oil, turmeric and sandalwood body wraps, and green tea body cocoons.

Hotel De Russie Spa (Map p300; ☑06 3288 8820; www.roccofortehotels.com/it; Via del Babuino 9; ⊙6.30am-10pm; Ⓜ Flaminio) In one of Rome's top hotels, this glamorous and gorgeous day spa boasts a salt water pool, steam room, Finnish sauna and well-equipped gym. A wide choice of treatments are available (for him and her), including shiatsu and deep-tissue massages; count at least €100 for a 50-minute massage.

★**ARTISANAL CORNUCOPIA**   DESIGN

Map p300 (☑342 871 4597; www.artisanal cornucopia.com; Via dell'Oca 38a; ⊙10am-7pm; Ⓜ Flaminio) One of several stylish independent boutiques on Via dell'Oca, this chic concept store showcases exclusive handmade pieces by Italian designers: think a trunk full of Anthony Peto hats, bold sculpture-like lamps by Roman designer Vincenzo Del Pizzo, and delicate gold necklaces and other jewellery crafted by Giulia Barela. It also sells artisan bags, shoes, candles, homewares and other lovely homemade objects.

FLUMEN PROFUMI   PERFUME

Map p296 (☑06 6830 7635; www.flumenprofumi. com; Via della Fontanella di Borghese 41; ⊙11am-2pm & 3.30-8pm Mon-Sat, 11am-2pm & 3-7.30pm Sun; ⎕ Via del Corso) Unique 'made in Rome' scents is what this artisan perfumery on Tridente's smartest shopping strip is all about. Natural perfumes are oil-based, contain four to eight base notes and evoke la dolce vita in Italy. Incantro fuses pomegranate with white flower, while Ritrovarsi Ancora is a nostalgic fragrance evocative of long, lazy, family meals around a shared countryside table (smell the fig!).

LA BOTTEGA DEL MARMORARO   ART

Map p300 (☑06 320 76 60; Via Margutta 53b; ⊙8am-7.30pm Mon-Sat; Ⓜ Flaminio) Watch *marmoraro* (marble artist) Sandro Fiorentini chip away in this enchanting Aladdin's cave filled, floor to ceiling, with his decorative marble plaques engraved with various inscriptions: la dolce vita, *la vita e bella* (life is beautiful) etc. Plaques start at €10 and Sandro will engrave any inscription you like (from €15). On winter days, warm your hands with Sandro in front of the open log fire.

I VIPPINI   CHILDREN'S CLOTHING

Map p296 (☑06 6880 3754; Via della Fontanella di Borghese 65; ⊙10am-7pm Wed-Sat, 3-7pm Mon; ⎕ Via del Corso) This pretty little boutique sells exquisite designer fashion for *bambini*, from newborns to teens. It stocks Italian designers in the main, alongside its own exclusive handmade label.

BORSALINO   FASHION & ACCESSORIES

Map p300 (☑06 3265 0838; www.borsalino.com; Piazza del Popolo 20; ⊙10am-7.30pm; Ⓜ Flaminio) This old-fashioned boutique is the Italian hatmaker favoured by 1920s criminal Al Capone, Japanese Emperor Hirohito and Humphrey Bogart. Think fedoras, pork-pie styles, felt cloches and woven straw caps. Service is English-speaking and naturally impeccable.

LAR   HOMEWARES

Map p296 (Lavori Artigiani Romani; ☑06 687 66 47; www.paralumi.it; Via del Leoncino 29; ⊙9am-7pm Mon-Fri, to 1pm Sat; ⎕ Via del Corso) Artisanal lamps and lampshades have been produced at this colourful family-run workshop since 1938. Their one-off creations, made from materials such as wood, brass and parchment, come in all shapes and sizes, from minimal free-standing white lights to cubist Mondrian-inspired table lamps.

FABRIANO   ARTS & CRAFTS

Map p300 (☑06 3260 0361; www.fabriano boutique.com; Via del Babuino 173; ⊙10am-8pm; Ⓜ Flaminio, Spagna) Fabriano makes stationery sexy, with deeply desirable leather-bound diaries, funky notebooks and products embossed with street maps of Rome. It's perfect for picking up a gift, with other items including beautifully made leather key rings and quirky paper jewellery by local designers.

TOD'S SHOES

Map p300 (☑06 6821 0066; www.tods.com; Via della Fontanella di Borghese 56a; ◷10.30am-7.30pm Mon-Sat, 11am-2pm & 3-7.30pm Sun; ⛙Via del Corso) The trademark of this luxury Italian brand, known more recently as the generous benefactor behind the much-needed clean-up of the northern and southern facades of the Colosseum facade, is its rubber-studded loafers – perfect weekend footwear for kicking back at your country estate.

🔒 Piazza di Spagna & Around

⭐**MANILA GRACE** FASHION & ACCESSORIES

Map p300 (☑06 679 78 36; www.manilagrace.com; Via Frattina 60; ◷10am-7.30pm; ⛙Spagna) An essential homegrown label for dedicated followers of fashion, Manila Grace mixes bold prints, patterns and fabrics to create a strikingly unique, assertive style for women who like to stand out in a crowd. Think a pair of red stiletto shoes with a fuchsia-pink pom pom on the toe, a striped jacket or a glittering gold bag with traditional tan-leather trim. Alessia Santi is the talented designer behind the brand.

⭐**GENTE** FASHION & ACCESSORIES

Map p300 (☑06 320 7671; www.genteroma.com; Via del Babuino 77; ◷10.30am-7.30pm Mon-Thu, to 8pm Fri & Sat, 11.30am-7.30pm Sun; ⛙Spagna) This multi label boutique was the first in Rome to bring all the big-name luxury designers – Italian, French and otherwise – under one roof and its vast emporium-styled space remains an essential stop for every serious fashionista. Labels include Dolce & Gabbana, Prada, Alexander McQueen, Sergio Rossi and Missoni.

It has a sparkling new store for women at **Via Frattini** (Map p300; ☑06 678 91 32; www.genteroma.com; Via Frattini 93; ◷10.30am-7.30pm Mon-Thu, to 8pm Fri & Sat, 11.30am-7.30pm Sun; ⛙Via del Corso).

BALENCIAGA FASHION & ACCESSORIES

Map p300 (☑06 8750 2260; www.balenciaga.com; Via Borgognona 7e; ◷10am-7pm Mon-Sat; ⛙Spagna) Design lovers will adore this boutique of French fashion label Balenciaga, inside a 19th-century *palazzo* with vintage furniture and fabulous 'aristocratic residence' vibe. Bold marquetry mixes rare woods in geometric zigzags and the theatrical overhead lighting is by Italian architect and lighting designer Gae Aulenti (1927–2012), best known for transforming an abandoned Parisian train station into Paris' Musée d'Orsay.

FEDERICO BUCCELLATI JEWELLERY

Map p300 (☑06 679 03 29; www.buccellati.com; Via dei Condotti 31; ◷3-7pm Mon, 10am-1.30pm & 3-7pm Tue-Fri, 10am-1.30pm & 2-7pm Sat; ⛙Spagna) Run today by the third generation of one of Italy's most prestigious silver- and goldsmiths, this historical shop opened in 1926. Everything is handcrafted and often delicately engraved with decorative flowers, leaves and nature-inspired motifs. Don't miss the Silver Salon on the 1st floor showcasing some original silverware and jewellery pieces by grandfather Mario.

FENDI FASHION & ACCESSORIES

Map p300 (☑06 33 45 01; www.fendi.com; Largo Carlo Goldoni 420, Palazzo Fendi; ◷10am-7.30pm Mon-Sat, 10.30am-7.30pm Sun; ⛙Spagna) With traverstine walls, stunning contemporary art and sweeping red-marble staircase, the flagship store of Rome's iconic fashion house inside 18th-century Palazzo Fendi is dazzling. Born in Rome in 1925 as a leather and fur workshop on Via del Plebiscit, this luxurious temple to Roman fashion is as much concept store as *maison*, selling ready-to-wear clothing for men and women (including its signature leather and fur pieces).

LEAVES OF STONE

In a city essentially known for its extraordinary ancient art and architecture, contemporary art installations in public spaces are a rare breed in conservative Rome. Enter *Foglie di Pietra* (2016), a sensational new sculpture outside the Fendi flagship store on posh shopping strip Largo Carlo Goldoni in Tridente. Donated to the city of Rome by the homegrown Fendi fashion house and unveiled in spring 2017, the sculpture by Italian artist Giuseppe Penone comprises two life-sized bronze trees supporting an 11-tonne marble block with their interlocked branches. The trees tower 18m and 9m high into the sky and represent a definite breath of contemporary fresh air on Rome's art scene.

FAUSTO SANTINI SHOES

Map p300 (☑06 678 41 14; www.faustosantini.com; Via Frattina 120; ⊗11am-7.30pm Mon-Sat, to 7pm Sun; MSpagna) Rome's best-known shoe designer, Fausto Santini, is famous for his beguilingly simple, architectural shoe designs, with beautiful boots and shoes made from butter-soft leather. Colours are beautiful, and the quality, impeccable. Seek out the end-of-line **discount shop** (Map p312; ☑06 488 09 34; Via Cavour 106; ⊗10am-1pm & 3.30-7.30pm Tue-Fri, 10am-1pm & 3-7.30pm Sat; MCavour) if the shoes here are out of your price range.

LAURA BIAGIOTTI FASHION & ACCESSORIES

Map p300 (☑06 679 1205; www.laurabiagiotti.it; Via Mario de' Fiori 26; ⊗10.30am-7pm Tue-Sat; MSpagna) A stiletto strut from the Spanish Steps, the neon-red entrance of this well-established Roman fashion designer is impossible to miss. Inside, ethnic-inspired printed fabrics and cashmere and silk pieces woo fashionistas on the lookout for the latest bold design by one of Italy's best known high-street designers.

PATRIZIA PEPE FASHION & ACCESSORIES

Map p300 (☑06 9437 78 91; www.patriziapepe.com; Via del Corso 141; ⊗10am-8pm; ☐Via del Corso) The most recent Patrizia Pepe boutique to open in Rome, this Florentine brand is known for its 'elegant yet still rock' fashion for men, women and children. Designs are contemporary, functional, glamorous and just a little bit sexy.

PELLETTERIA NIVES FASHION & ACCESSORIES

Map p300 (☑333 337 08 31; Via delle Carrozze 16, 2nd fl; ⊗9am-7pm Mon-Sat; MSpagna) Take the rickety lift to this workshop, choose from the softest leathers, and you will shortly be the proud owner of a handmade, designer-style bag, wallet, belt or briefcase – take a design with you. Bags cost €150 to €350 and take around a week to make.

SERMONETA FASHION & ACCESSORIES

Map p300 (☑06 679 19 60; www.sermonetagloves.com; Piazza di Spagna 61; ⊗9.30am-8pm Mon-Sat, 10am-7pm Sun; MSpagna) Buying leather gloves in Rome is a rite of passage for some, and its most famous glove-seller opposite the Spanish Steps is the place to go. Choose from a kaleidoscopic range of quality leather and suede gloves lined with silk and cashmere. An expert assistant will size up your hand in a glance.

VIA MARGUTTA

Small independent antique shops, art galleries and boutiques pepper **Via Margutta** (Map p300; MSpagna), one of Rome's prettiest pedestrian cobbled lanes strung with ivy-laced *palazzi*, decorative potted plants, marble-engraved shop plaques and the odd monumental fountain. The street is named after a 16th-century family of barbers but has long been associated with art and artists: bijou antique and art galleries line its length today; Picasso worked at a gallery at No 54 and the Italian Futurists had their first meeting here in 1917.

C.U.C.I.N.A. HOMEWARES

Map p300 (☑06 679 12 75; www.cucinastore.com; Via Mario de' Fiori 65; ⊗3.30-7.30pm Mon, 10am-7.30pm Tue-Fri, 10.30am-7.30pm Sat; MSpagna) Make your own *cucina* (kitchen) look the part with the designer goods from this famous kitchenware shop, with everything from classic *caffettiere* (Italian coffee makers) to cutlery and myriad devices you'll decide you simply must have.

🔒 Piazza di Trevi, Quirinale Hill & Around

GALLERIA ALBERTO SORDI SHOPPING CENTRE

Map p300 (☑06 6919 0769; www.galleriaalbertosordi.it; Piazza Colonna, Galleria di Piazza Colonna; ⊗8.30am-9pm Mon-Sat, 9.30am-9pm Sun; ☐Via del Corso) This elegant stained-glass arcade appeared in Alberto Sordi's 1973 classic, *Polvere di stelle* (Stardust), and has since been renamed for Rome's favourite actor, who died in 2003. It's a serene place to browse stores such as Zara and Feltrinelli, and there's an airy cafe ideal for a quick coffee break.

VIGANO' FRATELLI FASHION & ACCESSORIES

Map p300 (☑06 679 51 47; Via Marco Minghetti 8; ⊗hours vary; ☐Via del Corso) Piled high with head candy, Vigano opened in 1873 and sells top hats, bowlers and deerstalkers, as well as hacking jackets, to a princely clientele, as if nothing much has changed since it first opened its doors. The hours are quintessentially Roman, too – they open when they feel like it.

Vatican City, Borgo & Prati

VATICAN CITY | BORGO | PRATI

Neighbourhood Top Five

❶ Sistine Chapel (p126) Gazing heavenwards at Michelangelo's most celebrated masterpieces: his cinematic Genesis frescoes on the ceiling, and his terrifying vision of the *Last Judgment* on the western wall.

❷ St Peter's Basilica (p118) Being blown away by the super-sized opulence

of this, the most important church in the Catholic world.

❸ St Peter's Square (p130) Trying to line up the columns on the Vatican's central square – it is possible.

❹ Castel Sant'Angelo (p130) Revelling in the wonderful rooftop views

from this landmark castle on the Tiber.

❺ Stanze di Raffaello (p122) Marvelling at the vibrant colours of these fabulously frescoed chambers, home to Raphael's greatest painting, *La Scuola di Atene*.

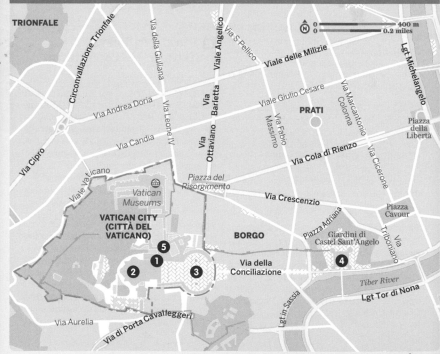

For more detail of this area see Map p304 ➡

Explore: Vatican City, Borgo & Prati

The Vatican stands atop the low-lying Vatican hill west of the Tiber. Much of its 44 hectares are covered by the Vatican Gardens, which can only be visited by guided tour, and the Palazzo Apostolico, which houses the pope's official residence and the Vatican Museums.

You'll need at least a morning to do justice to the Vatican Museums (p122). The highlight is the Michelangelo-frescoed Sistine Chapel (p126), but there's enough art on display to keep you busy for years. If you're with a tour guide, you can pass directly from the Chapel through to St Peter's Basilica (p118); otherwise you'll have to walk around and approach from St Peter's Square (p130). Once finished in the basilica, you'll be ready for a break. There are few good eating options in the Vatican itself, but the nearby Prati district is full of trattorias and takeaways.

Between the Vatican and the river lies the Borgo. Little remains of the original medieval district, which was largely destroyed by Mussolini in 1936 to make way for Via della Conciliazione, the monumental road that runs from St Peter's Square to Castel Sant'Angelo (p130), the large, drum-shaped castle overlooking the river.

Local Life

→**Fast food** Rather than having a full-length midday meal, local office workers tend to grab a snack from the many excellent takeaways in Prati. Join them for *pizza al taglio* at Pizzarium (p132), *panini* at Fa-Bìo (p131), or *arancine* at Mondo Arancina (p131).

→**Shopping** Prati is prime shopping territory. Spearing off Piazza del Risorgimento, Via Cola di Rienzo is lined with department stores and clothing shops. Boutique hunters should check out Rechicle (p133) for vintage fashions and Il Sellaio (p133) for handmade leather bags.

→**Catch a gig** Join the locals for sweet melodies at Alexanderplatz (p133), Rome's oldest jazz joint. Another top venue is the pub Fonclea (p133), which offers an eclectic program of nightly gigs.

Getting There & Away

→**Bus** From Termini, bus 40 is the quickest one to the Vatican – it'll drop you off near Castel Sant'Angelo. You can also take the 64, which runs a similar route but stops more often. Bus 81 runs to Piazza del Risorgimento, passing through San Giovanni and the *centro storico* (historic centre).

→**Metro** Take metro line A to Ottaviano-San Pietro. From the station, signs direct you to St Peter's.

→**Tram** Number 19 serves Piazza del Risorgimento by way of San Lorenzo, Viale Regina Margherita and Villa Borghese.

Lonely Planet's Top Tip

Be wary of the touts around Ottaviano metro station selling skip-the-line tours of the Vatican Museums. These guys are on commission to round up clients and the tours they're pushing could cost you more than the museums' own official tours.

The Vatican Museums' website lists an impressive array of tour packages. These take in the museums and sites across Vatican territories, including subterranean archaeological areas, the Vatican Gardens, and the papal palace at Castel Gandolfo.

✕ Best Places to Eat

- → Pizzarium (p132)
- → Enoteca La Torre (p132)
- → Ristorante L'Arcangelo (p132)
- → Fa-Bìo (p131)
- → Fatamorgana (p131)

For reviews, see p131.

🍸 Best Places to Drink

- → Sciascia Caffè (p133)
- → Makasar Bistrot (p133)
- → Passaguai (p133)
- → Be.re (p133)

For reviews, see p133.

⊙ Best Above & Below Ground

- → St Peter's Basilica Dome (p120)
- → Terrace of Castel Sant'Angelo (p130)
- → Tomb of St Peter (p121)
- → Vatican Grottoes (p121)
- → Necropoli Via Triumphalis (p130)

For reviews, see p130.

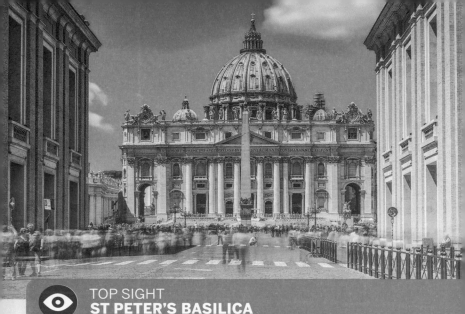

TOP SIGHT
ST PETER'S BASILICA

In a city of outstanding churches, none can hold a candle to St Peter's, Italy's largest, richest and most spectacular basilica. A monument to centuries of artistic genius, it boasts many spectacular works of art, including three of Italy's most celebrated masterpieces: Michelangelo's *Pietà*, his soaring dome, and Bernini's 29m-high baldachin over the papal altar.

History

The original St Peter's – which lies beneath the current basilica – was commissioned by the Emperor Constantine and built around 349 on the site where St Peter is said to have been buried between AD 64 and 67. But like many medieval churches, it eventually fell into disrepair and it wasn't until the mid-15th century that efforts were made to restore it, first by Pope Nicholas V and then, rather more successfully, by Julius II.

In 1506 construction began on Bramante's design for a new basilica based on a Greek-cross plan, with four equal arms and a huge central dome. But on Bramante's death in 1514, building ground to a halt as architects, including Raphael and Antonio da Sangallo, tried to modify his original plans. Little progress was made and it wasn't until Michelangelo took over in 1547 at the age of 72 that the situation changed. Michelangelo simplified Bramante's plans and drew up designs for what was to become his greatest architectural achievement, the dome. He never lived to see it built, though, and it was left to Giacomo della Porta and Domenico Fontana to finish it in 1590.

With the dome in place, Carlo Maderno inherited the project in 1605. He designed the monumental facade and lengthened the nave towards the piazza.

The basilica was finally consecrated in 1626.

DON'T MISS

→ *Pietà*
→ Statue of St Peter
→ The dome
→ The baldachin
→ *Cattedra di San Pietro*

PRACTICALITIES

→ Basilica di San Pietro
→ Map p304, C5
→ ☏06 6988 5518
→ www.vatican.va
→ St Peter's Square
→ admission free
→ ⏱7am-7pm summer, to 6.30pm winter
→ 🚌Piazza del Risorgimento, ⓂOttaviano-San Pietro

The Facade

Built between 1608 and 1612, Maderno's immense facade is 48m high and 115m wide. Eight 27m-high columns support the upper attic on which 13 statues stand representing Christ the Redeemer, St John the Baptist and the 11 apostles. The central balcony is known as the **Loggia della Benedizione**, and it's from here that the pope delivers his *Urbi et Orbi* blessing at Christmas and Easter.

Running across the entablature is an inscription, 'IN HONOREM PRINCIPIS APOST PAVLVS V BVRGHESIVS ROMANVS PONT MAX AN MDCXII PONT VII' which translates as 'In honour of the Prince of Apostles, Paul V Borghese, Roman, Pontiff, in the year 1612, the seventh of his pontificate'.

In the grand atrium, the **Porta Santa** (Holy Door) is opened only in Jubilee Years.

Interior – The Nave

Dominating the centre of the basilica is Bernini's 29m-high **baldachin**. Supported by four spiral columns and made with bronze taken from the Pantheon, it stands over the **papal altar**, also known as the Altar of the Confession. In front, Carlo Maderno's **Confessione** stands over the site where St Peter was originally buried.

Above the baldachin, Michelangelo's **dome** soars to a height of 119m. Based on Brunelleschi's design for the Duomo in Florence, it's supported by four massive stone **piers**, each named after the saint whose statue adorns its Bernini-designed niche. The saints are all associated with the basilica's four major relics: the lance **St Longinus** used to pierce Christ's side; the cloth with which **St Veronica** wiped Jesus' face; a fragment of the Cross collected by **St Helena**; and the head of **St Andrew**.

At the base of the **Pier of St Longinus** is Arnolfo di Cambio's much-loved 13th-century bronze **statue of St Peter**, whose right foot has been worn down by centuries of caresses.

Behind the altar, the tribune is home to Bernini's extraordinary **Cattedra di San Pietro**. A vast gilded bronze throne held aloft by four 5m-high saints, it's centred on a wooden seat that was once thought to have been St Peter's but in fact dates to the 9th century. Above, light shines through a yellow window framed by a gilded mass of golden angels and adorned with a dove to represent the Holy Spirit.

To the right of the throne, Bernini's **monument to Urban VIII** depicts the pope flanked by the figures of Charity and Justice.

For all its artistic treasures, St Peter's is still a working church and mass is held daily in the basilica's chapels. For a timetable, in Italian, see www.vatican.va/various/basiliche/san_pietro/it/vita_liturgica/orari.htm.

VATICAN CITY, BORGO & PRATI ST PETER'S BASILICA

Interior – Left Aisle

In the roped-off left transept, the **Cappella della Madonna della Colonna** takes its name from the Madonna that stares out from Giacomo della Porta's marble altar. To its right, above the **tomb of St Leo the Great**, is a fine relief by Alessandro Algardi. Under the next arch is Bernini's last work in the basilica, the **monument to Alexander VII**.

Halfway down the left aisle, the **Cappella Clementina** is named after Clement VIII, who had Giacomo della Porta decorate it for the Jubilee of 1600. Beneath the altar is the **tomb of St Gregory the Great** and, to the left, a **monument to Pope Pius VII** by Thorvaldsen.

The next arch shelters Alessandro Algardi's 16th-century **monument to Leo XI**. Beyond it, the richly decorated **Cappella del Coro** was created by Giovanni Battista Ricci to designs by Giacomo della Porta. The **monument to Innocent VIII** by Antonio Pollaiuolo in the next aisle arch is a re-creation of a monument from the old basilica.

Continuing on, the **Cappella della Presentazione** contains two of St Peter's most modern works: a black relief **monument to John XXIII** by Emilio Greco, and a **monument to Benedict XV** by Pietro Canonica.

Under the next arch are the so-called **Stuart monuments**. On the right is the monument to Clementina Sobieska, wife of James Stuart, by Filippo Barigioni, and on the left is Canova's vaguely erotic monument to the last three members of the Stuart clan, the pretenders to the English throne who died in exile in Rome.

Interior – Right Aisle

At the head of the right aisle is Michelangelo's hauntingly beautiful **Pietà**. Sculpted when he was only 25 (in 1499), it's the only work the artist ever signed – his signature is etched into the sash across the Madonna's breast.

Nearby, a **red floor disk** marks the spot where Charlemagne and later Holy Roman emperors were crowned by the pope.

On a pillar just beyond the *Pietà,* Carlo Fontana's gilt and bronze **monument to Queen Christina of Sweden** commemorates the far-from-holy Swedish monarch who converted to Catholicism in 1655.

Moving on, you'll come to the **Cappella di San Sebastiano**, home of Pope John Paul II's tomb, and the **Cappella del Santissimo Sacramento**, a sumptuously decorated baroque chapel with works by Borromini, Bernini and Pietro da Cortona.

Beyond the chapel, the grandiose **monument to Gregory XIII** sits near the roped-off **Cappella Gregoriana**, a chapel built by Gregory XIII from designs by Michelangelo.

Much of the right transept is closed off but you can still make out the **monument to Clement XIII**, one of Canova's most famous works.

Dome

From the **dome** (with/without lift €8/6; ⊙8am-6pm summer, to 5pm winter) entrance on the right of the basilica's main portico, you can walk the 551 steps to the top or take a small lift halfway and then follow on foot for the last 320 steps. Either way, it's a long, steep climb. But make it to the top, and you're rewarded with stunning views from a perch 120m above St Peter's Square.

Museo Storico Artistico

Accessed from the left nave, the **Museo Storico Artistico** (Tesoro, Treasury; adult/reduced €7/5; ⊙8am-6.50pm summer, to 5.50pm winter) sparkles with sacred relics. Highlights include a tabernacle by Donatello; the *Colonna Santa,* a 4th-century Byzantine column from the earlier church; and the 6th-century *Crux Vaticana*

Michelangelo's *Pietà*

FACE IN THE BALDACHIN

The frieze on Bernini's baldachin contains a hidden narrative that begins at the pillar to the left (looking with your back to the entrance). As you walk clockwise around the baldachin note the woman's face carved into the frieze of each pillar. On the first three pillars her face seems to express the increasing agony of childbirth; on the last one, it's replaced by that of a smiling baby. The woman was a niece of Pope Urban VIII, who gave birth as Bernini worked on the baldachin.

(Vatican Cross), a jewel-encrusted crucifix presented by the emperor Justinian II to the original basilica.

Vatican Grottoes

Extending beneath the basilica, the **Vatican Grottoes** (⊙8am-6pm summer, to 5.30pm winter) FREE contain the tombs and sarcophagi of numerous popes, as well as several columns from the original 4th-century basilica. The entrance is in the Pier of St Andrew.

Tomb of St Peter

Excavations beneath the basilica have uncovered part of the original church and what archaeologists believe is the **Tomb of St Peter** (☑06 6988 5318; www. scavi.va; €13, over 15s only). In 1942 the bones of an elderly, strongly built man were found in a box hidden behind a wall covered by pilgrims' graffiti. And while the Vatican has never definitively claimed that the bones belong to St Peter, in 1968 Pope Paul VI said that they had been identified in a way that the Vatican considered 'convincing'.

The excavations can only be visited by guided tour. For further details, and to book a tour, check out the website of the **Ufficio Scavi** (Excavations Office; Fabbrica di San Pietro; Map p304; ☑06 6988 5318; www. scavi.va; ⊙9am-6pm Mon-Fri, 9am-5pm Sat).

Contrary to popular opinion, St Peter's Basilica is not the world's largest church – the Basilica of Our Lady of Peace in Yamoussoukro on the Ivory Coast is bigger. Still, its measurements are pretty staggering – it's 187m long and covers more than 15,000 sq m. Bronze floor plates in the nave indicate the respective sizes of the 14 next-largest churches.

TOP SIGHT
VATICAN MUSEUMS

Visiting the Vatican Museums is a thrilling and unforgettable experience. With some 7km of exhibitions and more masterpieces than many small countries can call their own, this vast museum complex boasts one of the world's greatest art collections. Highlights include a spectacular collection of classical statuary in the Museo Pio-Clementino, a suite of rooms frescoed by Raphael, and the Michelangelo-decorated Sistine Chapel.

Founded by Pope Julius II in the early 16th century, the museums are housed in the lavishly decorated halls and galleries of the Palazzo Apostolico Vaticano. This immense 5.5-hectare complex consists of two palaces – the original Vatican palace (nearer to St Peter's) and the 15th-century Palazzetto di Belvedere – joined by two long galleries. On the inside are three courtyards: the Cortile della Pigna, the Cortile della Biblioteca and, to the south, the Cortile del Belvedere. You'll never cover it all in one day, so it pays to be selective.

Pinacoteca

Often overlooked by visitors, the papal picture gallery displays paintings dating from the 11th to 19th centuries, with works by Giotto, Fra Angelico, Filippo Lippi, Perugino, Titian, Guido Reni, Guercino, Pietro da Cortona, Caravaggio and Leonardo da Vinci.

Look out for a trio of paintings by Raphael in Room VIII – the *Madonna di Foligno* (Madonna of Folignano), the *Incoronazione della Vergine* (Crowning of the Virgin), and *La Trasfigurazione* (Transfiguration), which was completed by his students after his death in 1520. Other highlights include Filippo Lippi's

DON'T MISS

➡ Sistine Chapel
➡ Stanze di Raffaello
➡ *Apollo Belvedere* and *Laocoön,* Museo Pio-Clementino
➡ *La Trasfigurazione,* Pinacoteca

PRACTICALITIES

➡ Musei Vaticani
➡ Map p304, C4
➡ ☏ 06 6988 4676
➡ www.museivaticani.va
➡ Viale Vaticano
➡ adult/reduced €16/8, last Sun of month free
➡ ⊙9am-6pm Mon-Sat, 9am-2pm last Sun of month, last entry 2hr before close
➡ ▣Piazza del Risorgimento, ⓂOttaviano-San Pietro

L'Incoronazione della Vergine con Angeli, Santo e donatore (Coronation of the Virgin with Angels, Saints, and donors), Leonardo da Vinci's haunting and unfinished *San Gerolamo* (St Jerome), and Caravaggio's *Deposizione* (Deposition from the Cross).

Museo Chiaramonti & Braccio Nuovo

This museum is effectively the long corridor that runs down the lower east side of the Palazzetto di Belvedere. Its walls are lined with thousands of statues and busts representing everything from immortal gods to playful cherubs and ugly Roman patricians.

Near the end of the hall, off to the right, is the **Braccio Nuovo** (New Wing), which contains a celebrated statue of the Nile as a reclining god covered by 16 babies.

Museo Pio-Clementino

This stunning museum contains some of the Vatican's finest classical statuary, including the peerless *Apollo Belvedere* and the 1st-century BC *Laocoön*, both in the **Cortile Ottagono** (Octagonal Courtyard).

Before you go into the courtyard, take a moment to admire the 1st-century *Apoxyomenos*, one of the earliest known sculptures to depict a figure with a raised arm.

To the left as you enter the courtyard, the *Apollo Belvedere* is a 2nd-century Roman copy of a 4th-century-BC Greek bronze. A beautifully proportioned representation of the sun god Apollo, it's considered one of the great masterpieces of classical sculpture. Nearby, the *Laocoön* depicts the mythical death of the Trojan priest who warned his fellow citizens not to take the wooden horse left by the Greeks.

Back inside, the **Sala degli Animali** is filled with sculpted creatures and some magnificent 4th-century mosaics. Continuing on, you come to the **Sala delle Muse** (Room of the Muses), centred on the *Torso Belvedere*, another of the museum's must-sees. A fragment of a muscular 1st-century-BC Greek sculpture, this was found in Campo de' Fiori and used by Michelangelo as a model for his *ignudi* (male nudes) in the Sistine Chapel.

The next room, the **Sala Rotonda** (Round Room), contains a number of colossal statues, including a gilded-bronze *Ercole* (Hercules) and an exquisite floor mosaic. The enormous basin in the centre of the room was found at Nero's Domus Aurea and is made out of a single piece of red porphyry stone.

Museo Gregoriano Egizio

Founded by Pope Gregory XVI in 1839, this Egyptian museum displays pieces taken from Egypt in ancient Roman times. The collection is small, but there are

JUMP THE QUEUE

To avoid queues book tickets online (http://biglietteriamusei.vatican.va/musei/tickets/do; plus €4 booking fee) or check the museums' website for details of tours and visitor packages. Also try to time your visit to minimise waiting: Tuesdays and Thursdays are quietest; Wednesday mornings are good as everyone is at the pope's weekly audience; afternoon is better than morning; avoid Mondays, when many other museums are shut.

Exhibits are not well labelled, so consider hiring an audio guide (€7) or buying the *Guide to the Vatican Museums and City* (€14). Free guided tours are available for blind and deaf visitors; wheelchairs are available to borrow from the Special Permits desk in the entrance hall. Strollers are permitted in the museums. For further details, see the Services for Visitors section of the museums' website.

fascinating exhibits, including a fragmented statue of the pharaoh Ramses II on his throne, vividly painted sarcophagi dating from around 1000 BC, and a macabre mummy.

Museo Gregoriano Etrusco

At the top of the 18th-century Simonetti staircase, this fascinating museum contains artefacts unearthed in the Etruscan tombs of northern Lazio, as well as a superb collection of vases and Roman antiquities. Of particular interest is the *Marte di Todi* (Mars of Todi), a black bronze of a warrior dating to the late 5th century BC.

Galleria dei Candelabri & Galleria degli Arazzi

Originally an open loggia, the **Galleria dei Candelabri** is packed with classical sculpture and several elegantly carved candelabras that give the gallery its name. The corridor continues through to the **Galleria degli Arazzi** (Tapestry Gallery) and its huge hanging tapestries. The best, on the left, were woven in Brussels in the 16th century.

continued on p126

Museum Tour
Vatican Museums

LENGTH THREE HOURS

Follow this tour to see the museums' greatest hits, culminating in the Sistine Chapel.

Once you've passed through the entrance complex, head up the modern spiral ramp (or escalator) to ❶ **Cortile delle Corazze**, the start point for all routes through the museums. While here take a moment to nip out to the terrace for views over St Peter's dome and the Vatican Gardens. Re-enter and follow through to ❷ **Cortile della Pigna**, named after the huge Augustan-era bronze pine cone in the monumental niche. Cross the courtyard and enter the long corridor that is ❸ **Museo Chiaramonti**. Don't stop here, but continue left, up the stairs, to the Museo Pio-Clementino, home of the Vatican's finest classical statuary. Follow the flow of people through to the ❹ **Cortile Ottagono** (Octagonal Courtyard), where you'll find the mythical masterpieces, the *Laocoön* and *Apollo Belvedere*. Continue through a series of rooms – ❺ **Sala degli Animali** (Animal Room), ❻ **Sala delle Muse** (Room of the Muses), home of the famous *Torso Belvedere*, and ❼ **Sala Rotonda** (Round Room), centred on a vast red basin. From neighbouring ❽ **Sala Croce Greca** (Greek Cross Room), the Simonetti staircase leads up to ❾ **Galleria dei Candelabri** (Gallery of the Candelabra), the first of three galleries along a lengthy corridor. It gets very crowded up here as you're funnelled through ❿ **Galleria degli Arazzi** (Tapestry Gallery) and onto ⓫ **Galleria delle Carte Geografiche** (Map Gallery), a 120m-long hall hung with huge topographical maps. At the end of the corridor, carry on through ⓬ **Sala Sobieski** to ⓭ **Sala di Costantino**, the first of the four Stanze di Raffaello (Raphael Rooms) – the others are ⓮ **Stanza d'Eliodoro**, ⓯ **Stanza della Segnatura**, featuring Raphael's superlative *La Scuola di Atene*, and ⓰ **Stanza dell'Incendio di Borgo**. Anywhere else these magnificent frescoed chambers would be the star attraction, but here they serve as the warm-up for the grand finale, the ⓱ **Sistine Chapel**.

VATICAN MUSEUMS

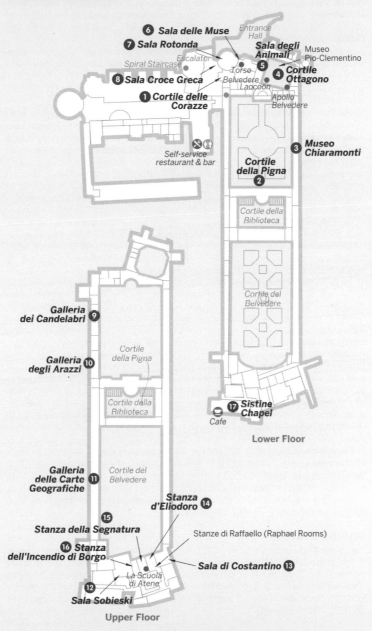

6 **Sala delle Muse**
Entrance Hall

7 **Sala Rotonda**

Spiral Staircase

Sala degli Animali
Museo Pio-Clementino

Escalator

5

4 **Cortile Ottagono**

Torso Belvedere
Laocoön

8 **Sala Croce Greca**

1 **Cortile delle Corazze**

Apollo Belvedere

Self-service restaurant & bar

3 **Museo Chiaramonti**

2 **Cortile della Pigna**

Cortile della Biblioteca

Cortile del Belvedere

9 **Galleria dei Candelabri**

Cortile della Pigna

10 **Galleria degli Arazzi**

Cortile della Biblioteca

17 **Sistine Chapel**

Cafe

Lower Floor

11 **Galleria delle Carte Geografiche**

Cortile del Belvedere

14 **Stanza d'Eliodoro**

Stanze di Raffaello (Raphael Rooms)

15

Stanza della Segnatura

16 **Stanza dell'Incendio di Borgo**

13 **Sala di Costantino**

La Scuola di Atene

12

Sala Sobieski

Upper Floor

Galleria delle Carte Geografiche & Sala Sobieski

One of the unsung heroes of the Vatican Museums, the 120m-long Map Gallery is hung with 40 huge topographical maps. These were created between 1580 and 1583 for Pope Gregory XIII based on drafts by Ignazio Danti, one of the leading cartographers of his day.

Beyond the gallery, the **Sala Sobieski** is named after an enormous 19th-century painting depicting the victory of the Polish King John III Sobieski over the Turks in 1683.

Stanze di Raffaello

These four frescoed chambers, currently undergoing partial restoration, were part of Pope Julius II's private apartments. Raphael himself painted the **Stanza della Segnatura** (1508–11) and the **Stanza d'Eliodoro** (1512–14), while the **Stanza dell'Incendio di Borgo** (1514–17) and **Sala di Costantino** (1517–24) were decorated by students following his designs.

The first room you come to is the **Sala di Costantino**, originally a ceremonial reception room, which is dominated by the *Battaglia di Costantino contro Maxentius* (Battle of the Milvian Bridge) showing the victory of Constantine, Rome's first Christian emperor, over his rival Maxentius.

Leading off the *sala*, but often closed to the public, the **Cappella Niccolina**, Pope Nicholas V's private chapel, boasts a superb cycle of frescoes by Fra Angelico.

The **Stanza d'Eliodoro**, which was used for the pope's private audiences, takes its name from the *Cacciata d'Eliodoro* (Expulsion of Heliodorus from the Temple), reflecting Pope Julius II's policy of forcing foreign powers off Church lands. To its right, the *Messa di Bolsena* (Mass of Bolsena) shows Julius paying homage to the relic of a 13th-century miracle at the lakeside town of Bolsena. Next is the *Incontro di Leone Magno con Attila* (Encounter of Leo the Great with Attila), and, on the fourth wall, the *Liberazione di San Pietro* (Liberation of St Peter), a brilliant work illustrating Raphael's masterful ability to illustrate light.

The **Stanza della Segnatura**, Julius' study and library, was the first room that Raphael painted, and it's here that you'll find his great masterpiece, *La Scuola di Atene* (The School of Athens), featuring philosophers and scholars gathered around Plato and Aristotle. The seated figure in front of the steps is believed to be Michelangelo, while the figure of Plato is said to be a portrait of Leonardo da Vinci, and Euclide (the bald man bending over) is Bramante. Raphael also included a self-portrait in the lower right corner – he's the second figure from the right in the black hat. Opposite is *La Disputa del Sacramento* (Disputation on the Sacrament), also by Raphael.

The most famous work in the **Stanza dell'Incendio di Borgo**, the former seat of the Holy See's highest court and later a dining room, is the *Incendio di Borgo* (Fire in the Borgo). This depicts Leo IV extinguishing a fire by making the sign of the cross. The ceiling was painted by Raphael's master, Perugino.

From the Raphael Rooms, stairs lead to the **Appartamento Borgia** and the Vatican's collection of modern religious art.

Sistine Chapel

The jewel in the Vatican crown, the *Cappella Sistina* (**Sistine Chapel** (Cappella Sistina; Map p304; www.museivaticani.va; Viale Vaticano; adult/reduced €16/8, last Sun of the month free; ⊙9am-6pm Mon-Sat, 9am-2pm last Sun of the month, last entry 2hr before close; ▣Piazza del Risorgimento, ⓂOttaviano-San Pietro) is home to two of the world's most famous works of art – Michelangelo's ceiling frescoes and his *Giudizio Universale* (Last Judgment).

History

The chapel was originally built for Pope Sixtus IV, after whom it's named, and consecrated on 15 August 1483. It's a big, barn-like structure, measuring 40.2m long, 13.4m wide and 20.7m high – the same size as the Temple of Solomon – and even pre-Michelangelo it would have been impressive. Frescoes by the leading artists of the day adorned the walls and the vaulted ceiling was coloured to resemble a blue sky with golden stars. Underneath everything was a patterned floor inlaid with polychrome marble.

However, apart from the wall frescoes and floor, little remains of the original decor, which was sacrificed to make way for Michelangelo's two masterpieces. The first, the ceiling, was commissioned by Pope Julius II and painted between 1508 and 1512; the second, the spectacular *Giudizio Universale* (Last Judgment), was completed almost 30 years later in 1541.

Both were controversial works influenced by the political ambitions of the popes who commissioned them. The ceiling came as part of Julius II's drive to transform Rome into the Church's showcase capital, while Pope Paul III intended the *Giudizio Universale* to serve as a warning to Catholics to toe the line during the Reformation, which was then sweeping through Europe.

Restoration

In recent years debate has centred on the chapel's multimillion dollar restoration, which finished in 1999 after nearly 20 years. In removing almost 450 years' worth of dust and candle soot, restorers finally revealed the frescoes in their original technicolour glory. But some critics claimed that they also removed a layer of varnish that Michelangelo had added to darken them and enhance their shadows. Whatever the truth, the Sistine Chapel remains a truly spectacular sight.

The Ceiling & the Ignudi

The Sistine Chapel provided the greatest challenge of Michelangelo's career and painting the entire 800-sq-m vaulted ceiling at a height of more than 20m pushed him to the limits of his genius.

When Pope Julius II first approached him – some say at the suggestion of his chief architect, Bramante, who was keen for Michelangelo to fail – he was reluctant to accept. He regarded himself as a sculptor and had no experience of painting frescoes. However, Julius persisted and in 1508 he persuaded Michelangelo to accept the commission for a fee of 3000 ducats (more or less €1.5 to €2 million in today's money).

Originally, Pope Julius wanted Michelangelo to paint the 12 apostles and a series of decorative

CONCLAVE

The Sistine Chapel is where the conclave meets to elect a new pope. Dating to 1274, give or take a few modifications, the rules of the voting procedure are explicit: between 15 and 20 days after the death of a pope, the entire College of Cardinals (comprising all cardinals under the age of 80) is locked in the chapel to elect a new pontiff. Four secret ballots are held a day until a two-thirds majority has been secured. News of the election is communicated by emitting white smoke through a specially erected chimney.

From mid-April to October, the Museums open late every Friday evening (7pm to 11pm). To visit at this time you'll need to book online.

VISITOR CAP

The heat and humidity caused by the Sistine Chapel's six million annual visitors pose a constant threat to its frescoes. To counter this, the Vatican Museums' management has hinted at the possibility of introducing a visitor cap, limiting the number of daily admissions to 20,000.

SISTINE CHAPEL CEILING

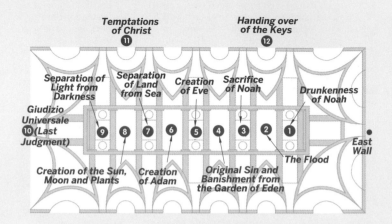

🏃 Museum Tour
Sistine Chapel

LENGTH 30 MINUTES

On entering the chapel head over to the main entrance in the far (east) wall for the best views of the ceiling.

Michelangelo's design, which took him four years to complete, covers the entire 800-sq-m surface. With painted architectural features and a colourful cast of biblical figures, it centres on nine panels depicting stories from the book of Genesis.

As you look up from the east wall, the first panel is the ❶ **Drunkenness of Noah**, followed by ❷ **The Flood**, and the ❸ **Sacrifice of Noah**. Next, ❹ **Original Sin and Banishment from the Garden of Eden** famously depicts Adam and Eve being sent packing after accepting the forbidden fruit from Satan, represented by a snake with the body of a woman coiled around a tree. The ❺ **Creation of Eve** is then followed by the ❻ **Creation of Adam**. This, one of the most famous images in Western art, shows a bearded God

pointing his finger at Adam, thus bringing him to life. Completing the sequence are the ❼ **Separation of Land from Sea**; the ❽ **Creation of the Sun, Moon and Plants**; and the ❾ **Separation of Light from Darkness**, featuring a fearsome God reaching out to touch the sun. Set around the central panels are 20 athletic male nudes, the so-called *ignudi*.

Straight ahead of you on the west wall is Michelangelo's mesmeric ❿ **Giudizio Universale** (Last Judgment), showing Christ – in the centre near the top – passing sentence over the souls of the dead as they are torn from their graves to face him. The saved get to stay up in heaven (in the upper right) while the damned are sent down to face the demons in hell (in the bottom right).

The chapel's side walls also feature stunning Renaissance frescoes, representing the lives of Moses (to your left) and Christ (to the right). Look out for Botticelli's ⓫ **Temptations of Christ** and Perugino's great masterpiece, the ⓬ **Handing over of the Keys**.

architectural elements. But the artist rejected this and came up with a more complex design based on stories from the book of Genesis. And it's this that you see today.

The focus of the ceiling frescoes are the nine central panels, but set around them are 20 athletic male nudes, known as *ignudi*. These muscle-bound models caused a scandal when they were first revealed and still today art historians are divided over their meaning – some claim they are angels, others that they represent Michelangelo's neo-Platonic vision of ideal man.

Also depicted are five sibyls and seven prophets. These pagan and Christian figures are thought to symbolise mankind's continuous wait for redemption.

Wall Frescoes

If you can tear your eyes from the Michelangelos, the Sistine Chapel also boasts some superb wall frescoes. These formed part of the original chapel decoration and were painted between 1481 and 1482 by a crack team of Renaissance artists, including Botticelli, Ghirlandaio, Pinturicchio, Perugino and Luca Signorelli. They represent events in the lives of Moses (to the left, looking at the *Giudizio Universale*) and Christ (to the right). Most famous of all is Perugino's masterpiece showing Christ handing the keys of heaven to a kneeling St Peter.

Giudizio Universale (Last Judgment)

Michelangelo's second stint in the Sistine Chapel, from 1535 to 1541, resulted in the *Giudizio Universale* (Last Judgment), his highly-charged depiction of Christ's second coming on the 200-sq-m western wall.

The project, which was commissioned by Pope Clement VII and encouraged by his successor Paul III, was controversial from the start. Critics were outraged when Michelangelo destroyed two Perugino frescoes while preparing the wall – it had to be replastered so that it tilted inwards to protect it from dust – and when it was unveiled in 1541, five years after Michelangelo had started painting, its swirling mass of 391 predominantly naked bodies provoked outrage. So fierce were feelings that the Church's top brass, meeting at the 1564 Council of Trent, ordered the nudity to be covered up. The task fell to Daniele da Volterra, one of Michelangelo's students, who added fig leaves and loincloths to 41 nudes, earning himself the nickname *il braghettone* (the breeches maker).

For his part Michelangelo rejected the criticism. He even got his own back on one of his loudest critics, Biagio de Cesena, the papal master of ceremonies, by depicting him as Minos, judge of the underworld, with donkey ears and a snake wrapped around him.

HEAVENLY BLUE

One of the striking features of the *Giudizio Universale* is the amount of ultramarine blue in the painting – in contrast with the ceiling frescoes, which don't have any. In the 16th century, blue paint was made from the hugely expensive stone lapis lazuli, and artists were reluctant to use it unless someone else was paying. In the case of the *Giudizio Universale*, the pope picked up the tab for all Michelangelo's materials; on the ceiling, however, the artist had to cover his own expenses and so used less costly colours.

Hidden amid the mass of bodies in the Sistine Chapel frescoes are two Michelangelo self-portraits. On the *Giudizio Universale* look for the figure of St Bartholomew, holding his own flayed skin beneath Christ. The face in the skin is said to be Michelangelo's, its anguished look reflecting the artist's tormented faith. His stricken face is also said to be that of the prophet Jeremiah on the ceiling.

⊙ SIGHTS

Boasting priceless treasures at every turn, the Vatican is home to some of Rome's most popular attractions. The Vatican Museums and St Peter's Basilica are the star turns, but Castel Sant'Angelo, one of the city's most recognisable landmarks, is also well worth a visit.

⊙ Vatican City

ST PETER'S BASILICA   BASILICA
See p118.

VATICAN MUSEUMS   MUSEUM
See p122.

ST PETER'S SQUARE   PIAZZA
Map p304 (Piazza San Pietro; MOttaviano-San Pietro) Overlooked by St Peter's Basilica, the Vatican's central square was laid out between 1656 and 1667 to a design by Gian Lorenzo Bernini. Seen from above, it resembles a giant keyhole with two semicircular colonnades, each consisting of four rows of Doric columns, encircling a giant ellipse that straightens out to funnel believers into the basilica. The effect was deliberate – Bernini described the colonnades as representing 'the motherly arms of the church'.

The scale of the piazza is dazzling: at its largest it measures 320m by 240m. There are 284 columns and, atop the colonnades, 140 saints. The 25m **obelisk** in the centre was brought to Rome by Caligula from Heliopolis in Egypt and later used by Nero as a turning post for the chariot races in his circus.

Leading off the piazza, the monumental approach road, **Via della Conciliazione**, was commissioned by Mussolini and built between 1936 and 1950.

VATICAN GARDENS   GARDENS
Map p304 (www.museivaticani.va; adult/reduced incl Vatican Museums €32/24; ⊙by reservation only; 🚌Piazza del Risorgimento, MOttaviano-San Pietro) Up to a third of the Vatican is covered by the perfectly manicured Vatican Gardens, which contain fortifications, grottoes, monuments, fountains, and the state's tiny heliport. Visits are by two-hour guided tour only, for which you'll need to book at least a week in advance.

Note that after the tour you're free to visit the Vatican Museums on your own.

NECROPOLI VIA TRIUMPHALIS   ARCHAEOLOGICAL SITE
Map p304 (www.museivaticani.va; adult/reduced incl Vatican Museums €26/20, incl Vatican Museums & Gardens €37/29; ⊙by reservation only; MOttaviano-San Pietro) Not to be confused with the Tomb of St Peter, this ancient Roman cemetery extends beneath the Vatican hill. Guided tours, which must be pre-booked, take in the tombs and burial chambers that extended along the ancient road known as Via Triumphalis.

⊙ Borgo

★CASTEL SANT'ANGELO   MUSEUM, CASTLE
Map p304 (📞06 681 91 11; www.castelsantangelo.beniculturali.it; Lungotevere Castello 50; adult/reduced €10/5; ⊙9am-7.30pm, ticket office to 6.30pm; 🚌Piazza Pia) With its chunky round keep, this castle is an instantly recognisable landmark. Built as a mausoleum for the emperor Hadrian, it was converted into a papal fortress in the 6th century and named after an angelic vision that Pope Gregory the Great had in 590. Nowadays, it houses the **Museo Nazionale di Castel Sant'Angelo** and its eclectic collection of paintings, sculpture, military memorabilia and medieval firearms.

Many of these weapons were used by soldiers fighting to protect the castle, which, thanks to a secret 13th-century passageway to the Vatican (the *Passetto di Borgo*), provided sanctuary to many popes in times of danger. Most famously, Pope Clemente VI holed up here during the 1527 sack of Rome.

The castle's upper floors are filled with elegant Renaissance interiors, including the lavish **Sala Paolina** with frescoes depicting episodes from the life of Alexander the Great. Two storeys up, the **terrace**, immortalised by Puccini in his opera *Tosca,* offers unforgettable views over Rome.

Note that ticket prices may increase during temporary exhibitions.

PONTE SANT'ANGELO   BRIDGE
Map p304 (🚌Piazza Pia) The emperor Hadrian built the Ponte Sant'Angelo in 136 to provide an approach to his mausoleum, but it was Bernini who brought it to life, designing the angel sculptures in 1668. The three central arches of the bridge are part of the original structure; the end arches were restored and enlarged in 1892–94 during the construction of the Lungotevere embankments.

 EATING

Beware, hungry travellers: there are an unholy number of overpriced tourist-traps around the Vatican and St Peter's. A much better bet is nearby Prati, which has everything from gourmet takeaways and artisanal gelaterie to old-school trattorias and hybrid restaurant-cafes.

✖ Vatican City

OLD BRIDGE   GELATO €
Map p304 (Viale dei Bastioni di Michelangelo 5; gelato €2-6; ⊙9am-2am Mon-Sat, 2.30pm-2am Sun; ☐Piazza del Risorgimento) Ideal for a pre- or post-Vatican pick-me-up, this tiny gelateria draws long lines of gasping tourists. It's been in the business for more than 25 years and still does a roaring trade in creamy gelato, served in regular flavours and huge portions. As an alternative, it also has yoghurts and refreshing sorbets.

✖ Borgo

COTTO CRUDO   SANDWICHES €
Map p304 (www.cottocrudo.it; Borgo Pio 46; panini from €4.50; ⊙10am-6pm Tue-Sun; ☐Piazza del Risorgimento, MOttaviano-San Pietro) Among the tourist traps on Borgo Pio, the main drag through what's left of the medieval Borgo neighbourhood, this hole-in-the-wall sandwich shop is ideal for a Vatican pit stop. Specialising in produce from Emilia-Romagna, it serves *panini* laden with delectable fillings such as aged Parma ham, *mortadella* (aka baloney) and *culatella* (a type of salami), as well as cheeses and vegetables.

LA VERANDA   RISTORANTE €€€
Map p304 (⊉06 687 29 73; www.laveranda.net; Borgo Santo Spirito 73; lunch €40, dinner €60-70, brunch €15-29; ⊙12.30-3pm & 7.30-11pm Tue-Sun; ☐Piazza Pia) Featured in Paolo Sorrentino's Oscar-winning film *The Great Beauty,* this fine-dining restaurant is as memorable for its setting – in the Renaissance Palazzo della Rovere – as its quality Italian cuisine. Inside, you can dine under 15th-century Pinturicchio frescoes, while in the warmer months, you can go alfresco in the garden. To enjoy the atmosphere for a snip of the regular price, stop by for Sunday brunch.

✖ Prati

★FA-BÌO   SANDWICHES €
Map p304 (⊉06 6452 5810; www.fa-bio.com; Via Germanico 43; sandwiches €5; ⊙10.30am-5.30pm Mon-Fri, to 4pm Sat; ☐Piazza del Risorgimento, MOttaviano-San Pietro) ⊘ Sandwiches, wraps, salads and fresh juices are all prepared with speed, skill and fresh organic ingredients at this friendly takeaway. Locals, Vatican tour guides and in-the-know visitors come here to grab a quick lunchtime bite and if you can find room in the tiny interior, you'd do well to follow suit.

★FATAMORGANA   GELATO €
Map p304 (www.gelateriafatamorgana.it; Via Leone IV 52; gelato €2.50-5; ⊙noon-11pm summer, to 9pm winter; MOttaviano-San Pietro) The Prati branch of hit gelateria chain. As well as all the classic flavours there are some wonderfully left-field creations, including a strange but delicious *basilico, miele e noci* (basil, honey and hazelnuts).

MO'S GELATERIE   GELATO €
Map p304 (⊉06 687 43 57; Via Cola di Rienzo 174; gelato €2.50-6; ⊙11am-8pm; ☐Piazza del Risorgimento) Chocoholics should make a beeline for Mo's, a small gelateria nestled between the shops on Via Cola di Rienzo. The choice of flavours is limited, but the artisanal gelato really hits the mark.

MONDO ARANCINA   FAST FOOD €
Map p304 (⊉06 9761 9213; Via Marcantonio Colonna 38; arancini from €2.50, ⊙10am-midnight; MLepanto) All sunny yellow ceramics, hungry crowds and tantalising deep-fried snacks, this bustling takeaway brings a little corner of Sicily to Rome. Stars of the show are the classic fist-sized *arancine,* fried rice balls stuffed with fillers ranging from the classic *ragù* to more exotic fare such as *zucca* (pumpkin) and gorgonzola.

DOLCE MANIERA   BAKERY €
Map p304 (Via Barletta 27; snacks €0.50-1; ⊙24hr; MOttaviano-San Pietro) For that late-night snack, nowhere beats this historic 24-hour basement bakery. When the munchies strike, head here to load up on cheap-as-chips *cornetti,* slabs of pizza, *panini,* pastries, cakes and biscuits.

LOCAL KNOWLEDGE

SLICED PIZZA TO DIE FOR

When a pizza joint is packed on a wet winter's lunch, you know it's something special. **Pizzarium** (Map p304; ☑06 3974 5416; Via della Meloria 43; pizza slices €5; ☺11am-10pm; ⓜCipro-Musei Vaticani), the takeaway of Gabriele Bonci, Rome's acclaimed pizza king, serves Rome's best sliced pizza, bar none. Scissor-cut squares of soft, springy base are topped with original combinations of seasonal ingredients and served on paper trays for immediate consumption.

IL SORPASSO   ITALIAN €€

Map p304 (☑06 8902 4554; www.sorpasso.info; Via Properzio 31-33; meals €20-35; ☺7am-1am Mon-Fri, 9am-1am Sat; ⓠPiazza del Risorgimento) A bar-restaurant hybrid sporting a vintage cool look – vaulted stone ceilings, exposed brick, rustic wooden tables – Il Sorpasso is a Prati hotspot. Open throughout the day, it caters to a fashionable crowd, serving everything from salads and pasta specials to *trappizini* (pyramids of stuffed pizza), cured meats and cocktails.

VELAVEVODETTO AI QUIRITI   ROMAN €€

Map p304 (☑06 3600 0009; www.ristorante velavevodetto.it; Piazza dei Quiriti 5; meals €30-35; ☺12.30-3pm & 7.45-11pm; ⓜLepanto) This welcoming restaurant wins you over with its unpretentious, earthy food and honest prices. The menu reads like a directory of Roman staples, and while it's all pretty good, standout choices include *fettuccine con asparagi, guanciale e pecorino* (pasta ribbons with asparagus, guanciale and pecorino cheese) and *polpette di bollito* (meat balls).

HOSTARIA DINO E TONI   ROMAN €€

Map p304 (☑06 3973 3284; Via Leone IV 60; meals €25-30; ☺12.30-3pm & 7-11pm, closed Sun & Aug; ⓜOttaviano-San Pietro) A bustling old-school trattoria, Dino e Toni offers simple, no-frills Roman cooking. Kick off with its house antipasto, a minor meal of fried *supplì*, olives and pizza, before plunging into its signature pasta dish, *rigatoni all'amatriciana* (pasta tubes with bacon-like guanciale, chilli and tomato sauce). No credit cards.

DAL TOSCANO   TUSCAN €€

Map p304 (☑06 3972 5717; www.ristorantedal toscano.it; Via Germanico 58-60; meals €40; ☺12.30-3pm & 8-11.15pm Tue-Sun; ⓜOttaviano-San Pietro) Immerse yourself in the tastes of Tuscany at this old-fashioned *ristorante*. Meat is a highlight, with cured hams and salamis served as starters, and grilled steaks providing the mains.

OSTERIA DELL'ANGELO   TRATTORIA €€

Map p304 (☑06 372 94 70; Via Bettolo 24; fixed-price menu €25-35; ☺12.30-2.30pm Mon-Fri & 8-11pm Mon-Sat; ⓜOttaviano-San Pietro) With rugby paraphernalia on the walls and basic wooden tables, this cheerfully hectic eatery is a choice spot for an authentic trattoria experience. The fixed-price menu features a mixed antipasti, a robust Roman-style pasta and a choice of hearty mains with a side dish.

DEL FRATE   WINE BAR €€

Map p304 (☑06 323 64 37; www.enotecadelfrate. it; Via degli Scipioni 122; meals €40-45; ☺12.30-3pm & 6.30-11.45pm Mon-Sat; ⓜOttaviano-San Pietro) Locals love this upmarket *enoteca* (wine bar) with its simple wooden tables and high-ceilinged brick-arched rooms. Dishes are designed to complement the extensive wine list, so there's a formidable selection of cheeses (everything from Sicilian ricotta to Piedmontese robiola), alongside a refined menu of tartars, salads, fresh pastas and main courses.

ENOTECA LA TORRE   RISTORANTE €€€

(☑06 4566 8304; www.enotecalatorreroma.com; Villa Laetitia, Lungotevere delle Armi 22; fixed-price lunch menu €60, tasting menus €95-120; ☺12.30-2.30pm Tue-Sat & 7.30-10.30pm Mon-Sat; ⓠLungotevere delle Armi) The romantic art nouveau Villa Laetitia provides an aristocratic setting for this refined Michelin-starred restaurant. Since opening in 2013, it has firmly established itself on Rome's fine-dining scene with its sophisticated brand of contemporary creative cuisine and a stellar wine list.

RISTORANTE
L'ARCANGELO   RISTORANTE €€€

Map p304 (☑06 321 09 92; www.larcangelo.com; Via Guiseppe G Belli 59; meals €50; ☺1-2.30pm Mon-Fri & 8-11pm Mon-Sat; ⓠPiazza Cavour) Styled as an informal bistro with wood panelling, leather banquettes and casual table settings, L'Arcangelo enjoys a stellar local reputation. Dishes are modern and creative yet still undeniably Roman in their use of traditional ingredients such as sweetbreads and *baccalà* (cod). A further plus is the wine list, which boasts some interesting Italian labels.

DRINKING & NIGHTLIFE

Once the Vatican tourists have left and Prati's army of office workers have gone home for the day, this is a quiet part of town. There are a few bars and cafes dotted around the place but the local drinking scene is pretty low-key, and nightlife is limited to a few live music venues and theatres.

★SCIASCIA CAFFÈ — CAFE

Map p304 (☎06 321 15 80; Via Fabio Massimo 80/A; ⏰7am-8.30pm Mon-Sat, 8am-8pm Sun; Ⓜ Ottaviano-San Pietro) There are several contenders for the best coffee in town but in our opinion, nothing tops the *caffè eccellente* served at this polished old-school cafe. A velvety smooth espresso served in a delicate cup lined with melted chocolate, it's nothing short of magnificent.

BE.RE — CRAFT BEER

Map p304 (☎06 9442 1854; www.be-re.eu; Piazza del Risorgimento, cnr Via Vespasiano; ⏰10am-2am; 🚊Piazza del Risorgimento) Rome's craft-beer fans keenly applauded the opening of this contemporary bar in late 2016. With its copper beer taps, exposed brick decor and high vaulted ceilings, it's a good-looking spot for an evening of Italian beers and cask ales.

PASSAGUAI — WINE BAR

Map p304 (☎06 8745 1358; www.passaguai.it; Via Leto 1; ⏰10am-2am Mon-Fri, 6pm-2am Sat & Sun; 📶; 🚊Piazza del Risorgimento) A basement bar with tables in a cosy stone-clad interior and on a quiet side street, Passaguai feels pleasingly off-the-radar. It's a great spot for a post-sightseeing cocktail or glass of wine – there's an excellent choice of both – accompanied by cheese and cold cuts, or even a full meal from the small menu.

MAKASAR BISTROT — WINE BAR, TEAHOUSE

Map p304 (☎06 687 46 02; www.makasar.it; Via Plauto 33; ⏰noon-midnight Mon-Thu, to 2am Fri & Sat, 5pm-midnight Sun; 🚊Piazza del Risorgimento) Recharge your batteries with a quiet drink at this bookish *bistrot*. Pick your tipple from the 250-variety tea menu or opt for an Italian wine and sit back in the softly lit earthenware-hued interior. For something to eat, there's a small menu of salads, bruschetta, baguettes and hot dishes.

ENTERTAINMENT

ALEXANDERPLATZ — JAZZ

Map p304 (☎06 8377 5604; www.facebook.com/alexander.platz.37; Via Ostia 9; ⏰8.30pm-1.30am; Ⓜ Ottaviano-San Pietro) Intimate, underground, and hard to find – look for the discreet black door – Rome's most celebrated jazz club draws top Italian and international performers and a respectful cosmopolitan crowd. Book a table for the best stage views or to dine here, although note that it's the music that's the star act, not the food.

FONCLEA — LIVE MUSIC

Map p304 (☎06 689 63 02; www.fonclea.it; Via Crescenzio 82a; ⏰6pm-2am Sep-May, concerts 9.30pm; 🚊Piazza del Risorgimento) Fonclea is a great little pub venue, with nightly gigs by bands playing everything from jazz and soul to pop, rock and doo-wop. Get in the mood with a drink during happy hour (6pm to 8.30pm daily). In summer, the pub ups sticks and moves to a site by the Tiber.

SHOPPING

Unless you're in the market for rosary beads and religious souvenirs, the Vatican has little in the way of shopping. Prati is a different story, and its shop-lined streets offer plenty of scope for browsing.

★IL SELLAIO — FASHION & ACCESSORIES

Map p304 (☎06 321 17 19; www.serafinipelletteria.it; Via Caio Mario 14; ⏰9.30am-7.30pm Mon-Fri, 9.30am-1pm & 3.30-7.30pm Sat; Ⓜ Ottaviano-San Pietro) During the 1960s Ferruccio Serafini was one of Rome's most sought-after artisans, making handmade leather shoes and bags for the likes of John F Kennedy, Liz Taylor and Marlon Brando. Nowadays, his daughter Francesca runs the family shop where you can pick up beautiful hand-stitched bags, belts and accessories. You can also have your own designs made to order.

★RECHICLE — VINTAGE

Map p304 (☎06 3265 2469; Piazza dell' Unità 21; ⏰10.30am-2pm & 3.30-7.30pm Mon-Sat; 🚊Via Cola di Rienzo) Lovers of vintage fashions should make a beeline for this fab boutique. Furnished with antique family furniture and restored cabinets, it's full of wonderful finds such as Roger Vivier comma heels (with their original box), iconic Chanel jackets, Hermès bags, Balenciaga coats and much more.

Rome's Churches

Rome is a feast, and whatever your faith, it's impossible not to be awestruck by its riches. Nowhere will you be able to visit such a splendid array and wealth of ecclesiastic architecture, from the stark simplicity of Basilica di Santa Sabina (p171) and the tiny perfection of Bramante's Tempietto (p157) to the awe-inspiring grandeur of St Peter's Basilica (the world's greatest church; p118) and the Sistine Chapel (p126). Rome's other inspirational pilgrimage sites include huge edifices such as the basilicas of San Lorenzo Fuori le Mura (p143), Santa Maria Maggiore (p139), San Giovanni in Laterano (p168) and the Chiesa di Santa Croce in Gerusalemme (p141).

Ancient Architecture

Whether they're baroque, medieval or Renaissance, many churches also feature a form of recycling that's uniquely Roman, integrating leftover architectural elements from imperial Rome. For example, you'll see ancient columns in Basilica di Santa Maria in Trastevere (p154), and the famous ancient mask, the Bocca della Verità (p67), in the beautiful medieval Chiesa di Santa Maria in Cosmedin. Taking the idea to the limit, the mesmerising Pantheon (p72) is an entire Roman temple converted into a church.

Divine Art

Rome's churches, which dot almost every street corner, also serve as free art galleries, bedecked in gold, inlay-work, mosaic and carvings. The wealth of the Roman Catholic church has benefited from centuries of virtuoso artists, architects and artisans who descended here to create their finest and most heavenly works in the glorification of God. Without paying a cent, anyone can wander in off the street to see this glut of masterpieces, including works by Michelangelo (in San Pietro in Vincoli, p140, and St Peter's Basilica), Caravaggio (in Santa Maria del Popolo, p99 and San Luigi dei Francesi, p76) and Bernini (in Santa Maria della Vittoria, p105).

1. The courtyard garden of Basilica di San Paolo Fuori le Mura (p195) **2.** Basilica di Santa Maria in Trastevere (p154) **3.** *Ecstasy of St Teresa* by Gian Lorenzo Bernini, in Chiesa di Santa Maria della Vittoria (p105)

Monti, Esquilino & San Lorenzo

MONTI | ESQUILINO | PIAZZA DELLA REPUBBLICA & AROUND | SAN LORENZO & BEYOND

Neighbourhood Top Five

❶ Palazzo Massimo alle Terme (p138) Time-travelling back to the magnificent frescoed, mosaic-carpeted villas of imperial Rome at one of Rome's finest unsung art museums.

❷ Monti (p140) Pottering around Rome's romantic, bohemian-chic neighbour-hood, lingering at old-world wine bars, sipping coffee on quaint pavement terraces and browsing independ-ent specialist boutiques en route.

❸ Pigneto (p148) Hob-nobbing with bohos in the iconic working-class district immortalised by film direc-tor Pasolini.

❹ Basilica di Santa Maria Maggiore (p139) Marvel-ling at the splendours of one of Rome's four patriarchal basilicas.

❺ Domus Aurea (p140) Exploring the underground wonders of Nero's great golden palace that lies today beneath Oppian Hill.

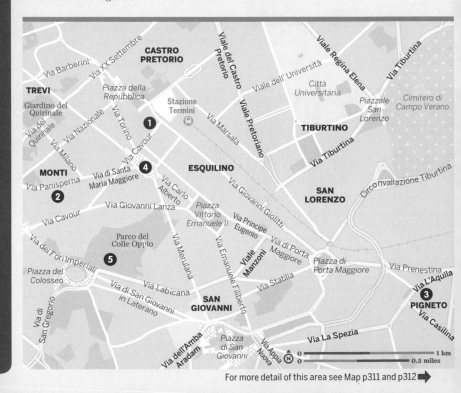

For more detail of this area see Map p311 and p312 ➡

Explore: Monti, Esquilino & San Lorenzo

Allow a full day to explore Esquilino, named after one of Rome's seven hills and embracing the increasingly scrubbed-up mesh of streets around Stazione Termini and Piazza Vittorio Emanuele II (Rome's largest city square), probably best avoided at night. The stunning classical art showcased in the Palazzo Massimo alle Terme (p138) alone warrants two or three hours.

Heading downhill, Monti was the ancient city's notorious Suburra slum – a red-light district and the childhood home of Julius Caesar. A welcome overdose of tasty eateries, shops and *enoteche* (wine bars) lend gentrified Monti bags of charm, a fact that is never more apparent than on weekends when seemingly half of Rome flocks here to shop, drink and eat. Follow suit for a day at least.

East of Termini, the lively student quarter of San Lorenzo, won't appeal to everyone – it was the area most damaged by Allied bombing during WWII and by day it feels hung-over. Plan to visit the beautiful Basilica di San Lorenzo Fuori le Mura (p143) in the late afternoon, followed by dinner in one of San Lorenzo's excellent restaurants. The student nightlife scene kicks in after dark.

Pigneto (p148), a quick tram ride southeast, is the Roman equivalent of London's Dalston. Devote an evening to exploring its ever-burgeoning bars and restaurants enlivened by local artists and boho urbanites.

Local Life

→**Coffee hangouts** Every neighbourhood has its own iconic cafe in which to while away an hour or so: try Monti's La Bottega del Caffè (p147); Esquilino's Yellow Bar (p148); San Lorenzo's Gente di San Lorenzo (p150); or Pigneto's Necci dal 1924 (p149).

→**Aperitivo** Esquilino's *aperitivo* (pre-dinner drinks) bar has been seriously raised with the opening of Gatsby Café (p148); for wine lovers, Il Sorì (p149) in San Lorenzo is the spot.

Getting There & Away

→**Metro** The Cavour metro stop (line B) is most convenient for Monti, while the Termini (lines A and B), Castro Pretorio (line B) and Vittorio Emanuele (line A) stations are useful for Esquilino. The section of Line C that will serve Pigneto is not scheduled for completion until 2020.

→**Bus** Termini is the city's main bus hub, connected to places all over the city. Access Monti from buses stopping on Via Nazionale or Via Cavour. San Lorenzo is served by buses 71 and 492; Pigneto is served by buses 81, 810 and 105, and night bus n12.

→**Tram** An easy way to access San Lorenzo (tram 3) or Pigneto and Centocelle (trams 5, 14 or 19).

Lonely Planet's Top Tip

Don't neglect to visit the oft-overlooked patriarchal **Basilica di San Lorenzo Fuori le Mura** (p143) – it's starkly beautiful and far from crowded, ensuring a refreshingly serene moment or three.

✖ Best Places to Eat

→ Antonello Colonna Open (p146)
→ Panella (p145)
→ Said (p147)
→ Ai Tre Scalini (p144)
→ Mercato Centrale (p145)

For reviews, see p143.

🍷 Best Places to Drink

→ Gatsby Café (p148)
→ Il Sorì (p149)
→ La Bottega del Caffè (p147)
→ Spirito (p148)
→ Co.So (p149)
→ Necci dal 1924 (p149)

For reviews, see p147.

⊙ Best Works of Art

→ Palazzo Massimo alle Terme (p138)
→ Michelangelo's colossal *Moses* (p140)
→ Fuga's 13th-century facade mosaics (p139)

For reviews, see p140.

TOP SIGHT **MUSEO NAZIONALE ROMANO: PALAZZO MASSIMO ALLE TERME**

One of Rome's finest museums, this light-filled treasure trove is packed with spectacular classical art yet remains off the beaten track. It's not to be missed.

We recommend you start your visit on the 2nd floor, so you see its wonders when you're fresh – the sensational frescoes here give a more complete picture of the inside of grand ancient Roman villas than you'll see anywhere else in the world. They include scenes from nature, mythology, and domestic and sensual life, using rich, vivid (and expensive) colours. The showstopper is the decoration covering an entire room from **Villa Livia**, one of the homes of Augustus' wife Livia Drusilla. The frescoes depict a paradisiacal garden full of a wild tangle of roses, violets, pomegranates, irises and camomile under a deep-blue sky. These decorated a summer triclinium, a large living and dining area built half underground to provide protection from the heat. The lighting mimics the modulation of daylight and highlights the richness of the millennia-old colours.

The ground and 1st floors are devoted to sculpture, examining imperial portraiture as propaganda and including some breathtaking works of art, including the 2nd-century-BC Greek bronzes, the *Boxer* and the *Prince,* a crouching *Aphrodite* from Villa Adriana, the 2nd-century-BC *Sleeping Hermaphrodite,* and the idealised vision of the *Discus Thrower.* Also fascinating are the elaborate bronze fittings that belonged to Caligula's ceremonial ships.

In the basement, the coin collection is far more absorbing than you might expect, tracing the Roman Empire's propaganda offensive via coinage. There's also jewellery dating back several millennia that looks as good as new, and the disturbing remains of a mummified eight-year-old girl, the only known example of mummification dating from the Roman Empire.

DON'T MISS

➡ The *Boxer*
➡ *Sleeping Hermaphrodite*
➡ Villa Livia frescoes

PRACTICALITIES

➡ Map p312, E3
➡ ☑ 06 3996 7700
➡ www.coopculture.it
➡ Largo di Villa Peretti 1
➡ adult/reduced €7/3.50
➡ ⊙9am-7.45pm Tue-Sun
➡ Ⓜ Termini

TOP SIGHT
BASILICA DI SANTA MARIA MAGGIORE

One of Rome's four patriarchal basilicas, this monumental church stands on the summit of the Esquilino Hill, on the spot where snow is said to have fallen in the summer of AD 358.

The basilica exterior is decorated with glimmering 13th-century mosaics, protected by Ferdinand Fuga's baroque porch (1741). The 18.78m-high column outside came from the Basilica of Massenzio in the Roman Forum and the 75m belfry, the highest in Rome, is 14th-century Romanesque.

The vast interior retains its original 5th-century structure as well as the original mosaics in the triumphal arch and nave. The central image in the apse, signed by Jacopo Torriti, dates from the 13th century and represents the coronation of the Virgin Mary. Beneath your feet, the nave floor is a fine example of 12th-century Cosmati paving.

The baldachin over the high altar is heavy with gilt cherubs; the altar itself is a porphyry sarcophagus, said to contain the relics of St Matthew and other martyrs. A plaque embedded in the floor to the right of the altar marks the spot where Gian Lorenzo Bernini and his father Pietro are buried. Steps lead down to the *confessio* (a crypt in which relics are placed), where a statue of Pope Pius IX kneels before a reliquary containing a fragment of Jesus' manger.

Don't miss the Loggia delle Benedizioni (accessible only by 30-minute guided tours), the extraordinary creation of Ferdinando Fuga, where you can get a close look at both the facade's iridescent 13th-century mosaics created by Filippo Rusuti, and Bernini's magnificent baroque helical staircase.

Through the souvenir shop on the right-hand side of the church is the Museo del Tresoro (Treasury Museum) with a glittering collection of religious artefacts.

DON'T MISS

→ Loggia delle Benedizioni
→ Cosmatesque floor
→ Jacopo Torriti apse mosaics

PRACTICALITIES

→ Map p312, E5
→ ☎06 6988 6800
→ Piazza Santa Maria Maggiore
→ basilica free, adult/reduced museum €3/2, museum & loggia €5/4
→ ⊙7am-7pm, loggia guided tours 9.30am-5.45pm
→ 🚇Piazza Santa Maria Maggiore

⊙ SIGHTS

Grand 19th-century buildings line the streets of Esquilino, the area around Rome's central train station, Termini. It might not be Rome's prettiest 'hood, and some parts feel downright shady, but it's studded with some stupendous art and museums. To the southeast, the student district of San Lorenzo, and bohemian Pigneto, south again, are street-art hot spots.

⊙ Monti

BASILICA DI SAN PIETRO
IN VINCOLI   BASILICA
Map p312 (Piazza di San Pietro in Vincoli 4a; ⊙8am-12.30pm & 3-7pm summer, to 6pm winter; Ⓜ Cavour) Pilgrims and art lovers flock to this 5th-century basilica for two reasons: to marvel at Michelangelo's colossal *Moses* (1505) sculpture and to see the chains that supposedly bound St Peter when he was imprisoned in the Carcere Mamertino (near the Roman Forum). Access to the church is via a flight of steps through a low arch that leads up from Via Cavour.

The church was built specially to house the shackles of St Peter, which had been sent to Constantinople after the saint's death, but were later returned as relics. They arrived in two pieces and legend has it that when they were reunited they miraculously joined together. They are now displayed under the altar.

To the right of the altar, Michelangelo's *Moses* forms the centrepiece of his unfinished tomb for Pope Julius II. The prophet strikes a muscular pose with well-defined biceps, a magnificent waist-length beard and two small horns sticking out of his head. These were inspired by a mistranslation of a biblical passage: where the original said that rays of light issued from Moses' face, the translator wrote 'horns'. Michelangelo was aware of the mistake, but gave Moses horns anyway. Flanking Moses are statues of Leah and Rachel, probably completed by Michelangelo's students.

The tomb, despite its imposing scale, was never finished – Michelangelo originally envisaged 40 statues, but got sidetracked by the Sistine Chapel – and Pope Julius II was buried in St Peter's Basilica.

⊙ Esquilino

BASILICA DI SANTA
MARIA MAGGIORE   BASILICA
See p139.

BASILICA DI SANTA PRASSEDE   CHURCH
Map p312 (🖉06 488 24 56; Via Santa Prassede 9a; ⊙7am-noon & 4-6.30pm; 🚇Piazza Santa Maria Maggiore) Famous for its brilliant Byzantine mosaics, this tiny gem of a 9th-century church is dedicated to St Praxedes, an early Christian heroine who hid Christians fleeing persecution and buried those she couldn't save in a well. The position of the well is now marked by a marble disc on the floor of the nave.

The mosaics, produced by artists whom Pope Paschal I had brought in specially from Byzantium, bear all the hallmarks of their eastern creators, with bold gold backgrounds and a marked Christian symbolism. The apse mosaics depict Christ flanked by Sts Peter, Pudentiana and Zeno on the right, and Paul, Praxedes and Pope Paschal on the left. All the figures have golden halos except for Paschal, whose head is shadowed by a blue nimbus to indicate that he was still alive at the time.

Further treasures await in the heavily mosaiced **Cappella di San Zenone**, including a piece of the column to which Christ was tied when he was flogged, brought back from Jerusalem – it's in the glass case on the right.

DOMUS AUREA   ARCHAEOLOGICAL SITE
Map p312 (Golden House; 🖉06 3996 7700; www.coopculture.it; Viale della Domus Aurea; adult/under 6yr €14/free; ⊙9am-4.45pm Sat & Sun; Ⓜ Colosseo) Nero had his Domus Aurea constructed after the fire of AD 64 (which he is rumoured to have started to clear the area). Named after the gold that lined its facade and interiors, it was a huge complex covering up to a third of the city. Making full use of virtual reality, superb state-of-the-art guided tours shed light on just how grand the Golden House – a lavish villa with porticoes – was. Advance online reservations are obligatory.

The palace was full of architectural invention, a more splendid palace than had ever been seen before. However, Nero's successors attempted to raze all trace of his megalomania. Vespasian drained Nero's ornamental lake and, in a symbolic gesture, built the Colosseum in its place. Domitian

VILLA ALDOBRANDINI

If you're in need of a breather around Via Nazionale or are in search of somewhere for a picnic, follow Via Mazzarino off the main road and walk up the steps, past 2nd-century ruins to **Villa Aldobrandini** (Map p312; Via Mazzarino; ☉dawn-dusk; ◻Via Nazionale), a graceful, sculpture-dotted garden with gravel paths and benches beneath fragrant orange trees, palms and camellias.

Raised around 10m above street level, these are the grounds of 16th-century Villa Aldobrandini, built to house the extensive art collection of Cardinal Pietro Aldobrandini. The villa, which is closed to the public, today houses the headquarters of an international law institute.

built a palace on the Palatino, while Trajan sacked and destroyed the 1st floor and then entombed the lower level in earth and used it for the foundations of his public baths complex, which was abandoned by the 6th century. This burial of the palace preserved it; the section that has been excavated lies beneath Oppian Hill. Wear warm clothes to visit as the palace now lies underground and is damp. Remarkably, the humidity has helped preserve the frescoes in the chambers, though this may only be seen in one small cleaned area – the rest have not been restored. Tours last an hour and 15 minutes and are guided by archaeologists who are extremely knowledgeable about the site.

During the Renaissance, artists (including Raphael and Pinturicchio) lowered themselves into the ruins, climbing across the top of Trajan's rubble in order to study the frescoed grottoes, and Raphael reproduced some of their motifs in his work on the Vatican.

CHIESA DI SANTA CROCE IN GERUSALEMME   CHURCH

Map p311 (www.santacroceroma.it; Piazza di Santa Croce in Gerusalemme 12; ☉7am-12.45pm & 3.30-7.30pm; ◻Piazza di Porta Maggiore) One of Rome's seven pilgrimage churches, this church was founded in 320 by St Helena, mother of the emperor Constantine, in the grounds of her palace. It takes its name from the Christian relics here – including a piece of Christ's cross and St Thomas'

doubting finger – that St Helena brought to Rome from Jerusalem, housed in a chapel to the left of the altar.

MUSEO NAZIONALE DEGLI STRUMENTI   MUSEUM

Map p311 (National Museum of Musical Instruments; ☎06 3 28 10; Piazza di Santa Croce in Gerusalemm; adult/reduced €5/2.50; ☉9am-7pm Tue-Sun; ◻Piazza di Porta Maggiore) This little-known museum behind the church of Santa Croce stands on the site of the former home of St Helena. It's undeservedly but refreshingly deserted, with a collection of over 3000 exquisite musical instruments that includes gorgeously painted, handle-operated 18th-century Neapolitan street pianos, and one of the oldest known pianos (1722).

CHIESA DI SAN MARTINO AI MONTI   CHURCH

Map p312 (Viale del Monte Oppio 28; ☉9am-noon & 4.30-7pm; ◻Cavour) This was already a place of worship in the 3rd century, when Christians would meet in what was then the home of a Roman named Equitius. In the 4th century, after Christianity was legalised, a church was constructed, and later rebuilt in the 6th and 9th centuries. It was then completely transformed by Filippo Gagliardi in the 1650s.

It's of particular interest for Gagliardi's frescoes showing the Basilica di San Giovanni in Laterano before it was rebuilt in the mid-17th century and St Peter's Basilica before it assumed its present 16th-century look. Remnants of the more distant past include the ancient Corinthian columns dividing the nave and aisles.

PIAZZA VITTORIO EMANUELE II   PIAZZA

Map p312 (◻Vittorio Emanuele) Laid out in the late 19th century as the centrepiece of an upmarket residential district, but today with a rundown, seedy feel, Rome's biggest square is a grassy expanse, surrounded by speeding traffic, porticoes and bargain stores. Within the fenced-off central section are the ruins of **Trofei di Mario**, once a fountain at the end of an aqueduct.

In the northern corner, the **Chiesa di Sant'Eusebio** (www.santeusebioroma.org; ☉7-9am & 5.30-7pm Mon, 7.30-noon & 5-7.30pm Tue-Sat, 8.30-1pm & 5.30-7.30pm Sun) is popular with pet owners who bring their companions to be blessed on St Anthony's feast day (17 January).

MONTI, ESQUILINO & SAN LORENZO SIGHTS

MUSEO STORICO DELLA LIBERAZIONE
MUSEUM

Map p311 (Museum of Liberation of Rome; ☑06 700 38 66; www.museoliberazione.it; Via Tasso 145; ⊙9.30am-12.30pm Tue-Sun, plus 3.30-7.30pm Tue, Thu, Fri & 1st Sun of month; MⓂManzoni) FREE Now a small, chilling museum, Via Tasso 145 was the headquarters of the German SS during the Nazi occupation of Rome (1943–44). Members of the Resistance were interrogated, tortured and imprisoned in the cells and you can still see graffiti scrawled on the walls by condemned prisoners. Exhibits, which include photos, documents and improvised weapons, chart the events of the occupation, covering the persecution of the Jews, the underground resistance and the Fosse Ardeatina massacre.

FONTANA DELLE NAIADI

Piazza della Repubblica's elegant **Fontana delle Naiadi** (Map p312), built in 1888, was designed by Alessandro Guerrieri, who decorated it with four lions; they were replaced by sculptor Mario Rutelli's bronze nymphs in 1901, which aroused puritanical ire when unveiled. The nudity of the four naiads, or water nymphs, who surround the central figure of Glaucus wrestling a fish, was considered too provocative – how Italy has changed! Each reclines on a creature symbolising water in a different form: a water snake (rivers), a swan (lakes), a lizard (streams) and a seahorse (oceans).

◉ Piazza della Repubblica & Around

MUSEO NAZIONALE ROMANO: PALAZZO MASSIMO ALLE TERME
MUSEUM

See p138.

PIAZZA DELLA REPUBBLICA
PIAZZA

Map p312 (MⓂRepubblica) Flanked by grand 19th-century neoclassical colonnades, this landmark piazza was laid out as part of Rome's post-unification makeover. It follows the lines of the semicircular *exedra* (benched portico) of Diocletian's baths complex and was originally known as Piazza Esedra.

MUSEO NAZIONALE ROMANO: TERME DI DIOCLEZIANO
MUSEUM

Map p312 (☑06 3996 7700; www.coopculture.it; Viale Enrico de Nicola 78; adult/reduced €7/3.50; ⊙9am-7.30pm Tue-Sun; MⓂTermini) The Terme di Diocleziano was ancient Rome's largest bath complex, covering about 13 hectares and able to accommodate some 3000 people. Today its ruins house a branch of the impressive Museo Nazionale Romano. Exhibits, which include memorial inscriptions, bas-reliefs and archaeological artefacts, provide a fascinating insight into Roman life. Outside, the vast cloister, constructed from drawings by Michelangelo, is lined with classical sarcophagi, headless statues and huge sculptured animal heads, thought to have come from the Foro di Traiano.

Elsewhere in the museum, look out for exhibits relating to cults and the early development of Christianity and Judaism. There's a particularly interesting section about amulets and spells, which were cast on neighbours and acquaintances to bring them bad luck and worse. Upstairs you'll find tomb objects dating from the 11th to 9th centuries BC, including jewellery and amphorae.

As you wander around the museum, you'll see glimpses of the original complex, which was completed in the early 4th century as a state-of-the-art combination of baths, libraries, concert halls and gardens – the Aula Ottagona and Basilica di Santa Maria degli Angeli buildings were also once part of this enormous endeavour. It fell into disrepair after the aqueduct that fed the baths was destroyed by invaders in about AD 536.

Note that the museum is one of four that collectively make up the Museo Nazionale Romano. The ticket, which is valid for three days, also gives admission to the other three sites: the Palazzo Massimo alle Terme, Palazzo Altemps and the Crypta Balbi.

PALAZZO DELLE ESPOSIZIONI
CULTURAL CENTRE

Map p312 (☑06 3996 7500; www.palazzo esposizioni.it; Via Nazionale 194; ⊙10am-8pm Tue-Thu & Sun, to 10.30pm Fri & Sat; ⒽVia Nazionale) This huge neoclassical palace was built in 1882 as an exhibition centre, though it has since served as headquarters for the Italian Communist Party, a mess hall for Allied servicemen, a polling station and even a public loo. Nowadays it's a splendid cultural hub, with cathedral-scale exhibition spaces hosting blockbuster art exhibitions and sleekly designed art labs, as well as a bookshop, cafe and Michelin-starred restaurant (p146) serving a bargain lunch or brunch beneath a dazzling all-glass roof. Occasional concerts, performances and film screenings are also held here.

⊙ San Lorenzo & Beyond

BASILICA DI SAN LORENZO FUORI LE MURA   BASILICA

Map p311 (Piazzale San Lorenzo; ⊘8am-noon & 4-6.30pm; 📮Piazzale del Verano) This is one of Rome's four patriarchal basilicas. It's an atmospheric, tranquil edifice that's starker than many of the city's grand churches, a fact that only adds to its breathtaking beauty. It was the only one of Rome's major churches to have suffered bomb damage in WWII, and is a hotchpotch of rebuilds and restorations, yet still feels harmonious.

St Lawrence was burned to death in AD 258, and Constantine had the original basilica constructed in the 4th century over his burial place, which was rebuilt 200 years later. Subsequently, a nearby 5th-century church dedicated to the Virgin Mary was incorporated into the building, resulting in the church you see today. The nave, portico and much of the decoration date to the 13th century.

Highlights are the Cosmati floor and the frescoed portico, depicting events from St Lawrence's life. The remains of St Lawrence and St Stephen are in the church crypt beneath the high altar. A pretty barrel-vaulted cloister contains inscriptions and sarcophagi and leads to the Catacombe di Santa Ciriaca, where St Lawrence was initially buried.

CIMITERO DI CAMPO VERANO   CEMETERY

Map p311 (☏06 4923 6349; www.cimiteri capitolini.it; Piazzale del Verano 1; ⊘7.30am-6pm Apr-Sep, to 5pm Oct-Mar; 📮Piazzale del Verano) The city's largest cemetery dates to the Napoleonic occupation of Rome between 1804 and 1814, when an edict ordered that the city's dead must be buried outside the city walls. Between the 1830s and the 1980s virtually all Catholics who died in Rome (with the exception of popes, cardinals and royalty) were buried here. If you're in the area, it's worth a look for its grand tombs. On All Souls' Day (2 November), thousands of Romans flock to the cemetery to leave flowers on the tombs of loved ones.

✗ EATING

Monti, an ancient slum with funky bars and restaurants, cooks up fantastic dining options for all tastes and budgets. In the less endearing Esquilino district, fine dines are hard to find, but the area does hide away some of Rome's best ethnic eats, while east in vibrant San Lorenzo, you'll find an enticing mix of restaurants.

✗ Monti

AROMATICUS   HEALTH FOOD €

Map p312 (☏06 488 13 55; www.aromaticus. it; Via Urbana 134; meals €10-15; ⊘11am-3pm & 6-8.30pm; 🛜; Ⓜ Cavour) Few addresses exude such a healthy vibe. Set within a shop selling aromatic plants and edible flowers, this inventive little cafe is the perfect place to satisfy green cravings. Its short but sweet menu features lots of creative salads, soups and gaspacho, tartare and carpaccio, juices and detox smoothies – all to stay or go.

ZIA ROSETTA   SANDWICHES €

Map p312 (☏06 3105 2516; www.ziarosetta.com; Via Urbana 54; salads €4.50-6, panini mini €2-3.50, regular €4.50-7; ⊘11am-4pm Mon-Thu, to 10pm Fri & Sat; Ⓜ Cavour) Grab a pew at a marble-topped table and brace your taste buds for a torturous choice of 25-odd different gourmet *panini* and another dozen monthly specials – all creatively stuffed with unexpected combinations, and with catchy names like Amber Queen, Strawberry Hill and Lady Godiva. If you really can't decide, pick a trio of mini *panini*. Freshly squeezed juices (€3.5) too. Glam and gluten-free.

ALLE CARETTE   PIZZA €

Map p292 (☏06 679 27 70; www.facebook.com/allecarrette; Via della Madonna dei Monti 95; pizza €5.50-8; ⊘11.30am-4pm & 7pm-midnight; 👪; Ⓜ Cavour) Honest pizza, super thin and swiftly cooked in a wood-burning oven, is what this traditional Roman pizzeria on one of Monti's prettiest car-free streets has done well for decades. Tobacco-coloured walls give the place a vintage vibe and Roman families pile in here at weekends. Begin your local feast with some battered and deep-fried zucchini flowers or *baccalà* (salted cod).

PASTA CHEF
FAST FOOD €

Map p312 (☑06 488 31 98; www.pastachefroma.it; Via Baccina 42; pasta €5-8; ☺12.30-9.30pm Mon-Sat; MCavour) 'Gourmet street food' is the strapline of this fast-food pasta joint where chefs Mauro and Leopoldo whip up steaming bowls of perfectly cooked pasta laced with carbonara, *pomodoro e basilico* (tomato and basil), bolognese and other classic sauces for a discerning, budget-conscious crowd. There's a veggie lasagne and other vegetarian options. The dynamic duo also run pasta cooking classes.

TRIESTE PIZZA
PIZZA €

Map p312 (☑366 8251313; www.trieste.pizza; Via Urbana 112; pizzas €2.20-3.60; ☺10am-11pm Sun-Thu, to 2am Fri & Sat; MCavour) A newcomer to the bohemian Monti neighbourhood, this welcoming takeaway joint serves excellent *pizzette* (small round pizzas). There are plenty to choose from, including the ever-present *margherita,* which comes with a soft, well-cooked base and a flavoursome coupling of tomato and melted mozzarella. Liquid sustenance is available in the form of bottled craft beers.

GREZZO
PASTRIES €

Map p312 (☑06 48 34 43; www.grezzoitalia.it; Via Urbana 130; ice cream €3-6, desserts & smoothies €6; ☺11am-11pm Mon-Thu & Sun, to midnight Fri & Sat; ☑; MCavour) 'Raw chocolate' is the strapline of this gourmet boutique where a knowing crowd hobnobs over exquisite tiramisu miniatures, raw chocolate tarts, cheese cakes, Sicilian almond and pistachio gelato (made with fresh almond milk) and one-bite pralines. Smoothies, desserts and sweets are all raw, organic and gluten-free. Take away or squat on stools around low coffee tables crafted from corrugated cardboard and woodchip.

GREEN & GO
HEALTH FOOD €

Map p312 (www.greenandgo-roma.it; Via del Boschetta 22; lunch menu €8.50; ☺11am-4pm Mon-Sat; MCavour) When the urge for hardcore green strikes, duck into this pocket-sized organic salad bar for homemade soups, gazpacho and made-to-measure salads topped with smoked salmon, tofu, prosciutto crudo, *pecorino* – in fact, absolutely anything you fancy. Freshly pressed juices and smoothies too, all to enjoy around a couple of bar-stool tables or to take away.

GELATERIA DELL'ANGELETTO
GELATERIA €

Map p312 (☑06 487 47 60; Via dell'Angeletto 15; gelato from €2.50; ☺11am-11pm; MCavour) An outpost of gelato-masters Dei Gracchi, who have their original gelateria close to the Vatican, this has many wonderful seasonal flavours, from pear and caramel to apple and cinnamon, and particularly *fantastico* pistachio.

CIURI CIURI
PASTRIES €

Map p312 (☑06 4544 4548; www.ciuri-ciuri.it; Via Leonina 18; snacks around €3; ☺8.30am-midnight Sun-Thu, to 2am Fri & Sat; MCavour) What's not to love about a Sicilian ice cream and pastry shop? Pop in for delectable homemade sweets such as *cannoli* freshly filled with ricotta, *cassata* and *pasticini di mandorla* (almond pastries), all available in bite-sized versions. It's not all sweet, though; there are also excellent freshly made *arancini* (deep-fried rice balls) and other snacks. Eat in or out.

★AI TRE SCALINI
WINE BAR €€

Map p312 (☑06 4890 7495; www.aitrescalini.org; Via Panisperna 251; meals €25; ☺12.30pm-1am; MCavour) A firm favourite since 1895, the 'Three Steps' is always packed, with crowds spilling out of the funky violet-painted door and into the street. Tuck into a heart-warming array of cheeses, salami and dishes such as *polpette al sugo* (meatballs with sauce), washed down with superb choices of wine or beer.

TEMAKINHO
SUSHI €€

Map p312 (☑06 4201 6656; www.temakinho.com; Via dei Serpenti 16; meals €40; ☺12.30-3.30pm & 7pm-midnight; MCavour) In a city where most food is still resolutely (though deliciously) Italian, this Brazilian-Japanese hybrid serving up sushi and ceviche makes for a sensationally refreshing change. As well as delicious, strong caipirinhas, which combine Brazilian *cachaça,* sugar, lime and fresh fruit, there are 'sakehinhas' made with sake. It's very popular; book ahead.

DA VALENTINO
TRATTORIA €€

Map p312 (☑06 488 06 43; Via del Boschetto 37; meals €30; ☺12.30-2.45pm & 8-11pm Mon-Sat; ☑Via Nazionale) The 1930s sign outside says 'Birra Peroni' and its enchanting vintage interior feels little changed. Come to this mythical dining address for delicious bruschetta,

MERCATO CENTRALE

A gourmet oasis for hungry travellers at Stazione Termini, this dazzling three-storey **food hall** (Map p312; www.mercatocentrale.it/roma; Via Giolitti 36, Stazione Termini; snacks/meals from €3/10; ⊗7am-midnight; 🔊; MTermini) is the latest project of Florence's savvy Umberto Montano. You'll find breads, pastries, cakes, veggie burgers, fresh pasta, truffles, pizza and a whole lot more beneath towering vaulted 1930s ceilings, as well as some of the city's most prized producers, including Gabriele Bonci (breads, focaccia and pizza), Roberto Liberati (salami) and Marcella Bianchi (vegetarian).

grilled meats, the purest of hamburgers and *scamorza,* a type of Italian cheese that is grilled and melted atop a myriad of different ingredients: tomato and rocket, artichokes, wafer-thin slices of aromatic *lardo di colonnata* (pork fat) from Tuscany and porcini mushrooms. No coffee.

L'ASINO D'ORO ITALIAN €€
Map p312 (📞06 4891 3832; www.facebook.com/asinodoro; Via del Boschetto 73; weekday lunch menu €16, meals €45; ⊗12.30-2.30pm & 7.30-11pm Tue-Sat; MCavour) This fabulous restaurant was transplanted from Orvieto, and its Umbrian origins resonate in Lucio Sforza's exceptional cooking. Unfussy yet innovative dishes feature bags of flavourful contrasts, like lamb meatballs with pear and blue cheese. Save room for the equally amazing desserts. Intimate, informal and classy, this is one of Rome's best deals – its lunch menu is a steal.

LA CARBONARA TRATTORIA €€
Map p312 (📞06 482 51 76; www.lacarbonara.it; Via Panisperna 214; meals €35-40; ⊗12.30-2.30pm & 7-11pm Mon-Sat; MCavour) On the go since 1906, this busy restaurant was favoured by the infamous Ragazzi di Panisperna, the group of young physicists whose discoveries led to the construction of the first atomic bomb. The waiters are brusque, the atmosphere crackles with energy, and the interior is covered in graffiti – tradition dictates that diners should leave their mark in a message on the wall.

DOOZO JAPANESE €€
Map p312 (📞06 481 56 55; www.doozo.it; Via Palermo 51; meals €15-30; ⊗12.30-3pm & 7.30-11pm Tue-Sat, 7.30-10.30pm Sun; 🔊Via Nazionale) Doozo (meaning 'welcome') is a spacious, Zen restaurant, bookshop and art gallery that serves traditional Japanese staples including tofu, sushi, sashimi, miso soup and tempura fries. The ambience is elegant and serene and the icing on the cake is a glorious courtyard garden, which, in summer, is a hidden oasis of peace, tranquillity and much-welcomed shade.

✕ Esquilino

★PANELLA BAKERY, CAFE €
Map p312 (📞06 487 24 35; www.panellaroma.com; Via Merulana 54; meals €7-15; ⊗8am-11pm Mon-Thu, to midnight Fri & Sat, 8.30am-4pm Sun; MVittorio Emanuele) Pure heaven for foodies, this enticing bakery is littered with well-used trays of freshly baked pastries loaded with confectioner's custard, wild-cherry fruit tartlets, *pizza al taglio, arancini* and focaccia – the smell alone is heavenly. Grab a bar stool between shelves of gourmet groceries inside or congratulate yourself on scoring a table on the flowery, sun-flooded terrace – one of Rome's loveliest.

PASTICCERIA REGOLI BAKERY €
Map p312 (📞06 487 2812; www.pasticceriaregoli.com; Via dello Statuto 60; ⊗cafe 6.30am-7.45pm Wed-Sun, shop to 8.20pm, MVittorio Emanuele) At weekends a queue marks the entrance to this elegant chandelier-lit *pasticceria*, much-loved since 1916. Its *crostate* (latticed jam tarts) are iconic, and a *maritozzi con panna* (sweet bread bun filled to bursting with whipped cream) is the downright wicked speciality to order in the neighbouring cafe – spot the secret hatch hidden in a mirror through which cakes are passed between the two. Excellent ice cream too.

FORNO ROSCIOLI PIETRO PIZZA, BAKERY €
Map p312 (📞06 446 71 46; www.facebook.com/fornorosciolipietro; Via Buonarroti 46-48; pizza slices €3.50; ⊗7am-8pm Mon-Sat; MVittorio Emanuele) The off-the-beaten-track branch of this splendid deli-bakery-pizzeria has utterly delicious *pizza al taglio,* pasta dishes and other goodies that make it ideal for a swift lunch or stocking up for picnic. It's on a road leading off Piazza Vittorio Emanuele II.

PALAZZO DEL FREDDO DI GIOVANNI FASSI GELATERIA €

Map p311 (☎06 446 47 40; www.palazzodelfreddo.it; Via Principe Eugenio 65; cones €1.60-3; ⊙noon-midnight Mon-Thu, to 12.30pm Fri & Sat, to 11pm Sun; MVittorio Emanuele) A vast temple to gelato, decked out with plenty of marble-topped table seating and decorated with antique gelato-making machinery, Fassi is a classic Rome experience. Funky flavours include *riso* (rice) and *nocciola* (hazelnut), and its *tramezzini* (ice-cream wafer 'sandwiches') and granita – served with dollops of cream – both deserve special mention.

MEID IN NAPOLS NEAPOLITAN €€

Map p312 (☎06 4470 4131; www.meidinnepols.com; Via Varese 54; pizza €4.50-12.50, meals €40; ⊙12.30-3pm & 7.30-11.30pm Mon-Sat; MTermini) For a steaming bowl of *impepata di cozze* (pepper-spiced mussels) or *frittura Napoletana* (fry-up of battered anchovies and salmon) near Stazione Termini, try this casual Neapolitan eatery. Or follow the young Roman crowd and choose from a couple of dozen different pizzas and a craft beer. Chocolate lovers, note, the house-special *pizza sciù sciù* is a calzone filled with warm gooey Nutella.

TRATTORIA DA DANILO TRATTORIA €€

Map p312 (☎06 7720 0111; www.trattoriadadanilo.com; Via Petrarca 13; meals €40; ⊙1-3.30pm & 6.30-11pm Tue-Sat, 6.30-11pm Mon; MVittorio Emanuele, Manzoni) Ideal if you're looking for a fine robust meal, this upmarket version of the classic neighbourhood trattoria offers icons of Roman cooking in a rustic, classical trattoria atmosphere. It's renowned for its *pasta cacio e pepe* (pasta with caciocavallo cheese and pepper) and carbonara. Top marks for its roll-down shutter, a street-art lesson in spaghetti-eating etiquette.

TRATTORIA MONTI TRATTORIA €€

Map p312 (☎06 446 65 73; Via di San Vito 13a; meals €45; ⊙1-1.45pm & 8-10.45pm Tue-Sat, 1-1.45pm Sun; MVittorio Emanuele) The Camerucci family runs this elegant brick-arched trattoria proffering top-notch traditional cooking from the Marches region. There are wonderful *fritti* (fried things), delicate pastas and ingredients such as *pecorino di fossa* (sheep's milk cheese aged in caves), goose, swordfish and truffles. Try the egg-yolk *tortelli* pasta. Desserts are delectable, including apple pie with *zabaglione* (egg and marsala custard). Book ahead.

Piazza della Repubblica & Around

★ANTONELLO COLONNA OPEN ITALIAN €€€

Map p312 (☎06 4782 2641; www.antonellocolonna.it; Via Milano 9a; lunch/brunch €16/30, meals €16-100; ⊙12.30-3.30pm & 8-11pm Tue-Sat, 12.30-3.30pm Sun; ❄; 🚌Via Nazionale) Spectacularly set at the back of Palazzo delle Esposizioni, super-chef Antonello Colonna's Michelin-starred restaurant lounges dramatically under a dazzling all-glass roof. Cuisine is new Roman – innovative takes on traditional dishes, cooked with wit and flair – and the all-you-can-eat lunch buffet and weekend brunch are unbeatable value. On sunny days, dine alfresco on the rooftop terrace.

San Lorenzo & Beyond

MOZZICO BURGERS €

Map p311 (☎06 9453 2800; www.mozzico.it; Via dei Volsci 80; burgers €8-14; ⊙noon-2am; 🚌Via Tiburtina) This bistro and *birreria* (beer house) in San Lorenzo cooks up burgers, fried meatballs and *mozzichi* (deep-fried bread-ball bombs, hollowed out and filled with various savoury combos) in an unpretentious, shabby chic interior: think salvaged vintage furnishings and random objects as wall art. Beer aficionados will adore the 10 Italian craft beers on tap, and the cocktails are not bad either.

TACOS & BEER MEXICAN €

Map p311 (www.facebook.com/tacosandbeersanlorenzo; Via dei Latini 37; ⊙12.30-3pm & 7.30pm-1am; 🚌Via Tiburtina, 🚋Via dei Reti) At home in an old *perfumeria* (perfumery) and *drogheria* (grocery), this hugely popular Mexican joint in San Lorenzo cooks up well-filled tacos to an appreciative student crowd. Count €7 for three tacos and a drink.

PIZZERIA FORMULA UNO PIZZA €

Map p311 (☎06 445 38 66; Via degli Equi 13; pizzas from €6.50; ⊙7.30pm-1.30am Mon-Sat; 🚌Via Tiburtina, 🚋Via dei Reti) This basic, historic San Lorenzo pizzeria is as adrenaline-fuelled as its name: waiters zoom around under whirring fans, delivering tomato-loaded bruschetta, fried courgette flowers, *supplì al telefono* and bubbling thin-crust pizza to eternal crowds of feasting students and wallet-savvy locals and tourists.

PASTIFICIO SAN LORENZO
ITALIAN €€

Map p311 (☑06 9727 3519; www.pastificiosan
lorenzo.com; Via Tiburtina 196; lunch/dinner
€25/40; ☺12.30-3pm & 8-11.30pm Mon-Fri,
8-11.30pm Sat; ☎; ☐Via Tiburtina, ☐Via dei
Reti) With a vintage horse vault serving as
a bench, saggy ginger-leather armchairs in
the *salotto* (salon), a white ceramic-tiled
bar and edgy brasserie-style seating, this
restaurant is a stylish place to hang out. It
is the dining arm of the **Pastificio Cerere
art gallery** (Map p311; ☑06 4542 2960; www.
pastificiocerere.com; Via degli Ausoni 7; ☺3-7pm
Mon-Fri, 4-8pm Sat; ☐Via Tiburtina), in an old
pasta factory around the corner, and cuisine
is predictably creative.

TRAM TRAM
OSTERIA €€

Map p311 (☑06 49 04 16; www.tramtram.it; Via dei
Reti 44; meals €35-45; ☺12.30-3.30pm & 7.30-
11.30pm Tue-Sun; ☐Via Tiburtina, ☐Via dei Reti)
This wildly popular, old-style trattoria with
lace curtains takes its name from the trams
that rattle by outside. It's a family-run affair
with a kitchen that unusually mixes classical
Roman dishes with seafood from Puglia in
Italy's hot south. Taste sensation *tiella riso,
patata* and *cozze* (baked rice dish with rice,
potatoes and mussels) is not to be missed.
Book well ahead.

POMMIDORO
TRATTORIA €€

Map p311 (☑06 445 26 92; Piazza dei Sanniti 44;
meals €33; ☺12.30-3.30pm & 7-11pm Mon-Sat,
closed Aug; ☐Via Tiburtina) Throughout San
Lorenzo's metamorphosis from down-at-heel
working-class district to down-at-heel student enclave, Pommidoro has remained the
same. It was a favourite of controversial film
director Pasolini and contemporary celebs
sometimes stop by, but it's an unpretentious
place with traditional food of superb quality,
specialising in grilled meats.

★SAID
ITALIAN €€€

Map p311 (☑06 446 92 04; www.said.it; Via
Tiburtina 135; meals €50; ☺6pm-12.30am Mon,
10am-12.30am Tue-Fri, to 1.30am Sat, to midnight
Sun; ☎; ☐Via Tiburtina, ☐Via dei Reti) Housed
in an early 1920s chocolate factory, this hybrid cafe-bar, restaurant and boutique in San
Lorenzo's coolest hipster haunt. Its Japanese
pink-tea pralines, indulged in with a coffee
or bought wrapped to take home, are glorious, and dining here is urban chic, with battered sofas, industrial antiques and creative
cuisine.

DRINKING &
NIGHTLIFE

**Few districts buzz after dark quite like
Monti, a neighbourhood littered with
quaint cafe pavement terraces, old-
world *enoteche* (wine bars) and a slew
of contemporary bar openings. For edgy
clubs and live music, wander off the
beaten track into the grungy student
'hood of San Lorenzo or further east into
boho Pigneto.**

❦ Monti

★LA CASETTA A MONTI
CAFE

Map p312 (☑06 482 7756; www.facebook.com/
lacasettadeimonti; Via della Madonna dei Monti
62; ☺9.30am-8pm Mon-Thu, to 10pm Fri & Sat,
8.30am-9pm Sun; ☎; ⓂCavour) Delicious
cakes, pastries and the finest chocolate salami in town is the name of the game at this
uber cute cafe, dolls house in size, run with
much love and passion by Eugenio and Alessandro. Find the cafe, all fresh and sassy after a 2017 restyle, in a low-lying house with
big windows and foliage-draped facade in
the cobbled heart of Monti. There's breakfast, lunch, drinks and music too.

LA BOTTEGA DEL CAFFÈ
CAFE

Map p312 (☑06 4/4 15 78; Piazza Madonna dei
Monti 5; ☺8am-2am; ☎; ⓂCavour) On one of
Rome's prettiest squares in Monti, La Bottega del Caffè – named after a comedy by
Carlo Goldoni – is the hot spot in Monti for
lingering over coffee, drinks, snacks and
lunch or dinner. Heaters in winter ensure
balmy alfresco action year-round.

ICE CLUB
BAR

Map p292 (☑06 9784 5581; www.iceclubroma.it;
Via della Madonna dei Monti 18; ☺5pm-1am Mon-
Thu & Sun, to 2am Fri & Sat; ⓂCavour) Novelty
value is what the Ice Club is all about. Pay
€15 (you get a free vodka cocktail served in a
glass made of ice), don a (completely unflat-
tering) hospital-blue thermal cloak and mit-
tens, and enter the bar, in which everything
is made of ice (temperature: –5°C). Most
people won't chill here for too long.

LIBRERIA CAFFÈ BOHEMIEN
BAR

Map p312 (☑339 722 46 22; www.caffebohemien.
it; Via degli Zingari 33-36; ☺2pm-1am Sun, Mon,
Wed & Thu, to 2am Fri & Sat; ⓂCavour) This hybrid wine bar, tearoom and bookshop with

WORTH A DETOUR

PIGNETO & CENTOCELLE

If you feel like a night bar-hopping to see where the evening takes you, head to **Pigneto**. Over the last decade, this working-class quarter has undergone a rapid metamorphosis to arty, hipster nightlife zone. The action centres on pedestrian **Via del Pigneto**, but there are also bars in the surrounding streets. The area also harbours some of Rome's best street art (listed on the street-art map available from tourist kiosks). To get here, take a tram from Termini to Via Prenestina.

The nearby suburban district of **Centocelle** is becoming a good place to go out to eat amid in-the-know Roman foodies. It's accessible via Tram 5, the Metro Parco di Centocelle, or buses 14, 105 or 150.

Eating

Burbée (☑06 701 1695; www.burbee.it; Via La Spezia 127a; burger €13.50-23; ⊙12.30-3.30pm & 7.30-11.30pm; 🛜; 🚋Via La Spezia) When the urge for a meaty *cavállo* (horse), Irish Black Angus or Japanese wagyu beef burger strikes, head to this thoroughly modern burger bar within frolicking distance of Pigneto.

Vitaminas 24 (Map p311; ☑331 204 5535; Via Ascoli Piceno 40-42; meals €15; ⊙11am-midnight Tue-Sun, to 4pm Mon; 🛜🌱; 🚋Circonvallazione Casilina) Produce from Rome's agricultural surrounds goes into the delicious smoothies, soups, wraps, salads, burgers and other vegetarian and vegan cuisine cooked up at this stylish bistro.

Primo (Map p311; ☑06 701 38 27; www.primoalpigneto.it; Via del Pigneto 46; meals €40-50; ⊙7pm-2am Tue-Sat, noon-3pm Sun; 🛜; 🚋Via Prenestina) Flagship of the Pigneto food scene, Primo is still buzzing after several years in business. Food wise, the onus is on modern Italian with dishes such as duck breast with honey chutney and chickpeas.

Drinking & Nightlife

Spirito (☑327 2983900; www.club-spirito.com; Via Fanfulla da Lodi 53; ⊙7.30pm-3am Wed-Mon; 🚋Via Prenestina) Spirited away behind a simple white door at the back of a sandwich shop, this is a Prohibition speakeasy with expertly mixed craft cocktails (around €10), gourmet food, live music and a fun-loving crowd.

fantastic paint-peeling front door lives up to its name; it feels like something you might stumble on in Left Bank Paris. It's small, with mismatched vintage furniture and an eclectic crowd drinking wine by the glass, aperitifs, tea and coffee.

AL VINO AL VINO　　　　　　WINE BAR
Map p312 (☑06 48 58 03; Via dei Serpenti 19; ⊙10.30am-2.30pm & 6pm-12.30am; MCavour) Mixing lovely ceramic-topped bistro tables with bottle-lined walls and the odd contemporary painting, this rustic *enoteca* is an attractive spot in which to linger over a fine collection of wine, including several *passiti* (sweet wines). The other speciality is *distillati* – grappa, whisky and so on.

🍷 Esquilino

★GATSBY CAFÉ　　　　　　BAR, CAFE
Map p312 (☑06 6933 9626; Piazza Vittorio Emanuele II 106; cocktails €7-10; ⊙8am-midnight Mon-

Thu, to 2am Fri & Sat; MTermini) There's good reason why the friendly bar staff here all wear flat caps, feather-trimmed trilbys and other traditional gents hats: this fabulous 1950s-styled space with salvaged vintage furniture and flashes of funky geometric wallpapering was originally a milliner's shop called Galleria Venturini. Brilliant rhubarb or elderflower *spritz,* craft cocktails, gourmet *panini* (€5) and *taglieri* (salami and cheese platters) make it a top *aperitivo* spot.

YELLOW BAR　　　　　　BAR
Map p312 (☑06 446 35 54; www.the-yellow.com; Via Palestro 40; ⊙24hr; 🛜; MCastro Pretorio) With its vintage zinc bar, high vaulted ceiling and amusing house rules chalked on the blackboard, this is a notch up from your bog-standard pub. Across the street from the hostel of the same name, around-the-clock Yellow is constantly packed with young, fun, international travellers. DJs spin tunes from 10pm until 4am, there are live bands at weekends and themed parties galore.

Co.So (📞06 4543 5428; Via Braccio da Montone 80; ⏰7pm-3am Mon-Sat; 🚌Via Prenestina)
The chicest bar in Pigneto, tiny Co.So is hipster to the hilt. Think Carbonara Sour cocktails (with pork-fat-infused vodka), bubblewrap coasters, and popcorn and M&M bar snacks.

Necci dal 1924 (📞06 9760 1552; www.necci1924.com; Via Fanfulla da Lodi 68; ⏰8am-2am; 🛜; 🚌Via Prenestina) An all-round hybrid, iconic Necci opened as a gelateria in 1924. These days, it caters to a buoyant hipster crowd with its laid-back vibe, retro interior and food served all day.

Cargo (Map p311; 📞349 740 4620; www.cargopigneto.com; Via del Pigneto 20; ⏰5pm-2am; 🛜; 🚌Circonvallazione Casilina, 🚌Via Prenestina) Year-round the steely black street terrace of Cargo is the hottest spot to lounge on Pigneto's main pedestrian drag. The bar rocks during its sacrosanct, aperitivo-fuelled 'happy hour' (actually from 5.30pm to 9.30pm).

Yeah! Pigneto (📞06 6480 1456; www.yeahpigneto.com; Via Giovanni de Agostini 41; ⏰7.30pm-2am; 🚌Via Casilina) We say 'si!' to Yeah! Pigneto, a relaxed boho-feeling bar with a mismatched vintage look, DJs playing jazz and the walls covered in collages and classic album covers.

Vini e Olii (Map p311; Via del Pigneto 18; ⏰11am-2pm & 6pm-midnight Mon-Sat; 🚌Circonvallazione Casilina) If you want authenticity, this traditional 'wine and oil' shop is the place, with its cheap beer and wine and menu of antipasti and porchetta.

Il Tiaso (Map p311; 📞06 4547 4625; www.iltiaso.com; Via Ascoli Piceno 25; ⏰6pm-2am; 🛜; 🚌Circonvallazione Casilina) Think living room with zebra-print chairs, walls of indie art, and the odd neighbourhood dog. Expect well-priced wine, an intimate chilled vibe, regular live music and lovely pavement terrace.

Birra Più (📞06 7061 3106; www.birrapiu.it; Via del Pigneto 105; ⏰5pm-1am Mon-Thu, to 2am Fri & Sat, 6pm-1am Sun; 🚌Circonvallazione Casilina) A small, relaxed bar, with a laid-back crowd draped over blonde-wood bar stools and tables, and a wide variety of craft beers (around €5), with names such as 'brown sugar' and 'parrot invasion'.

ZEST BAR
BAR

Map p312 (Radisson Blu es. Hotel; 📞06 4448 4384; Via Filippo Turati 171; ⏰9am-1am; 🛜; Ⓜ Vittorio Emanuele) In need of a cocktail in the Termini district? Pop up to the 7th-floor bar at the slinkily designed **Radisson Blu es. hotel**. Chairs are by Jasper Morrison, views are through plate-glass, and there's a sexy outdoor rooftop pool to gaze at, open May to September.

TRIMANI
WINE BAR

Map p312 (📞06 446 96 30; www.trimani.com; Via Cernaia 37b; meals €45; ⏰11.30am-3pm & 5.30pm-12.30am Mon-Sat; Ⓜ Termini) Part of the Trimani family's wine empire (their vast shop around the corner on Via Goito stocks 4000-odd international labels), this is an unpretentious yet highly professional *enoteca*, with knowledgeable, multilingual staff. It's Rome's biggest wine bar and has a vast selection of Italian regional wines as well as an ever-changing food menu including local salami, cheese, oysters and the like.

San Lorenzo & Beyond

★IL SORÌ
WINE BAR

Map p311 (📞393 4318661; www.ilsori.it; Via dei Volsci 51; ⏰7.30pm-2am Mon-Sat; 🚌Via Tiburtina) Every last salami slice and chunk of cheese has been carefully selected from Italy's finest artisanal and small producers at this gourmet wine bar and *bottega* (shop), an unexpected pearl of a stop for dedicated foodies in student-driven San Lorenzo. Interesting and unusual wine tastings, theme nights, 'meet the producer' soirées and other events cap off what is already a memorable drinking (and dining) experience.

VICIOUS CLUB
CLUB

Map p311 (📞345 845 65 91; www.viciousclub.com; Via Achille Grandi 7a; ⏰10pm-late Mon-Sat; 🚌Piazza di Porta Maggiore) This hugely trendy, gay-friendly club and cocktail bar near Termini station is the hottest kid on the block (not to

MONTI, ESQUILINO & SAN LORENZO DRINKING & NIGHTLIFE

mention a little wild around the edges) on Rome's fairly conservative clubbing scene. Expect an underground vibe, unfamiliar to Romans, with its dark-black interior covered almost entirely in mirrors, sultry twinset of DJ booths and smoking room.

STREAT SAN LORENZO
LOUNGE, BAR

Map p311 (☑06 6401 3486; www.facebook.com/streatSL; Piazza dei Campani 6-8; ⊘11am-2am; ⏹; ◙Via dei Reti) The sort of place where you can really kick back and relax, this lounge bar is an enticing all-rounder for meals, late-night cocktails or afternoon lounging over drinks. Vintage curiosities – an old Polaroid camera, printing blocks, copper teapots – add visual interest and mixed-bag seating covers everything from bar stools and beanbags to saggy leather sofa.

BAR CELESTINO
BAR

Map p311 (☑06 4547 2483; Via degli Ausoni 62; ⊘7.30am-2am; ◙Via Tiburtina) Few places evoke the San Lorenzo student vibe quite like this grungy, shabby drinking den near Piazza dei Sanniti. A die-hard icon of this working-class neighbourhood, Celestino first opened its doors in 1904 and is still going strong thanks to its simple, unpretentious vibe. Grab a seat on the pavement terrace or head inside.

GENTE DI SAN LORENZO
BAR

Map p311 (☑06 445 44 25; Via degli Aurunci 42; ⊘7am-2am; ⏹; ◙Via dei Reti) San Lorenzo's signature neighbourhood bar is a chilled place to hang with students over a drink, snack or meal. The interior is airy, with warm wooden floors, brick arches and a couple of sofas, but the real action happens outside on the pavement terrace where there are prime people-watching views of Piazza dell'Immacolata and its throngs of students lazing beneath orange trees on balmy nights.

LOCANDA ATLANTIDE
CLUB

Map p311 (☑06 9604 5875; www.facebook.com/locanda.atlantide; Via dei Lucani 22b; cover varies; ⊘9.30pm-late Oct-Jun; ◙Scalo San Lorenzo) Come and tickle Rome's grungy underbelly. Descend through a door in a graffiti-covered wall into this cavernous basement dive, packed to the rafters with studenty, alternative crowds and featuring everything from prog-folk to techno and psychedelic trance. It's good to know that punk is not dead.

☆ ENTERTAINMENT

NUOVO CINEMA PALAZZO
ARTS CENTER

Map p311 (www.nuovocinemapalazzo.it; Piazza dei Sanniti 9a; ⊘hours vary; ◙Via Tiburtina) Students, artists and activists are breathing new life into San Lorenzo's former Palace Cinema with a bevy of exciting creative happenings: think film screenings, theatre performances, DJ sets, concerts, live music, break dance classes and a host of other artsy events. In warm weather, the action spills outside onto the street terrace, overlooked by a B&W stencil mural by Rome street artists Sten & Lex.

TEATRO DELL'OPERA DI ROMA
OPERA, BALLET

Map p312 (☑06 48 16 01; www.operaroma.it; Piazza Beniamino Gigli 1; ⊘box office 10am-6pm Mon-Sat, 9am-1.30pm Sun; MRepubblica) Rome's premier opera house boasts a plush gilt interior, a Fascist 1920s exterior and an impressive history: it premiered Puccini's *Tosca*, and Maria Callas once sang here. Opera and ballet performances are staged between September and June.

WISHLIST
LIVE MUSIC

Map p311 (☑349 749 4659; www.facebook.com/wishlistclub; Via dei Volsci 126b; €5; ⊘Wed, Fri & Sat; ◙Via Tiburtina, ◙Via dei Reti) A black door marks the entrance to this eternally popular music club, in a low-lying building on one of San Lorenzo's grungiest streets. Gigs cover all sounds, kicking off at 9.30pm or 10pm.

BLACKMARKET
LIVE MUSIC

Map p312 (www.blackmarketartgallery.it/monti; Via Panisperna 101; ⊘7.30pm-2am; MCavour) A bit outside the main Monti hub, this charming, living-room-style bar filled with eclectic vintage furniture is a small but rambling place, great for sitting back on mismatched armchairs and having a leisurely, convivial drink. It hosts regular acoustic indie and folk gigs, which feel a bit like having a band in your living room.

CHARITY CAFÉ
LIVE MUSIC

Map p312 (☑06 4782 5881; www.charitycafe.it; Via Panisperna 68; ⊘7pm-2am Tue-Sun; MCavour) Think narrow space, spindly tables, dim lighting and laid-back vibe: this is a place to snuggle down and listen to some slinky live jazz and blues. Civilised, relaxed, untouristy and very Monti. Gigs usually take place from 10pm, with live music and *aperitivo*.

TEATRO AMBRA JOVINELLI
THEATRE

Map p311 (⏩06 8308 2884; www.ambrajovinelli. org; Via G Pepe 43-47; Ⓜ Vittorio Emanuele) A home away from home for many famous Italian comics, the Ambra Jovinelli is a historic venue for alternative comedians and satirists. Its program is still geared towards comedians today, although it also stages the odd drama, musical and contemporary work.

 SHOPPING

TINA SONDERGAARD
FASHION & ACCESSORIES

Map p312 (⏩334 385 07 99; Via del Boschetto 1d; ⏰3-7.30pm Mon, 10.30am-1pm & 1.30-7.30pm Tue-Sat, closed Aug; Ⓜ Cavour) Sublimely cut and whimsically retro-esque, Tina Sondergaard's handmade threads for women are a hit with fashion cognoscenti, including Italian rock star Carmen Consoli and the city's theatre and TV crowd. You can have adjustments made (included in the price); dresses cost around €150.

FELTRINELLI INTERNATIONAL
BOOKS

Map p312 (⏩06 482 78 78; www.lafeltrinelli.it; Via VE Orlando 84-86; ⏰9am-8pm Mon-Sat, 10.30am-1.30pm & 4-8pm Sun; Ⓜ Repubblica) The international branch of Italy's ubiquitous bookseller has a splendid collection of books in English, Italian, Spanish, French, German and Portuguese. You'll find everything from recent bestsellers to dictionaries, travel guides, DVDs and an excellent assortment of maps.

ROMA LIUTERIA DI MATHIAS MENANTEAU
MUSICAL INSTRUMENTS

Map p312 (⏩339 351 7677; www.romaliuteria.it; Via di Santa Maria Maggiore 150; ⏰10am-1pm & 3-7pm Mon-Sat; Ⓜ Cavour) A vintage ceramic-tiled wood burner casts a golden glow on this old-fashioned artisan workshop where French luthier Mathias Menanteau crafts and restores cellos and violins by hand.

TRANSMISSION
MUSIC

Map p311 (⏩06 4470 4370; www.transmissionroma.com; Via Salentini 27; ⏰10am-2pm & 3-6pm Mon-Sat; 🚋 Via Tiburtina) One of a handful of shops serving Rome's record collectors, this San Lorenzo store is vinyl nirvana. Its eclectic collection of LPs, CDs, 7-inch singles, DVDs and Blu-rays covers the whole musical gamut, ranging from classical music and 1950s oldies to jazz, reggae, punk, new wave and modern dance.

MERCATO MONTI URBAN MARKET
MARKET

Map p312 (www.mercatomonti.com; Via Leonina 46; ⏰10am-8pm Fri-Sun Sep-Jun; Ⓜ Cavour) Vintage clothes, accessories, one-off pieces by local designers: this market in the hip 'hood of Monti is well worth a rummage.

PODERE VECCIANO
FOOD

Map p312 (⏩06 4891 3812; www.poderevecciano.com; Via dei Serpenti 33; ⏰10am-8pm; Ⓜ Cavour) Selling produce from its Tuscan farm, this shop is a great place to pick up presents, such as different varieties of pesto, honey and marmalade, selected wines, olive-oil-based cosmetics and beautiful olive wood chopping boards. There's even an olive tree growing in the middle of the shop.

ABITO
FASHION & ACCESSORIES

Map p312 (⏩06 488 10 17; www.legallinelle.it; Via Panisperna 61; ⏰11am-8pm Mon-Sat, 3-8pm Sun; Ⓜ Cavour) Wilma Silvestre, founder of local label Le Gallinelle, designs elegant clothes with a difference. Here at her Monti boutique you can browse her chic, laid-back styles and buy off the rack.

PERLEI
JEWELLERY

Map p312 (⏩06 4891 3862; Via del Boschetto 35; ⏰10am-8pm Mon-Thu, to 9pm Fri & Sat, 11am-2pm & 3-8pm Sun; Ⓜ Cavour) Contemporary women's jewellery created by Noritamy, a collaboration between Tammar Edelman and Elinor Avni, is showcased in this tiny artisan boutique. Think bright polished stones, organic shapes and architectural structures.

NUOVO MERCATO ESQUILINO
MARKET

Map p311 (Via Filippo Turati 160; ⏰5am-3pm Mon-Thu, to 5pm Fri & Sat; Ⓜ Vittorio Emanuele) Lap up the real Rome at this buzzing covered food market where budget-conscious Romans and students shop for fresh fruit, veg, exotic herbs, spices and more.

LA BOTTEGA DEL CIOCCOLATO
FOOD

Map p312 (⏩06 482 14 73; www.labottegadelcioccolato.it; Via Leonina 82; ⏰9.30am-7.30pm; Ⓜ Cavour) Run by the younger generation of a long line of *chocolatiers,* this is an exotic world of scarlet walls and old-fashioned glass cabinets set into black wood, with irresistible smells wafting in from the kitchen and rows of lovingly homemade chocolates on display.

Trastevere & Gianicolo

EAST OF VIALE DI TRASTEVERE | WEST OF VIALE DI TRASTEVERE | GIANICOLO

Neighbourhood Top Five

❶ Basilica di Santa Maria in Trastevere (p154) Admiring the exquisite interior and exterior mosaics of this beautiful church.

❷ Trattoria dining (p158) Feasting on the perfect Roman carbonara or *pasta cacio e pepe* at traditional trattorias hidden away on tiny cobbled piazzas – try Da Enzo.

❸ Villa Farnesina (p155) Savouring the breathtaking interior decor by Raphael inside Trastevere's elegant Renaissance villa.

❹ Cocktails (p161) Sampling a Carbonara Sour, knocking back shots served in chocolate cups or hobnobbing with local hipsters in a secret speakeasy in Trastevere, starting at fashionable Freni e Frizioni.

❺ Gianicolo Hill (p157) Hiking to the top of Rome's second-largest hill for a magnificent panorama of the city.

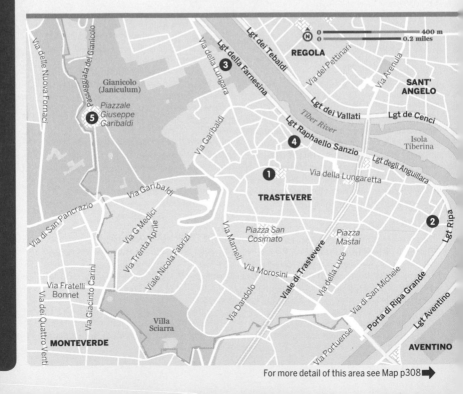

For more detail of this area see Map p308 ➡

Explore: Trastevere & Gianicolo

Cradled in a left-bank curve of the River Tiber, medieval Trastevere is made for walking – or rather aimless, contented wandering punctuated by endless photo stops, lazy coffee breaks in local cafes, and some of Rome's finest home cooking in vintage trattorias. Allow at least a full day to explore: key sights include glittering Basilica di Santa Maria in Trastevere (p154); Villa Farnesina (p155), one of the most breathtaking frescoed mansions you're ever likely to see; and Galleria Corsini (p156) with its dazzling art collection. End your sightseeing foray with a green moment in Trastevere's botanical gardens or, should you be up for the stiff hike, atop Gianicolo Hill (p157) – don't neglect to see Bramante's perfect little Tempietto (p157) on your way up.

Come dusk, bars unveil sumptuous banquets of nibbles for that sacrosanct *aperitivo* (pre-dinner drinks). Many are clustered in the small lanes around Piazza Trilussa; Via Benedetta is the street for international-style pubs (much loved by American students from the nearby John Cabot University).

Local Life

➜**Cafe culture** No cafe terrace is as no-frills or busy as veteran favourite Bar San Calisto (p161), notorious for serving the cheapest beer in Rome.

➜**Home-cooking** Join locals queuing at Antica Caciara Trasteverina (p163) for ingredients to make an authentic Roman carbonara.

➜**Summer nights** Trendy pop-up outdoor bars pepper Trastevere's riverside quays between Ponte Mazzoni and Ponte Cesto in summer, making the river the cool place to be.

➜**Meeting point** Locals always meet up at 'the steps', the wide short flight of steps leading up to the 17th-century fountain on Piazza Trilussa; in summer the steps are packed with people sitting here, drink in hand.

Getting There & Away

➜**Tram** From Largo di Torre Argentina tram 8 runs along the main drag of Viale di Trastevere, ending up at Villa Doria Pamphilj. Tram 3 also stops at the southern end of Viale Trastevere, connecting with Testaccio (Via Marmorata), Colosseo, San Giovanni and Villa Borghese.

➜**Bus** From Termini, bus H runs to Viale di Trastevere, while the 780 runs from Piazza Venezia. For Gianicolo, if you don't fancy the steep steps from Via G Mameli, take bus 870 from Piazza delle Rovere.

Lonely Planet's Top Tip

With its century-old biscuit shops and bakeries, family-run trattorias, open-air food market and tiny grocery stores packed to the hilt with carefully sourced, zero-kilometre farm produce, Trastevere is naturally a gourmet destination – its gourmandise is a major attraction in itself. To get the most out of it, consider a guided food tour with locals-in-the-know: **Casa Mia** (p159) or **GT Food & Travel** (p159).

TRASTEVERE & GIANICOLO

✕ Best Places to Eat

➜ Da Enzo (p158)
➜ Da Augusto (p159)
➜ La Prosciutteria (p159)
➜ Panattoni (p158)
➜ Litro (p160)

For reviews, see p158.

🍷 Best Places to Drink

➜ Freni e Frizioni (p161)
➜ Bar San Calisto (p161)
➜ Rivendita Libri, Cioccolata e Vino (p161)
➜ Keyhole (p161)
➜ Pimm's Good (p161)

For reviews, see p161.

◉ Best Works of Art

➜ Basilica di Santa Maria in Trastevere (p154)
➜ Basilica di Santa Cecilia in Trastevere (p156)
➜ Villa Farnesina (p155)
➜ Galleria Corsini (p156)

For reviews, see p156.

TOP SIGHT
BASILICA DI SANTA MARIA IN TRASTEVERE

This glittering church is said to be the oldest church in Rome dedicated to the Virgin Mary. Its facade is decorated with a beautiful medieval mosaic depicting Mary feeding Jesus surrounded by 10 women bearing lamps. Two are veiled and hold extinguished lamps, symbolising widowhood, while the lit lamps of the others represent their virginity.

The church was first constructed in the early 3rd century over the spot where, according to legend, a fountain of oil miraculously sprang from the ground. Its current Romanesque form is the result of a 12th-century revamp. The portico was added by Carlo Fontana in 1702, with its balustrade decorated with statues of four popes.

Inside, it's the golden 12th-century mosaics that stand out. In the apse, look out for the dazzling depiction of Christ and his mother flanked by various saints and, on the far left, Pope Innocent II holding a model of the church. Beneath this is a series of six mosaics by Pietro Cavallini (c 1291) illustrating the life of the Virgin.

Note the 21 Roman columns, some plundered from the Terme di Caracalla; the wooden ceiling designed in 1617 by Domenichino; and, on the right of the altar, a spiralling Cosmati candlestick, on the exact spot where the oil fountain is said to have sprung. The Cappella Avila is also worth a look for its stunning 17th-century dome. The spiralling Cosmatesque floor was relaid in the 1870s, a re-creation of the 13th-century original.

DON'T MISS

➡ Facade mosaics

➡ 13th-century Cavallini mosaics in the apse

➡ Ancient Roman granite columns

PRACTICALITIES

➡ Map p298

➡ 📞06 581 4802

➡ Piazza Santa Maria in Trastevere

➡ ⏱7.30am-9pm Sep-Jul, 8am-noon & 4-9pm Aug

➡ 🚌Viale di Trastevere, 🚊Viale di Trastevere

TOP SIGHT
VILLA FARNESINA

This 16th-century villa is serenely and symmetrically proportioned on the outside and fantastically frescoed from top to bottom on the inside.

Villa Farnesina was built for Agostino Chigi, the immensely wealthy papal banker. At his banquets he'd encourage his guests to throw their solid gold plates out of the window once they'd finished (servants would stand beneath the windows to catch them in nets). The house was bought by Cardinal Alessando Farnese in 1577.

The architect was Baldassare Peruzzi, formerly Bramante's assistant; he also painted several of the frescoes. On the ground floor is the **Loggia of Galatea**, attributed to Raphael and depicting a sea nymph, with the vault frescoed by Peruzzi, and mythological scenes by Sebastiano del Piombio. Next door, the **Loggia of Cupid and Psyche** was also frescoed by Raphael and seethes with naked figures and muscular cupids.

On the 1st floor, Peruzzi's frescoes in the **Salone delle Prospettive** are a superb illusionary perspective of a panorama of 16th-century Rome, while Chigi's bedchamber is filled with cavorting cherubs, gods and goddesses.

DON'T MISS...

➡ Frescoes by Sebastiano del Piombo
➡ Raphael-attributed loggia decoration
➡ Peruzzi's panoramas in the Salone delle Prospettive

PRACTICALITIES

➡ Map p308, D1
➡ ☎06 6802 7268
➡ www.villafarnesina.it
➡ Via della Lungara 230
➡ adult/reduced €6/5, guided tour €4
➡ ⊘9am-2pm Mon-Sat, to 5pm 2nd Sun of the month
➡ ⛱Lungotevere della Farnesina

◉ SIGHTS

Trastevere tucks away a peppering of exquisite churches and Renaissance *palazzi* (mansions) amid its picturesque narrow lanes. North of Trastevere rise the hilly slopes of Gianicolo. It's difficult to imagine that in 1849 the Gianicolo, today a tranquil and leafy area, was the scene of fierce and bloody fighting against French troops sent to restore papal rule.

◉ East of Viale di Trastevere

★BASILICA DI SANTA CECILIA IN TRASTEVERE
BASILICA

Map p308 (☑06 589 9289; www.benedettine santacecilia.it; Piazza di Santa Cecilia; fresco & crypt each €2.50; ⊙basilica & crypt 10am-1pm & 4-7pm, fresco 10am-12.30pm Mon-Sat; ☐Viale di Trastevere, ☐Viale di Trastevere) The last resting place of the patron saint of music features Pietro Cavallini's stunning 13th-century fresco, in the nuns' choir of the hushed convent adjoining the church. Inside the church itself, Stefano Maderno's mysterious sculpture depicts St Cecilia's miraculously preserved body, unearthed in the Catacombs of San Callisto in 1599. You can also visit the excavations of Roman houses, one of which was possibly that of Cecilia.

CHIESA DI SAN FRANCESCO D'ASSISI A RIPA GRANDE
CHURCH

Map p308 (☑06 581 9020; www.sanfrancesco aripa.com/la-chiesa; Piazza di San Francesco d'Assisi 88; ⊙7am-1pm & 3-7pm; ☐Viale di Trastevere, ☐Viale di Trastevere) St Francis is said to have stayed here in 1219, and in his cell you can still see the rock that he purportedly used as a pillow and his crucifix. Rebuilt several times, the church's current incarnation dates from the 1680s. It contains one of Bernini's most daring works, the *Beata Ludovica Albertoni* (Blessed Ludovica Albertoni; 1674), a work of highly charged sexual ambiguity.

◉ West of Viale di Trastevere

BASILICA DI SANTA MARIA IN TRASTEVERE
BASILICA

See p154.

★GALLERIA CORSINI
GALLERY

Map p308 (Palazzo Corsini; ☑06 6880 2323; www.barberinicorsini.org; Via della Lungara 10; adult/reduced €5/2.50, incl Palazzo Barberini €10/5; ⊙8.30am-7.30pm Wed-Mon; ☐Lungotevere della Farnesina) Once home to Queen Christina of Sweden, whose richly frescoed bedroom witnessed a steady stream of male and female lovers, the 16th-century Palazzo Corsini was designed by Ferdinando Fuga in grand Versailles style, and houses part of Italy's national art collection. Highlights include Caravaggio's mesmerising *San Giovanni Battista* (St John the Baptist), Guido Reni's unnerving *Salome con la Testa di San Giovanni Battista* (Salome with the Head of John the Baptist), and Fra Angelico's Corsini Triptych, plus works by Rubens, Poussin and Van Dyck.

TRIUMPHS & LAMENTS
PUBLIC ART

Map p308 (Lungotevere della Farnesina; ☐Lungotevere dei Tebaldi) A bold new addition to

---

STUMBLING STONES

Watch your footing when meandering Trastevere's impossibly quaint, old-world lanes and alleys. Among the uneven, well-worn square-shaped cobblestones (dangerously slippy in rain), you will occasionally stumble across a *pietri d'inciampo* (literally 'stumbling stone' in Italian) glinting in the sunlight. Each one of these polished brass stones, shaped square like a Roman cobble and engraved with the name of a local Jewish resident, marks the exact spot where the Holocaust victim was rounded up by Nazi soldiers during WWII and deported to Auschwitz or other death camp. Most stumbling blocks are embedded in pavements in front of private homes and invariably count more than one – a stone for each member of entire Jewish families deported.

The stumbling stones are part of a Europe-wide memorial project initiated by German artist Gunter Demning. Some 200 pave the historic streets of Rome to date, predominantly in Trastevere and the old Jewish Ghetto directly across the river.

Rome's cityscape, this vast frieze adorns the River Tiber walls between Ponte Sisto and Ponte Mazzini. The creation of South African artist William Kentridge, it stretches for 550m and comprises more than 80 figures, some up to 12m high, illustrating episodes from Rome's history. Look for depictions of Roman emperor Marcus Aurelius, Mussolini, and actor Marcello Mastroianni who's shown kissing Anita Ekberg in a re-creation of the famous Trevi Fountain scene from *La Dolce Vita*.

PIAZZA DI SANTA MARIA IN TRASTEVERE PIAZZA

Map p308 (◻Viale di Trastevere, ◻Viale di Trastevere) Trastevere's focal square is a prime people-watching spot. By day it's full of parents with strollers, chatting locals and guidebook-toting tourists; by night it's the domain of foreign students, young Romans and out-of-towners, all out for a good time in its many cafes and bars. The fountain piercing the centre of the square, of Roman origin, was restored by Carlo Fontana in 1692. The beautiful Romanesque facade of Basilica di Santa Maria in Trastevere (p154), currently under wraps as painstaking restoration takes place, lords over all this.

◉ Gianicolo

GIANICOLO HILL HILL

Map p308 (Janiculum) The verdant hill of Gianicolo is dotted by monuments to Garibaldi and his makeshift army, who fought pope-backing French troops in one of the fiercest battles in the struggle for Italian unification on this spot in 1849. The Italian hero is commemorated with a massive **monument** (Map p308; Piazzale Giuseppe Garibaldi; ◻Passeggiata del Gianicolo) in Piazzale Giuseppe Garibaldi, while his Brazilian-born wife, Anita, has her own **equestrian monument** (Map p308; Piazzale Anita Garibaldi; ◻Passeggiata del Gianicolo) about 200m away in Piazzale Anita Garibaldi; she died from malaria, together with their unborn child, shortly after the siege.

Rome's highest hill is a superb viewpoint with sweeping panoramas over Rome's rooftops, and has several summer-only bars that are blessed with thrilling views. There are also weekend children's puppet shows on the hill, a long-standing tradition.

ORTO BOTANICO GARDENS

Map p308 (Botanical Garden; ☎06 4991 7107; Largo Cristina di Svezia 24; adult/reduced €8/4; ⊙9am-6.30pm Mon-Sat Apr-Oct, to 5.30pm Nov-Mar; ◻Lungotevere della Farnesina, Piazza Trilussa) Formerly the private grounds of Palazzo Corsini, Rome's 12-hectare botanical gardens are a little-known, slightly neglected gem and a great place to unwind in a tree-shaded expanse covering the steep slopes of the Gianicolo. Plants have been cultivated here since the 13th century and the current gardens were established in 1883, when the grounds of Palazzo Corsini were given to the University of Rome. They now contain up to 8000 species, including some of Europe's rarest plants.

TEMPIETTO DI BRAMANTE & CHIESA DI SAN PIETRO IN MONTORIO CHURCH

Map p308 (☎06 581 3940; www.sanpietroinmontorio.it; Piazza San Pietro in Montorio 2; ⊙chiesa 8.30am-noon & 3-4pm Mon-Fri, tempietto 10am-6pm Tue-Sun; ◻Via Garibaldi) Considered the first great building of the High Renaissance, Bramante's sublime Tempietto (Little Temple; 1508) is a perfect surprise, squeezed into the courtyard of the Chiesa di San Pietro in Montorio, on the spot where St Peter is said to have been crucified. It's small, but perfectly formed; its classically inspired design and ideal proportions epitomise the Renaissance zeitgeist.

FONTANA DELL'ACQUA PAOLA FOUNTAIN

Map p308 (Via Garibaldi; ◻Via Garibaldi) Featured in the opening scene of Paolo Sorrentino's Oscar-winning *La grande bellezza* (The Great Beauty), this monumental white fountain was built in 1612 to celebrate the restoration of a 2nd-century aqueduct that supplied (and still supplies) water from Lago di Bracciano, 35km to the north of Rome. Four of the fountain's six pink-stone columns came from the facade of the old St Peter's Basilica, while much of the marble was pillaged from the Roman Forum.

VILLA DORIA PAMPHILJ MONUMENT, PARK

(⊙sunrise-sunset; ◻Via di San Pancrazio) Lorded over by the 17th-century Villa Doria Pamphilj is Rome's largest landscaped park – many a Roman's favourite place to escape the city noise and bustle. Once a vast private estate, it was laid out around 1650 for Prince Camillo Pamphilj, nephew of Pope Innocent X. It's a huge expanse of rolling parkland, shaded by Rome's distinctive umbrella pines. At its centre is the prince's summer residence, Casino del Belrespiro (used for official government functions today), with its manicured gardens and citrus trees.

✖ EATING

Picturesque Trastevere is packed with restaurants, trattorias, cafes and pizzerias. The better places dot the maze of side streets, and it pays to be selective, as many of the restaurants are bog-standard tourist traps.

✖ East of Viale di Trastevere

★ DA ENZO   TRATTORIA €
Map p308 (☏06 581 22 60; www.daenzoal29.com; Via dei Vascellari 29; meals €30; ⊙12.30-3pm & 7-11pm Mon-Sat; ᯼Viale di Trastevere, ᯼Viale di Trastevere) Vintage buttermilk walls, red-checked tablecloths and a traditional menu featuring all the Roman classics: what makes this staunchly traditional trattoria exceptional is its careful sourcing of local, quality products, many from nearby farms in Lazio. The seasonal, deep-fried Jewish artichokes and the *pasta cacio e pepe* (cheese-and-black-pepper pasta) in particular are among the best in Rome.

PANATTONI   PIZZA €
Map p308 (Ai Marmi; ☏06 580 09 19; Viale di Trastevere 53; pizzas €6.50-9; ⊙6.30pm-1am Thu-Tue; ᯼Viale di Trastevere, ᯼Viale di Trastevere) Also called 'ai Marmi' or *l'obitorio* (the morgue) because of its vintage marble-slab tabletops, this is Trastevere's most popular pizzeria. Think super-thin pizzas, a clattering buzz, testy waiters, a street terrace and some fantastic fried starters – the *supplì* (Roman rice ball), *baccalà* (salted cod) and zucchini flowers are all heavenly.

DON   PIZZA €
Map p308 (www.donpizzafritta.com; Via di San Francesco a Ripa 103; pizzas €4-6.50; ⊙noon-3pm & 7pm-midnight Tue-Sun; ᯼Viale di Trastevere, ᯼Viale di Trastevere) A small corner of Naples in Trastevere, Don serves authentic fried pizzas. These golden half-moons of comforting doughiness and melted cheese are delicious and joyfully messy to eat – be

GRATTACHECCA
It's summertime, the living is easy, and Romans like nothing better in the sultry evening heat than to amble down to the river and partake of some *grattachecca* (crushed ice covered in fruit and syrup). It's the ideal way to cool down and there are kiosks along the riverbank satisfying this very Roman need; try **Sora Mirella Caffè** (Map p308; Lungotevere degli Anguillara; grattachecca €3-6; ⊙11am-3am May-Sep; ᯼Lungotevere degli Anguillara), next to Ponte Cestio.

careful not to burn your mouth on the first bite! Pizzas come in two sizes (*sorriso* and *Napoli d'Oro*) and feature fillers such as San Marzano tomatoes, sausage and *mozzarella di bufala*.

LOCANDA DEL GELATO   GELATO €
Map p308 (www.locandadelgelato.it; Via di San Francesco a Ripa 71; tubs & cones €2-4.50; ⊙noon-midnight, shorter hours in winter; ᯼Viale di Trastevere, ᯼Viale di Trastevere) This artisanal gelateria has quickly risen to the top of the ice-cream charts since it opened in April 2016. It serves classic flavours alongside more adventurous creations such as *prosecco* and pear. The house speciality is *gelato al vino* (wine ice cream). Alternatively, there are crêpes and great creamy smoothies.

DA TEO   TRATTORIA €€
Map p308 (☏06 581 83 55; www.trattoriadateo.it; Piazza dei Ponziani 7; meals €30; ⊙12.30-3pm & 7.30-11.30pm Mon-Sat; ᯼Viale di Trastevere, ᯼Viale di Trastevere) One of Rome's classic trattoria, Da Teo buzzes with locals digging into steaming platefuls of Roman standards, such as carbonara, *pasta cacio e pepe* (cheese-and-black-pepper pasta) and the most fabulous seasonal artichokes out – both Jewish (deep-fried) and Roman-style (stuffed with parsley and garlic, and boiled). In keeping with hardcore trattoria tradition, Teo's homemade gnocchi is only served on Thursday. Reservations essential.

ROMA SPARITA   TRATTORIA €€
Map p308 (☏06 580 07 57; www.romasparita.com; Piazza di Santa Cecilia 1; meals €30; ⊙12.30-2.30pm & 7.30-11.30pm Tue-Sat, 12.30-2.30pm Sun, closed last two weeks Aug; ᯼Viale

di Trastevere, ⌂Viale di Trastevere) With its traditional country-style interior – all whitewashed beams, terracotta tiled floor and pretty pastel colour palette – and summertime terrace overlooking one of Trastevere's most peaceful car-free piazzas, Roma Sparita is something of a find. The cuisine is Roman, with house speciality *pasta cacio e pepe* (cheese and black pepper pasta) served in an edible bowl made of crisp, golden Parmesan. Don't hold back.

✕ West of Viale di Trastevere

★LA PROSCIUTTERIA   TUSCAN €

Map p308 (✆06 6456 2839; www.laprosciutteria.com/roma-trastevere; Via della Scala 71; chopping board €5 per person; ⊗11am-11.30pm; ⌂Piazza Trilussa) For a gratifying taste of Tuscany in Rome, consider lunch or a decadent *aperitivo* at this Florentine *prosciutteria* (salami shop). Made-to-measure *taglieri* (wooden chopping boards) come loaded with different cold cuts, cheeses, fruit and veg and are best devoured over a glass of Brunello di Montalcino or simple Chianti Classico. Bread comes in peppermint-green tin saucepans and dozens of hams and salami dangle overhead.

★DA AUGUSTO   TRATTORIA €

Map p308 (✆06 580 37 98; Piazza de' Renzi 15; meals €25; ⊗12.30-3pm & 8-11pm; ⌂Viale di Trastevere, ⌂Viale di Trastevere) Bag one of Augusto's rickety tables outside and tuck into some truly fabulous mamma-style cooking on one of Trastevere's prettiest piazza terraces. Hearty portions of all the Roman classics are dished up here as well as lots of rabbit, veal, hare and *pajata* (calf intestines). Winter dining is around vintage formica tables in a bare-bones interior, unchanged for decades. Be prepared to queue. Cash only.

LE LEVAIN   BAKERY €

Map p308 (✆06 6456 2880; www.lelevainroma.it; Via Luigi Santini 22-23; meals €5.50-10; ⊗8am-8.30pm Tue-Sat, 9am-7.30pm Sun; ⌂Viale di Trastevere, ⌂Viale di Trastevere) Many a foreigner living in Rome swears by this *pâtisserie au beurre fin* for their daily dose of rich and creamy butter, albeit it in the guise of authentic croissants, *pains au chocolat* and other irresistible French pastries. Traditional French cakes – colourful cream-filled macarons, flaky millefeuilles, miniature *tartes aux pommes* (apple tarts) – are equally authentic.

FOOD & WINE TOURS & COURSES

Casa Mia (✆346 800 17 46; www.italyfoodandwinetours.com; 3hr tour with tastings 2/4 people €360/420) Food and wine tours with tastings and behind-the-scene meetings with local shopkeepers, producers, chefs and restaurateurs.

Vino Roma (Map p312; ✆328 487 44 97; www.vinoroma.com; Via in Selci 84g; 2hr tastings per person €50; ⓂCavour) Wine-tasting classes in a state-of-the-art tasting studio.

GT Food & Travel (✆320 720 42 22; www.gtfoodandtravel.com; 3hr tour with tastings per person around €120) Themed food-lover tours, as well as cooking classes and in-home dining experiences.

Eating Italy Food Tours (✆06 9480 4492; www.eatingitalyfoodtours.com; tours €77-94) Informative four-hour tours around Testaccio or Trastevere.

Elizabeth Minchilli (www.elizabethminchilliinrome.com) Small-group food tours, pasta workshops, olive-oil tasting and more with one of Rome's best-known food bloggers.

Città di Gusto (✆06 5511 2211; www.gamberorosso.it; Via Ottavio Gasparri 13-17; ⌂Viale dei Colli Portuensi) Demonstrations, workshops, lessons and courses in the headquarters of Italian food organisation Gambero Rosso.

Latteria Studio (✆835 29 990; https://latteriastudio.com; Via di Ponziano 29; ⌂Viale di Trastevere, ⌂Viale di Trastevere) Highly personalised market tours and cooking classes in a stylish food-photography studio in backstreet Trastevere.

FIOR DI LUNA
GELATERIA €

Map p308 (☑06 6456 1314; http://fiordiluna. com; Via della Lungaretta 96; gelato from €1.70; ☉11.30am-11.30pm Easter-Oct, to 9pm Tue-Sun Nov-Easter; ☐Viale di Trastevere, ☐Viale di Trastevere) For many Romans this busy little hub makes the best handmade gelato and sorbet in the world. Produced in small batches using natural, seasonal ingredients – a few flavours are even made from donkeys' milk. Favourites include walnut and honey, blueberry yoghurt, kiwi (complete with seeds) and pistachio (the nuts are ground by hand).

FORNO LA RENELLA
BAKERY €

Map p308 (☑06 581 72 65; www.panificiola renella.com; Via del Moro 15-16; pizza slices from €2.50; ☉7am-2am Tue-Sat, to 10pm Sun & Mon; ☐Piazza Trilussa) Watch urban pizza masters at work behind glass at this historic Trastevere bakery, a fantastic space to hang out in with its wood-fired ovens, bar-stool seating and heavenly aromas of pizza (€9 to €18 per kilo), bread and biscuits baking throughout the day. Piled-high toppings (and fillings) vary seasonally, to the joy of everyone from punks with big dogs to old ladies with little dogs. It's been in the biz since 1870.

RUMI BOTTEGA ORGANICA
DELI €

Map p308 (☑06 581 49 88; http://rumibottega organica.tumblr.com; Via di San Francesco a Ripa 133; meals €10; ☉10am-9.30pm Mon-Sat; ☐Viale di Trastevere, ☐Viale di Trastevere) There is a real charm to this down-to-earth, rustic *bottega organica* (organic grocery store) in Trastevere where a knowing crowd lingers over zero-kilometre veggie burgers doused in artisanal pesto, sassy farro- and pulse-packed salads, and sandwiches made from organic naturally leavened bread. Craft beer and organic wine are natural companions, and the picnic-handy deli doubles as fruit, veg and grocer shop, too.

DA OLINDO
TRATTORIA €

Map p308 (☑06 581 88 35; Vicolo della Scala 8; meals €25; ☉noon-2.30pm & 7.30-11pm Mon-Sat; ☐Piazza Trilussa) This is your classic family affair – the menu is short, the cuisine is robust, the portions are huge, and the atmosphere is lively. Expect *baccalà con patate* (salted cod stewed with potatoes) on Friday and *trippa* (tripe) on Saturday, but other dishes – such as *coniglio all cacciatore* (rabbit, hunter-style) or *polpette al sugo* (meatballs in sauce) – whichever day you like.

MERCATO DI PIAZZA SAN COSIMATO
MARKET

Map p308 (Piazza San Cosimato; ☉7am-2pm Mon-Sat; ☐Viale di Trastevere, ☐Viale di Trastevere) Trastevere's neighbourhood open-air market is a top spot to stock up on globe and violet artichokes, *Romanesco broccoli* (Roman cauliflower), dandelion greens and other seasonal foodstuffs, as has been the case for at least a century. Bring your own bag or basket.

LITRO
ITALIAN €€

Map p308 (☑06 4544 7639; http://vinerialitro. it; Via Fratelli Bonnet 5, Monteverde; meals €25; ☉12.30pm-3.30am & 5.30-midnight Mon-Fri, 12.30pm-12.30am Sat; ☎; ☐Via Fratelli Bonnet) Crunchy brown bread comes in a paper bag and the 1950s clocks on the wall – all three dozen them – say a different time at this understated vintage-styled bistro-bar in wonderfully off-the-beaten-tourist-track Monteverde. The creative Roman kitchen is predominantly organic, with ingredients sourced from small local producers, and the choice of natural and biodynamic wines is among the best in Rome.

PARIS IN TRASTEVERE
RISTORANTE €€€

Map p308 (di Dario Cappellani; ☑06 581 53 78; www.ristoranteparis.it; Piazza San Calisto 7a; meals €45-55; ☉12.30-3pm & 7.30-11pm Tue-Sun; ☐Viale di Trastevere, ☐Viale di Trastevere) An old-school restaurant set in a 17th-century building with outdoor tables on a buzzing piazza, Paris – named for its founder, not the French capital – is the best place outside the Ghetto to sample Roman-Jewish cuisine. Signature dishes include *gran fritto vegetale con baccalà* (deep-fried vegetables with salted cod) and *carciofi alla giudia* (fried artichoke).

GLASS HOSTARIA
ITALIAN €€€

Map p308 (☑06 5833 5903; www.glass-restaur ant.it; Vicolo del Cinque 58; menus €85-140, meals €90; ☉7.30-11.30pm Tue-Sun; ☐Piazza Trilussa) Trastevere's foremost foodie address, Michelin-starred Glass cooks up innovative cuisine in a contemporary, sophisticated space with mezzanine. Female law graduate-turned-chef Cristina Bowerman creates inventive, delicate dishes that combine seasonal ingredients with traditional elements to delight and surprise the palate – best experienced with her tasting menu. There's also a vegetarian menu, too.

🍷 DRINKING & NIGHTLIFE
⚓

Trastevere is one of the city's most popular areas to wander, drink and decide what to do afterwards.

🍷 East of Viale di Trastevere

HÝBRIS
BAR

Map p308 (📞06 9437 6374; www.hybrisartgallery. com; Via della Lungaretta 164; 🚇; 🚊Viale di Trastevere, 🚊Viale di Trastevere) This modish cafe-bar on pedestrian, shop-strewn Via della Lungaretta is an artsy spot for early-evening drinks between marble busts and art works. Vintage typewriters, a piano and armchairs add a generous dose of trendy old-world ambience, and the marble balustrade bar gets top marks for design. Live jazz and blues, DJ sets and art exhibitions too.

TERRA SATIS
CAFE, WINE BAR

Map p308 (📞06 9893 6909; Piazza di Ponziani 1a; ⏰7am-1am Mon-Thu, to 2am Fri & Sat; 🚇; 🚊Viale di Trastevere, 🚊Viale di Trastevere) This hip neighbourhood cafe and wine bar in Trastevere has it all: newspapers, great coffee and charming bar staff, not to mention vintage furniture, a fantastic peppermint-green 1950s dresser, and comfy banquette seating with polka-dot and striped cushions. On warm days the laid-back action spills out onto its bijou terrace on cobbled Piazza di Ponziani.

🍷 West of Viale di Trastevere

★RIVENDITA LIBRI, CIOCCOLATA E VINO
COCKTAIL BAR

Map p308 (📞06 5830 1868; www.facebook.com/cioccolateriatrastevere; Vicolo del Cinque 11a; shot €3-5; ⏰7pm-2am Mon-Fri, 2pm-2am Sat & Sun; 🚊Piazza Trilussa) There is no finer – or funnier – spot in the whole of Rome for a swift French Kiss, Orgasm or One Night Stand than this highly inventive cocktail bar, packed every night from around 10pm with a fun-loving, post-dinner crowd. Cocktails are served in miniature chocolate cups, filled with various types of alcohol and topped with whipped cream.

★KEYHOLE
COCKTAIL BAR

Map p308 (Via Arco di San Calisto 17; ⏰10pm-2am; 🚊Viale di Trastevere, 🚊Viale di Trastevere) The latest in a growing trend of achingly hip, underground speakeasies in Rome, Keyhole ticks all the boxes: no identifiable name or signage outside the bar; a black door smothered in keys; and Prohibition-era decor including leather Chesterfield sofas, dim lighting and an electric craft cocktail menu. Not sure what to order? Ask the talented mixologists to create your own bespoke cocktail (around €10).

★PIMM'S GOOD
BAR

Map p308 (📞06 9727 7979; www.facebook.com/pimmsgood; Via di Santa Dorotea 8; ⏰10am-2am; 🚇; 🚊Piazza Trilussa) 'Anyone for Pimm's?' is the catchline of this eternally popular bar with part red-brick ceiling that does indeed serve Pimm's – the classic way or in a variety of cocktails (€10). The party-loving guys behind the bar are serious mixologists and well-crafted cocktails is their thing. Look for the buzzing street-corner pavement terrace – lit up in winter with flaming outdoor heaters.

★FRENI E FRIZIONI
BAR

Map p308 (📞06 4549 7499; www.freniefrizioni. com; Via del Politeama 4-6; ⏰7pm-2am; 🚊Piazza Trilussa) This perennially cool Trastevere bar is housed in an old mechanic's workshop – hence its name ('brakes and clutches') and tatty facade. It draws a young *spritz*-loving crowd that swells onto the small piazza outside to sip superbly mixed cocktails (€10) and seasonal punches, and fill up on its lavish early-evening *aperitivo* buffet (7pm to 10pm). Table reservations are essential on Friday and Saturday evenings.

★BAR SAN CALISTO
CAFE

Map p308 (Piazza San Calisto 3-5; ⏰6am-2am Mon-Sat; 🚊Viale di Trastevere, 🚊Viale di Trastevere) Those in the know head to 'Sanca' for its basic, stuck-in-time atmosphere and cheap prices (beer from €1.50). It attracts everyone from intellectuals to keeping-it-real Romans, alcoholics and foreign students. It's famous for its chocolate – come for hot chocolate with cream in winter, and chocolate gelato in summer. Try the *sambuca con la mosca* ('with flies' – raw coffee beans). Expect occasional late-night jam sessions.

BIR & FUD
CRAFT BEER

Map p308 (📞06 589 40 16; www.birandfud.it; Via Benedetta 23; ⏰noon-2am; 🚋Piazza Trilussa) On a narrow street lined with raucous drinking holes, this brick-vaulted bar-pizzeria wins plaudits for its outstanding collection of craft *bir* (beer), many on tap, and equally tasty *fud* (food) for when late-night munchies strike. Its Neapolitan-style wood-fired pizzas are particularly excellent.

CAFFÈ LUNGARA 1940
CAFE

Map p308 (📞06 687 56 26; www.facebook.com/lungara1940; Via della Lungara 14; ⏰6.30am-10pm Mon-Fri, 7am-10pm Sat, 7am-3pm Sun; 🛜; 🚋Piazza Triussa) Run with much pride, passion and creativity by the Nardecchia family for 70-odd years, Caffè Lungara is an address every Roman loves, from students to arts-loving elderly couples. Pop in before or after visiting the neighbouring botanical gardens, Galleria Corsini or Villa Farnesina for a cappuccino, Aperol *spritz* sundowner or full meal in a sharp, contemporary interior.

MECCANISMO
BAR

Map p308 (📞06 581 61 11; www.meccanismoroma.com; Piazza Trilussa 34; ⏰7.30am-2am Mon-Sat, to midnight Sun; 🛜; 🚋Piazza Trilussa) This welcoming all-rounder is an easy spot in tourist-busy Trastevere to lounge in comfort (grab an armchair if you can) over breakfast, lunch, an afternoon tea or dusk-time *aperitivo* with nibbles (€9) until 9pm. Burgers, salads and some vegetarian dishes appease hunger pangs and there's ample pavement seating to people-watch on Piazza Trilussa. Monday is live music night.

MA CHE SIETE VENUTI A FÀ
PUB

Map p308 (📞06 6456 2046; www.football-pub.com; Via Benedetta 25; ⏰11am-2am; 🚋Piazza Trilussa) Named after a football chant, which translates politely as 'What did you come here for?', this pint-sized Trastevere pub is a beer-buff's paradise, packing in around 15 international craft beers on tap and even more by the bottle. Expect some rowdy drinking.

🍷 Gianicolo

IL BARETTO
BAR

Map p308 (📞06 589 60 55; www.ilbarettoroma.com; Via Garibaldi 27; ⏰7am-2am Mon-Sat; 🚋Via Garibaldi) Venture a little way up the Gianicolo, up a steep flight of steps from Trastevere – go on, it's worth it. Because there you'll discover this good-looking cocktail bar where the basslines are meaty, the bar staff hip, and the interior a mix of vintage and pop art.

☆ ENTERTAINMENT

LETTERE CAFFÈ
LIVE MUSIC

Map p308 (📞340 004 41 54; www.letterecaffe.org; Vicolo di San Francesco a Ripa 100-101; ⏰6pm-2am, closed mid-Aug–mid-Sep; 🚋Viale di Trastevere, 🚋Viale di Trastevere) Like books? Poetry? Blues and jazz? Then you'll love this place, a clutter of bar stools and books, where there are regular live gigs, poetry slams, comedy and gay nights, plus DJ sets playing electronic, indie and new wave. *Aperitivo,* with a tempting vegetarian buffet, is served between 7pm and 9pm.

BIG MAMA
BLUES

Map p308 (📞06 581 25 51; www.bigmama.it; Vicolo di San Francesco a Ripa 18; ⏰9pm-1.30am, shows 10.30pm, closed Jun-Sep; 🚋Viale di Trastevere, 🚋Viale di Trastevere) Head to this cramped Trastevere basement for a mellow night of Eternal City blues. A long-standing venue, it also stages jazz, funk, soul and R&B acts, as well as popular cover bands.

TEATRO VASCELLO
THEATRE

Map p308 (📞06 588 10 21; www.teatrovascello.it; Via Giacinto Carini 72, Monteverde; 🚋Via Giacinto Carini) Left-field in vibe and location, this independent fringe theatre in off-the-beaten-tourist-track Monteverde stages interesting, cutting-edge new work, including avant-garde dance, multimedia events and works by emerging playwrights.

SHOPPING

★BENHEART
FASHION & ACCESSORIES

Map p308 (📞06 5832 0801; www.benheart.it; Via del Moro 47; ⏰11am-11pm; 🚋Piazza Triussa) From the colourful resin floor papered with children's drawings to the vintage typewriter, dial-up telephone and old-fashioned tools decorating the interior, everything about this artisanal leather boutique is achingly cool. Benheart, a young Florentine designer, is one of Italy's savviest talents and his fashionable handmade shoes (from €190) and jackets for men and women are glorious.

★**ANTICA CACIARA**
TRASTEVERINA FOOD & DRINKS
Map p308 (☎06 581 28 15; www.anticacaciara.
it; Via San Francesco a Ripa 140; ⊗7am-2pm &
4-8pm Mon-Sat; ⊠Viale di Trastevere, ⊠Viale di
Trastevere) The fresh ricotta is a prized possession at this century-old deli, and it's all
usually snapped up by lunchtime. If you're
too late, take solace in the to-die-for *ricotta
infornata* (oven-baked ricotta), 35kg wheels
of famous, black-waxed *pecorino romano*
DOP (€16.50 per kilo), and aromatic garlands of *guanciale* (pig's jowl) begging to be
chopped up, pan-fried and thrown into the
perfect carbonara.

★**BISCOTTIFICIO INNOCENTI** FOOD
Map p308 (☎06 580 39 26; www.facebook.com/
biscottificioInnocenti; Via delle Luce 21; ⊗8am-
8pm Mon-Sat, 9.30am-2pm Sun; ⊠Viale di Trastevere, ⊠Viale di Trastevere) For homemade
biscuits, bite-sized meringues and tiny fruit
tarts, there is no finer address in Rome than
this vintage *biscottificio* with ceramic-tiled
interior, fly-net door curtain and a set of
old-fashioned scales on the counter to weigh
out biscuits (€16 to €24 per kilo). The shop
has been run with much love and passion
for several decades by the ever-dedicated
Stefania.

LES VIGNERONS WINE
Map p308 (☎06 6477 1439; www.lesvignerons.
it; Via Mameli 61; ⊗4-9pm Mon, 11am-9pm Tue-
Thu, 11am-9 30pm Fri & Sat; ⊠Viale di Trastevere,
⊠Viale di Trastevere) If you're looking for some
interesting wines to take home, search out

this lovely Trastevere wine shop. It boasts
one of the capital's best collections of natural wines, mainly from small Italian and
French producers, as well as a comprehensive selection of spirits and international
craft beers.

PORTA PORTESE MARKET MARKET
Map p308 (Piazza Porta Portese; ⊗6am-2pm
Sun; ⊠Viale di Trastevere, ⊠Viale di Trastevere)
To see another side of Rome, head to this
mammoth flea market. With thousands of
stalls selling everything from rare books
and fell-off-a-lorry bikes to Peruvian shawls
and MP3 players, it's crazily busy and a lot of
fun. Keep your valuables safe and wear your
haggling hat.

ALMOST CORNER BOOKSHOP BOOKS
Map p308 (☎06 583 69 42; Via del Moro 45;
⊗10am-8pm Mon-Sat, 11am-8pm Sun; ⊠Piazza
Trilussa) This is how a bookshop should look:
a crammed haven full of rip-roaring reads,
with every millimetre of wall space containing English-language fiction and nonfiction
(including children's) and travel guides.
Heaven to browse.

ROMA-STORE PERFUME
Map p308 (☎06 581 87 89; www.romastore
profumi.it; Via della Lungaretta 63; ⊗10am-8pm;
⊠Viale di Trastevere, ⊠Viale di Trastevere) An
enchanting perfume shop crammed full of
deliciously enticing bottles of scent, including lots of small, lesser-known brands that
will have perfume-lovers practically fainting
with joy.

Rome Street Life

As in many sunny countries, much of life in Rome is played out on the street. In the morning, you can watch the city slowly wake up. Shop shutters are cranked open, rubbish collectors do the rounds, restaurants set out their tables: Rome is readying itself for its close-up.

Day to Night

During the next phase, the fruit and veg markets in every *rione* (neighbourhood) will swell with people, with a predominance of matriarchs wielding grocery trolleys and showing a reckless disregard for queuing.

Throughout the day, people come and go on Rome's piazzas and public spaces. In Campo de' Fiori (p77), there's a busy food market during the day, then the character of the piazza changes towards the evening when its bars become busy, taking over corners of the square.

Pedestrianised Via del Pigneto (p148), to Rome's northeast, follows a similar trajectory: market in the morning, bars and cafes creating a party atmosphere in the evening. In the historic centre, locals and tourists gather to rest and people-watch on the Spanish Steps (p98), but these empty as night falls.

Day or evening, the stadium-sized Piazza Navona (p74) ebbs and flows with people-watching entertainment, with hawkers, caricaturists and occasional street performers.

La Passeggiata

In the early evening, the *passeggiata* (an early evening stroll) is an important

1. Dinner in the *centro storico* (p70) 2. Daily market, Campo de' Fiori (p77) 3. Portrait artist in Piazza Navona (p74)

part of Roman life, as it is elsewhere in Italy. Locals will usually dress up before heading out. Like many other parts of everyday life, such as coffee-drinking, Italians have elevated a seemingly simple practice into something special.

Romans will usually head to the area that's most convenient for them. Trastevere (p156) tends to be a broader mix of tourists and young people. Villa Borghese (p181) and the Pincio Hill Gardens (p101) attract more families and are more tranquil. Via del Corso is popular among younger window-shoppers, while Rome's smartest shopping strip, Via dei Condotti (p102), attracts a mix of ages. In summer, there's the Lungo il Tevere festival (p23) on Isola Tiberina, and stalls along the riverside create a new area for early evening wanders.

Many people out on the stroll will opt, instead of paying €6 or so to sit and drink at a bar, to stop for a more affordable gelato, which they can eat on their way. In summer, you'll see lots of people enjoying *grattachecca* – flavoured, crushed ice – along the banks of the Tiber.

The *bella figura* ('beautiful figure', better explained as 'keeping up appearances') is important here, and the *passeggiata* is as much about checking everyone else out as it is about enjoying the atmosphere. The *passeggiata* reaches its height in summer, as 5pm or 6pm is when the heat of the day subsides. There's not much else to do, so why not head out into the street?

San Giovanni & Testaccio

SAN GIOVANNI & THE CELIO | AVENTINO & AROUND | TESTACCIO

Neighbourhood Top Five

❶ Basilica di San Giovanni in Laterano (p168) Facing up to the monumental splendour of what was once Rome's most important church. You'll feel very small as you explore the echoing baroque interior of Rome's oldest Christian basilica.

❷ Terme di Caracalla (p169) Being over-awed by the colossal remnants of this vast baths complex.

❸ Villa del Priorato di Malta (p171) Looking through the unmarked keyhole to enjoy a magical view of St Peter's dome.

❹ Basilica di San Clemente (p170) Going underground at this beautiful medieval basilica. Before you go, check the church's glittering 12th-century apse mosaic.

❺ Cimitero Acattolico per gli Stranieri (p172) Grave-spotting in Rome's non-Catholic cemetery.

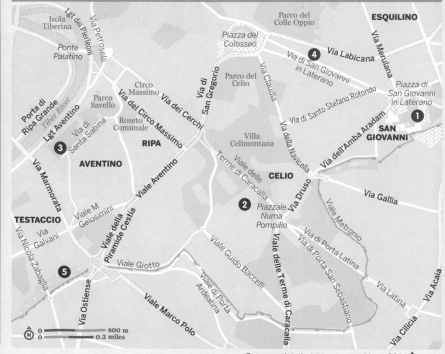

For more detail of this area see Map p306 ➡

Explore: San Giovanni & Testaccio

Extending south of the city centre, this is a large area that rewards a measured approach. To get the best out of it, take it slow and savour the various neighbourhoods. The district can easily be divided into two separate patches: San Giovanni and the Celio; and Aventino and Testaccio. A day in each is more than enough to cover the main sights.

Start off at the landmark Basilica di San Giovanni in Laterano (p168), the focal point of the largely residential San Giovanni neighbourhood. It's easily accessible by metro and quite magnificent, both inside and out. Once you've explored the basilica and surrounding piazza, head down Via di San Giovanni in Laterano towards the Colosseum. Near the bottom, the Basilica di San Clemente (p170) is a fascinating church with some exciting underground ruins. From there, you can walk across to the Celio, the green hill that rises south of the Colosseum. There's not a lot to see, but the graceful Villa Celimontana (p171) park is a great place to escape the crowds. Further south, the towering ruins of the Terme di Caracalla (p169) are a thrilling sight.

To the west, on the banks of the Tiber, the once working-class area of Testaccio is a foodie hotspot with a number of excellent trattorias and a popular nightlife strip. Rising above it, the Aventino hill boasts a number of serene medieval churches and one of Rome's great curiosities – the famous keyhole view of St Peter's dome.

Local Life

→**Romance** Local Lotharios out to impress their loved ones take them to enjoy the sunset views from the Parco Savello (p171) on the Aventino.

→**Offal** Testaccio is the spiritual home of Roman 'blood-and-guts' cooking. It's not for everyone, but savvy locals head to trattorias such as Da Felice (p173) to indulge.

→**Market food** In recent years, a number of foodie stalls have sprouted at Testaccio's covered market, including the hugely popular Mordi e Vai (p173), and Cups (p173), specialising in fresh soups and sauces.

Getting There & Away

→**Bus** Useful bus routes include 85 and 87, both of which stop near the Basilica di San Giovanni in Laterano, and 714, which serves San Giovanni and the Terme di Caracalla.

→**Metro** San Giovanni is accessible by metro line A. For Testaccio take line B to Piramide. The Aventino is walkable from Testaccio, and Circo Massimo station (line B).

→**Tram** Number 3 runs from San Giovanni along Viale Aventino, through Testaccio and on to Trastevere.

Lonely Planet's Top Tip

If you like opera and ballet, check www.operaroma.it for details of summer performances at the Terme di Caracalla. If contemporary art in a gritty urban setting is more your thing, look out for exhibitions and installations at **MACRO Testaccio** (p172), a gallery space in Rome's former abattoir.

SAN GIOVANNI & TESTACCIO

 Best Places to Eat

→ Sbanco (p172)
→ Trapizzino (p173)
→ Aroma (p173)
→ Flavio al Velavevodetto (p173)
→ Da Felice (p173)
→ Pizzeria Da Remo (p173)

For reviews, see p172.

Best Places to Drink

→ Rec 23 (p174)
→ Coming Out (p175)
→ L'Oasi della Birra (p174)
→ Bibenda Wine Concept (p174)
→ Anticafé Roma (p174)

For reviews, see p174.

Best Off-the-Radar Gems

→ Villa del Priorato di Malta (p171)
→ Cimitero Acattolico per gli Stranieri (p172)
→ Chiesa di Santo Stefano Rotondo (p171)
→ Basilica dei SS Quattro Coronati (p170)
→ Parco Savello (p171)

For reviews, see p170.

TOP SIGHT
BASILICA DI SAN GIOVANNI IN LATERANO

For a thousand years this monumental cathedral was the most important church in Christendom. Dating to the 4th century, it was the first Christian basilica built in the city and, until the late 14th century, it was the pope's main place of worship. It's still Rome's official cathedral and the pope's seat as the bishop of Rome.

The oldest of Rome's four papal basilicas, it was commissioned by the Emperor Constantine and consecrated by Pope Sylvester I in AD 324. From then until 1309, when the papacy moved to Avignon, it was the principal pontifical church, and the adjacent Palazzo Laterano was the pope's official residence. Both buildings fell into disrepair during the pope's French interlude and when Pope Gregory XI returned to Rome in 1377 the papal court decamped to the fortified Vatican.

The basilica has been revamped several times over the centuries, most notably by Francesco Borromini in the 17th century, and by Alessandro Galilei, who added the immense white facade in 1735.

DON'T MISS

➡ Monument to Pope Sylvester II
➡ The nave
➡ The baldachin
➡ The cloister

PRACTICALITIES

➡ Map p306, H2
➡ Piazza di San Giovanni in Laterano 4
➡ basilica/cloister free/€5 with audio guide
➡ ⊘7am-6.30pm, cloister 9am-6pm
➡ Ⓜ San Giovanni

The Facade

Surmounted by 15 7m-high statues – Christ with St John the Baptist, John the Evangelist and the 12 Apostles – Galilei's huge facade is an imposing work of late-baroque classicism. Behind the colossal columns there are five sets of doors in the portico. The **central bronze doors** were moved here from the Curia in the Roman Forum, while, on the far right, the **Holy Door** is only opened in Jubilee years.

The Interior

The cavernous interior owes much of its present look to Francesco Borromini, who styled it for the 1650 Jubilee. It's a breathtaking sight with a golden gilt **ceiling**, a 15th-century **mosaic floor**, and a wide **nave** lined with 18th-century sculptures of the apostles, each 4.6m high and each set in its own dramatic niche.

At the end of the nave, an elaborate Gothic **baldachin** stands over the papal altar. Dating to the 14th century, this is said to contain the relics of the heads of Sts Peter and Paul. In front, a double staircase leads down to the **confessio** and the Renaissance tomb of Pope Martin V.

Behind the altar, the massive **apse** is decorated with sparkling mosaics. Parts of these date to the 4th century, but most were added in the 1800s.

At the other end of the basilica, on the first pillar in the right-hand aisle, is an incomplete Giotto fresco. While admiring this, cock your ear towards the next column, where a monument to Pope Sylvester II (r 999–1003) is said to creak when the death of a pope is imminent.

The Cloister

To the left of the altar, the basilica's 13th-century cloister is a lovely, peaceful place with graceful twisted columns set around a central garden. Lining the ambulatories are marble fragments from the original church, including the remains of a 5th-century papal throne and inscriptions of two papal bulls.

TOP SIGHT
TERME DI CARACALLA

The remains of the emperor Caracalla's vast baths complex are among Rome's most awe-inspiring ruins. Inaugurated in AD 216, the original 10-hectare site, which comprised baths, gyms, libraries, shops and gardens, was used by up to 8000 people daily, while below ground hundreds of slaves sweated in a 9.5km tunnel network, tending to the complex plumbing systems.

The baths remained in continuous use until AD 537, when the invading Visigoths cut off Rome's water supply. Excavations in the 16th and 17th centuries unearthed a number of important sculptures, many of which later found their way into the Farnese family's art collection. More recently, archaeologists discovered an underground **Mithraeum** (temple) dedicated to the Persian god Mithras. Unfortunately, this is off-limits to visitors.

Most of the ruins are what's left of the central bath house. This was a huge rectangular edifice bookended by two **palestre** (gyms) and centred on a **frigidarium** (cold room), where bathers would stop after spells in the warmer **tepidarium** and dome-capped **caldaria** (hot room).

DON'T MISS...

- The *frigidarium*
- The *caldaria*
- The *palestre*

PRACTICALITIES

- Map p306, E4
- ☑ 06 3996 7700
- www.coopculture.it
- Viale delle Terme di Caracalla 52
- adult/reduced €6/3
- ⊙ 9am-1hr before sunset Tue-Sun, 9am-2pm Mon
- ☐ Viale delle Terme di Caracalla

◉ SIGHTS

Rome is a city of churches and this district boasts some of the capital's finest. There are also underground treasures, towering ancient ruins, and a couple of beautiful parks.

◉ San Giovanni & the Celio

BASILICA DI SAN GIOVANNI IN LATERANO   BASILICA
See p168.

★ BASILICA DI SAN CLEMENTE   BASILICA
Map p306 (www.basilicasanclemente.com; Piazza San Clemente; excavations adult/reduced €10/5; ⊙9am-12.30pm & 3-6pm Mon-Sat, 12.15-6pm Sun; 🚍Via Labicana) Nowhere better illustrates the various stages of Rome's turbulent past than this fascinating multi-layered church. The ground-level 12th-century basilica sits atop a 4th-century church, which, in turn, stands over a 2nd-century pagan temple and a 1st-century Roman house. Beneath everything are foundations dating from the Roman Republic.

The street-level *basilica superiore* features a marvellous 12th-century apse mosaic depicting the *Trionfo della Croce* (Triumph of the Cross) and some wonderful 15th-century frescoes by Masolino in the **Cappella di Santa Caterina** showing a crucifixion scene and episodes from the life of St Catherine.

Steps lead down to the 4th-century *basilica inferiore,* mostly destroyed by Norman invaders in 1084, but with some faded 11th-century frescoes illustrating the life of San Clement. Follow the steps down another level and you'll come to a 1st-century Roman house and a dark, 2nd-century temple to Mithras, with an altar showing the god slaying a bull. Beneath it all, you can hear the eerie sound of a subterranean river flowing through a Republic-era drain.

PALAZZO LATERANO   HISTORIC BUILDING
Map p306 (Piazza di San Giovanni in Laterano; Ⓜ San Giovanni) Adjacent to the Basilica di San Giovanni in Laterano, Palazzo Laterano was the official papal residence until the pope moved to the Vatican in 1377. It's still technically Vatican property and today houses offices of the Vicariate of Rome. Much altered over the centuries, it owes its current form to a 16th-century facelift by Domenico Fontana.

Overlooking the *palazzo* is Rome's oldest and tallest **obelisk**.

SANTUARIO DELLA SCALA SANTA & SANCTA SANCTORUM   CHRISTIAN SITE
Map p306 (www.scala-santa.it; Piazza di San Giovanni in Laterano 14; Scala free, Sancta with/without audio guide €5/3.50; ⊙Scala 6am-2pm & 3-7pm summer, to 6pm winter, Sancta Sanctorum 9.30am-12.45pm & 3-4.45pm Mon-Sat; Ⓜ San Giovanni) The Scala Santa, said to be the staircase that Jesus walked up in Pontius Pilate's Jerusalem palace, was brought to Rome by St Helena in the 4th century. Pilgrims consider it sacred and climb it on their knees, saying a prayer on each of the 28 steps. At the top, behind iron grating, is the richly decorated **Sancta Sanctorum** (Holy of Holies), formerly the pope's private chapel.

Behind the sanctuary building you'll see a cut-off cross-section of a building adorned with a showy gold mosaic. This is the **Triclinium Leoninum** (Map p306; Ⓜ San Giovanni), an 18th-century reconstruction of a wall from the original Palazzo Laterano.

BASILICA DEI SS QUATTRO CORONATI   BASILICA
Map p306 (☎06 7047 5427; Via dei Santi Quattro 20; cloisters €2, Oratorio di San Silvestro €1; ⊙basilica 6.30am-12.45pm & 3.30-8pm, cloister 9.45-11.45am & 3.45-5.45pm Mon-Sat; 🚍Via di San Giovanni in Laterano) This brooding fortified church harbours some lovely 13th-century frescoes and a delightful hidden **cloister**, accessible from the left-hand aisle. The frescoes, in the **Oratorio di San Silvestro**, depict the story of Constantine and pope Sylvester I and the so-called Donation of Constantine (p225), a notorious forged document with which the emperor supposedly ceded control of Rome and the Western Roman Empire to the papacy.

To access the Oratorio, ring the bell in the entrance courtyard.

CASE ROMANE   CHRISTIAN SITE
Map p306 (☎06 7045 4544; www.caseromane.it; Clivo di Scauro; adult/reduced €8/6; ⊙10am-1pm & 3-6pm Thu-Mon; 🚍Via Claudia) According to tradition, two martyred Roman soldiers, John and Paul, lived in these subterranean houses beneath the **Basilica dei SS Giovanni e Paolo al Celio** (Map p306; Piazza dei Santi Giovanni e Paolo; ⊙8.30am-noon & 3.30-6pm; 🚍Via Claudia) before they were beheaded

SUBTERRANEAN CULT

The cult of Mithraism was hugely popular in ancient military circles. According to its mythology, the Sun ordered Mithras, a young, handsome god, to slay a wild bull. As the animal died, it gave life, its blood causing wheat and other plants to grow.

Mithraic temples, known as Mithraeums, were almost always in underground locations or caves, reflecting the cult's belief that caverns represented the cosmos. In these Mithraeums, devotees underwent complex initiation rites, and ate bread and water to symbolise the body and blood of the bull. Sound familiar? The early Christians thought so too, and were fervently opposed to the cult.

by the emperor Julian. There's actually no direct evidence for this, although research has revealed that the houses were used for Christian worship. There are more than 20 rooms, many of them richly decorated.

Entry is to the side of the basilica on the Clivo di Scauro.

VILLA CELIMONTANA   PARK

Map p306 (⊙7am-sunset; 🚊Via della Navicella) With its grassy banks and colourful flower beds, this leafy park is a wonderful place to escape the crowds and enjoy a summer picnic. At its centre is a 16th-century villa housing the Italian Geographical Society, while to the south stands a 12m-plus Egyptian obelisk.

CHIESA DI SANTO
STEFANO ROTONDO   CHURCH

Map p306 (www.santo-stefano-rotondo.it; Via di Santo Stefano Rotondo 7; ⊙10am-1pm & 2.30-5.30pm winter, 10am-1pm & 3.30-6.30pm summer; 🚊Via Claudia) Set in its own secluded grounds, this haunting church boasts a porticoed facade and a round, columned interior. But what really gets the heart racing is the graphic wall decor – a cycle of 16th-century frescoes depicting the tortures suffered by many early Christian martyrs.

Describing them in 1846, Charles Dickens wrote: 'Such a panorama of horror and butchery no man could imagine in his sleep, though he were to eat a whole pig, raw, for supper'.

The church, one of Rome's oldest, dates to the late 5th century, although it was subsequently altered in the 12th and 15th centuries.

◉ Aventino & Around

BASILICA DI SANTA SABINA   BASILICA

Map p306 (☑06 57 94 01; Piazza Pietro d'Illiria 1; ⊙8.15am-12.30pm & 3.30-6pm; 🚊Lungotevere Aventino) This solemn basilica, one of Rome's most beautiful early Christian churches, was founded by Peter of Illyria in around AD 422. It was enlarged in the 9th century and again in 1216, just before it was given to the newly founded Dominican order – note the tombstone of Muñoz de Zamora, one of the order's founding fathers, in the nave floor. A 20th-century restoration returned it to its original look.

One of the few features to have survived since the 5th century are the basilica's cypress-wood doors. These feature 18 carved panels depicting biblical events, including one of the oldest Crucifixion scenes in existence. It's quite hard to make out in the top left, but it depicts Jesus and the two thieves, although, strangely, not their crosses.

Inside, 24 custom-made columns support an arcade decorated with a faded red-and-green frieze. Light streams in from high nave windows that were added in the 9th century, along with the carved choir, pulpit and bishop's throne.

Behind the church is a garden and a meditative 13th-century cloister.

PARCO SAVELLO   PARK

Map p306 (Via di Santa Sabina; ⊙7am-6pm Oct-Feb, to 8pm Mar & Sep, to 9pm Apr-Aug; 🚊Lungotevere Aventino) Known to Romans as the *Giardino degli Aranci* (Orange Garden), this walled park is a romantic haven. Head down the central avenue, passing towering umbrella pines and lawns of blooming orange trees, to bask in heavenly sunset views of St Peter's dome and the city's rooftops.

★ VILLA DEL PRIORATO
DI MALTA   HISTORIC BUILDING

Map p306 (Villa Magistrale; Piazza dei Cavalieri di Malta; 🚊Lungotevere Aventino) Fronting an ornate cypress-shaded piazza, the Roman headquarters of the Sovereign Order of Malta, aka the *Cavalieri di Malta* (Knights of Malta), boasts one of Rome's most celebrated views. It's not immediately apparent, but look through the keyhole in the Villa's green door and you'll see the dome of St Peter's Basilica perfectly aligned at the end of a hedge-lined avenue.

Unfortunately, that's as close as you'll get to entering the building, which is closed to the public except for rare special openings.

The piazza, which sits on the summit of the Aventino hill, owes its ornamental look to a late 18th-century overhaul by the artist and architect Giovanni Battista Piranesi.

⊙ Testaccio

CIMITERO ACATTOLICO
PER GLI STRANIERI   CEMETERY
Map p306 (www.cemeteryrome.it; Via Caio Cestio 5; voluntary donation €3; ☺9am-5pm Mon-Sat, to 1pm Sun; MPiramide) Despite the roads that surround it, Rome's 'non-Catholic' Cemetery is a verdant oasis of peace. An air of Grand Tour romance hangs over the site where up to 4000 people lie buried, including poets Keats and Shelley, and Italian political thinker Antonio Gramsci.

Among the gravestones and cypress trees, look out for the *Angelo del Dolore* (Angel of Grief), a much-replicated 1894 sculpture that US artist William Wetmore Story created for his wife's grave.

MACRO TESTACCIO   GALLERY
(☑06 06 08; www.museomacro.org; Piazza Orazio Giustiniani 4; adult/reduced €6/5; ☺2-8pm Tue-Sun; ☐Via Marmorata) Housed in Rome's former slaughterhouse, MACRO Testaccio (the second of MACRO's two exhibition spaces) is part of a cultural complex that also includes a seat of Rome's Accademia di Belle Arti and the University of Roma Tre's Architecture Department. Contemporary art exhibitions are staged in two cavernous industrial halls.

Note that the gallery opens only when there's an exhibition on – check the website for details.

MONTE TESTACCIO   HISTORIC SITE
Map p306 (☑06 06 08; Via Nicolo Zabaglia 24, cnr Via Galvani; adult/reduced €4/3, plus cost of tour; ☺group visits only, reservation necessary; ☐Via Marmorata) In the heart of the eponymous neighbourhood, Monte Testaccio, aka Monte dei Cocci, is an artificial grass-covered hill made of smashed amphorae (*testae* in Latin, hence the area's name, Testaccio).

Between the 2nd century BC and the 3rd century AD, Testaccio was Rome's river port. Supplies of olive oil were transported here in huge terracotta amphorae, which, once emptied, were broken and the fragments stacked in a huge pile near the storehouses. Over time, this pile grew into a substantial 49m-high hill – Monte Testaccio.

✖ EATING

Testaccio's workaday streets harbour some wonderful old-school trattorias, as well as a growing number of trendy takeaways. Elsewhere, you'll find some surprisingly good eateries among the tourist traps southeast of the Colosseum.

✖ San Giovanni & the Celio

CAFÈ CAFÈ   BISTRO €
Map p306 (☑06 700 87 43; www.cafecafe bistrot.it; Via dei Santi Quattro 44; meals €15-20; ☺9.30am-8.50pm; ☐Via di San Giovanni in Laterano) Cosy, relaxed and welcoming, this cafe-bistro is a far cry from the usual impersonal eateries in the Colosseum area. With its rustic wooden tables, butternut walls and wine bottles, it's a charming spot in which to charge your batteries over an egg-and-bacon breakfast, a light lunch, or afternoon tea and homemade cake.

★SBANCO   PIZZA €€
Map p318 (☑06 78 93 18; Via Siria 1; pizzas €7.50-12.50; ☺7.30pm-midnight; ☐Piazza Zama) With its informal warehouse vibe and buzzing atmosphere, Sbanco is one of the capital's hottest pizzerias. Since opening in 2016, it has quickly made a name for itself with its creative, wood-fired pizzas and sumptuous fried starters – try the carbonara *supplì* (risotto balls). To top things off, it serves some deliciously drinkable craft beer.

DIVIN OSTILIA   WINE BAR, TRATTORIA €€
Map p306 (☑06 7049 6526; Via Ostilia 4; meals €30-35; ☺noon-1am; ☐Via Labicana) Ever popular Divin Ostilia is a model wine bar with wooden shelves lined with bottles and a high brick ceiling. It's a well-known spot and its cosy interior gets busy at mealtimes as diners squeeze in to feast on cheese and cured meats, grilled steaks and classic pasta dishes.

IL BOCCONCINO
LAZIO CUISINE €€

Map p306 (📞06 7707 9175; www.ilbocconcino.com; Via Ostilia 23; meals €30-35; ⊘12.30-3.30pm & 7.30-11.30pm Thu-Tue; 🚇Via Labicana) One of the better options in the touristy pocket near the Colosseum, this easy-going trattoria stands out for its authentic regional cooking and use of locally sourced seasonal ingredients. Daily specials are chalked up on blackboards or there's a regular menu of classic Roman pastas, grilled meats, fish and imaginative desserts.

AROMA
RISTORANTE €€€

Map p306 (📞06 9761 5109; www.aromarestaurant.it; Via Labicana 125; meals €120-150; ⊘12.30-3pm & 7.30-11.30pm; 🚇Via Labicana) One for a special occasion, the rooftop restaurant of the Palazzo Manfredi hotel offers once-in-a-lifetime views of the Colosseum and Michelin-starred food that rises to the occasion. Overseeing the kitchen is chef Giuseppe Di Iorio, whose seasonal menus reflect his passion for luxurious, forward-thinking Mediterranean cuisine.

✖ Aventino & Around

IL GELATO
GELATO €

Map p306 (Viale Aventino 59; gelato €2-4.50; ⊘10am-midnight summer, 11am-9pm winter; 🚇Viale Aventino) This is the Aventine outpost of Rome's ice-cream king, Claudio Torcè. His creamy creations are seasonal and preservative free, ranging from the classic to the decidedly not – anyone for green tea or gorgonzola?

✖ Testaccio

★TRAPIZZINO
FAST FOOD €

Map p306 (📞06 4341 9624; www.trapizzino.it; Via Branca 88; trapizzini from €3.50; ⊘noon-1am Tue-Sun; 🚇Via Marmorata) The original of what is now a growing countrywide chain, this is the birthplace of the *trapizzino*, a kind of hybrid sandwich made by stuffing a cone of doughy focaccia with fillers like *polpette al sugo* (meatballs in tomato sauce) or *pollo alla cacciatore* (stewed chicken). They're messy to eat but quite delicious.

MORDI E VAI
STREET FOOD €

Map p306 (www.mordievai.it; Box 15, Nuovo Mercato di Testaccio; panini €3.50-5; ⊘8am 3pm Mon-Sat; 🚇Via Galvani) Chef Sergio Esposito's critically acclaimed and much frequented market stall – 'Bite and Go' in English – is all about the unadulterated joy of traditional Roman street food. That means *panini* such as his signature *allesso di scottona*, filled with tender slow-cooked beef, and plastic plates of no-nonsense meat-and-veg dishes.

CUPS
STREET FOOD €

Map p306 (Box 44, Nuovo Mercato di Testaccio; dishes €5-8; ⊘8am-4pm Mon-Sat; 🚇Via Galvini) This gourmet food stall at Testaccio market is the latest venture of local celebrity chef Cristina Bowerman. It takes its name from the carton cups used to serve dishes such as meatballs in tomato sauce and *brodo di pho*, a scorching take on the traditional Vietnamese soup dish. You can also order *panini*, focaccias, pastries and artisanal gelato.

PIZZERIA DA REMO
PIZZA €

Map p306 (📞06 574 62 70; Piazza Santa Maria Liberatrice 44; meals €15; ⊘7pm-1am Mon-Sat; 🚇Via Marmorata) For an authentic Roman experience, join the noisy crowds here, one of the city's best-known and most popular pizzerias. It's a spartan-looking place, but the fried starters and thin-crust Roman pizzas are the business, and there's a cheerful, boisterous vibe. Expect to queue after 8.30pm.

FLAVIO AL VELAVEVODETTO
ROMAN €€

Map p306 (📞06 574 41 94; www.ristorantevelavodetto.it; Via di Monte Testaccio 97-99; meals €30-35; ⊘12.30-3pm & 7.45-11pm; 🚇Via Galvani) Housed in a rustic Pompeian-red villa set into the side of Monte Testaccio, a man-made hill of smashed Roman amphorae, this casual eatery is celebrated locally for its earthy, no-nonsense *cucina romana* (Roman cuisine). Expect *antipasti* of cheeses, cured meats and fried titbits, huge helpings of homemade pastas, and uncomplicated meat dishes.

DA FELICE
ROMAN €€

Map p306 (📞06 574 68 00; www.feliceatestaccio.it; Via Mastro Giorgio 29; meals €30-40; ⊘noon-3pm & 7.30-11pm; 🚇Via Marmorata) Much loved by local foodies and well-dressed diners, this historic stalwart is famous for its unwavering dedication to Roman culinary traditions. In contrast to the light-touch modern decor, the menu is pure old school with a classic weekly timetable: *pasta e fagioli* (pasta and beans) on Tuesdays, *bollito di manzo* (boiled beef) on Thursdays, fish on Fridays. Reservations essential.

TAVERNA VOLPETTI
ITALIAN €€

Map p306 (Via Volta 8; meals €20-35; ⏱11am-11pm Mon-Sat; ☐Via Marmorata) Join the neighbourhood's lunching locals at this casually smart eatery. An offshoot of the Volpetti deli, it serves a popular lunchtime buffet of pastas and vegetables, as well as *supplì* (risotto balls) and fried snacks. For dinner, expect fine cheeses, cured meats, and a selection of daily specials such as calamari salad with fresh anchovies and pecorino.

🍷 DRINKING & NIGHTLIFE

🍷 San Giovanni & the Celio

ANTICAFÉ ROMA
CAFE

(📞06 7049 4442; Via Veio 4B; ⏱9am-10pm; 📶; Ⓜ San Giovanni) Something of a novelty in Rome, Anticafé doesn't charge for its drinks. Instead you pay for the time you spend there – €4 for the first hour, then €3 for successive hours. With that you're free to hang out and do pretty much whatever – use the wi-fi, play board games, read on the sofa, drink. You can BYO or there's a bar with free drinks and snacks.

BIBENDA WINE CONCEPT
WINE BAR

Map p306 (📞06 7720 6673; www.wineconcept.it; Via Capo d'Africa 21; ⏱noon-3pm & 6pm-midnight Mon-Thu, to 2am Fri & Sat, closed Sat lunch & Sun; ☐Via Labicana) Wine buffs looking to excite their palate should search out this smart modern *enoteca* (wine bar). Boasting a white, light-filled interior, it has an extensive list of Italian regional labels and European vintages, as well as a small daily food menu. Wines are available to drink by the glass or buy by the bottle.

IL PENTAGRAPPOLO
WINE BAR

Map p306 (📞06 709 63 01; Via Celimontana 21b; ⏱noon-3pm & 6pm-1am Mon-Thu, 6pm-2am Fri-Sun; Ⓜ Colosseo) This vaulted, softly lit wine bar is the perfect antidote to sightseeing overload. Join the mellow crowd for an evening of wine, piano music and jazz courtesy of the frequent live gigs. There's also a full menu served at lunch and dinner.

🍷 Aventino & Around

CASA MANFREDI
CAFE

Map p306 (📞06 9760 5892; Viale Aventino 93; ⏱7am-9pm; ☐Viale Aventino, ☐Viale Aventino) Very 'in' when we visited, Casa Manfredi is a good-looking cafe in the wealthy Aventine neighbourhood. Join well-dressed locals for a quick coffee in the gleaming glass and chandelier interior, a light alfresco lunch or chic evening *aperitivo*. It also does a tasty line in artisanal gelato.

🍷 Testaccio

REC 23
BAR

Map p306 (📞06 8746 2147; www.rec23.com; Piazza dell'Emporio 2; ⏱6.30pm-2am daily & 12.30-3.30pm Sat & Sun; ☐Via Marmorata) All exposed brick and mismatched furniture, this large, New York–inspired venue caters to all moods, serving *aperitivo*, restaurant meals, and a weekend brunch. Arrive thirsty to take on a Bud Spencer, one from the ample list of cocktails, or get to grips with the selection of Scottish whiskies and Latin American rums. Thursday's blues aperitif is a popular weekly appointment.

LINARI
CAFE

Map p306 (📞06 578 23 58; Via Nicola Zabaglia 9; ⏱7am-9.30pm Wed-Mon; ☐Via Marmorata) An authentic local hang-out, this cafe-*pasticceria* has the busy clatter of a good bar, with excellent pastries, splendid coffee and plenty of bar-side banter. There are a few outside tables, ideal for a cheap lunch, but you'll have to outfox the neighbourhood ladies to get one.

L'OASI DELLA BIRRA
BAR

Map p306 (📞06 574 61 22; Piazza Testaccio 41; ⏱4pm-12.30am; ☐Via Marmorata) Housed in the Palombi Enoteca, a longstanding bottle shop on Piazza Testaccio, this is exactly what it says it is – an Oasis of Beer. With hundreds of labels, from Teutonic heavyweights to British bitters and Belgian brews, as well as wines, cheeses and cold cuts, it's ideally set up for an evening's quaffing, either in the cramped cellar or piazza-side terrace.

GAY STREET

· ·

The bottom end of Via di San Giovanni in Laterano, the sloping street that runs from the Basilica di San Giovanni in Laterano to near the Colosseum, is a favourite haunt of Rome's gay community. In the evenings, and not so much during the day, bars like **Coming Out** (Map p306; ☑ 06 700 98 71; www.coming out.it; Via di San Giovanni in Laterano 8; ⊘ 7.30am-2am; ꇤ Via Labicana) and **My Bar** (Map p306; Via di San Giovanni in Laterano 12; ⊘ 9am-2am; ꇤ Via Labicana) burst into life, attracting large crowds of mostly gay men.

L'ALIBI
CLUB

Map p306 (☑ 06 574 34 48; Via di Monte Testaccio 44; ⊘ 11.30pm-5am Fri & Sat; ꇤ Via Galvani) A historic gay club, L'Alibi is still kicking, hosting regular weekend parties and serving up a mixed mash of house, techno, hip hop, Latino, pop and dance to a mixed gay and straight crowd. It's spread over three floors, so if the sweaty atmosphere on the dance floors gets too much, head up to the spacious summer terrace.

 **ENTERTAINMENT**

TERME DI CARACALLA
OPERA

Map p306 (www.operaroma.it; Viale delle Terme di Caracalla 52; tickets €20-150; ꇤ Viale delle Terme di Caracalla) The hulking ruins of this vast 3rd-century baths complex set the memorable stage for the Teatro dell'Opera's summer season of music, opera and ballet, as well as shows by big-name Italian performers.

CONTESTACCIO
LIVE MUSIC

Map p306 (☑ 06 5728 9712; www.contestaccio. com; Via di Monte Testaccio 65b; ⊘ 8pm-4am Thu-Sun; ꇤ Via Galvani) With an under-the-stars terrace and buzzing vibe, ConteStaccio is one of the top venues on the Testaccio clubbing strip. It's something of a multipurpose outfit with a cocktail bar, pizzeria and restaurant, but is best known for its free live music. Gigs by emerging groups set the tone, spanning indie, rock, acoustic, funk and electronic genres.

 SHOPPING

VOLPETTI
FOOD & DRINKS

Map p306 (www.volpetti.com; Via Marmorata 47; ⊘ 8.30am-2pm & 4.30-8.15pm Mon-Wed, 8.30am-8.15pm Thu-Sat; ꇤ Via Marmorata) This super-stocked deli, considered by many the best in town, is a treasure trove of gourmet delicacies. Helpful staff will guide you through the extensive selection of smelly cheeses, homemade pastas, olive oils, vinegars, cured meats, veggie pies, wines and grappas. It also serves excellent sliced pizza.

NUOVO MERCATO DI TESTACCIO
MARKET

Map p306 (entrances Via Galvani, Via Beniamino Franklin, Via Volta, Via Manuzio, Via Ghiberti; ⊘ 7am-3.30pm Mon-Sat; ꇤ Via Marmorata) A trip to Testaccio's neighbourhood market is always fun. Occupying a modern, purpose-built site, it hums with morning activity as locals go about their daily shopping, picking, prodding and sniffing the brightly coloured produce and browsing displays of shoes and clothes. You'll also find several stalls serving fantastic street food.

SOUL FOOD
MUSIC

Map p306 (☑ 06 7045 2025; www.haterecords. com; Via di San Giovanni in Laterano 192; ⊘ 10.30am-1.30pm & 3.30-7.30pm Tue-Sat; ꇤ Via di San Giovanni in Laterano) Run by Hate Records, Soul Food is a laid-back record store with an eclectic collection of vinyl that runs the musical gamut, from '60s garage and rockabilly to punk, indie, new wave, folk, funk and soul. You'll also find retro T-shirts, fanzines and other groupie clobber.

Villa Borghese & Northern Rome

VILLA BORGHESE & AROUND | FLAMINIO | SALARIO | NOMENTANO | PARIOLI

Neighbourhood Top Five

1 **Museo e Galleria Borghese** (p178) Getting to grips with artistic genius at this lavish gallery.

2 **Villa Borghese** (p181) Escaping the crowds as you explore the leafy lanes and glades of Rome's most famous park.

3 **Museo Nazionale Etrusco di Villa Giulia** (p182) Applauding Italy's most comprehensive collection of Etruscan treasures at this splendid museum.

4 **La Galleria Nazionale** (p181) Coming face to face with the giants of modern art in the halls of a stately belle-époque palace.

5 **Auditorium Parco della Musica** (p186) Catching a world-class concert and admiring Renzo Piano's trend-setting architecture at this eye-catching cultural centre.

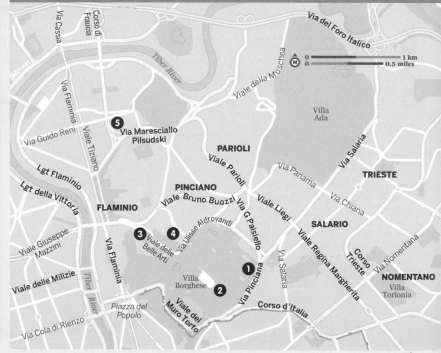

For more detail of this area see Map p316 ➡

Explore: Villa Borghese & Northern Rome

Although less packed with traditional sights than elsewhere, this large swathe of northern Rome is rich in interest. The obvious starting point is Villa Borghese (p181), an attractive park counting the city's zoo, its largest modern art gallery, and a stunning Etruscan museum among its myriad attractions. But its great scene-stealing highlight is the Museo e Galleria Borghese (p178), one of Rome's top art museums.

From Piazzale Flaminio, a tram heads up Via Flaminia to two of Rome's most important modern buildings: the Auditorium Parco della Musica (p186), Renzo Piano's concert centre, and MAXXI (p181), Zaha Hadid's contemporary art gallery. Continue up the road and you come to Ponte Milvio (p182), a handsome footbridge and scene of an ancient Roman battle. Over the river, Piazzale Ponte Milvio is a favourite hang-out, its busy eateries much frequented by the area's well-to-do residents. To the west, crowds flock to the Stadio Olimpico (p186) for top-flight football and Six Nations rugby.

To the east of Villa Borghese, Via Salaria, the old Roman *sale* (salt) road, runs through a smart residential and business district. To the north, Villa Ada park expands northwards while, to the south, Via Nomentana traverses acres of housing as it heads out of town. On Via Nomentana, Villa Torlonia (p183) is a captivating park, and the Basilica di Sant'Agnese Fuori le Mura (p184) claims Rome's oldest Christian mosaics.

Local Life

➡ **Concerts and events** Rome's culture vultures keep a close eye on what's going on at the Auditorium Parco della Musica (p186), which stages a year-round program of concerts, screenings and festivals.

➡ **Parks** Tourists tend to stop at Villa Borghese (p181), but locals often head to Villa Torlonia (p183) on Via Nomentana or Villa Ada (p183).

➡ **Football** For football fans, Sunday is match day. And for Rome's ardent fans that means a pilgrimage to the Stadio Olimpico (p186) to cheer their team on.

Getting There & Away

➡ **Bus** Buses 53 and 160 go to Villa Borghese from Via Vittorio Veneto near Barberini metro station. There are also regular buses along Via Nomentana and Via Salaria.

➡ **Metro** Villa Borghese is accessible from Flaminio and Spagna stations (both line A).

➡ **Tram** Tram 2 trundles up Via Flaminia and Viale Tiziano from Piazzale Flaminio; number 3 connects Villa Borghese with San Lorenzo, San Giovanni, Testaccio and Trastevere; number 19 runs from Piazza del Risorgimento to Villa Borghese and Viale Regina Margherita.

Lonely Planet's Top Tip

Monday is not a good day to explore Villa Borghese. Sure, you can walk in the park, but all of the museums and galleries are shut – they open Tuesday through Sunday. Also remember to book tickets for the **Museo e Galleria Borghese** (p178). It's easy to do, either online (plus a €2 booking fee) or by phoning the museum directly, and you won't get in without a reservation.

VILLA BORGHESE & NORTHERN ROME

Best Places to Eat

➡ Metamorfosi (p185)
➡ Osteria Flaminio (p184)
➡ Pro Loco Pinciano (p185)
➡ Neve di Latte (p185)
➡ Serenella (p184)

For reviews, see p184. ➡

Best Places to Drink

➡ Momart (p185)
➡ Lanificio 159 (p186)
➡ Chioschetto di Ponte Milvio (p186)
➡ Lemoncocco (p186)

For reviews, see p185. ➡

Best Museums & Galleries

➡ Museo e Galleria Borghese (p178)
➡ Museo Nazionale Etrusco di Villa Giulia (p182)
➡ La Galleria Nazionale (p181)
➡ MAXXI (p181)
➡ MACRO (p182)

For reviews, see p181. ➡

TOP SIGHT
MUSEO E GALLERIA BORGHESE

If you only have the time or inclination for one art gallery in Rome, make it this one. Housing what's often referred to as the 'queen of all private art collections', it boasts some of the city's finest art treasures, including a series of sensational sculptures by Gian Lorenzo Bernini and important paintings by the likes of Caravaggio, Titian, Raphael and Rubens.

The Villa

The museum's collection was formed by Cardinal Scipione Borghese (1579–1633), the most knowledgeable and ruthless art collector of his day. It was originally housed in the cardinal's residence near St Peter's but in the 1620s he had it transferred to his new villa just outside Porta Pinciana. And it's in the villa's central building, the Casino Borghese, that you'll see it today.

Over the centuries the villa has undergone several overhauls, most notably in the late 1700s when Prince Marcantonio Borghese added much of the lavish neoclassical decor. But while the villa remained intact, the collection did not. Much of the antique statuary was carted off to the Louvre in the early 19th century, and other pieces were gradually sold off. In 1902 the Italian State bought the casino, but it wasn't until 1997 that the collection was finally put on public display.

The villa is divided into two parts: the ground-floor museum, with its superb sculptures, intricate Roman floor mosaics and hypnotic trompe l'œil frescoes; and the upstairs picture gallery.

DON'T MISS

➡ *Ratto di Proserpina*
➡ *Venere vincitrice*
➡ *Ragazzo col Canestro di Frutta*
➡ *La Deposizione di Cristo*
➡ *Amor Sacro e Amor Profano*

PRACTICALITIES

➡ Map p316, F6
➡ 📞06 3 28 10
➡ www.galleriaborghese.it
➡ Piazzale del Museo Borghese 5
➡ adult/reduced €15/8.50
➡ 🕑9am-7pm Tue-Sun
➡ 🚌Via Pinciana

Ground Floor

From the basement entrance, stairs lead up to **Sala IV**, home of Gian Lorenzo Bernini's *Ratto di Proserpina* (1621–22). This flamboyant sculpture, one of a series depicting pagan myths, brilliantly reveals the artist's virtuosity – just look at Pluto's hand pressing into the seemingly soft flesh of Persephone's thigh. Further on, in **Sala III**, he captures the exact moment Daphne's hands start morphing into leaves in *Apollo e Dafne* (1622–25).

Another statuesque scene-stealer is Antonio Canova's daring depiction of Napoleon's sister, Paolina Bonaparte Borghese, reclining topless as *Venere vincitrice* (1805–08) in **Sala I**. Its suggestive pose and technical virtuosity is typical of Canova's elegant, mildly erotic neoclassical style.

Caravaggio dominates **Sala VIII**. There's a dissipated-looking *Bacchino malato* (Young Sick Bacchus; 1592–95), the strangely beautiful *La Madonna dei Palafenieri* (Madonna with Serpent; 1605–06), and *San Giovanni Battista* (St John the Baptist; 1609–10), probably Caravaggio's last work. There's also the much-loved *Ragazzo col Canestro di Frutta* (Boy with a Basket of Fruit; 1593–95), and the dramatic *Davide con la Testa di Golia* (David with the Head of Goliath; 1609–10) – Goliath's severed head is said to be a self-portrait.

Beyond Sala VIII, a portico flanks the grand **entrance hall**, decorated with 4th-century floor mosaics of fighting gladiators and a 2nd-century *Satiro Combattente* (Fighting Satyr). High on the wall is a gravity-defying bas-relief of a horse and rider falling into the void *(Marco Curzio a Cavallo)* by Pietro Bernini (Gian Lorenzo's father).

Pinacoteca

Upstairs, the picture gallery offers a wonderful snapshot of Renaissance art.

Don't miss Raphael's extraordinary *La Deposizione di Cristo* (The Deposition; 1507) in **Sala IX**, and his *Dama con Liocorno* (Lady with a Unicorn; 1506). In the same room is Fra Bartolomeo's *Adorazione del Bambino* (Adoration of the Christ Child; 1495) and Perugino's *Madonna con Bambino* (Madonna and Child; first quarter of the 16th century).

Next door, Correggio's *Danäe* (1530–31) shares the room with a willowy Venus, as portrayed by Cranach in his *Venere e Amore che Reca Il Favo do Miele* (Venus and Cupid with Honeycomb; 1531).

Moving on, **Sala XIV** boasts two self-portraits by Bernini, and **Sala XVIII** contains two portraits by Pietro da Cortona and Rubens' *Susanna e I Vecchioni* (Susanna and the Elders; 1605–07).

To finish off, Titian's early masterpiece *Amor Sacro e Amor Profano* (Sacred and Profane Love; 1514), in **Sala XX**, is one of the collection's most prized works.

CARDINAL SCIPIONE BORGHESE

Cardinal Scipione Caffarelli Borghese (1576–1633) was one of the most influential figures in Rome's baroque art world. Nephew of Pope Paul V, he sponsored the greatest artists of the day, including Caravaggio, Bernini, Domenichino, Rubens and Guido Reni. Yet while he promoted the artists, he didn't always see eye to eye with them and was quite prepared to play dirty to get his hands on their works: he had Cavaliere d'Arpino jailed in order to confiscate his canvases and Domenichino arrested to force him to surrender *La Caccia di Diana* (The Hunt of Diana).

To limit numbers, visitors are admitted at two-hourly intervals, so you'll need to pre-book your ticket and get an entry time. To book, either phone the museum directly or buy tickets online at www.tosc.it (plus €2 booking fee). Note that if you have a Roma Pass you can only book by phone. Pick up your ticket from the ticket office 30 minutes before your entry time and remember to take ID.

MUSEO E GALLERIA BORGHESE

**Services and Amenities Level
(Basement)**

First Floor

Ground Floor

⊙ SIGHTS

Ballooning northwards from the city centre, Villa Borghese is the obvious focus of this extensive area. Elsewhere, you'll find several top sights, including Rome's flagship cultural centre and two contemporary art museums.

⊙ Villa Borghese & Around

MUSEO E GALLERIA
BORGHESE   MUSEUM
See p178.

VILLA BORGHESE   PARK
Map p316 (www.sovraintendenzaroma.it; entrances at Piazzale San Paolo del Brasile, Piazzale Flaminio, Via Pinciana, Via Raimondo, Largo Pablo Picasso; ☉sunrise-sunset; 🚊Via Pinciana) Locals, lovers, tourists, joggers – no one can resist the lure of Rome's most celebrated park. Originally the 17th-century estate of Cardinal Scipione Borghese, it covers about 80 hectares of wooded glades, gardens and grassy banks. Among its attractions are several excellent museums, the landscaped **Giardino del Lago** (boat hire per 20min €3; ☉7am-9pm summer, to 6pm winter), **Piazza di Siena**, a dusty arena used for Rome's top equestrian event in May, and a panoramic terrace on the Pincio Hill (p101).

Film buffs should head to the area around the Piazzale San Paolo del Brasile entrance, where the **Casa del Cinema** (Map p316; ☑06 06 08; www.casadelcinema.it; Largo Marcello Mastroianni 1) hosts regular film-related events, and the **Cinema dei Piccoli** (Map p316; ☑06 855 34 85; www.cinemadeipiccoli.it; Viale della Pineta 15; tickets Mon-Fri €5, Sat & Sun €6) is one of the world's smallest cinemas.

★LA GALLERIA NAZIONALE   GALLERY
Map p316 (☑06 3229 8221; http://lagalleria nazionale.com; Viale delle Belle Arti 131, accessible entrance Via Antonio Gramsci 71; adult/reduced €10/5; ☉8.30am-7.30pm Tue-Sun; 🚊Piazza Thorvaldsen) Housed in a vast belle-époque palace, this oft-overlooked modern art gallery, known locally as GNAM, is an unsung gem. Its superlative collection runs the gamut from neoclassical sculpture to abstract expressionism with works by many of the most important exponents of 19th- and 20th-century art.

There are canvases by the *macchiaioli* (Italian Impressionists) and futurists Boccioni and Balla, as well as sculptures by Canova and major works by Modigliani, de Chirico and Guttuso. International artists represented include Van Gogh, Cézanne, Monet, Klimt, Kandinskij, Mondrian and Man Ray.

⊙ Flaminio

AUDITORIUM PARCO
DELLA MUSICA   CULTURAL CENTRE
Map p316 (☑06 8024 1281; www.auditorium. com; Viale Pietro de Coubertin; guided tours adult/reduced €9/5; ☉11am-8pm Mon-Sat, 10am-8pm Sun summer, to 6pm winter; 🚊Viale Tiziano) Designed by archistar Renzo Piano and inaugurated in 2002, Rome's flagship cultural centre is an audacious work of architecture consisting of three grey pod-like concert halls set round a 3000-seat amphitheatre.

Excavations during its construction revealed remains of an ancient Roman villa, which are now on show in the Auditorium's small **Museo Archeologico** (Map p316; ☑06 8024 1281; www.auditorium.com; Auditorium Parco della Musica, Viale Pietro de Coubertin; ☉10am-8pm summer, 11am-6pm Mon-Sat, 10am-6pm Sun winter; 🚊Viale Tiziano) **FREE**.

Guided tours (for a minimum of 10 people) depart hourly between 11.30am and 4.30pm Saturday and Sunday, and by arrangement from Monday to Friday.

MUSEO NAZIONALE DELLE
ARTI DEL XXI SECOLO   GALLERY
Map p316 (MAXXI; ☑06 320 19 54; www.fonda zionemaxxi.it; Via Guido Reni 4a; adult/reduced €12/8, permanent collection free Tue-Fri & 1st Sun of month; ☉11am-7pm Tue-Fri & Sun, to 10pm Sat; 🚊Viale Tiziano) As much as the exhibitions, the highlight of Rome's leading contemporary art gallery is the Zaha Hadid–designed building it occupies. Formerly a barracks, the curved concrete structure is striking inside and out with a multilayered geometric facade and a cavernous light-filled interior full of snaking walkways and suspended staircases.

The gallery has a permanent collection of 20th- and 21st-century works, of which a selection are on free display in Gallery 4, but more interesting are its international exhibitions.

TOP SIGHT **MUSEO NAZIONALE ETRUSCO DI VILLA GIULIA**

Pope Julius III's 16th-century villa provides the charming setting for Italy's finest collection of Etruscan and pre-Roman treasures. Exhibits, many of which came from tombs in the surrounding Lazio region, range from bronze figurines and black *bucchero* tableware to temple decorations, terracotta vases and dazzling jewellery.

Must-sees include a polychrome terracotta statue of Apollo from the Etruscan town of Veio, just north of Rome, and the so-called *Lamine di Pyrgi* (Pyrgi Tablets), three gold sheets discovered during excavations of Pyrgi, Cerveteri's ancient sea port. Dating to the end of the 6th century BC, they are inscribed with texts written in both Etruscan and Phoenician. Perhaps the museum's most famous piece, however, is the 6th-century BC *Sarcofago degli Sposi* (Sarcophagus of the Betrothed). This astonishing work, originally unearthed in a tomb in Cerveteri, depicts a husband and wife reclining on a stone banqueting couch. And although called a sarcophagus, it was actually designed as an elaborate urn for the couple's ashes.

Further finds are housed in the nearby **Villa Poniatowski**, which is currently closed to visitors.

DON'T MISS...

➡ *Sarcofago degli Sposi*

➡ *Apollo di Veio*

➡ *Lamine di Pyrgi*

PRACTICALITIES

➡ Map p316, D5

➡ 🗐 06 322 65 71

➡ www.villagiulia. beniculturali.it

➡ Piazzale di Villa Giulia

➡ adult/reduced €8/4

➡ 🕑8.30am-7.30pm Tue-Sun

➡ 🗐Via delle Belle Arti

PONTE MILVIO BRIDGE

Map p316 (🗐 Lungotevere Maresciallo Diaz) A cobbled footbridge, Ponte Milvio is best known as the site of the ancient Battle of the Milvian Bridge. It was first built in 109 BC to carry Via Flaminia over the Tiber and survived intact until 1849, when Garibaldi's troops partially destroyed it to stop advancing French soldiers. Pope Pius IX had it rebuilt a year later.

FORO ITALICO ARCHITECTURE

Map p316 (Viale del Foro Italico; 🗐Lungotevere Maresciallo Cadorna) At the foot of the heavily wooded **Monte Mario**, the Foro Italico is a grandiose Fascist-era sports complex, centred on the Stadio Olimpico (p186), Rome's 70,000-seat football stadium. Most people pass through en route to a football or rugby match, but if you're interested in Fascist architecture, it's worth a look.

EXPLORA – MUSEO DEI BAMBINI DI ROMA MUSEUM

Map p316 (🗐06 361 37 76; www.mdbr.it; Via Flaminia 80-86; adult/reduced €8/5; 🕑entrance 10am, noon, 3pm & 5pm Tue-Sun; 🗐Flaminio) Rome's only dedicated kids' museum, Explora is aimed at the under-12s. It's divided into thematic sections and with everything from a play pool and fire engine to a train driver's cabin, it's a hands-on, feet-on, full-on experience that your nippers will love. Outside there's also a free play park open to all.

⊙ Salario

MUSEO D'ARTE CONTEMPORANEA DI ROMA GALLERY

Map p316 (MACRO; 🗐06 06 08; www.museomacro.org; Via Nizza 138, cnr Via Cagliari; adult/reduced €11/9; 🕑10.30am-7.30pm Tue-Sun; 🗐Via Nizza) Along with MAXXI, this is Rome's most important contemporary art gallery. Occupying a converted Peroni brewery, it hosts exhibitions by international artists such as Anish Kapoor, and displays works from its permanent collection of post-1960s Italian art.

Vying with the exhibits for your attention is the museum's sleek black-and-red interior design. The work of French architect Odile Decq, this retains much of the building's original structure while also incorporating a sophisticated steel-and-glass finish.

CATACOMBE DI PRISCILLA CHRISTIAN SITE

Map p316 (🗐06 8620 6272; www.catacombepriscilla.com; Via Salaria 430; guided visit adult/

reduced €8/5; ⊗9am-noon & 2-5pm Tue-Sun; 🖳Via Salaria) Dug between the 2nd and 5th centuries, this network of creepy tunnels was known as the Queen of Catacombs. It was an important early Christian burial site and numerous martyrs and popes were buried in the tombs and chambers that line the 13km of tunnels.

Visits take in a decorated Greek chapel and a scratchy fresco of the Virgin Mary with the baby Jesus on her lap. Dating to around AD 230, this is thought to be the oldest existing image of the Madonna.

VILLA ADA   PARK

Map p316 (entrances at Via Salaria, Via di Ponte Salario, Via di Monte Antenne, Via Panama; ⊗7am-sunset; 🖳Via Salaria) Once the private estate of King Vittorio Emanuele III, Villa Ada is a big rambling park, about 160 hectares, with shady paths, lakes, lawns and woods. It's popular with locals and explodes into life in summer when outdoor concerts are staged during the Roma Incontro il Mondo festival.

⊙ Nomentano

PORTA PIA   GATE

Map p316 (Piazzale Porta Pia; 🖳Via XX Settembre) Michelangelo's last architectural work, this crenellated structure was commissioned by Pope Pius IV to replace Porta Nomentana, one of the original gates in the Aurelian Walls, and built between 1561 and 1564.

Bitter street fighting took place here in 1870 as Italian troops breached the adjacent walls on 20 September to wrest the city from the pope and claim it for the nascent kingdom of Italy.

VILLA TORLONIA   PARK

Map p316 (Via Nomentana 70; ⊗7am-7pm winter, to 8.30pm summer; 🖳Via Nomentana) Full of towering pine trees, atmospheric palms and scattered villas, this splendid 19th-century park once belonged to Prince Giovanni Torlonia (1756–1829), a powerful banker and landowner. His large neoclassical villa, **Casino Nobile**, later became the Mussolini family home (1925–43) and, in the latter part of WWII, Allied headquarters (1944–47). These days it's part of the Musei di Villa Torlonia museum.

MUSEI DI VILLA TORLONIA   MUSEUM

Map p316 (📞06 06 08; www.museivillatorlonia.it; Via Nomentana 70; adult/reduced Casino Nobile €7.50/6.50, Casina delle Civette €6/5, combined

€9.50/7.50; ⊗9am-7pm Tue-Sun; 🖳Via Nomentana) Housed in three villas – Casino Nobile, Casina delle Civette and Casino dei Principi – this museum boasts an eclectic collection of sculpture, paintings, furnishings and decorative stained glass.

The main ticket office is just inside the Via Nomentana entrance to Villa Torlonia.

With its oversized neoclassical facade – added by architect Giovan Battista Caretti to embellish an earlier overhaul by Giuseppe Valadier – **Casino Nobile** (Map p316; www.museivillatorlonia.it; Villa Torlonia, Via Nomentana 70; adult/reduced €7.50/6.50; ⊗9am-7pm Tue-Sun; 🖳Via Nomentana) makes quite an impression. In the lavishly decorated interior you can admire the Torlonia family's fine collection of classically inspired sculpture and early-20th-century paintings from the *Scuola Romana* (Roman School of Art).

To the northeast, the much smaller **Casina delle Civette** (Map p316; www.museivillatorlonia.it; Villa Torlonia, Via Nomentana 70; adult/reduced €6/5; ⊗9am-7pm Tue-Sun; 🖳Via Nomentana) is a bizarre mix of Swiss cottage, Gothic castle and twee farmhouse decorated in art-nouveau style. Built between 1840 and 1930, it's now a museum dedicated to stained glass.

Casino dei Principi (Map p316; www.museivillatorlonia.it; Villa Torlonia, Via Nomentana 70; adult/reduced incl Casino Nobile €7.50/6.50; ⊗only for exhibitions 9am-7pm Tue-Sun, 🖳Via Nomentana) houses the archive of the *Scuola Romana* and opens only to stage temporary exhibitions.

QUARTIERE COPPEDÈ

The compact **Quartiere Coppedè** (Map p316; 🖳Viale Regina Margherita), best entered from the corner of Via Tagliamento and Via Dora, is one of Rome's most extraordinary neighbourhoods. Conceived and built by the little-known Florentine architect, Gino Coppedè, between 1913 and 1926, it's a fairy-tale mix-match of Tuscan turrets, Liberty sculptures, Moorish arches, Gothic gargoyles, frescoed facades and palm-fringed gardens.

At its heart, the whimsical **Fontana delle Rane** (Fountain of the Frogs; Map p316; Piazza Mincio; 🖳Viale Regina Margherita) is a modern take on the better known Fontana delle Tartarughe in the Jewish Ghetto.

VILLA TORLONIA BUNKER   HISTORIC SITE

Map p316 (Villa Torlonia; ⊙currently closed; 🚇Via Nomentana) Beneath the greenery of Villa Torlonia lie reminders of a dark chapter in Rome's history. Between 1940 and 1943, Mussolini had two air raid shelters and an underground bunker built beneath what was, at the time, his family estate. Guided tours take you down into these bare underground chambers, complete with anti-gas doors and air filtration systems. The bunker, whose 4m-thick walls lie 6m below the Casino Nobile (p183), was still being worked on when the Duce was arrested on 25 July 1943.

★BASILICA DI SANT'AGNESE FUORI LE MURA & MAUSOLEO DI SANTA COSTANZA   BASILICA

(www.santagnese.com; entrances at Via Nomentana 349 & Via di Sant'Agnese 3; basilica & mausoleo free, catacombs guided visit adult/reduced €8/5; ⊙basilica 8am-noon & 4-7.30pm, mausoleo 9am-noon & 3-6pm, catacombs 9am-noon Mon-Sat & 3-5pm daily; 🚇Via Nomentana) Although a bit of a hike, it's well worth searching out this intriguing medieval church complex. Set over the **catacombs** where St Agnes was buried, it comprises the **Basilica di Sant'Agnese Fuori le Mura**, home to a stunning Byzantine mosaic of the saint, and the **Mausoleo di Santa Costanza**, a circular 4th-century mausoleum decorated by some of Christendom's oldest mosaics.

The original basilica, remains of which can be seen in a field adjacent to the current complex, was built in the 4th century for Costanza, daughter of the emperor Costantino. It was subsequently abandoned in the 7th century and replaced by the current basilica, which has itself been much modified over the centuries. Its star attraction, and one of the few original features, is its golden **apse mosaic**, one of the best examples of Byzantine art in Rome, has survived intact. It shows St Agnes, flanked by Popes Honorius and Symmachus, standing over the signs of her martyrdom – a sword and a flame. According to tradition, the 13-year-old Agnes was sentenced to be burnt at the stake, but when the flames failed to kill her she was beheaded on Piazza Navona and buried beneath this church.

Up from the main basilica is the Mausoleo di Santa Costanza. This squat circular building has a dome supported by 12 pairs of granite columns and a vaulted ambulatory decorated with beautiful 4th-century mosaics.

✗ EATING

✗ Villa Borghese & Around

SERENELLA   PIZZA €

Map p316 (☎06 6478 1660; Via Salaria 70; pizza slices from €2; ⊙8am-10pm; 🚇Via Salaria) For the best sliced pizza near Villa Borghese park, search out this humble takeaway. Pizzas come capped with a selection of imaginative toppings and a light, fluffy base, the result of a 72-hour preparation and the use of natural yeast. For a cheap, easy-to-eat snack, the pizza *bianca* (plain white pizza) is excellent.

CAFFÈ DELLE ARTI   CAFE, RISTORANTE €€

Map p316 (☎06 3265 1236; www.caffedelleartiroma.com; Via Gramsci 73; meals €40-45; ⊙8am-5pm Mon, 8am-midnight Tue-Sun; 🚇Piazza Thorvaldsen) The cafe-restaurant of La Galleria Nazionale (p181) sits in neoclassical splendour in a tranquil corner of Villa Borghese. An elegant venue, it's at its best on warm sunny days when you can sit on the terrace and enjoy the romantic setting over a lunch salad, cocktail or al fresco dinner of classic Italian cuisine.

✗ Flaminio

BAR POMPI   PASTRIES €

Map p316 (☎06 333 34 88; Via Cassia 8; tiramisu €4; ⊙7am-midnight Wed-Mon, 4pm-12.30pm Tue; 🚇Ponte Milvio) This renowned *pasticceria* is celebrated for its tiramisu. Alongside the classic coffee, liqueur and cocoa combination, there are several other versions including strawberry, pistachio, and banana and chocolate.

OSTERIA FLAMINIO   RISTORANTE €€

Map p316 (☎06 323 69 00; www.osteriaflaminio.com; Via Flaminia 297; lunch buffet €8-12, meals €30-35; ⊙12.30-3.30pm & 7.30pm-midnight; 🚇Via Flaminia) This friendly eatery makes for a fine lunch stop after a visit to the MAXXI art museum. The vibe is casual and its interior is a handsome mix of dark wood floors, large street-facing windows and muted greys and whites. Foodwise, it serves a popular lunch buffet (vegetarian on Mondays, fish on Fridays) and a full menu of modern Italian and international fare.

ALL'ORO
RISTORANTE €€€

Map p316 (☑06 9799 6907; www.ristorante alloro.it; Via Giuseppe Pisanelli 23-25; tasting menus €78-130; ⊘7-11pm daily & 1-2.45pm Sat & Sun; ⓂFlaminio) This Michelin-starred restaurant, recently re-located to the five-star H'All Tailor Suite hotel, is one of Rome's top fine dining tickets. At the helm is chef Riccardo Di Giacinto whose artfully presented food is modern and innovative whilst still being recognisably Italian. Complementing the cuisine, the decor strikes a contemporary club look with dark wood ceilings, brass lamps and a fireplace.

✗ Salario

PASTICCERIA GRUÈ
PASTRIES €

Map p316 (☑06 841 22 20; Viale Regina Margherita 95; pastries from €1.50; ⊘7am-9pm Sun-Fri; ☐Viale Regina Margherita) One of many eateries on Viale Regina Margherita, this sleek *pasticceria*-cafe is a local hotspot – suits and sharply dressed office workers lunch here on delicate *panini* and daily pastas while evening sees the aperitif crowd move in. But its real calling cards are the exquisitely designed pastries and chocolates that stare out from beneath the counter.

PRO LOCO PINCIANO
LAZIO CUISINE, PIZZA €€

Map p316 (☑06 841 41 36; www.prolocopinciano. it; Via Bergamo 18; meals €25-30; ⊘12.30-3pm & 7.30-11pm; ☐Via Salaria) Like a number of Rome's newer eateries – it opened in late 2014 – Pro Loco Pinciano is something of a culinary all-rounder. It serves regional cured meats and cheeses from a well-furnished deli counter, wood-fired pizzas, and a menu of salads, pastas and mains. All this in a good-looking interior of exposed brick walls and trendy mismatched furniture.

✗ Parioli

METAMORFOSI
RISTORANTE €€€

Map p316 (☑06 807 68 39; www.metamorfosi roma.it; Via Giovanni Antonelli 30; tasting menus €100-130; ⊘12.30-2.30pm & 8-10.30pm, closed Sat lunch & Sun; ☐Via Giovanni Antonelli) This Michelin-starred Parioli restaurant is one of Rome's top dining tickets offering international fusion cuisine and a contemporary look that marries linear clean-cut lines with

---

> **LOCAL KNOWLEDGE**
>
> ### HIDDEN GELATO GEMS
> ●
>
> This neck of the woods harbours some outstanding gelaterie, but they're not the easiest to find. A case in point is **Neve di Latte** (Map p316; ☑06 320 84 85; Via Poletti 6; gelato €2.50-5; ⊘noon-11pm Sun-Thu, to midnight Fri & Sat; ☐Viale Tiziano), an innocuous-looking place that serves some of the best classical gelato in town. Over the river, **Al Settimo Gelo** (Map p316; www.alsetti mogelo.it; Via Vodice 21a; gelato €2-5; ⊘10am-8.30pm Tue-Sat, 11am-2pm & 3.30-8.30pm Sun winter, 10am-11.30pm Tue-Sat, 11am-2pm & 4-11.30pm Sun summer; ☐Piazza Giuseppe Mazzini) is another much-lauded gelateria.

warm earthy tones. Chef Roy Careeres' cooking is eclectic, often featuring playful updates of traditional Roman dishes, such as his signature Uovo 65° carbonara antipasto, a deconstruction of Rome's classic pasta dish.

MOLTO
RISTORANTE €€€

Map p316 (☑06 808 79 00; www.moltoitaliano.it; Viale dei Parioli 122; meals €50-60; ⊘12.30-3pm & 7.30-11pm; ☐Viale Parioli) Fashionable and quietly chic, Molto is a Parioli favourite. The discreet entrance gives onto an elegant, modern interior and open-air terrace, while the menu offers everything from cured meat and cheese starters to traditional Roman pastas and succulent roast meats. Saturday features a burger menu and there's brunch on Sunday (€40).

🍷 DRINKING & NIGHTLIFE

MOMART
CAFE

(☑06 8639 1656; www.momartcafe.it; Viale XXI Aprile 19; ⊘noon-2am, to 3am Sat & Sun; ☐Viale XXI Aprile) A modish restaurant-cafe in the university district near Via Nomentana, Momart serves one of Rome's most bountiful *apericena* (an informal evening meal involving *aperitivi* and tapas-style food) spreads. A mixed crowd of students and local professionals flocks here to fill up on the ample buffet and kick back over cocktails on the pavement terrace.

KIOSK BARS

A recurring feature of Rome's streetscape are its green kiosks. Many of these are occupied by vendors selling newspapers, magazines and public transport tickets. Some, however, harbour long-standing and much-loved bars. On the river, the **Chioschetto di Ponte Milvio** (Map p316; Piazzale Ponte Milvio; ⊘6pm-2am summer, 5pm-2am Thu-Sat, 9am-11pm Sun winter; 🚇Ponte Milvio) is a classic case in point: a neighbourhood meeting point that buzzes on warm summer nights. Another prime example is **Lemoncocco** (Map p316; Piazza Buenos Aires; ⊘11am-2.30am; 🚇Viale Regina Margherita), a local institution famous for its trademark lemon-and-coconut drink.

LANIFICIO 159   CLUB
(✆06 4178 0081; www.lanificio.com; Via Pietralata 159a; ⊘club nights 11pm-4.30am Fri-Sun; 🚇Via Pietralata) Occupying an ex-wool factory in Rome's northeastern suburbs, this cool underground venue hosts live gigs and hot clubbing action, led by top Roman crews and international DJs. The club is part of a larger complex that stages more reserved events such as Sunday markets, exhibitions and *aperitivi*.

ENTERTAINMENT

★AUDITORIUM PARCO DELLA MUSICA   CONCERT VENUE
Map p316 (✆06 8024 1281; www.auditorium.com; Viale Pietro de Coubertin; 🚇Viale Tiziano) The hub of Rome's thriving cultural scene, the Auditorium is the capital's premier concert venue. Its three concert halls offer superb acoustics, and together with a 3000-seat open-air arena, stage everything from classical music concerts to jazz gigs, public lectures and film screenings.

The Auditorium is also home to Rome's world-class **Orchestra dell'Accademia Nazionale di Santa Cecilia** (www.santacecilia.it).

FORO ITALICO   SPECTATOR SPORT
Map p316 (✆800 622662; www.foroitalico ticketing.it; Viale del Foro Italico; 🚇Lungotevere Maresciallo Cadorna) This grand Fascist-era sports complex, built between 1928 and 1938, is centred on Rome's 70,000-seat Stadio Olimpico, home of the capital's two *Serie A* football teams. It also hosts Italy's premier tennis tournament, the Internazionali BNL d'Italia, in May.

STADIO OLIMPICO   STADIUM
Map p316 (✆06 3685 7563; Viale dei Gladiatori 2, Foro Italico; 🚇Lungotevere Maresciallo Cadorna) A trip to Rome's impressive Stadio Olimpico offers an unforgettable insight into Rome's sporting heart. Throughout the football season (September to May) there's a game on most Sundays featuring one of the city's two Serie A teams (Roma or Lazio), and during the six nations rugby tournament (February to March) it hosts Italy's home games.

TEATRO OLIMPICO   THEATRE
Map p316 (✆06 326 59 91; www.teatroolimpico. it; Piazza Gentile da Fabriano 17; 🚇Piazza Mancini, 🚇Piazza Mancini) The Teatro Olimpico hosts a varied program of opera, dance, one-man shows, musicals and comedies, as well as classical music concerts by the Accademia Filarmonica Romana.

SHOPPING

BIALETTI   HOMEWARES
Map p316 (Via Salaria 52; ⊘10am-8pm; 🚇Via Salaria) In 1933 Alfonso Bialetti revolutionised domestic coffee-making by creating his classic *moka caffettiera*. His design has by now become a household staple, as ubiquitous in Italian kitchens as kettles in British homes. Here at this gleaming shop you'll find a full range as well as all manner of cool kitchenware.

LIBRERIA L'ARGONAUTA   BOOKS
Map p316 (✆06 854 34 43; www.librerialargo nauta.com; Via Reggio Emilia 89; ⊘10am-8pm Mon-Fri, 10am-1pm & 4-8pm Sat winter, 10am-8pm Mon-Fri summer; 🚇Via Nizza) Near the MACRO contemporary art museum, this travel bookshop is a lovely place for browsing. With its serene atmosphere and shelves of travel literature, guides, maps and photo tomes, it can easily spark daydreams of far-off places. It also hosts regular talks and cultural events.

Southern Rome

VIA APPIA ANTICA | OSTIENSE, SAN PAOLO & GARBATELLA

Neighbourhood Top Five

❶ Via Appia Antica (p189) Tracing the route of a thousand ancient Roman footsteps by bike or on foot along this urban 'countryside' trail, sprinkled with ancient Roman ruins.

❷ Catacombe di San Sebastiano (p191) Exploring ancient Christian burial catacombs of subterranean Rome.

❸ Street art (p195) Checking out the vibrant, edgy gallery of open-air art in ex-industrial and alternative Ostiense.

❹ Museo Capitoline Centrale Montemartini (p195) Wandering around the ingenious location for the overflow from the Capitoline Museums – a former power station.

❺ Basilica de San Paolo Fuori le Mura (p195) Feeling dwarfed by the majesty of the second-largest church in Rome after St Peter's.

For more detail of this area see Map p318 ➡

Lonely Planet's Top Tip

Originally paved with huge *basoli* (polygonal cobbles of basalt rock) and wide enough for two carriages to pass, the Appian Way is today something of a hair-raising racetrack for loony Roman drivers out for a Sunday spin – visit on a weekday when the road is quieter.

X Best Places to Eat

➡ Eataly (p197)

➡ Doppiozeroo (p197)

➡ Seacook (p197)

➡ Verde Pistacchio (p197)

➡ L'Archeologia Ristorante (p196)

For reviews, see p196.➡

● Best Places to Drink

➡ Circolo Illuminati (p197)

➡ Goa (p198)

➡ Vinile (p198)

➡ Neo Club (p198)

➡ Appia Antica Caffè (p198)

For reviews, see p197.➡

◉ Best Roman Ruins

➡ Circo di Massenzio (p189)

➡ Mausoleo di Cecilia Metella (p189)

➡ Mausoleo di Romolo (p189)

➡ Villa di Massenzio (p189)

For reviews, see p194.➡

Explore: Southern Rome

Southern Rome is a sprawling neighbourhood that comprises four distinct areas of interest to tourists: the Via Appia Antica (p189), famous for its Roman ruins, catacombs and bucolic country air; hip, post-industrial Ostiense with its rainbow of street art (p195) and cutting-edge nightlife; picturesque Garbatella (p196); and EUR (p196), Mussolini's futuristic building development spearheaded today by Italian fashion house Fendi, which has its global headquarters here. It's all quite spread out, but public transport connections are good.

Count at least a day for the Appian Way, best kept for a day when you have the urge to 'get out of town'. Fields surround the rickety old, stone-paved road – one of the world's oldest roads and a much-prized Roman address. The main sights can be done on foot, but to get the most out of the road, originally 212km long and requiring a journey of five days when the Romans built it in 312 BC, rent a bicycle at the Info Point (p189) by the bus stop at the start of the road.

To the west, Via Ostiense presents a very different picture. Explore by day if you are here to track down street art, admire superb classical statuary in defunct power station Centrale Montemartini (p195), or visit the gargantuan Basilica di San Paolo Fuori le Mura (p195), one step removed from Ostiense's gritty soul. Otherwise, come after dark when tagged, disused factories and warehouses buzz with some of the best clubs in town.

Local Life

➡**Clubbing** Some of the coolest clubs on Roman earth – Vinile (p198), Neo Club (p198), Circolo Illuminati (p197), Goa (p198) – are clustered on and around Via Libetta, at the southern end of Via Ostiense.

➡**Weekend brunch** Roman families pile into Porto Fluviale (p197) for Sunday brunch, while cent-saving students ram Vinile (p198) to the rafters.

➡**Cycling** Escape from the frenetic city centre along the beautiful Appian Way (p189).

➡**Food, glorious food** There is no finer spot to shop for, and taste, the very best of Italian food products than at Eataly (p197). This glorious food emporium also hosts cooking classes and shows.

Getting There & Away

➡**Metro** Metro line B runs to Piramide, Garbatella, Basilica San Paolo, EUR Palasport and EUR Fermi.

➡**Bus** There are bus connections to Porta San Sebastiano (118, 218 and 714), Via Ostiense (23 and 716) and Via Appia Antica (118, 660).

TOP SIGHT
VIA APPIA ANTICA

The Appian Way was known to the Romans as *Regina Viarum* (Queen of Roads). Named after Appius Claudius Caecus, who laid the first 90km section in 312 BC, it was extended in 190 BC to reach Brindisi on the southern Adriatic coast. Today it is one of Rome's most exclusive addresses, a beautiful cobbled thoroughfare flanked by fields, Roman ruins and towering pines.

Villa di Massenzio

The outstanding feature of Maxentius' enormous 4th-century **palace complex** (☑06 06 08; www.villadimassenzio.it; ☺10am-4pm Tue-Sun) FREE is the **Circo di Massenzio**, Rome's best-preserved ancient racetrack – you can still make out the starting stalls used for chariot races. The 10,000-seat arena was built by Maxentius around 309, but he died before ever seeing a race here. Above the arena are the ruins of Maxentius' imperial residence. Near the racetrack, the **Mausoleo di Romolo** (Tombo di Romolo; Map p318; ☑06 06 08; www.villadimassenzio.it; ☺10am-4pm Tue-Sun) FREE was built by Maxentius for his 17-year-old son Romulus.

Mausoleo di Cecilia Metella

Dating to the 1st century BC, this great drum of a **mausoleum** (Map p318; ☑06 3996 7700; www.coopculture.it; adult/reduced incl Terme di Caracalla & Villa dei Quintili €6/3; ☺9am-1hr before sunset Tue-Sun) encloses a burial chamber, now roofless. In the 14th century it was converted into a fort by the Caetani family, who were related to Pope Boniface VIII and used to frighten passing traffic into paying a toll.

DON'T MISS

➡ The catacombs
➡ Cycling along the Appia
➡ Villa dei Quintili

PRACTICALITIES

➡ Appian Way
➡ Map p318, E3
➡ ☑06 513 53 16
➡ www.parcoappia antica.it
➡ ☺Info Point 9.30am-sunset summer, 9.30am-1pm & 2-5pm Mon-Fri, 9.30am-5pm Sat & Sun winter
➡ ▢Via Appia Antica

THE APPIAN WAY

The most pleasurable way of exploring the Appian Way is by bicycle. Rent a set of wheels and pick up maps at the **Info Point Appia Antica** (Map p318; ☑06 513 53 16; www.parcoappiaantica. it; Via Appia Antica 58-60; ⊙9.30am-sunset summer, 9am-1pm & 2-5pm Mon-Fri, 9.30am-5pm Sat & Sun winter; ⊟Via Appia Antica) at the northern end of the road.

The Info Point also sells the **Appia Antica Card** (€6), valid seven days and covering admission to three key sights along the way (Villa dei Quintili, Mausoleo di Cecilia Metella, Terme di Caracalla).

Mausoleo di Cecilia Metella (p189)

Villa dei Quintili

Towering over green fields, this 2nd-century **villa** (☑06 3996 7700; www.coopculture.it; Via Appia Nuova 1092; adult/reduced incl Terme di Caracalla & Mausoleo di Cecilia Meteappialla €6/3; ⊙9am-1hr before sunset Tue-Sun; ⊟Via Appia Antica) is one of Rome's unsung splendours. It was the luxurious abode of two consuls, the Quintili brothers, but its splendour was their downfall: the emperor Commodus had them both killed, taking over the villa for himself. The emperor added to the complex and the ruins are fabulously impressive. The highlight is the well-preserved baths complex with a pool, *caldarium* (hot bath room) and *frigidarium* (cold bath room). There's an interesting small museum as well.

Catacombs

The Appia Antica, peaceful today, resounds with history: it's where Spartacus and 6000 of his slave rebels were crucified in 71 BC, and around it lie 300km of underground tunnels carved out of soft tufa rock, used as burial chambers by the early Christians. Corpses were wrapped in simple white sheets and usually placed in rectangular niches carved into the walls, which were then closed with marble or terracotta slabs. You can't visit all 300km, but three major catacombs – San Callisto (p194), San Sebastiano (p191) and Santa Domitilla (p194) – are open for guided exploration.

TOP SIGHT
BASILICA & CATACOMBE DI SAN SEBASTIANO

The most famous of the Appian Way catacombs contain frescoes, stucco work, epigraphs and several immaculately preserved mausoleums. The catacombs extend for more than 12km and are divided into three levels, 3m, 9m and 12m deep. They once harboured more than 65,000 tombs.

DON'T MISS
....

➡ Graffiti to St Peter and St Paul

➡ Mausoleums

➡ Basilica di San Sebastiano

Basilica

The 4th-century **basilica** (Via Appia Antica 136; ⊘8am-1pm & 2-5.30pm) that was built here by the emperor Constantine was mostly destroyed by Saracen raids in the 9th century, and the church you see today dates mainly from the reconstruction initiated by Cardinal Borghese in the 17th century. It is dedicated to St Sebastian, who was martyred and buried here in the late 3rd century. In 826 his body was transferred to St Peter's for safekeeping, but he was re-interred here in the 12th century. In the Capella delle Reliquie you'll find one of the arrows used to kill him and the column to which he was tied. On the other side of the church is a marble slab with Jesus' footprints.

PRACTICALITIES
....

➡ Map p318, F5

➡ ☑06 785 03 50

➡ www.catacombe.org

➡ Via Appia Antica 136

➡ adult/reduced €8/5

➡ ⊘10am-5pm Mon-Sat Jan-Nov

➡ 🚌Via Appia Antica

➡ Map p318, F5

➡ Via Appia Antica 136

➡ ⊘8am-1pm & 2-5.30pm

➡ 🚌Via Appia Antica

Catacombs

A warren of tunnels that lie beneath the church and beyond, the Catacombe di San Sebastiano were the first catacombs to be so called, the name deriving from the Greek *kata* (near) and *kymbas* (cavity), because they were located near a cave. During the persecution of Christians by the emperor Vespasian from AD 258, it's believed that the catacombs were used as a safe haven for the remains of St Peter and St Paul and became a popular pilgrimage site. A plastered wall is covered with hundreds of invocations, engraved by worshippers in the 3rd and 4th centuries, featuring personalised entreaties such as 'Peter and Paul, pray for Victor'. However, it may be the case that the remains were never kept here, and the catacombs simply served as a focus for worship during those difficult times.

Mausoleums

Within the catacombs there are three beautifully preserved, decorated mausoleums. Each of the monumental facades feature a door, above which are inscribed symbols and the names of the owners. The first mausoleum belonged to Marcus Clodius Ermete, while the second one is named 'of the innocentiores', which is thought to have been the name of an association. During the 3rd century the area was filled in to build a place of pilgrimage where visitors could come to honour St Peter and St Paul, which is why the delicate stucco has remained so immaculately well preserved.

Roman Catacombs

Ancient Roman law forbade burying the dead within the city walls, for reasons of hygiene. Rome's persecuted Christian community didn't have their own cemeteries, so in the 2nd century AD they began to build an extensive network of subterranean burial grounds outside the city.

The tombs were dug by specialised gravediggers, who tunnelled out the galleries. Bodies were wrapped in simple shrouds and then either placed individually in carved-out niches, called *loculi*, or in larger family tombs. Many tombs were marked with elaborate decorations, from frescoes to stucco work, which remain remarkably well preserved. A great many tombs discovered here bear touching inscriptions, such as the following: 'Apuleia Crysopolis, who lived for 7 years, 2 months; (her) parents made (this) for their dearest daughter'.

Symbolism

An almost secretive language of symbols had evolved to represent elements of the Christian faith. Since many early Christians could not read and write, these symbols served as both a secret code and a means to communicate among the illiterate. The most common of the symbols include the fish, the Greek word for which is *ichthys*, standing for Iesous Christos Theou Yios Soter (Jesus Christ, son of God, Saviour). The anchor, which also appears regularly, symbolises the belief in Christ as a safe haven, a comforting thought in times of persecution. It's thought, too, that this was again an example of Greek wordplay: *ankura* resembling *en kuriol*, which means 'in the Lord'. A dove with an olive

1. Crypt of the Popes, Catacombe di San Callisto (p194) **2.** Catacombe di Priscilla (p182) **3.** Wall fresco in Catacombe di San Callisto (p194)

branch in the beak is a reference to the biblical dove, meaning salvation.

Abandonment

The catacombs began to be abandoned as early as 313, when Constantine issued the Milan decree of religious tolerance and Christians were thus able to bury their dead in churchyards.

In about 800, after frequent incursions by invaders, the bodies of the martyrs and first popes were transferred to the basilicas inside the city walls for safe keeping. The catacombs were abandoned and by the Middle Ages many had been forgotten.

Since the 19th century, more than 30 catacombs have been uncovered in the area. The warren of tunnels are fascinating to explore, and sections of three sets of catacombs are accessible via guided tour. Unless you're passionate about catacombs, visiting one set will be sufficient.

TOP 5 CATACOMB READS

➡ *The Roman Catacombs*, by James Spencer Northcote (1859)

➡ *Tombs and Catacombs of the Appian Way: History of Cremation*, by Olinto L Spadoni (1892)

➡ *Valeria, the Martyr of the Catacombs*, by WH Withrow (1892)

➡ *Christian Rome: Past and Present: Early Christian Rome Catacombs and Basilicas*, by Philippe Pergola (2002)

➡ *The Churches and Catacombs of Early Christian Rome: A Comprehensive Guide* by Matilda Webb (2001)

⊙ SIGHTS

⊙ Via Appia Antica

VIA APPIA ANTICA HISTORIC SITE
See p189.

**BASILICA DI SAN
SEBASTIANO** BASILICA
See p191.

**CATACOMBE DI SAN
SEBASTIANO** CATACOMB
See p191.

MUSEO DELLE MURA MUSEUM
Map p318 (⌨06 7047 5284; www.museodelle
muraroma.it; Via di Porta San Sebastiano 18; ⏲9am-2pm Tue-Sun; ⛳Porta San Sebastiano) FREE Marking the start of Via Appia Antica, the 5th-century Porta San Sebastiano is the largest of the gates in the Aurelian Wall. During WWII the Fascist Party secretary Ettore Muti lived here; today it houses the modest Museo delle Mure, which offers the chance to walk along the top of the walls for around 50m as well as displaying the history of the city's fortifications. The gate was originally known as Porta Appia but took on its current name in honour of the thousands of pilgrims who passed under it on their way to the Catacombe di San Sebastiano (p191).

CHIESA DEL DOMINE QUO VADIS CHURCH
Map p318 (⌨06 512 04 41; Via Appia Antica 51; ⏲8am-7.30pm summer, to 6.30pm winter; ⛳Via Appia Antica) This pint-sized church marks the spot where St Peter, fleeing Rome, met a vision of Jesus going the other way. When Peter asked, *'Domine, quo vadis?'* (Lord, where are you going?), Jesus replied, *'Venio Roman iterum crucifigi'* (I am coming to Rome to be crucified again). Reluctantly deciding to join him, Peter tramped back into town where he was arrested and executed. In the aisle are copies of Christ's footprints; the originals are in Basilica di San Sebastiano (p191).

**CATACOMBE DI SANTA
DOMITILLA** CATACOMB
Map p318 (⌨06 511 03 42; www.domitilla.info; Via delle Sette Chiese 282; adult/reduced €8/5; ⏲9am-noon & 2-5pm Wed-Mon mid-Jan–mid-Dec; ⛳Via Appia Antica) Among Rome's largest and oldest, these catacombs stretch for about 17km. They were established on the private burial ground of Flavia Domitilla, niece of the emperor Domitian and a member of the wealthy Flavian family. They contain Christian wall paintings and the haunting underground **Chiesa di SS Nereus e Achilleus**, a 4th-century church dedicated to two Roman soldiers martyred by Diocletian.

**MAUSOLEO DELLE
FOSSE ARDEATINE** MONUMENT
Map p318 (⌨06 513 67 42; www.mausoleo fosseardeatine.it; Via Ardeatina 174; ⏲8.15am-3.30pm Mon-Fri, to 4.30pm Sat & Sun; ⛳Via Appia Antica) FREE This moving mausoleum is dedicated to the victims of Rome's worst WWII atrocity. Buried here, outside the Ardeatine Caves, are 335 Italians shot by the Nazis on 24 March 1944. Following the massacre, ordered in reprisal for a partisan attack, the Germans used mines to explode sections of the caves and bury the bodies. After the war, the bodies were exhumed, identified and reburied in a mass grave, now marked by a huge concrete slab and sculptures.

CATACOMBE DI SAN CALLISTO CATACOMB
Map p318 (⌨06 513 01 51; www.catacombe.roma.it; Via Appia Antica 110-126; adult/reduced €8/5; ⏲9am-noon & 2-5pm Thu-Tue Mar-Jan; ⛳Via Appia Antica) These are the largest and busiest of Rome's catacombs. Founded at the end of the 2nd century and named after Pope Calixtus I, they became the official cemetery of the newly established Roman Church. In the 20km of tunnels explored to date, archaeologists have found the tombs of 16 popes, dozens of martyrs and thousands upon thousands of Christians.

The patron saint of music, St Cecilia, was also buried here, though her body was later removed to Basilica di Santa Cecilia in Trastevere (p156). When her body was exhumed in 1599, more than a thousand years after her death, it was apparently perfectly preserved, as depicted in Stefano Maderno's softly contoured sculpture, a replica of which is here.

CAPO DI BOVE ARCHAEOLOGICAL SITE
(⌨06 7839 2729; http://archeoroma.beniculturali.it/siti-archeologici/capo-bove; Via Appia Antica 222; ⏲9am-5pm winter, to 6.30pm summer; ⛳Via Appia Antica) Discovered when excavating the grounds of a private villa to build a swimming pool, the remains of this Roman villa give a sense of how a gracious ancient Roman life was lived, with mosaics and the remains of its private bath house, set amid the countryside of the Appia Antica Regional Park.

☉ Ostiense, San Paolo & Garbatella

★BASILICA DI SAN PAOLO
FUORI LE MURA
BASILICA

Map p318 (☑06 6988 0803; www.basilica sanpaolo.org; Via Ostiense 190; adult/reduced €4/3; ☉7am-6.30pm; ⓂBasilica San Paolo) The largest church in Rome after St Peter's (and the world's third-largest), this magnificent basilica stands on the site where St Paul was buried after being decapitated in AD 67. Built by Constantine in the 4th century, it was largely destroyed by fire in 1823 and much of what you see is a 19th-century reconstruction.

However, many treasures survived, including the 5th-century **triumphal arch**, with its heavily restored mosaics, and the Gothic marble **tabernacle** over the high altar. This was designed around 1285 by Arnolfo di Cambio together with another artist, possibly Pietro Cavallini. To the right of the altar, the elaborate Romanesque Pas-

chal candlestick was fashioned by Nicolò di Angelo and Pietro Vassalletto in the 12th century and features a grim cast of animal-headed creatures. St Paul's tomb is in the nearby **confessio**.

Looking upwards, doom-mongers should check out the papal portraits beneath the nave windows. Every pope since St Peter is represented here, and legend has it that when there is no longer room for the next portrait, the world will fall.

Also well worth a look is the stunning 13th-century Cosmati mosaic work that decorates the columns of the **cloisters** of the adjacent Benedictine abbey.

MUSEO CAPITOLINE CENTRALE
MONTEMARTINI
MUSEUM

Map p318 (Museums at Centrale Montemartini; ☑06 06 08; www.centralemontemartini.org; Via Ostiense 106; adult/reduced €7.50/6.50, incl Capitoline Museums €16/14, ticket valid 7 days; ☉9am-7pm Tue-Sun; ⓠVia Ostiense) Housed in a former power station, this fabulous outpost of the Capitoline Museums (Musei

---

STREET ART IN THE SUBURBS

With over 30 works, ex-industrial and alternative Ostiense is one of the best parts of Rome to lap up an outdoor gallery of colourful wall murals. Highlights include the murals at **Caserma dell'Aeronautica** (Map p318; Via del Porto Fluviale; ⓂPiramide), a former military warehouse where Bolognese artist **Blu** (www.blublu.org) painted a rainbow of sinister faces across the entire building in 2014. Further up Via Ostiense is another work by Blu, depicting interlocking yellow cars, that covers the entire facade of a now-derelict building. Known as **Alexis** (Map p318; Via Ostiense 122; ⓠVia Ostiense), the mural immortalises Alexis Grigoropoulos, the 15-year-old student who was killed, allegedly by a police bullet, during demonstrations in Greece in 2008.

The signature stencil art of well-known Italian street artists **Sten & Lex** (www. stenlex.com) is well-represented in Ostiense with a B&W wall mural of an anonymous student at Via delle Conce 14, and the giant **Peassagio Urbano XVIII** (2016) emblazoning the pedestrian entrance to Stazione Roma-Ostiense on Piazzale XII Octobre. Nearby, on Via dei Magazzini Generali, a line-up of larger-than-life portraits by Sten & Lex provide an admiring audience for the iconic *Wall of Fame* by Rome's very own **JBRock** (www.jbrock.it).

Two experimental museums give Rome's street-art scene instant cred. East of the Appian Way, in the off-beat district of Quadraro, **M.U.Ro** (Museo di Urban Art di Roma; www.muromuseum.blogspot.it; Via dei Lentuli, Quadraro; walking/bicycle tour €10/20; ⓂPorta Furba Quadraro) runs highly recommended guided tours of the wealth of murals decorating the neighbourhood streets. In Ostiense the ruins of the 19th-century soap factory Mira Lanza recently opened its doors as a **museum** (Map p318; ☑351 031 75 63; www.999contemporary.com/exmiralanza; Via Amedeo Avogadro; ☉24hr; ⓂStazione Trastevere) **FREE**, the result of a public-art project by **999Contemporary**, which invited French globe-painter **Seth** (www.seth.fr) to spruce up the site with a series of large-scale art installations and murals.

For more info, tourist kiosks have maps marked up with key street-art works, and street-art itineraries can be found at www.turismoroma.it and www.ostiensedistrict.it.

WORTH A DETOUR

ROMAN UNIVERSAL EXHIBITION (EUR) DISTRICT

One of the few planned developments in Rome's history, **EUR** (MEUR Palasport) was built for an international exhibition in 1942. There are a few museums here, but the area's interest lies in its spectacular rationalist architecture, beautifully expressed in a number of distinctive *palazzi*, including the iconic **Palazzo della Civiltà Italiana** (Palace of Italian Civilisation; ☑06 33 45 01; www.fendi.com; Quadrato della Concordia; ⊗8am-6pm Mon-Sat, 10am-7pm Sun; MEUR Magliana) FREE. Other monumentalist architecture includes the **Chiesa Santi Pietro e Paolo** (www.santipietroepaoloroma.it; Piazzale Santi Pietro e Paolo; ⊗6.30am-noon & 4-7pm Mon-Sat, 7.30am-1pm & 4-8pm Sun; MEUR Palasport), the **Palazzetto dello Sport** (Palalottomatica; Piazza Apollodoro 10; MEUR Palasport) and the **Palazzo dei Congressi** (Piazza JF Kennedy 1; MEUR Fermi).

Massimiliano and Doriana Fuksas' cutting-edge 2016 **Rome Convention Centre La Nuvola** (☑06 5451 3710; www.nellanuvola.it; Viale Asia, entrance cnr Via Cristoforo Colombo; MEUR Fermi) – the largest new building to open in Rome in half a century – is the most dramatic piece of contemporary architecture. The striking building comprises a transparent, glass-and-steel box called 'Le Theca' (The Shrine), inside of which hangs the organically shaped *Nuvola* (Cloud).

Also in EUR is Rome's largest public swimming pool, **Piscina delle Rose** (☑06 5422 0333; www.piscinadellerose.it; Viale America 20; adult/reduced €16/14, 3hr pass Mon-Fri €10, under 10yr free; ⊗10am-10pm Mon-Fri, 9am-7pm Sat & Sun mid-May–Sep; MEUR Palasport); it gets crowded, so arrive early to grab a deck chair.

Capitolini) boldly juxtaposes classical sculpture against diesel engines and giant furnaces. The collection's highlights are in the Sala Caldaia, where ancient statuary strike poses around the giant furnace. Beautiful pieces include the *Fanciulla Seduta* (Seated Girl) and the *Musa Polimnia* (Muse Polyhymnia), and there are also some exquisite Roman mosaics, depicting favourite subjects such as hunting scenes and foodstuffs.

QUARTIERE GARBATELLA AREA
Map p318 (MGarbatella) A favourite location for TV and film-makers, Quartiere Garbatella was originally conceived as a workers' residential quarter, but in the 1920s the Fascists hijacked the project and used the area to house people who'd been displaced by construction work in the city. Many people were moved into *alberghi suburbani* (suburban hotels), big housing blocks designed by Innocenzo Sabbatini, the leading light of the Roman School of architecture; the most famous, **Albergo Rosso** (Map p318; Piazza Michele da Carbonara; MGarbatella), is typical of the style. Other trademark buildings are the **Scuola Cesare Battisti** (Map p318; Piazza Damiano Sauli; MGarbatella) and Teatro Palladium (p198).

✖ EATING

✖ Via Appia Antica

IL GIARDINO DI GIULIA E FRATELLI ITALIAN €
Map p318 (☑347 5092772; Via Appia Antica 176; panini €4, meals €20; ⊗noon-3pm & 7-11.30pm Tue-Sat; ☒Via Appia Antica) Almost opposite the tomb of Cecilia Metella, this garden restaurant is a bucolic delight. Snag a table laid with a red-and-white checked tablecloth beneath the orange trees, and feast on a light lunch or *panini* amid flowery green views.

★**L'ARCHEOLOGIA RISTORANTE** ITALIAN €€
Map p318 (☑06 788 04 94; www.larcheologia.it; Via Appia Antica 139; meals €50; ⊗12.30-3pm & 8-11pm; ☒Via Appia Antica) At home in an old horse exchange on the Appian Way, this 19th-century inn exudes vintage charm. Dining is elegant, with white-tablecloth-covered tables beneath age-old beams or in front of the fireplace. In summer, dining is alfresco and fragrant with the blooms of a magnificent 300-year-old wisteria. Cuisine is traditional Roman, and the wine list, exemplary. Reservations recommended.

QUI NUN SE MORE MAI ITALIAN €€

Map p318 (📞06 780 39 22; www.facebook.com/
qvinunsemoremai; Via Appia Antica 198; meals
around €40; ⊘noon-3pm & 7.30-11.45pm Tue-Sat,
noon-3pm Sun; 🚇Via Appia Antica) This small,
charismatic restaurant has an open fire for
grilling, plus a small terrace for when the
weather's good. The menu offers Roman
classics such as pasta *amatriciana*, carbonara, *alla gricia* and *cacio e pepe* – just the
thing to set you up for the road ahead.

✖ Ostiense, San Paolo & Garbatella

⭐**EATALY** ITALIAN €

Map p318 (www.eataly.net; Piazzale XII Ottobre
1492; meals €10-50; ⊘shops 9am-midnight,
restaurants typically noon-3.30pm & 7-11pm; 🛜;
🚇Piramide) Be prepared for some serious
taste bud titillation in this state-of-the-art
food emporium of gargantuan proportions.
Four shop floors showcase every conceivable
Italian food product (dried and fresh), while
multiple themed food stalls and restaurants
offer plenty of opportunity to taste or feast
on Italian cuisine.

⭐**DOPPIOZEROO** ITALIAN €

Map p318 (📞06 5730 1961; www.doppiozeroo.
com; Via Ostiense 68; meals €15; ⊘7am-2am;
🚇Via Ostiense, 🚇Piramide) This easygoing bar
was once a bakery, hence the name ('double
zero' is a type of flour). But today the sleek,
modern interior attracts hungry, trendy
Romans who pile in here for its cheap,
canteen style lunches, famously lavish *aperitivo* (6pm to 9pm) and abundant weekend
brunch (12.30pm to 3.30pm).

VERDE PISTACCHIO VEGETARIAN, VEGAN €

Map p318 (📞06 4547 5965; www.facebook.com/
verdepistacchioroma; Via Ostiense 181; lunch menu
€14; ⊘10am-3.30pm & 5.30pm-midnight Mon-
Thu, 10am-3.30pm & 5.30pm-2am Fri, 6pm-2am
Sat, 6pm-midnight Sun; 🛜; 🚇Via Ostiense, 🚇Gar-
batella) Camilla, Raffaele and Francesco are
the trio of friends behind Green Pistachio,
a stylish bistro and cafe with a minimalist,
vintage interior and streetside tables in the
sun in summer. The kitchen cooks up fantastic vegetarian and vegan cuisine, and the
lunchtime deal is a steal. Lunch here before or after visiting Rome's second-largest
church, a stone's throw away on the same
street.

PIZZA OSTIENSE PIZZA €

Map p318 (📞06 5730 5081; www.pizzeriaostiense.
com; Via Ostiense 56; pizzas from €5.50; ⊘6.30pm-
1am, closed Tue winter; 🚇Via Ostiense, 🚇Piramide)
Run by folk formerly of the much-lauded
classic Roman pizzeria Remo in Testaccio,
Pizza Ostiense offers similarly paper-thin,
crispy bases and delicious fresh toppings and
scrumptious *fritti* (fried things) in unfussy
surroundings. There's a friendly vibe.

ANDREOTTI PASTRIES €

Map p318 (📞06 575 07 73; www.andreottiroma.
it; Via Ostiense 54; pastries from €1.20; ⊘7.30am-
10pm; 🚇Via Ostiense, 🚇Piramide) Film director
and Ostiense local Ferzan Ozpetek is such
a fan of the pastries crafted at this 1934
pasticceria that he's known to cast them in
his films. They're all stars, from the buttery
crostate (tarts) to the piles of golden *sfogliatelle romane* (ricotta-filled pastries).

PORTO FLUVIALE ITALIAN €€

Map p318 (📞06 574 31 99; www.portofluviale.com;
Via del Porto Fluviale 22; meals €25; ⊘10.30am-
2am Sun-Thu, to 3am Fri & Sat; 🛜; 🚇Piramide) A
hip, buzzing restaurant-bar in the industri-
al-chic vein, Porto Fluviale attracts a mixed
crowd – lots of families included – with its
spacious lounge-style interior and good-
value kitchen that turns out everything from
pasta, pizza and *cicchetti* (tapas-style appe-
tisers) to burgers and meal-sized salads, all
available in half-portions too.

SEACOOK SEAFOOD €€€

Map p318 (📞06 5730 1512; www.seacook.it; Via
del Porto Fluviale 7d-e; meals €60; ⊘noon-3pm &
7pm-midnight; 🛜; 🚇Piramide) For stylish seafood dining in a chic aquatic ambience, look
no further than this glorious Scandinavian-
styled space in Ostiense with sea-blue bar-
stool seating, potted plants in white ceramic
jugs and bamboo lampshades. *Cuochi e
Pescatori* (Cooks and Fishermen) is the strapline and fish is fresh from seafaring Salento
in southern Italy.

🍷 DRINKING & NIGHTLIFE

⭐**CIRCOLO ILLUMINATI** CLUB, BAR

Map p318 (📞327 7615286; www.circolodegli
illuminati.it; Via Libetta 1a; ⊘midnight-late; 🚇Gar-
batella) Tech house, hip-hop and chill music
revs up clubbers at this wildly popular Ostiense club on the international DJ club

SOUTHERN ROME DRINKING & NIGHTLIFE

circuit. The vibe is very much underground, and its courtyard garden with potted plants and olive trees is a gorgeous space in which to kick-start the evening beneath the stars.

★GOA
CLUB

Map p318 (☑06 574 82 77; www.goaclub.com; Via Libetta 13; ☺11.30pm-4.30am Thu-Sat; ⓂGarbatella) At home in a former motorbike repair shop down a dead-end alley in industrial-style Ostiense, Goa is Rome's serious super-club with an exotic India-inspired decor and international DJs mixing house and techno. Expect a fashion-forward crowd, podium dancers, thumping dance floor, sofas to lounge on and heavies on the door.

VINILE
CLUB

Map p318 (☑06 5728 8666; www.vinileroma.it; Via Libetta 19; ☺8pm-2am Tue & Wed, to 3am Thu, to 4am Fri & Sat, 12.30-3pm & 8pm-2am Sun; ⓂGarbatella) On weekends a mixed bag of Romans of all ages hit the dance floor at Vinyl, a buzzing bar and club cooking up food, music and party happenings on the southern fringe of Ostiense. Inside its huge cavernous interior – with part-vegetal, part-frescoed ceiling – the night starts with an *aperitivo* banquet from 8pm; DJ sets start at 11.30pm. On Sunday students pile in here for the unbeatable-value brunch.

GAZOMETRO 38
COCKTAIL BAR

Map p318 (☑06 5730 2106; www.gazometro38. com; Via del Gazometro 38; ☺12.30-3pm & 6.30pm-2am Tue-Sat, 6.30pm-midnight Sun; ☐Via Ostiense, ⓂPiramide) It's not so much about the food as the eye-catching industrial design at this contemporary lounge bar-restaurant in edgy Ostiense. Hobnob over an Elderflower Mule or Raspberry Basil Smash cocktail and a plate of *fritti* (fried courgette flowers) or *supplì* (rice balls) in the lounge area with sofa seating or at a table in the alley-entrance, plastered with B&W murals of industrial scenes.

APPIA ANTICA CAFFÈ
CAFE

Map p318 (☑06 8987 9575; www.appiaantico caffe.it; Via Appia Antica 175; ☺9am-sunset; ☐Via Appia Antica) Heading south along the Appian Way, you come to this tiny streetside cafe with tree-shaded pavement terrace, hunger-appeasing selection of *panini*, pastries and light snacks, plus a fantastic garden out back. The cafe also rents bicycles and can provide you with a picnic lunch.

WORTH A DETOUR

ROME'S CINEMA CITY

Cinecittà (☑06 88816182; http:// cinecittastudios.it; Via Tuscolana 1055; adult/reduced incl guided tour €20/15; ☺9.30am-7pm Wed-Mon; ⓂCinecittà) is Italy's foremost film studio, founded in 1937 by Mussolini, and used for many iconic Italian and international films. It's possible to take a tour of the studios, where you get to visit several impressive sets, including 1500s Florence and ancient Rome, and there are interesting exhibitions, one dedicated to the work of Fellini, and another exploring the history of the studios, with some hands-on exhibits, and, most excitingly, an American submarine set.

NEO CLUB
CLUB

Map p318 (☑338 9492526; www.piovra.it; Via degli Argonauti 18; ☺11.30pm-6am Fri & Sat; ⓂGarbatella) This small, dark two-level club has an underground feel and it's one of the funkiest choices in the zone, featuring a dancetastic mish-mash of breakbeat, techno and old-school house.

☆ ENTERTAINMENT

CAFFÈ LETTERARIO
LIVE MUSIC

Map p318 (☑06 5730 2842; www.caffeletterario roma.it; Via Ostiense 95; ☺10am-2am Tue-Sat, 4pm-2am Sun; ☐Via Ostiense, ⓂPiramide) Caffè Letterario is an intellectual hangout housed in the funky converted, post-industrial space of a former garage. It combines designer looks, a bookshop, gallery, co-working space, performance area and lounge bar. There are regular gigs from 10pm to midnight, ranging from soul and jazz to Indian dance.

TEATRO PALLADIUM
THEATRE

Map p318 (☑box office 06 5733 2772; http:// teatropalladium.uniroma3.it; Piazza Bartolomeo Romano; ⓂGarbatella) Once at risk of being turned into a bingo hall, the historic Teatro Palladium (1926), with a beautifully renovated 1920s interior, stages a rich repertoire of theatre, classical music concerts, cinema and art exhibitions.

Day Trips from Rome

Ostia Antica p200
Wander through complete streets, gape at ancient toilets and clamber over an amphitheatre at the ancient port of Ostia Antica, Rome's very own Pompeii.

Tivoli p201
A hilltop town home to two Unesco World Heritage sites: Villa Adriana, the emperor Hadrian's colossal country estate, and Villa d'Este, famous for its landscaped gardens and lavish fountains.

Castelli Romani p202
Located south of Rome, the pretty Coli Albani (Alban Hills) and their 13 towns have long provided a green escape for overheated Romans.

Cerveteri p204
The evocative tombs and archaeological treasures of this once impor-tant Etruscan city provide a window into a mysterious ancient world.

Orvieto p206
Home to one of Italy's most awe-inspiring Gothic cathedrals, this hilltop Umbrian town makes for a rewarding day trip.

Ostia Antica

Explore

An easy train ride from Rome, Ostia Antica is one of Italy's finest and most under-appreciated archaeological sites.

Founded in the 4th century BC, the city started life as a fortified military camp guarding the mouth of the Tiber – hence the name: Ostia is a derivation of the Latin word *ostium* (mouth). It quickly grew, and by the 2nd century AD was a thriving port with a population of around 50,000.

Decline set in after the fall of the Roman Empire, and by the 9th century the city had largely been abandoned, its citizens driven off by barbarian raids and outbreaks of malaria. Over subsequent centuries, it was plundered of marble and building materials and its ruins were gradually buried in river silt, hence their survival.

The Best...

➡**Sight** Terme di Nettuno

Top Tip

Bring a picnic or time your visit so that you can eat at a restaurant as the on-site canteen gets extremely busy.

Getting There & Away

➡**Train** From Rome, take the Ostia Lido train from Stazione Porta San Paolo (next to Piramide metro station), getting off at Ostia Antica (25 minutes, every 15 minutes). The trip is covered by a standard Rome public transport ticket (€1.50).

➡**Car** Take Via del Mare, which runs parallel to Via Ostiense, and follow signs for the *scavi* (ruins).

Need to Know

➡**Location** 25km southwest of Rome

◉ SIGHTS

★**SCAVI ARCHEOLOGICI DI OSTIA ANTICA** ARCHAEOLOGICAL SITE
(☑06 5635 0215; www.ostiaantica.beniculturali. it; Viale dei Romagnoli 717; adult/reduced €8/4, free 1st Sun of month, exhibitions €3; ☉8.30am-6.15pm Tue-Sun summer, shorter hours winter) One of Lazio's prize sights, the ruins of ancient Rome's seaport are wonderfully complete, like a smaller version of Pompeii. Highlights include the Terme di Nettuno (Baths of Neptune), a steeply stacked amphitheatre, and an ancient cafe, complete with a bar and traces of the original menu frescoed on the wall.

Note that the site is pretty large and you'll need a few hours to do it justice. Also, it gets busy at weekends, but is much quieter on weekdays.

Near the entrance, **Porta Romana** gives onto the **Decumanus Maximus**, the site's central strip, which runs over 1km to **Porta Marina**, the city's original sea-facing gate.

On the Decumanus, the **Terme di Nettuno** is a must-see. This baths complex, one of 20 that originally stood in town, dates to the 2nd century and boasts some superb mosaics, including one of Neptune driving his sea-horse chariot. In the centre of the complex are the remains of an arcaded **Palestra** (gym).

Next to the *terme* is the **Teatro**, an amphitheatre originally built at the end of the 1st century BC by Agrippa and later enlarged to hold 4000 people.

The grassy area behind the amphitheatre is the **Piazzale delle Corporazioni** (Forum of the Corporations), home to the offices of Ostia's merchant guilds. The mosaics that line the perimeter – ships, dolphins, a lighthouse, an elephant – are thought to represent the businesses housed on the square: ships and dolphins indicated shipping agencies, while the elephant probably referred to a business involved in the ivory trade.

The **Forum**, Ostia's main square, is overlooked by what remains of the **Capitolium**, a temple built by Hadrian and dedicated to Jupiter, Juno and Minerva.

Nearby is another highlight: the **Thermopolium**, an ancient cafe, complete with a bar, frescoed menu, kitchen and small courtyard where customers would have relaxed by a fountain. Just to the north of the Thermopolium are two of the site's so-called **case decorate**. These frescoed houses are off-limits to unaccompanied visitors but can be visited on a guided tour at 10.30am each Sunday – book a place via email (ss-col. domusostia@beniculturali.it).

Over on the other side of the Decumanus are the remains of the 2nd-century **Terme del Foro**, originally the city's largest baths complex. Here, in the *forica* (public toilet), you can see 20 well-preserved latrines set sociably in a long stone bench.

For more modern facilities, there's a cafeteria-bar complex with toilets and a gift shop to the north of the Decumanus (head up Via dei Molini). Also at this complex is a small **museum** displaying statues and sarcophagi excavated at the site.

CASTELLO DI GIULIO II   CASTLE
(☑06 5635 8013; Piazza della Rocca; adult/reduced €3/1.50; ☺9.30am-6.30pm Sat & Sun) Rising above Ostia's medieval *borgo* (village), this landmark castle is a fine example of Renaissance military architecture. It's named after Pope Giulio II, who had it built at the end of the 15th century to guard the mouth of the Tiber, at the time one of the main access routes to Rome. It was eventually abandoned after the course of the Tiber was changed by heavy flooding in 1557.

✖ EATING

RISTORANTE MONUMENTO   RISTORANTE €€
(☑06 565 00 21; www.ristorantemonumento.it; Piazza Umberto I 8; meals €30-35; ☺12.30-3.30pm & 8-11pm Tue-Sun) In Ostia's small medieval centre, this long-standing restaurant started life in the 19th century, catering to the men working on reclaiming the local marshlands. Nowadays, it does a brisk business serving homemade pastas and seafood dishes to sightseers fresh out of the nearby ruins.

Tivoli

Explore
A summer retreat for ancient Romans and the Renaissance rich, the hilltop town of Tivoli is home to two Unesco World Heritage Sites: Villa Adriana, the sprawling estate of Emperor Hadrian, and the 16th-century Villa d'Este, a Renaissance villa famous for its landscaped gardens and lavish fountains.

The Best...
→**Sight** The *canopo* at Villa Adriana

Top Tip
Villa Adriana is at its best when the spring flowers are out, but if you suffer from hay fever, make sure you take antihistamines.

Getting There & Away
→**Bus** Tivoli is accessible by Cotral bus (€1.30, 50 minutes, at least twice hourly) from Ponte Mammolo metro station.
→**Car** Take Via Tiburtina or the quicker Rome–L'Aquila autostrada (A24).
→**Train** Trains run from Rome's Stazione Tiburtina to Tivoli (€2.60, one hour, at least hourly).

Need to Know
→**Area Code** ☑0774
→**Location** 30km east of Rome
→**Tourist Information Point** (☑0774 31 35 36; Piazzale delle Nazioni Unite; ☺10am-1pm & 4-6pm Tue-Sun)

◉ SIGHTS

★VILLA ADRIANA   ARCHAEOLOGICAL SITE
(☑0774 38 27 33; www.villaadriana.beniculturali.it; Largo Marguerite Yourcenar 1; adult/reduced €8/4; ☺9am-1hr before sunset) The ruins of Hadrian's vast country villa, 5km outside of Tivoli proper, are quite magnificent, and easily on a par with anything you'll see in Rome. Built between AD 118 and 138, the villa was one of the largest in the ancient world, encompassing more than 120 hectares – of which about 40 are now open to the public. You'll need up to three hours to explore it fully.

Must-sees include the **canopo**, a landscaped canal overlooked by a *nymphaeum* (shrine to the water nymph), and the **Teatro Marittimo**, Hadrian's personal refuge.

Hadrian, a great traveller and enthusiastic architect, designed much of the villa himself, basing his ideas on buildings he'd seen around the world. The **pecile**, the large pool area near the walls, is a reproduction of a building in Athens. Similarly, the *canopo* is a copy of a sanctuary in the Egyptian town of Canopus, with a narrow 120m-long pool flanked by sculptural figures. At its head, the **Serapaeum** is a semi-circular *nymphaeum* that was used to host summer banquets. Flanking the water, the **antiquarium** is used to stage temporary exhibitions (note that when these are on, admission to the villa costs slightly more than usual).

To the northeast of the *pecile*, the Teatro Marittimo is one of the villa's signature buildings, a mini-villa built on an island in an artificial pool. Originally accessible only by swing bridges, it's currently off-limits due to ongoing restoration.

To the east, **Piazza d'Oro** makes for a memorable picture, particularly in spring, when its grassy centre is cloaked in wild yellow flowers.

There are also several bath complexes, temples and barracks.

Parking (€3) is available at the site.

VILLA D'ESTE
HISTORIC BUILDING

(☑0774 33 29 20; www.villadestetivoli.info; Piazza Trento; adult/reduced €8/4; ☉8.30am-1hr before sunset Tue-Sun) In Tivoli's hilltop centre, the steeply terraced grounds of Villa d'Este are a superlative example of a Renaissance garden, complete with monumental fountains, elegant tree-lined avenues and landscaped grottoes. The villa, originally a Benedictine convent, was converted into a luxury retreat by Lucrezia Borgia's son, Cardinal Ippolito d'Este, in the late 16th century. It later provided inspiration for composer Franz Liszt who stayed here between 1865 and 1886 and immortalised it in his 1877 piano composition *The Fountains of the Villa d'Este*.

Before heading out to the gardens, take time to admire the villa's rich mannerist frescoes. Outside, the manicured park features water-spouting gargoyles and shady lanes flanked by lofty cypress trees and extravagant fountains, all powered by gravity alone. Look out for the Bernini-designed **Fountain of the Organ**, which uses water pressure to play music through a concealed organ, and the 130m-long **Avenue of the Hundred Fountains**.

✖ EATING

TRATTORIA DEL FALCONE
LAZIO €€

(☑0774 31 23 58; Via del Trevio 34; pizzas €5.50-9.50, meals €30; ☉noon-4pm & 6.30-11pm) Near Villa d'Este, this unpretentious trattoria lures in strolling visitors as they wander in to Tivoli's historic centre. There are pizzas but the speciality of the house is old-school Roman and Lazio cuisine such as *rigatoni alla amatriciana* (pasta tubes with pancetta and tomato sauce) or *saltimbocca alla romana* (veal cutlets with ham and sage).

 SLEEPING

★RESIDENZE GREGORIANE
BOUTIQUE HOTEL €€€

(☑347 7136854; www.residenzegregoriane.it; Via Domenico Giuliani 92; ste €230-250; ❄ 🛜 ⬛) For a night to remember, the Residenza Gregoriane is steeped in history. Its three spacious suites, all decorated in classic antique style, occupy the fabulous 15th-century Palazzo Mancini-Torlonia. Frescoes adorn the historic building, many by the same artists who worked on Villa d'Este, and there's a magnificent internal courtyard. Room rates also cover use of a small pool in the vaulted cellar.

Castelli Romani

Explore

A pretty pocket of verdant hills and volcanic lakes 20km southeast of Rome, the Colli Albani (Alban Hills) and their 13 towns are collectively known as the Castelli Romani. Since ancient times they've provided a green refuge from the city and still today Romans flock to the area on hot summer weekends. Highlights include the famous wine town of Frascati, hilltop Castel Gandolfo, and the scenic Lago Albano.

The Best...

➡ **Sight** Lake Albano

➡ **Place to Eat** Cacciani (p204)

➡ **Place to Drink** Frascati

Top Tip

In Frascati, search out a *cantina* (cellar-cum-trattoria) and settle down for a simple feast of *porchetta* (herb-roasted pork) and fresh local wine.

Getting There & Away

➡ **Train** Regular trains run from Rome's Stazione Termini to Frascati (€2.10, 30 minutes) and Castel Gandolfo (€2.10, 40 minutes) – for Castel Gandolfo, take the Albano Laziale train.

➡ **Car** Exit Rome on Via Tuscolana (SS215) for Frascati or Via Appia (SS7) for Castel Gandolfo and Lago Albano.

Getting Around

➡**Bus** To travel between the Castelli towns, you'll need to take the bus. From Frascati's Piazza Marconi, Cotral buses connect with Grottaferrata (€1.10, 10 minutes) and Castel Gandolfo (€1.30, 30 minutes).

Need to Know

➡**Location** 20km southeast of Rome

 SIGHTS

◉ Frascati

CATTEDRALE DI SAN PIETRO   CHURCH
(Piazza San Pietro; ⏰9am-noon & 4-7pm) Frascati is a long way from Scotland but it's here, in the town's 16th-century cathedral that the heart of Charles Edward Stuart, aka Bonnie Prince Charlie, is buried – the rest of his body is at St Peter's Basilica in Rome. The church's main feature is its bombastic two-tone baroque facade, the creation of architect Girolamo Fontana.

SCUDERIE ALDOBRANDINI   MUSEUM
(📞06 941 71 95; Piazza Marconi 6; adult/reduced €3/1.50, plus exhibition €5.50/3; ⏰10am-6pm Tue-Fri, to 7pm Sat & Sun) The former stables of Villa Aldobrandini, restored by architect Massimiliano Fuksas, house Frascati's single museum of note, the **Museo Tuscolano**. Dedicated to local history, its collection includes ancient Roman artefacts and several interesting models of local villas.

**VILLA ALDOBRANDINI
GARDENS**   GARDENS
(📞06 942 25 60; Via Cardinal Massai 18; ⏰8.30am-5.30pm Mon-Fri) **FREE** Looming over Frascati's main square, Villa Aldobrandini is a haughty 16th-century villa designed by Giacomo della Porta and built by Carlo Maderno. It's closed to the public, but you can visit its impressive baroque gardens during the week.

◉ Grottaferrata

ABBAZIA GRECA DI SAN NILO   MONASTERY
(📞06 945 93 09; www.abbaziagreca.it; Corso del Popolo 128, Grottaferrata; abbey free, museum adult/reduced €3/1.50; ⏰abbey 9am-noon &

3.30-7pm Mon-Sat, museum 10am-6pm Sat & Sun) Grottaferrata's fortified monastery, the last of the Byzantine-Greek abbeys that once dotted medieval Italy, was founded in 1004. The walls and battlements were added some 400 years later to provide a protective perimeter to the Chiesa di Santa Maria di Grottaferrata. This bejewelled, icon-laden church features a series of 17th-century frescoes by Domenichino and a revered Byzantine image of Santa Maria. Also in the abbey is a small museum dedicated to the the monastery's thousand-year-old history.

◉ Castel Gandolfo

GIARDINI DI VILLA BARBERINI   GARDENS
(Villa Barberini Gardens; www.museivaticani.va; Via Carlo Rosselli; adult/reduced €20/15, incl guided tour €26/15; ⏰8.30am-3pm Mon-Sat) Since 2014, the papal gardens in Castel Gandolfo have been open to guided visits. The regular one-hour tours involve a mini-train ride through the extensive gardens, taking in Roman ruins, artful flower displays, woods, fruit and veg patches, and the papal helipad. Guided tours on foot are also available but need to be booked in advance.

**MUSEO DEL PALAZZO
APOSTOLICO**   MUSEUM
(www.museivaticani.va; Piazza della Libertà; adult/reduced €10/5; ⏰9am-1pm Mon-Fri, 9am-4.30pm Sat) Housed in what was until recently the pope's traditional summer residence, the Palazzo Apostolico (also known as the Palazzo Pontificio), this museum displays portraits of around 50 popes as well as costumes, robes and assorted papal paraphernalia, including the BMW that Pope John Paul II used when he stayed at the palace.

◉ Lake Albano

LAGO ALBANO   LAKE
The largest and most developed of the Castelli's two volcanic lakes – the other is Lago di Nemi – Lago Albano is set in a steeply banked wooded crater. It's a popular hangout, particularly in spring and summer, when Romans flock here to top up their tans and eat in the many lakeside eateries.

EATING

Frascati

The real reason many come to Frascati is to eat and drink. There are plenty of good restaurants but for a more down-to-earth bite, pick up a *panino con porchetta* (sandwich filled with herb-roasted pork) from a stand on Piazza del Mercato, or head to a traditional *cantina* (cellar-cum-trattoria).

CANTINA SIMONETTI   OSTERIA €
(Piazza San Rocco 4; meals €25; ☺1-4pm Sat & Sun, 7.45pm-midnight Wed-Sun, longer hours summer) For an authentic *vino e cucina* (wine and food) experience, search out this traditional *cantina* and sit down to a meal of *porchetta*, cold cuts and cheese, accompanied by jugs of local white wine. No credit cards.

OSTERIA SAN ROCCO
PIACENTE   OSTERIA €
(☑06 9428 2786; Via Cadorna 1; meals €25; ☺12.30-4pm Sat & Sun, 7pm-12.30am Tue-Sun) To try a typical *osteria,* head to this popular spot. Just make sure you arrive hungry if you want to get beyond the rich starters of *porchetta* and cured meats. If you make it, there are classic Roman pastas and grilled meats to follow.

CACCIANI   RISTORANTE €€€
(☑06 942 03 78; www.cacciani.it; Via Armando Diaz 13; fixed-price lunch menu €25, meals €50; ☺1-2.30pm Tue-Sun & 8-10.30pm Tue-Sat) One of Frascati's most renowned restaurants, Cacciani offers fine food and twinkling terrace views of Rome. The menu lists various creative dishes, but it's the classics like *tonnarello a cacio e pepe* (egg spaghetti with pecorino cheese and black pepper) that really stand out. There's also a weighty wine list and a fixed-price lunch menu, available Tuesday through to Friday.

Castel Gandolfo

ANTICO RISTORANTE
PAGNANELLI   RISTORANTE €€€
(☑06 936 00 04; www.pagnanelli.it; Via Antonio Gramsci 4; meals €60; ☺noon-3.30pm & 6.30-11.45pm) Housed in a colourful wisteria-clad villa, this celebrated restaurant is a great place for a romantic meal. It's no casual trattoria, erring on the formal side, but the seasonally driven food is excellent. There's

a colossal wine list (and an amazing cellar carved into tufa rock), and the terrace views over Lago Albano are unforgettable.

Cerveteri

Explore

A quiet provincial town 35km northwest of Rome, Cerveteri is home to one of Italy's great Etruscan treasures – the Necropoli di Banditaccia. This ancient burial complex, now a Unesco World Heritage Site, is all that remains of the formidable Etruscan city that once stood here.

Founded in the 9th century BC, the city that the Etruscans knew as Kysry, and Latin-speakers called Caere, was a powerful member of the Etruscan League, and, for a period between the 7th and 5th centuries, one of the Mediterranean's most important commercial centres. It eventually came into conflict with Rome and, in 358 BC, was annexed into the Roman Republic.

The Best...
➔**Sight** Necropoli di Banditaccia

Top Tip
Don't miss Cerveteri's Etruscan museum, which provides context for the tombs and brings the ancient era to life.

Getting There & Away
➔**Bus** Take the Cotral bus (€2.80, one hour, up to twice hourly Monday to Saturday, 10 daily Sunday) from the Cornelia metro station (line A). To get to the necropolis from the town centre, take bus G from Piazza Aldo Moro (€1.10, five minutes, approximately hourly).
➔**Car** Take either Via Aurelia (SS1) or the Civitavecchia autostrada (A12) and exit at Cerveteri–Ladispoli.

Need to Know
➔**Area Code** ☑06
➔**Location** 35km northwest of Rome
➔**Tourist Information Point** (☑06 9955 2637; Piazza Aldo Moro; ☺9.30am-12.30pm & 5.30-7.30pm Mon-Sat & 10am-1pm Sun Apr, May, Jul & Aug, 9.30am-12.30pm Mon-Sat & 10am-1pm Sun Oct-Mar, Jun & Sep)

TARQUINIA

Some 90km northwest of Rome, Tarquinia is the pick of Lazio's Etruscan towns. The highlight is the magnificent Unesco-listed necropolis and its extraordinary frescoed tombs, but there's also a fantastic Etruscan museum (the best outside of Rome) and an atmospheric medieval centre.

Legend holds that Tarquinia was founded towards the end of the Bronze Age in the 12th century BC. It was later home to the Tarquin kings of Rome, reaching its peak in the 4th century BC, before a century of struggle ended with surrender to Rome in 204 BC.

The **Museo Archeologico Nazionale Tarquiniense** (☑0766 85 00 80; www. tarquinia-cerveteri.it; Via Cavour 1; adult/reduced €6/3, incl necropoli €8/4; ⊘8.30am-7.30pm Tue-Sun), beautifully housed in the 15th-century Palazzo Vitelleschi, is a treasure trove of locally found Etruscan artefacts.

To see one of Italy's most important Etruscan sites, head to **Necropoli di Tarquinia** (Necropoli dei Monterozzi; ☑0766 84 00 00; www.tarquinia-cerveteri.it; Via Ripagretta; adult/reduced €6/3, incl Museo €8/4; ⊘8.30am-7.30pm Tue-Sun summer, to 1hr before sunset winter), a remarkable 7th-century BC necropolis. At first sight, it doesn't look like much – a green field littered with corrugated huts – but once you start ducking into the tombs and seeing the vivid frescoes, you'll realise what all the fuss is about. Some 6000 tombs have been excavated in this area since digs began in 1489, of which 140 are painted and 20 are currently open to the public. For the best frescoes search out the **Tomba della Leonessa**, the **Tomba della Caccia e della Pesca**, the **Tomba dei Leopardi**, and the **Tomba della Fustigazione**.

To get to the necropolis, which is about 1.5km from the centre, take the free shuttle bus B from near the tourist office. Alternatively, it's about 20 minutes on foot – head up Corso Vittorio Emanuele, turn right into Via Porta Tarquinia and continue along Via Ripagretta.

The best way to reach Tarquinia from Rome is by train from Termini (€6.90, 1½ hours, hourly). From Tarquinia station, catch the hourly BC bus to the hilltop historic centre. By car, take the autostrada for Civitavecchia and then Via Aurelia (SS1).

 SIGHTS

⭐NECROPOLI DI BANDITACCIA
ARCHAEOLOGICAL SITE

(☑06 994 06 51; www.tarquinia-cerveteri.it; Piazzale Mario Moretti 32; adult/reduced €8/5, incl museum €10/6; ⊘8.30am-1hr before sunset) This haunting 12-hectare necropolis is a veritable city of the dead, with streets, squares and terraces of *tumuli* (circular tombs cut into the earth and capped by turf). Some tombs, including the 6th-century-BC **Tomba dei Rilievi**, retain traces of painted reliefs, many of which illustrate endearingly domestic household items, as well as figures from the underworld.

Another interesting tomb is the 7th-century BC **Tumulo Mengarelli**, whose plain interior shows how the tombs were originally structured.

Some *tumuli* can be lit with a remote control available from the ticket office – you'll need to leave ID.

MUSEO NAZIONALE CERITE
MUSEUM

(☑06 994 13 54; www.tarquinia-cerveteri.it; Piazza Santa Maria 1; adult/reduced €8/5, incl necropolis €10/6; ⊘8.30am-7.30pm Tue-Sun) Housed in a medieval fortress on what was once ancient Caere's acropolis, this splendid museum charts the history of the Etruscan city, housing archaeological treasures unearthed at the necropolis.

🍴 EATING

MILLE800 STAZIONE DEL GUSTO
RISTORANTE €€

(☑329 4970782, 06 9955 1565; Via Antonio Ricci 9; meals €30-35; ⊘noon-5pm & 6.30-12.30am Tue-Sun) Near the tourist information kiosk, this welcoming restaurant is styled as an old train station with brick arches, signs for *binari* (platforms) and leather suitcases as decor. Food-wise it's a cut above your average trattoria, serving a mixed menu of pizzas, fail-safe pastas and creative main courses.

Orvieto

Explore

Sitting astride a volcanic plug of rock above fields streaked with vines, and olive and cypress trees, Orvieto is visually stunning from the first. Like the love child of Rome and Florence and nestled midway between the two cities, history hangs over the cobbled lanes, medieval piazzas and churches of this cinematically beautiful city. And few churches in Italy can hold a candle to its wedding cake of a Gothic cathedral, which frequently elicits gasps of wonder at its layers of exquisite detail.

The Best...

➡**Sight** Duomo di Orvieto
➡**Place to Eat** Di Pasqualetti
➡**Place to Drink** Bottega Vera

Top Tip

Stay overnight to experience the medieval atmosphere of the town once all the day trippers have ebbed away.

Getting There & Away

➡**Bus** Buses depart from the station near Piazza Cahen, stopping at the train station, and include services to Todi (€6.30, two hours, one daily Sep-June) and Terni (€6.90, two hours, 6.35am, 5.20pm & 7.40pm).

➡**Car** Orvieto is on the Rome–Florence A1, while the SS71 heads north to Lago Trasimeno. There's plenty of metered parking on Piazza Cahen and in designated areas outside the city walls, including **Parcheggio Campo della Fiera** (Via Belisario 10; per hr €1-1.50).

➡**Train** Orvieto's **train station** (www.trenitalia.com; Via Antonio Gramsci, Orvieto Scalo) is located west of the *centro storico* (historic centre) in Orvieto Scalo. Hourly connections include Rome (€7.80 to €9.90, 1¼ hours), Florence (€11.80 to €16.10, 1½ to 2½ hours) and Perugia (€7.60 to €13.95, 1¾ to 2½ hours).

Getting Around

➡**Funicular** A century-old **funicular** (tickets €1.30; ⊙every 10min 7.20am-8.30pm Mon-Sat, every 15min 8am-8.30pm Sun) creaks up the wooded hill from the train station to Piazza Cahen. The fare includes a bus ride from Piazza Cahen to Piazza Duomo. Outside of funicular hours, bus 1 runs up to the old town from the train station (€1.30). An elevator connects Parcheggio Campo della Fiera with the old town on the western end.

➡**Bus** Bus A (€1.30) connects Piazza Cahen with Piazza Duomo and bus B (€1.30) runs to Via Garibaldi.

Need to Know

➡**Area Code** ☑0763
➡**Location** 120km northwest of Rome
➡**Tourist Office** (Via Postierla; ⊙10am-2.30pm summer)

◉ SIGHTS

★**DUOMO DI ORVIETO**   CATHEDRAL
(www.opsm.it; Piazza Duomo 26; €4, with Museo dell'Opera del Duomo di Orvieto €5; ⊙9.30am-7pm Mon-Sat, 1-5.30pm Sun summer, shorter hours winter) Nothing can prepare you for the visual feast that is Orvieto's soul-stirring Gothic cathedral. Dating to 1290, it sports a black-and-white banded exterior fronted by what is perhaps the most astonishing facade to grace any Italian church: a mesmerising display of rainbow frescoes, jewel-like mosaics, bas-reliefs and delicate braids of flowers and vines.

The building took 30 years to plan and three centuries to complete. It was started by Fra Bevignate and later additions were made by Sienese master Lorenzo Maitani, Andrea Pisano (of Florence Cathedral fame) and his son Nino Pisano, Andrea Orcagna and Michele Sanmicheli.

Of the art on show inside, it's Luca Signorelli's magnificent *Giudizio Universale* that draws the crowds. The artist began work on the vast fresco in 1499 and over the course of the next four years covered every inch of the **Cappella di San Brizio** with a swirling and, at times grotesque, depiction of the Last Judgment. Michelangelo is said to have taken inspiration from the work. Indeed, to some, Michelangelo's masterpiece runs a close second to Signorelli's creation.

On the other side of the transept, the **Cappella del Corporale** houses a 13th-century altar cloth stained with blood that miraculously poured from the communion bread of a priest who doubted the transubstantiation.

MUSEO DELL'OPERA DEL DUOMO DI ORVIETO
MUSEUM

(www.museomodo.it; Piazza Duomo 26; €4, with Duomo di Orvieto €5; ☺9.30am-7pm) Housed in the former papal palace, this museum contains a fine collection of religious relics from the cathedral, paintings by artists such as Arnolfo di Cambio and the three Pisanos (Andrea, Nino and Giovanni), and a separate permanent exhibit on sculptor and medallist Emilio Greco.

MUSEO ARCHEOLOGICO NAZIONALE
MUSEUM

(Palazzo Papale, Piazza Duomo; adult/reduced €4/2; ☺8.30am-7.30pm) Ensconced in the medieval Palazzo Papale, the archaeological museum holds plenty of interesting artefacts, some over 2500 years old. Etruscan ceramics, necropolis relics, bronzes and frescoed chamber tombs are among the items on display.

TORRE DEL MORO
HISTORIC BUILDING

(Moor's Tower; Corso Cavour 87; adult/reduced €2.80/2; ☺10am-8pm summer, shorter hours winter) From the Piazza Duomo, head northwest along Via del Duomo to Corso Cavour and the 13th-century Torre del Moro. Climb all 250 steps for sweeping views of the city.

ORVIETO UNDERGROUND
HISTORIC SITE

(www.orvietounderground.it; Piazza Duomo 23; adult/reduced €6/5) The coolest place in Orvieto (literally), this series of 440 caves (out of 1200 in the system) has been used for millennia by locals for various purposes, including WWII bomb shelters, refrigerators, wine storage, wells and, during many a pesky Roman or barbarian siege, as dovecotes to trap the usual one-course dinner: pigeon (still seen on local restaurant menus as *palombo*).

✖ EATING & DRINKING

DI PASQUALETTI
GELATO €

(www.facebook.com/PasqualettiSrl; Piazza Duomo 14; cones €2.50-5; ☺11am-10pm, to midnight Sat) This gelateria serves mouth-watering gelato, plus there are plenty of tables on the piazza for you to gaze at the magnificence of the cathedral while you gobble.

★AL POZZO ETRUSCO
UMBRIAN €€

(☎0763 34 10 50; www.alpozzoetruscodagiovanni.it; Piazza dei Ranieri 1a; meals €23-35; ☺12.30-2.30pm & 7.30-9.30pm Wed-Mon; ☎) Named after an ancient Etruscan well and silo that

graces its basement, this fan favourite has drawn quite a following in just a few short years. Your host, Giovanni, will guide you through his seasonal menu of Umbrian delights, best enjoyed alfresco on the charming candlelit patio.

I SETTE CONSOLI
ITALIAN €€€

(☎0763 34 39 11; www.isetteconsoli.it; Piazza Sant'Angelo 1a; meals around €45, 6-course tasting menu €42; ☺12.30-3pm & 7.30-10pm, closed Wed & dinner Sun) This refined restaurant walks the culinary high wire in Orvieto, with inventive, artfully presented dishes, from pasta so light it floats off the fork to beautifully cooked pigeon casserole with minced hazelnuts and cherry-beer sauce. In good weather, try to get a seat in the garden, with the *duomo* in view.

BOTTEGA VERA
WINE BAR

(www.casaveraorvieto.it; Via del Duomo 36; wines by the glass €3-7; ☺9am-8pm Mon-Thu, 8.30am-10pm Fri-Sun; ☎) It's no easy task sussing out a non-touristy *enoteca* (wine bar) in Orvieto, but this stylish gourmet deli and wine shop has been at it since 1938, when it was started by the grandmother of Cesare, who will expertly guide you – and mostly Italians! – through his daily changing offerings by the glass.

🛏 SLEEPING

★B&B RIPA MEDICI
B&B €

(☎0763 34 13 43; www.ripamedici.it; Vicolo Ripa Medici 14; s/d from €50/75; ❄☎♨) Hugging the cliff walls on the edge of Orvieto's old town, this B&B takes the concept of 'room with a view' to a whole new level, gazing longingly out across undulating countryside. The rooms have been given a pinch of romance, with antique furnishings, while the beamed apartment offers even more space and a kitchen.

★MISIA RESORT
BOUTIQUE HOTEL €€

(☎0763 34 23 36; www.misiaresort.it; Località Rocca Ripesena 51/52; s €70-80, d €110-130, ste €130-160; ℗❄☎♨) You won't regret going the extra mile to this boutique hotel on the rocks, with fabulous views of Orvieto from its hilltop hamlet perch surrounded by 500 planted roses. This stunning country-house conversion has been designed with the utmost taste. The light, spacious rooms in soft, earthy tones come with stylish vintage touches.

Sleeping

Rome is expensive and busy; book ahead to secure the best deal. Accommodation ranges from palatial five-star hotels to hostels, B&Bs, pensioni (pensions) and private rooms. Hostels are the cheapest, with dorm beds and private rooms. B&Bs and hotels cover every style and price range.

Pensions & Hotels

The bulk of Rome's accommodation consists of *pensioni* (pensions) and *alberghi* (hotels).

A *pensione* is a small, family-run hotel, often in a converted apartment. Rooms are usually fairly simple, though most come with a private bathroom.

Hotels are rated from one to five stars. Most hotels in Rome's historic centre tend to be three-star and up. As a rule, a three-star room will come with a hairdryer, a minibar (or fridge), a safe, air-con and wi-fi. Some have satellite TV. Roman hotel rooms tend to be small, especially in the *centro storico* (historic centre) and Trastevere, where hotels are often housed in centuries-old *palazzi* (mansions).

B&Bs & Guesthouses

Alongside traditional B&Bs, Rome has many boutique-style guesthouses offering upmarket rooms at midrange to top-end prices.

Breakfast in a Roman B&B usually consists of bread rolls, croissants, yoghurt, ham and cheese.

Hostels

Rome's hostels cater to everyone from backpackers to budget-minded families. Many offer hotel-style rooms alongside traditional dorms. Some hostels don't accept reservations for dorms, so it's first come, first served.

The city's new breed of hostels are chic, designer pads with trendy bar-restaurants, the occasional stunning rooftop garden and offer a fantastic array of organised tours and activities.

Rental Accommodation

For longer stays, renting an apartment will generally work out cheaper than an extended hotel sojourn. Bank on about €900 per month for a studio apartment or one-bedroom flat. For longer stays, you'll probably have to pay bills plus a building maintenance charge.

Seasons & Rates

Rome doesn't have a low season as such but rates are at their lowest from November to March (excluding Christmas and New Year) and from mid-July through August. Expect to pay top whack in spring (April to June) and autumn (September and October) and over the main holiday periods. Most midrange and top-end hotels accept credit cards, but it's always best to check in advance.

Useful Websites

➡ **Lonely Planet** (www.lonelyplanet. com/italy/rome/hotels) Author-reviewed accommodation options.

➡ **Cross Pollinate** (www.cross-pollinate.com) Personally vetted rooms and apartments by the team behind Rome's super-efficient and stylish Beehive (p214) hostel.

➡ **Bed & Breakfast Association of Rome** (www.b-b.rm.it) B&Bs and short-term apartment rentals.

➡ **Bed & Breakfast Italia** (www.bbitalia.it) Rome's longest-established B&B network.

➡ **Rome As You Feel** (www.romeasyoufeel. com) Apartment rentals; cheap studio flats to luxury apartments.

Lonely Planet's Top Choices

Palm Gallery Hotel (p216)
Arty retreat in elegant surroundings.

Generator Hostel (p214)
Chic design hostel with private rooms and sensational rooftop lounge.

Inn at the Roman Forum
(p211) Classy boutique hideaway near the Imperial Forums.

Villa Spalletti Trivelli (p215)
Stately style in a city-centre mansion.

Best by Budget

€

Althea Inn (p216) Designer comfort at budget prices.

Beehive (p214) Classy hostel near Termini.

Hotel Pensione Barrett
(p211) Welcoming old-school *pensione* with exuberant decor.

€€

Arco del Lauro (p215)
B&B bolthole in happening Trastevere.

Residenza Maritti (p211)
Hidden gem with captivating views over the Forums.

Nerva Boutique Hotel
(p211) Stylish hideaway at the back of the Imperial Forums.

€€€

Hotel Campo de' Fiori
(p211) Classy four-star in the heart of the action.

Gigli d'Oro Suite (p212)
Contemporary style in a 15th-century *palazzo*.

Fendi Private Suites (p213)
Live the fashion-designer dream.

Best Boutique Hotels

Villa Laetitia (p214) Revel

in tasteful decor at this Fendi-designed riverside villa.

Inn at the Roman Forum
(p211) Modern styling and Roman ruins meet at this elegant bolthole.

Relais Le Clarisse (p215)
Peaceful hotel with farmhouse charm in the heart of Trastevere.

Best B&Bs

Althea Inn (p216) A hidden gem near Testaccio.

Le Stanze di Orazio (p213)
An attractive home-away-from-home in upmarket Prati.

BDB Luxury Rooms (p212)
Designer pied-à-terre on mythical, car-free Via Margutta.

Best for Romance

Hotel Sant'Anselmo (p216)
Escape to this beautiful Liberty-style villa.

Hotel Locarno (p212) Star in your own romance at this art-deco gem.

Casa Fabbrini (p212)
Romance by design in an art-nouveau villa.

Buonanotte Garibaldi
(p216) B&B accommodation in a secret Giancolo courtyard.

Best for Greenery

Beehive (p214) Boutique hostel with bijou garden made for lounging around.

Villa Della Fonte (p215)
Cosy gem in a 17th-century townhouse with a trio of rooftop gardens.

Hotel Donna Camilla Savelli (p215) Luxury, 16th-century, convent hotel with two gardens.

Hotel Santa Maria (p216)
Fantastic midrange hotel with courtyard garden, peppered with orange trees.

NEED TO KNOW

Price Ranges

Price ranges refer to a high-season double room with private bathroom, including breakfast unless stated otherwise.

€	less than €110
€€	€110–€200
€€€	more than €200

Accommodation Tax

Everyone overnighting in Rome must pay a room-occupancy tax on top of their bill:

➡ €3 per person per night in one- and two-star hotels

➡ €3.50 in B&Bs and room rentals

➡ €4/6/7 in three-/four-/five-star hotels.

The tax is applicable for a maximum of 10 consecutive nights. Prices in reviews do not include the tax.

Reservations

➡ Always try to book ahead, especially in high season (Easter to September) and during major religious festivals.

➡ Ask for a *camera matrimoniale* for a room with a double bed; a *camera doppia* has twin beds.

Checking In & Out

➡ When you check in you'll need to present your passport or ID card.

➡ Checkout is usually between 10am and noon. In hostels it's around 9am.

➡ Most guesthouses and B&Bs require you to arrange, in advance, a time to check in.

Where to Stay

NEIGHBOURHOOD	FOR	AGAINST
Ancient Rome	Close to major sights such as Colosseum, Roman Forum and Capitoline Museums; quiet at night.	Not cheap and has few budget options; restaurants are touristy.
Centro Storico	Atmospheric area with everything on your doorstep – Pantheon, Piazza Navona, restaurants, bars, shops.	Most expensive part of town; few budget options; can be noisy.
Tridente, Trevi & the Quirinale	Good for Spanish Steps, Trevi Fountain and designer shopping; excellent midrange and top-end options; good transport links.	Upmarket area with prices to match; subdued after dark.
Monti, Esquilino & San Lorenzo	Many hostels and budget hotels around Stazione Termini; top eating options in Monti and thriving nightlife in studenty San Lorenzo; good transport links.	Some dodgy streets in Termini area, which is not Rome's most characterful.
San Giovanni & Testaccio	Authentic atmosphere with good eating and drinking options; Aventino is a quiet, romantic area; Testaccio is a top food and nightlife district.	Few options available; not many big sights.
Trastevere & Gianicolo	Gorgeous, atmospheric area; party vibe with hundreds of bars, cafes, and restaurants; some interesting sights.	Can be noisy, particularly on summer nights – try to stay in the 'quiet' side, east of Via di Trastevere.
Vatican City, Borgo & Prati	Near St Peter's Basilica and Vatican Museums; decent range of accommodation; some excellent shops and restaurants; on the metro.	Expensive near St Peter's; not much nightlife; sells out quickly for religious holidays.
Villa Borghese & Northern Rome	Largely residential area good for the Auditorium and some top museums; generally quiet after dark.	Out of the centre; few budget choices.

🛏 Ancient Rome

★RESIDENZA MARITTI
GUESTHOUSE €€

Map p292 (📞06 678 82 33; www.residenzamaritti.com; Via Tor de' Conti 17; s/d/tr €120/170/190; ❋🔋; MCavour) Boasting stunning views over the nearby forums and Vittoriano, this hidden gem has rooms spread over several floors. Some are bright and modern, others are more cosy in feel with antiques, original tiled floors and family furniture. There's a fully equipped kitchen and a self-service breakfast is provided.

NERVA BOUTIQUE HOTEL
BOUTIQUE HOTEL €€

Map p292 (📞06 678 18 35; www.hotelnerva.com; Via Tor de' Conti 3; d €143-300; ❋🔋; MCavour) Given a complete makeover in 2013, this friendly hotel is tucked away behind the Imperial Forums. Its snug rooms display a contemporary look in shades of cream, grey and black, with padded leather bedsteads, hanging lamps, and the occasional art tome.

★INN AT THE ROMAN FORUM
BOUTIQUE HOTEL €€€

Map p292 (📞06 6919 0970; www.theinnattheromanforum.com; Via degli Ibernesi 30; d €228-422; MCavour) Hidden behind a discreet entrance in a quiet street near the Imperial Forums, this chic boutique hotel is pure gold. From the friendly welcome to the contemporary-styled rooms and panoramic roof terrace, it hits the jackpot. It even has its own ancient ruins in the form of a small 1st-century BC tunnel complex.

🛏 Centro Storico

HOTEL PENSIONE BARRETT
PENSION €€

Map p296 (📞06 686 8481; www.pensionebarrett.com; Largo di Torre Argentina 47; s/d/tr €115/135/165; ❋🔋; 🔋Largo di Torre Argentina) This exuberant pension is quite unique. Boasting a convenient central location, its decor is wonderfully over the top with statues, busts and vibrant stucco set against a forest of leafy potted plants. Rooms are cosy and come with thoughtful extras like foot spas, coffee machines and fully stocked fridges.

ARGENTINA RESIDENZA
GUESTHOUSE €€

Map p296 (📞06 6819 3267; www.argentinaresidenza.com; Via di Torre Argentina 47, 3rd fl; d €170-240; ❋🔋; 🔋Largo di Torre Argentina) A classy boutique guesthouse, Argentina Residenza provides a stylish bolthole in the heart of the historic centre. Its six rooms, fresh from a recent facelift, cut a contemporary dash with their white and pearl-grey palettes, parquet floors, design touches and sparkling bathrooms.

ALBERGO CESÀRI
HISTORIC HOTEL €€

Map p296 (📞06 674 9701; www.albergocesari.it; Via di Pietra 89a; s €130-170, d €145-280; ❋🔋; 🔋Via del Corso) This friendly three-star has been welcoming guests since 1787 and both Stendhal and Mazzini are said to have slept here. Modern-day visitors can expect traditionally attired rooms, complete with creaky parquet floors, a stunning rooftop terrace, and a wonderful central location.

HOTEL MIMOSA
PENSION €€

Map p296 (📞06 6880 1753; www.hotelmimosa.net; Via di Santa Chiara 61, 2nd fl; s €110-135, d €120-145, tr €150-175; ❋@🔋; 🔋Largo di Torre Argentina) This long-standing *pensione* is an excellent budget option offering a warm welcome and a top location near the Pantheon. Rooms are spacious and comfortable with jazzy patterned wallpaper, laminated parquet floors and cooling low-key colours.

RELAIS PALAZZO TAVERNA
BOUTIQUE HOTEL €€

Map p296 (📞06 2039 8064; www.relaispalazzotaverna.com; Via dei Gabrielli 92; s/d/tr €140/210/240; ❋🔋; 🔋Corso del Rinascimento) Housed in a 15th-century *palazzo*, this six-room boutique hotel is just off Via dei Coronari, an elegant cobbled street north of Piazza Navona. Its rooms are simply furnished but come alive thanks to imaginative design touches, wood-beamed ceilings and dark-wood flooring. There's no dining area so breakfast is served in your room.

★HOTEL CAMPO DE' FIORI
BOUTIQUE HOTEL €€€

Map p296 (📞06 6880 6865; www.hotelcampodefiori.com; Via del Biscione 6; r €280-430, apt €230-350; ❋@🔋; 🔋Corso Vittorio Emanuele II) This rakish four-star has got the lot – enticing boudoir decor, an enviable location, professional staff and a fabulous panoramic roof terrace. The interior feels delightfully decadent with its boldly coloured walls, low wooden ceilings, gilt mirrors and crimson damask. Also available are 13 apartments, each sleeping two to five people.

GIGLI D'ORO SUITE
BOUTIQUE HOTEL €€€

Map p296 (☑06 6839 2055; www.giglidorosuite. com; Via dei Gigli d'Oro 12; r €215-410; ⌗ 🛜; 🚇Corso del Rinascimento) This classy hideaway offers six suites in a 15th-century *palazzo* that once belonged to Pope Sixtus V. Traces of the original building have been kept intact so you'll find stone doorways, antique fireplaces and, in the top-floor executive suite, a sloping wood-beamed ceiling. The suites, all named after roads that once crisscrossed the area, boast a chic white look and designer bathrooms.

HOTEL NAVONA
HOTEL €€€

Map p296 (☑06 6821 1392; www.hotelnavona. com; Via dei Sediari 8; s €110-170, d €125-260, q €195-400; ⌗🛜; 🚇Corso del Rinascimento) This recently renovated small hotel offers a range of handsome rooms in a 15th-century *palazzo* near Piazza Navona. The fresh, modern decor marries clean white walls with wooden floors, large padded bedsteads and the occasional ceiling fresco to striking effect. Family rooms, including a deluxe as large as a mid-size apartment, are also available. Breakfast costs €10 extra.

🛏 Tridente, Trevi & the Quirinale

LA CONTRORA
HOSTEL €

Map p300 (☑06 9893 7366; Via Umbria 7; dm €20-40, d €80-110; ⌗ @🛜; 🚇Barberini, 🚇Repubblica) Quality budget accommodation is thin on the ground in the upmarket area north of Piazza Repubblica, but this great little hostel is a top choice. It has a friendly laid-back vibe, cool staff, double rooms and bright, airy mixed dorms (for three and four people), with parquet floors, air-con and private bathrooms. Minimum two-nights stay at weekends.

★CASA FABBRINI
B&B €€

Map p300 (☑329 947 01 53; www.casafabbrini. it; Vicolo delle Orsoline 13; d €150; ⌗🛜; 🚇Spagna) In a part of Rome nicknamed 'Piccolo Londra' (Little London), Casa Fabbrini is a stunning art nouveau villa with an interior straight out of the glossy pages of *Elle Decoration* – host and owner Simone Fabbrini is, funnily enough, an interior designer. Weathered antique doors are upcycled as uber chic bedheads; coloured glass lamps light up rooms to romantic perfection; and rich fabrics make bold use of colour.

HOTEL MODIGLIANI
HOTEL €€

Map p300 (☑06 4281 5226; www.hotelmodigliani. com; Via della Purificazione 42; d/tr/q €195/260/340; ⌗🛜; 🚇Barberini) Run by Italian writer Marco and musician Giulia, this three-star hotel is all about attention to detail. Twenty-three modern, spacious rooms sport a soothing, taupe-and-white palette and some have balconies. Room 602 steals the show with a St Peter's view from its romantic rooftop terrace.

HOTEL LOCARNO
HOTEL €€

Map p300 (☑06 361 08 41; www.hotellocarno.com; Via della Penna 22; d from €200; 😊⌗@🛜; 🚇Flaminio) With its stained-glass doors and rattling cage-lift, this 1925 hotel is an art-deco classic – the kind of place Hercule Poirot might stay if he were in town. Many rooms have silk wallpaper, period furniture, marble bathrooms and are full of vintage charm, if in need of a little TLC. Roof garden, wisteria-draped courtyard, restaurant and fin de siècle cocktail bar (p111) with wintertime fireplace, too.

GIUTURNA BOUTIQUE HOTEL
BOUTIQUE HOTEL €€

Map p300 (☑06 6228 9629; www.giuturna boutiquehotel.com; Largo del Tritone 153; d from €180; 🕓reception 7am-9pm; ⌗@🛜; 🚇Barberini) A hop, skip and coin's throw from Trevi Fountain, this stylish boutique hotel is a peaceful and elegant retreat from the madding crowds. Rooms mix parquet flooring and original architectural features like polished 18th-century beams and exposed brickwork with soft taupe walls, beautiful fabrics and contemporary furniture.

HOTEL FORTE
HISTORIC HOTEL €€

Map p300 (☑06 320 7625; www.hotelforte.com; Via Margutta 61; d/tr €180/230; ⌗@🛜🌐; 🚇Spagna) At home in elegant 18th-century Palazzo Alberto, this three-star hotel from 1923 is a fabulous midrange choice for those seeking, peace, quiet and a room with a view on one of Rome's prettiest ivy-draped streets, peppered with art galleries and car free to boot. Its 20 classical rooms are comfortable, and spacious quads make it a sterling family choice.

BDB LUXURY ROOMS
GUESTHOUSE €€

Map p300 (☑06 6821 0020; www.bdbluxury rooms.com; Via Margutta 38; d from €160; ⌗🛜; 🚇Flaminio) For your own designer pied-à-terre on one of Rome's prettiest and most peaceful pedestrian streets, reserve yourself one of seven chic rooms on Via Margutta. The ground-floor reception is, in fact, a contemporary art gallery and bold wall art is a prominent feature of the stylish rooms inside the 17th-century *palazzo*.

GREGORIANA
HOTEL €€
Map p300 (✆06 679 42 69; www.hotelgregoriana. it; Via Gregoriana 18; d €190-220; ❄❀☏; ⓂSpagna) This low-key, polished art-deco hotel is fantastically set behind the Spanish Steps. Beds have beautiful, circular maple-wood headboards, snow-white linen and lots of gleaming rosewood. Staff are friendly and unpretentious. Its 19 rooms overlook elegant, *palazzo*-laced Via Gregoriana or a peaceful interior courtyard.

FIRST
DESIGN HOTEL €€€
Map p300 (✆06 4561 7070; www.thefirsthotel. com; Via del Vantaggio 14; d from €450; ❀@☏; ⓂFlaminio) Noble 19th-century *palazzo* turned 'luxury art hotel' is the essence of this boutique, five-star hotel. From the magnificent white cow in the lobby to the contemporary artworks exhibited (and for sale), this is one stylish urban retreat. The rooftop garden (with restaurant and cocktail bar) is one of Rome's best.

FENDI PRIVATE SUITES
DESIGN HOTEL €€€
Map p300 (✆06 9779 8080; www.fendiprivate suites.com; Via della Fontanella di Borghese 48, Palazzo Fendi; d from €900; Ⓟ❀@☏; ❑Via del Corso) Comfortably at home on the 2nd floor of Palazzo Fendi (the Roman fashion house's flagship store is right below), this exclusive boutique hotel is pure class. Original art works, photographs of the city snapped by Fendi creative director Karl Lagerfield, Fendi Casa furniture and haute-couture fabrics in soothing greys and blues dress the seven exquisite suites. Dress the part.

IL PALAZZETTO
BOUTIQUE HOTEL €€€
Map p300 (✆06 699 341 000; www.ilpalazzetto roma.com; Vicolo del Bottino 8; d €360; ❀@☏; ⓂSpagna) Something of a secret retreat, this luxury four-room hotel in a 16th-century *palazzo* treats guests to four beautifully appointed doubles with classical decor and spectacular views of the neighbouring Spanish Steps. Luxurious bathrooms are marble, guests share the roof terrace, and breakfast is served in the historic Hotel Hassler (p213), Il Palazzetto's big sister, up the hill; guests can also use its spa and business centre.

HOTEL HASSLER
HOTEL €€€
Map p300 (✆06 69 93 40; www.hotelhassler roma.com; Piazza della Trinità dei Monti 6; s/d from €415/550; ❀@☏; ⓂSpagna) Surmounting the Spanish Steps, the historic Hassler is a byword for old-school luxury. A long line of VIPs have stayed here, enjoying the ravishing views and sumptuous hospitality. Its Michelin-starred restaurant Imàgo (p109) has one of the finest city views. Under the same management is nearby boutique Il Palazzetto (p213), with views over the Spanish Steps.

HOTEL DE RUSSIE
HOTEL €€€
(✆06 32 88 81; www.roccofortehotels.com/it; Via del Babuino 9; d €980; Ⓟ❀@☏; ⓂFlaminio) The historic Hotel de Russie is almost on Piazza del Popolo and has exquisite terraced gardens. The decor is softly luxurious in many shades of grey, and the rooms offer state-of-the-art entertainment systems, massive mosaic-tiled bathrooms and all the luxuries. There's a lovely courtyard **bar** (⏰9am-1am) and a fab, five-star spa (p113).

🛏 Vatican City, Borgo & Prati

COLORS HOTEL
HOTEL €
Map p304 (✆06 687 40 30; www.colorshotel.com; Via Boezio 31; s €53-90, d €62-122, q €98-150; ❀☏; ❑Via Cola di Rienzo) Popular with young travellers, this welcoming hotel impresses with its fresh, artful design and clean, colourful rooms. These come in various shapes and sizes, including two or three cheaper ones with shared bathrooms and, from June to August, dorms for guests under 38 years.

CASA DI ACCOGLIENZA PAOLO VI
CONVENT €
Map p304 (✆06 390 91 41; www.casapaolosesto. it; Viale Vaticano 94; s/d/tr €45/73/92; ❀☏; ❑Viale Vaticano) Stay at this tranquil, palm-shaded convent and you're ideally placed to be first in the line at the Vatican Museums. The resident nuns keep everything ship-shape and the 30 small, sunny rooms are clean as a pin, if institutional in feel. No breakfast but there's a fridge, microwave and drinks dispenser for guests to use.

⭐LE STANZE DI ORAZIO
B&B €€
Map p304 (✆06 3265 2474; www.lestanzediorazio. com; Via Orazio 3; d €110-135; ❀☏; ❑Via Cola di Rienzo; ⓂLepanto) This friendly B&B makes for an attractive home away from home in

SLEEPING VATICAN CITY, BORGO & PRATI

the heart of the elegant Prati district, a single metro stop from the Vatican. It has five bright, playfully decorated rooms, designer bathrooms and a small breakfast area.

QUOD LIBET
GUESTHOUSE €€

Map p304 (☑347 1222642; www.quodlibetroma. com; Via Barletta 29, 4th fl; d €120-150; ✳☎; ⓂOttaviano-San Pietro) A friendly family-run guesthouse offering big colourful rooms and a convenient location near Ottaviano-San Pietro metro station. Rooms are spacious with hand-painted watercolours, parquet and homey furnishings, and there's a kitchen for guest use.

FABIO MASSIMO
DESIGN HOTEL
DESIGN HOTEL €€

Map p304 (☑06 321 30 44; www.hotelfabio massimo.com; Viale Giulio Cesare 71; r €139-229; ✳☎; ⓂOttaviano-San Pietro) Walkable from Ottaviano-San Pietro metro station, this design hotel is convenient as well as quietly stylish. From the 4th-floor reception and breakfast area, corridors lead off to nine rooms, each carpeted and coloured in slate greys and whites with touches of oxblood red, flower motifs and hanging lamps.

★VILLA LAETITIA
BOUTIQUE HOTEL €€€

(☑06 322 67 76; www.villalaetitia.com; Lungotevere delle Armi 22; r €179-390; ✳☎; 🖳Lungotevere delle Armi) Villa Laetitia is a stunning boutique hotel in a riverside art-nouveau villa. Its 20 rooms and mini-apartments, spread over the main building and a separate Garden House, were all individually designed by Anna Venturini Fendi of the famous fashion house. The result are interiors which marry modern design touches with family furniture, vintage pieces and rare finds, such as a framed Picasso scarf in the Garden Room.

🛌 Monti, Esquilino & San Lorenzo

★GENERATOR HOSTEL
HOSTEL €

Map p312 (☑06 492 330; https://generator hostels.com; Via Principe Amedeo 257; dm €17-70, d €50-200; ✳@☎🖳; ⓂVittorio Emanuele) Hostelling just got a whole lot smarter in Rome thanks to this designer hostel which, quite frankly, is more uber-cool hotel in mood – 72% of the 174 beds here languish in bright white private rooms with sharp bathrooms, and dorms max out at four beds. Check in at the bar, hang out in the stylish lounge, or chill on the sensational rooftop lounge.

★YELLOW HOSTEL
HOSTEL €

Map p312 (☑06 446 35 54; www.the-yellow.com; Via Palestro 51; dm €20-35, d €90-120, q €100-150; ✳@☎; ⓂCastro Pretorio) This sharp, 300-bed party hostel, with designer dorms, play area sporting comfy beanbags, escape room and kitchen you'd actually want to hang out in, is rapidly colonising the entire street – aka the 'Yellow Square' – with its top-notch facilities aimed squarely at young travellers.

★BEEHIVE
HOSTEL €

Map p312 (☑06 4470 4553; www.the-beehive.com; Via Marghera 8; dm €35-40, d without bathroom €80, s/d/tr €70/100/120; ⏱reception 7am-11pm; ✳☎🖳; ⓂTermini) 🗣 More boutique chic than backpacker dive, the Beehive is a small and stylish hostel with a glorious summer garden. Dynamic American owners Linda and Steve exude energy and organise cooking classes, storytelling evenings, weekly hostel dinners around a shared table, pop-up dinners with chefs, and so on. Pick from a spotless eight-bed dorm (mixed), a four-bed female dorm, or private rooms with ceiling fan and honey-based soap.

HOTEL LAURENTIA
HOTEL €€

Map p311 (☑06 445 02 18; www.hotellaurentia. com; Largo degli Osci 63, San Lorenzo; s/d/tr/q €110/125/145/170; ✳@☎🖳; 🖳Scalo San Lorenzo) At home in an attractive 19th-century townhouse with burnt-orange facade and green foliage, this elegant three-star hotel is the best spot to stay in San Lorenzo. Its 45 rooms are clean, comfortable and some overlook the pretty market square with bell tower; the best have a terrace.

HOTEL DUCA D'ALBA
HOTEL €€

Map p312 (☑06 48 44 71; www.hotelducadalba. com; Via Leonina 14; d from €180; ✳☎; ⓂCavour) This appealing four-star hotel with attractive ochre-coloured facade has 27 small but charming rooms, many with fabric-covered walls, wood-beamed ceilings and travertine marble bathrooms. Breakfast is served beneath red-brick vaults and the best rooms have gorgeous little balconies overlooking the Monti rooftops.

RESIDENZA CELLINI
GUESTHOUSE €€

Map p312 (☑06 4782 5204; www.residenzacellini. it; Via Modena 5; s €190, d €130-205; ✳@☎🖳; ⓂRepubblica) A beautiful 1920s cage lift with polished wood-panelled interior rattles its way up to this elegant 3rd-floor hotel on a quiet side road near busy Via Nazionale. Its

17 rooms are notably spacious, with floral fabrics, period furniture, kettle, and Jacuzzi or hydro-massage shower. Don't miss the rooftop terrace with lounge seating.

66 IMPERIAL INN
B&B €€

Map p312 (☑06 482 56 48; www.66imperialinn. com; Via del Viminale 66; d/tr/q €125/155/185; ❄️🛜; ☐Via Nazionale) Find this swish B&B on the 4th floor of a burnt-orange *palazzo* with aubergine wooden shutters and the odd frescoed hallway. Its five rooms, each named after a colour (or animal in the case of B&W-striped Zebra), combine designer wallpapers with vibrant silks, white linen and fabulous high ceilings.

HOTEL COLUMBIA
HOTEL €€

Map p312 (☑06 488 35 09; www.hotelcolumbia. com; Via del Viminale 15; d from €160; ❄️@🛜; MTermini or Repubblica) In a workaday area sandwiched between Rome's Brutalist opera house and Stazione Termini, family-run Columbia sports a polished look with beamed or exposed stone ceilings and Murano crystal chandeliers. Its 45 white-walled rooms are bright and characterful.

★VILLA SPALLETTI TRIVELLI
BOUTIQUE HOTEL €€€

Map p312 (☑06 4890 7934; www.villaspalletti. it; Via Piacenza 4; d €625; P❄️@🛜; MSpagna) This glorious boutique hotel resides in a mansion fitted out with 16th-century tapestries, antique books and original period furnishings. It was built by Gabriella Rasponi, niece of Carolina Bonaparte (Napoleon's sister), and much of the family's art collection remains. Its 14 romantic suites are elegantly decorated, with lovely green garden views. But nothing beats the rooftop terrace with sunloungers and bubbling Jacuzzis.

🛏 Trastevere & Gianicolo

★RELAIS LE CLARISSE
HOTEL €€

Map p308 (☑06 5833 4437; www.leclarisse trastevere.com; Via Cardinale Merry del Val 20; d €80-250; ❄️🛜; ☐Viale di Trastevere, ☐Viale di Trastevere) Set hacienda-style around a pretty internal courtyard with an 80-year-old olive tree, orange trees and a scattering of summertime breakfast tables, this is a peaceful 18-room oasis in Trastevere's bustling core. In contrast to the urban mayhem outside, the hotel is a picture of farmhouse charm with rooms decorated in rustic style.

★ARCO DEL LAURO
GUESTHOUSE €€

Map p308 (☑06 9784 0350; www.arcodellauro. it; Via Arco de' Tolomei 27; d €95-135, q €135-175; ❄️@🛜; ☐Viale di Trastevere, ☐Viale di Trastevere) Perfectly placed on a peaceful cobbled lane in the 'quiet side' of Trastevere, this ground-floor guesthouse sports six gleaming white rooms with parquet floors, a modern low-key look and well-equipped bathrooms.

★VILLA DELLA FONTE
B&B €€

Map p308 (☑06 580 37 97; www.villafonte.com; Via della Fonte dell'Olio 8; s €120-140, d €150-190; ❄️🛜; ☐Viale di Trastevere, ☐Viale di Trastevere) A lovely terracotta-hued, ivy-shrouded gem in a 17th-century townhouse, Villa della Fonte is precisely what Rome's la dolce vita is about. Five pretty rooms, some with original red brick and wood beam ceilings, exude old-world charm. But the crowning glory is the trio of rooftop gardens, strewn with sunloungers, potted pomegranate trees and fragrant citrus plants.

B&B SUITES TRASTEVERE
B&B €€

(☑347 074 40 86; www.trastevere.bbsuites.com; Viale di Trastevere 248; d €120-130; ❄️🛜; ☐Viale di Trastevere, ☐Viale di Trastevere) Find this guesthouse on the 4th floor of a honey-hued *palazzo* on the busy main drag and tramway running from Trastevere. Owner and ultimate-good-host Marco is an utter angel and you won't forget you're in Rome staying here – each of the suites is dramatically frescoed with local sights, such as the Colosseum, Pantheon and Trevi Fountain.

RESIDENZA ARCO DE' TOLOMEI
GUESTHOUSE €€

Map p308 (☑06 5832 0819; www.bbarcodei tolomei.com; Via Arco de' Tolomei 27; s/d €170/195; ❄️🛜; ☐Viale di Trastevere, ☐Viale di Trastevere) Polished antiques and rich fabrics decorate this old-world guesthouse, on the 2nd floor of an old building in backstreet Trastevere. There are six rooms, each named after a Roman road – Appia, Aurelia and so on.

★HOTEL DONNA CAMILLA SAVELLI
HOTEL €€€

Map p308 (☑06 588 861; www.hoteldonnacamilla savelli.com; Via Garibaldi 27; d €270; P❄️@🛜; ☐Viale di Trastevere, ☐Viale di Trastevere) It's seldom you can stay in a 16th-century convent designed by baroque genius Borromini. This four-star hotel is exquisitely appointed – muted colours complement the serene concave and convex curves of the architecture

– and the service is excellent. The best rooms overlook the cloister garden or have views of Rome.

★HOTEL SANTA MARIA　HOTEL €€€

Map p308 (☑06 5894 626; www.hotelsantamaria. info; Vicolo del Piede 2; d/tr/q €240/295/325; P❋@🖨🛗; 🚊Viale di Trastevere, 🚊Viale di Trastevere) Squirreled away behind a wall in the heart of Trastevere is this old convent, today an idyllic 20-room hotel arranged around a courtyard peppered with orange trees. An alley of potted lemon trees leads up to the modern, low-lying building and functional, if dated, rooms evoke the sun with terracotta floors and Provencal colour schemes.

BUONANOTTE GARIBALDI　B&B €€€

Map p308 (☑06 5833 0733; www.buonanotte garibaldi.com; Via Garibaldi 83; d €240-280; ⊗reception 9am-7pm; ☻❋@🖨; 🚊Viale di Trastevere, 🚊Viale di Trastevere) With only three rooms in a divinely pretty villa set around a courtyard in Giancolo, this upmarket B&B is a haven. The rooms – themed Rome (inspired by the magnificent sunsets over Rome as seen from Giancolo), Chocolate and Tinto – are beautifully decorated. There are works of art and sculpture all over the place.

🛏 San Giovanni & Testaccio

★ALTHEA INN　B&B €

Map p306 (☑06 9893 2666, 339 4353717; www. altheainn.com; Via dei Conciatori 9; d €120; ❋🖨; MPiramide) In a workaday apartment block near the Aurelian Walls, this friendly B&B offers superb value for money and easy access to Testaccio's bars, clubs and restaurants. Its spacious, light-filled rooms sport a modish look with white walls and tasteful modern furniture, and each has its own small terrace.

HOTEL LANCELOT　HOTEL €€

Map p306 (☑06 7045 0615; www.lancelothotel. com; Via Capo d'Africa 47; s €120-128, d €180-216, f €250-278; ❋🖨; 🚊Via di San Giovanni in Laterano) A great location near the Colosseum, striking views and super-helpful English-speaking staff – the family-run Lancelot scores across the board. The lobby and communal areas gleam with marble and crystal while the spacious rooms exhibit a more modest classic style. The best, on the 6th floor, also come with their own terrace.

★HOTEL SANT'ANSELMO　HOTEL €€€

Map p306 (☑06 57 00 57; www.aventinohotels. com; Piazza Sant'Anselmo 2; s €135-265, d €155-285; ❋🖨; 🚊Via Marmorata) A ravishing romantic hideaway in the hilltop Aventino district. Housed in an elegant villa, its individually named rooms are not the biggest but they are stylish, juxtaposing retro four-poster beds, Liberty-style furniture and ornate decorative flourishes with modern touches and contemporary colours.

🛏 Villa Borghese & Northern Rome

★PALM GALLERY HOTEL　HOTEL €€

Map p316 (☑06 6478 1859; www.palmgalleryhotel. com; Via delle Alpi 15d; s €130-160, d €150-210; ❋🖨🛏; 🚊Via Nomentana, 🚊Viale Regina Margherita) Housed in a 1905 Liberty-style villa, this gorgeous hotel sports an eclectic look that effortlessly blends African and Middle Eastern art with original art-deco furniture, exposed brickwork and hand-painted tiles. Rooms are individually decorated, with the best offering views over the wisteria and thick greenery in the surrounding streets.

CASA MONTANI　GUESTHOUSE €€€

Map p316 (☑06 3260 0421; www.casamontani. com; Piazzale Flaminio 9; d €168-260; ❋🖨; MFlaminio) An intimate and contemporary hideaway, Casa Montani has five rooms on the 3rd floor of a *palazzo* overlooking Porta del Popolo. The three deluxe rooms and two suites are all individually decorated but expect muted shades of grey, custom-designed furniture, hardwood floors and modern art. Bathrooms come with Hermès toiletries, and breakfast is served in your room on fine china.

🛏 Southern Rome

HOTEL ABITART　HOTEL €€

Map p318 (☑06 454 31 91; www.abitarthotel.com; Via Pellegrino Matteucci 10-20; d €140; 🚊Via Ostiense, MPiramide) Changing contemporary art exhibitions by local Roman artists decorate this hotel in gritty Ostiense. Standard doubles are a riot of bright colours and themed suites evoke different art periods (cubism, 1970s, pop art) and genres (poetry, photography). Pluses include the hotel restaurant-bar **Estrobar** (☑06 5728 9141; www.estro bar.com; menu/meals €27/40; ⊗9am-midnight) with attractive summertime terrace and garage parking (€24 per night) right next door.

Understand Rome

Rome Today

Political turmoil is part and parcel of Roman life as recent events have amply demonstrated. On the surface the news has been good – EU leaders met in town to mark 60 years of European unity; millions of pilgrims poured into St Peter's for Pope Francis' Holy Year; the Colosseum was unveiled after a lengthy restoration. But behind the scenes, the story has been one of controversy and crisis in City Hall and ferocious in-fighting at the Vatican.

Best on Film

La grande bellezza (The Great Beauty; 2013) Paolo Sorrentino's Fellini-esque homage to the Eternal City.
Roma Città Aperta (Rome Open City; 1945) A neo-realist study of desperation in Nazi-occupied Rome.
The Talented Mr Ripley (1999) Murderous intrigue on Piazza di Spagna and in other Italian locations.

Best in Print

The Secrets of Rome: Love & Death in the Eternal City (Corrado Augias; 2007) Journalist Augias muses on little-known historical episodes.
Four Seasons in Rome (Anthony Doerr; 2008) Intimate memoir of a year in Rome by Pulitzer Prize–winning writer.
Roman Tales (Alberto Moravia; 1954) Short stories set in Rome's poorest neighbourhoods.
Rome (Robert Hughes; 2012) A personal portrait of the city by the straight-talking Australian art critic.
Michelangelo & the Pope's Ceiling (Ross King; 2003) Fascinating account of the painting of the Sistine Chapel.

Chaos in City Hall

In summer 2016 Rome elected its first ever woman mayor. Virginia Raggi, a 37-year old city councillor swept to victory in the June elections, taking 67% of the vote as candidate for the populist Movimento 5 Stelle (5 Star Movement). Promising to take on corruption and improve the city's dire public services, her message struck a chord with a Roman public weary of cutbacks and political scandal. Her honeymoon period didn't last long, though, and within months her administration was mired in controversy.

By Christmas, she'd had to deal with the resignation of several key appointees, including the manager she'd tasked with cleaning up the city. Then, in early 2017, she was placed under investigation for abuse of office following the appointment of a city tourism official.

In the midst of all this, she did, however, make some big decisions. She scotched Rome's bid for the 2024 Olympic Games and gave the go-ahead for a new football stadium in the city's southern reaches. She also pushed through a €5.3 billion budget, earmarking €430 million for upgrading the city's public transport network, including buying new buses and funding construction on the city's third metro line.

Jubilee & Vatican Intrigue

Over on the west bank of the Tiber, the Vatican has been busy. Pope Francis declared 2016 a Jubilee, or Holy Year, and millions made the pilgrimage to Rome – according to Vatican estimates, 21 million people passed through the Holy Door at St Peter's Basilica over the course of the year.

A highlight event was the canonisation of Mother Teresa in September 2016, which drew crowds of up to 120,000 to St Peter's Square and featured a special pizza lunch for 1500 homeless people.

Behind the scenes, however, the atmosphere in the Vatican has become increasingly toxic as internal opposition has grown to Pope Francis' progressive politics. With his easy-going manner and popular charm, the Argentinian pontiff has won worldwide acclaim for giving the Church a friendlier face, but his liberal line has enraged powerful conservatives. Central to the dispute, which some commentators have likened to a civil war, is the pope's line on social issues such as the family, marriage and divorce.

Monumental Makeovers

For several years now, Rome's cultural administrators have been courting private money to shore up municipal budgets and help cover the cost of maintaining the city's historic sites and monuments. This policy has sparked heated debate but it is now showing signs of fruition. Most notably, the Colosseum is looking better than it has in centuries after the recent completion of a three-year clean-up. The work came as the first part of a comprehensive €25 million restoration project being sponsored by the designer shoemakers Tod's. Similarly, the Spanish Steps, which were reopened to the public in September 2016, are gleaming after a €1.5 million makeover financed by luxury jewellers Bulgari. Foreign organisations are also getting in on the act and, in March 2017, it was announced that the Danish Academy would be donating €1.5 million towards work on the Foro di Cesare.

As well as these high-profile projects, the city has also managed some quieter successes. At the Roman Forum, the Chiesa di Santa Maria Antiqua was reopened after a lengthy restoration, while at the Circo Massimo a renovated section of the original stadium was recently opened to guided tours.

Art on the Streets

While donations pour in for Rome's ancient sites and historic monuments, the state of the city's streets and parks remains a source of anger to many Romans. Litter in overgrown parks, roads full of potholes, pavements blocked by illegally parked cars – these are complaints you'll hear in bar conversations across the city.

The situation has sparked community action, which has often taken the form of street art. Giant murals have gone up on walls all over town, adding colour to abandoned buildings, disused factories and housing blocks. A more recent phenomenon has even seen immigrants taking to cleaning pavements and roadsides on their own initiative.

if Rome were 100 people

87 would be Italian
5 would be Eastern European
4 would be Asian
1 would be African
3 would be other

nationality
(% of population)

Italian 80

Others 20

population per sq km

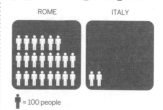

ROME   ITALY

👤 ≈ 100 people

History

Rome's history spans three millennia, from the classical myths of vengeful gods to the follies of Roman emperors, from Renaissance excess and papal plotting to swaggering 20th-century fascism. Everywhere you go in this remarkable city, you're surrounded by the past. Martial ruins, Renaissance *palazzi* (mansions) and flamboyant baroque basilicas all have tales to tell – of family feuding, historic upheavals, artistic rivalries, intrigues and dark passions.

Ancient Rome, The Myth

As much a mythical construct as a historical reality, ancient Rome's image has been carefully nurtured throughout history. Intellectuals, artists and architects have sought inspiration from this skilfully constructed legend, while political and religious rulers have invoked it to legitimise their authority and serve their political ends.

Imperial Spin Doctors

Rome's original myth-makers were the first emperors. Eager to reinforce the city's status as *caput mundi* (capital of the world), they turned to writers such as Virgil, Ovid and Livy to create an official Roman history. These authors, while adept at weaving epic narratives, were less interested in the rigours of historical research and frequently presented myth as reality. In the *Aeneid,* Virgil brazenly draws on Greek legends and stories to tell the tale of Aeneas, a Trojan prince who arrives in Italy and establishes Rome's founding dynasty. Similarly, Livy, a writer celebrated for his monumental history of the Roman Republic, makes liberal use of mythology to fill the gaps in his historical narrative.

Ancient Rome's rulers were sophisticated masters of spin and under their tutelage, art, architecture and elaborate public ceremony were employed to perpetuate the image of Rome as an invincible and divinely sanctioned power. Monuments such as the Ara Pacis, the Colonna di Traiano and the Arco di Costantino celebrated imperial glories, while gladiatorial games highlighted the Romans' physical superiority. The

In 2014 excavations under the Lapis Niger in the Roman Forum unearthed a wall dating to between the end of the 9th century BC and the early 8th century BC. This would suggest that Rome was founded a century or so before its traditional birth date of 753 BC.

TIMELINE	753 BC	509 BC	146 BC
	According to legend, Romulus kills his twin brother Remus and founds Rome. Archaeological evidence exists of an 8th-century settlement on the Palatino.	On the death of the king Tarquinius Superbus, the Roman Republic is founded, paving the way for Rome's rise to European domination.	Carthage is razed to the ground at the end of the Third Punic War and mainland Greece is conquered by rampant legionaries. Rome becomes undisputed master of the Mediterranean.

Colosseum, the Roman Forum and the Pantheon were not only sophisticated feats of engineering, they were also impregnable symbols of Rome's eternal might.

The Past as Inspiration

During the Renaissance, a period in which ancient Rome was hailed as the high point of Western civilisation, the city's great monuments inspired a whole generation of artists and architects. Bramante, Michelangelo and Raphael modelled their work on classical precedents as they helped rebuild Rome as the capital of the Catholic Church.

But more than anyone, it was Italy's 20th-century fascist dictator Benito Mussolini who invoked the glories of ancient Rome. Il Duce spared no effort in his attempts to identify his fascist regime with imperial Rome – he made Rome's traditional birthday, 21 April, an official fascist holiday, he printed stamps with images of ancient Roman emperors, and he commissioned archaeological digs to unearth further proof of Roman might. His idealisation of the Roman Empire underpinned much of his colonialist ideology.

Ancient Rome on Screen

Spartacus (1960; Stanley Kubrick)

Quo Vadis (1951; Mervyn LeRoy)

Gladiator (2000; Ridley Scott)

I, Claudius (1976; BBC)

Rome (2005–07; HBO, BBC)

HISTORY ANCIENT ROME, THE MYTH

ROMULUS & REMUS, ROME'S LEGENDARY TWINS

The most famous of Rome's many legends is the story of Romulus and Remus and the foundation of the city on 21 April 753 BC.

According to myth, Romulus and Remus were the children of the vestal virgin Rhea Silva and the god of war, Mars. While still babies they were set adrift on the Tiber to escape a death penalty imposed by their great-uncle Amulius, who at the time was battling their grandfather Numitor for control of Alba Longa. However, they were discovered near the Palatino by a she-wolf, who suckled them until a shepherd, Faustulus, found and raised them.

Years later the twins decided to found a city on the site where they'd originally been saved. They didn't know where this was, so they consulted the omens. Remus, on the Aventino, saw six vultures; his brother over on the Palatino saw 12. The meaning was clear and Romulus began building, much to the outrage of his brother. The two argued and Romulus killed Remus.

Romulus continued building and soon had a city. To populate it he created a refuge on the Campidoglio, Aventino, Celio and Quirinale Hills, to which a ragtag population of criminals, ex-slaves and outlaws soon decamped. However, the city still needed women. Romulus therefore invited everyone in the surrounding country to celebrate the Festival of Consus (21 August). As the spectators watched the festival games, Romulus and his men pounced and abducted all the women, an act that was to go down in history as the Rape of the Sabine Women.

73–71 BC	49 BC	44 BC	AD 14
Spartacus leads a slave revolt against dictator Cornelius Sulla. Defeat is inevitable; punishment is brutal. Spartacus and 6000 followers are crucified along Via Appia Antica.	'Alea iacta est' ('The die is cast'). Julius Caesar leads his army across the River Rubicon and marches on Rome. In the ensuing civil war, Caesar defeats rival Pompey.	On the Ides of March, soon after Julius Caesar is proclaimed dictator for life, he is stabbed to death in the Teatro di Pompeo (on modern-day Largo di Torre Argentina).	Augustus dies after 41 years as Rome's first emperor. His reign is successful, unlike those of his mad successors, Tiberius and Caligula, who go down in history for their cruelty.

A WHO'S WHO OF ROMAN EMPERORS

Of the 250 or so emperors of the Roman Empire, only a few were truly heroic. Here we highlight 10 of the best, worst and completely insane.

Augustus (27 BC–AD 14) Rome's first emperor. Ushers in a period of peace and security; the arts flourish and many monuments are built, including the Ara Pacis and the original Pantheon.

Caligula (37–41) The third emperor, after Augustus and Tiberius. Remains popular until illness leads to the depraved behaviour for which he becomes infamous. Is murdered by his bodyguards on the Palatino.

Claudius (41–54) Expands the Roman Empire and conquers Britain. Is eventually poisoned, probably at the instigation of Agrippina, his wife and Nero's mother.

Nero (54–68) Initially rules well but later slips into madness – he has his mother murdered, persecutes the Christians and attempts to turn half the city into a palace, the Domus Aurea. He is eventually forced into suicide.

Vespasian (69–79) First of the Flavian dynasty, he imposes peace and cleans up the imperial finances. His greatest legacy is the Colosseum.

Trajan (98–117) Conquers the east and rules over the empire at its zenith. He revamps Rome's city centre, adding a forum, marketplace and column, all of which still stand.

Hadrian (117–38) Puts an end to imperial expansion and constructs walls to mark the empire's borders. He rebuilds the Pantheon and has one of the ancient world's greatest villas built at Tivoli.

Aurelian (270–75) Does much to control the rebellion that sweeps the empire at the end of the 3rd century. Starts construction of the city walls that still today bear his name.

Diocletian (284–305) Splits the empire into eastern and western halves in 285. Launches a savage persecution of the Christians as he struggles to control the empire's eastern reaches.

Constantine I (306–37) Although based in Byzantium (later renamed Constantinople in his honour), he legalises Christianity and embarks on a church-building spree in Rome.

Nowadays, the myth of Rome is used less as a rallying cry and more as an advertising tool – and with some success. However cynical and world-weary you are, it's difficult to deny the thrill of seeing the Colosseum for the first time or of visiting the Palatino, the hill where Romulus is said to have founded the city in 753 BC.

64	67	80	285
Rome is ravaged by a huge fire that burns for five and a half days. Some blame Nero, although he was in Anzio when the conflagration broke out.	Sts Peter and Paul become martyrs as Nero massacres Rome's Christians. The persecution is a thinly disguised ploy to win back popularity after the great fire of AD 64.	The 50,000-seat Flavian Amphitheatre, better known as the Colosseum, is inaugurated by the emperor Titus. Five thousand animals are slaughtered in the 100-day opening games.	To control anarchy within the Roman Empire, Diocletian splits it into two. The eastern half is later incorporated into the Byzantine Empire; the western half falls to the barbarians.

Legacy of an Empire

Rising out of the bloodstained remains of the Roman Republic, the Roman Empire was the Western world's first great superpower. At its zenith under the emperor Trajan (r AD 98–117), it extended from Britannia in the north to North Africa in the south, from Hispania (Spain) in the west to Palestina (Palestine) and Syria in the east. Rome itself had more than 1.5 million inhabitants and the city sparkled with the trappings of imperial splendour: marble temples, public baths, theatres, circuses and libraries. Decline eventually set in during the 3rd century, and by the latter half of the 5th century, the city was in barbarian hands.

Europe Divided

The empire's most immediate legacy was the division of Europe into east and west. In AD 285 the emperor Diocletian, prompted by widespread disquiet across the empire, split the Roman Empire into eastern

The Roman Empire

313	476	754	800
A year after his victory at the Battle of Milvian Bridge, the emperor Constantine issues the Edict of Milan, officially establishing religious tolerance and legally ending Christian persecution.	The fall of Romulus Augustulus marks the end of the Western Empire. This had been on the cards for years: in 410 the Goths sacked Rome; in 455 the Vandals followed suit.	Pope Stephen II and Pepin, king of the Franks, cut a deal resulting in the creation of the Papal States. The papacy is to rule Rome until Italian unification.	Pope Leo III crowns Pepin's son, Charlemagne, Holy Roman Emperor during Christmas mass at St Peter's Basilica. A red disk in the basilica marks the spot where it happened.

and western halves – the west centred on Rome, the east on Byzantium (later called Constantinople) – in a move that was to have far-reaching consequences. In the west, the fall of the Western Roman Empire in AD 476 paved the way for the emergence of the Holy Roman Empire and the Papal States, while in the east, Roman (later Byzantine) rule continued until 1453 when the empire was conquered by Ottoman armies.

Democracy & the Rule of Law

In broader cultural terms, Roman innovations in language, law, government, art, architecture, engineering and public administration remain relevant to this day.

One of the Romans' most striking contributions to modern society was democratic government. Democracy had first appeared in 5th-century-BC Athens, but it was the Romans, with their genius for organisation, who took it to another level. Under the Roman Republic (509–47 BC), the Roman population was divided into two categories: the Senate and the Roman people. Both held clearly defined responsibilities. The people, through three assembly bodies – the Centuriate Assembly, the Tribal Assembly and the Council of the People – voted on all new laws and elected two annual tribunes who had the power of veto in the Senate. The Senate, for its part, elected and advised two annual consuls who acted as political and military leaders. It also controlled the Republic's purse strings and, in times of grave peril, could nominate a dictator for a six-month period.

This system worked well for the duration of the republic, and remained more or less intact during the empire – at least on paper. In practice, the Senate assumed the assemblies' legislative powers and the emperor claimed power of veto over the Senate, a move that pretty much gave him complete command.

The observance of law was an important feature of Roman society. As far back as the 5th century BC, the republic had a bill of rights, known as the Twelve Tables. This remained the foundation stone of Rome's legal system until the emperor Justinian (r 527–65) produced his mammoth *Corpus Iurus Civilis* (Body of Civil Law) in 529. This not only codified all existing laws, but also included a systematic treatise on legal philosophy. In particular, it introduced a distinction between *ius civilis* (civil law – laws particular to a state), *ius gentium* (law of nations – laws established and shared by states) and *ius naturale* (natural law – laws concerning male–female relationships and matrimony).

HISTORY LEGACY OF AN EMPIRE

Virgil (70–19 BC), real name Publius Vergilius Maro, was born near the northern Italian town of Mantua to a wealthy family. He studied in Cremona, Milan, Rome and Naples, before becoming Rome's best-known classical poet. His most famous works are the *Eclogues, Georgics* and the *Aeneid*.

1084	1300	1309	1347
Rome is sacked by a Norman army after Pope Gregory VII invites them in to help him against the besieging forces of the Holy Roman Emperor Henry IV.	Pope Boniface VIII proclaims Rome's first ever Jubilee, offering a full pardon to anyone who makes the pilgrimage to the city. Up to 200,000 people are said to have come.	Fighting between French-backed pretenders to the papacy and Roman nobility ends in Pope Clement V transferring to Avignon. Only in 1377 does Pope Gregory XI return to Rome.	Cola di Rienzo, a local notary, declares himself dictator of Rome. Surprisingly, he's welcomed by the people; less surprisingly he's later driven out of town by the hostile aristocracy.

Latin

More than the laws themselves, Rome's greatest legacy to the legal profession was the Latin language. Latin was the lingua franca of the Roman Empire and was later adopted by the Catholic Church, a major reason for its survival. It is still one of the Vatican's official languages and until the second Vatican Council (1962–65) it was the only language in which Catholic Mass could be said. As the basis for modern Romance languages such as Italian, French and Spanish, it provides the linguistic roots of many modern words.

Christianity & Papal Power

For much of its history Rome has been ruled by the pope, and still today the Vatican wields immense influence over the city.

Before the arrival of Christianity, the Romans were remarkably tolerant of foreign religions. They themselves worshipped a cosmopolitan pantheon of gods, ranging from household spirits and former emperors to deities appropriated from Greek mythology (Jupiter, Juno, Neptune, Minerva etc). Religious cults were also popular – the Egyptian gods Isis and Serapis enjoyed a mass following, as did Mithras, a heroic saviour-god of vaguely Persian origin, who was worshipped by male-only devotees in underground temples.

The patron saints of Rome, Peter and Paul, were both executed during Nero's persecution of the Christians between 64 and 68. Paul, who as a Roman citizen was entitled to a quick death, was beheaded, while Peter was crucified head down on Nero's Circus on the Vatican Hill.

HISTORY CHRISTIANITY & PAPAL POWER

DONATION OF CONSTANTINE

The most famous forgery in medieval history, the Donation of Constantine is a document with which the emperor Constantine purportedly grants Pope Sylvester I (r 314–35) and his successors control of Rome and the Western Roman Empire, as well as primacy over the holy sees of Antioch, Alexandria, Constantinople, Jerusalem and all the world's churches.

No one is exactly sure when the document was written but the consensus is that it dates to the mid- or late 8th century. Certainly this fits with the widespread theory that the author was a Roman cleric, possibly working with the knowledge of Pope Stephen II (r 752–57).

For centuries the donation was accepted as genuine and used by popes to justify their territorial claims. But in 1440 the Italian philosopher Lorenzo Valla proved that it was a forgery. By analysing the Latin used in the document he was able to show that it was inconsistent with the Latin used in the 4th century.

1378–1417	1506	1508	1527
Squabbling between factions in the Catholic Church leads to the Great Schism. The pope rules in Rome while the alternative anti-pope sits in Avignon.	Pope Julius II employs 150 Swiss mercenaries to protect him. The Swiss Guard, all practising Catholics from Switzerland, are still responsible for the pope's personal safety.	Michelangelo starts painting the Sistine Chapel, while down the hall Raphael decorates Pope Julius II's private apartments, now known as the Stanze di Raffaello (Raphael Rooms).	Pope Clement VII takes refuge in Castel Sant'Angelo as Rome is sacked by troops loyal to Charles V, king of Spain and Holy Roman Emperor.

Emergence of Christianity

The Roman Inquisition was set up in the 16th century to counter the threat of Protestantism. It was responsible for prosecuting people accused of heresy, blasphemy, immorality and witchcraft, and although it did order executions, it often imposed lighter punishments such as fines and the recital of prayers.

Christianity entered Rome's religious cocktail in the 1st century AD, sweeping in from Judaea, a Roman province in what is now Israel and the West Bank. Its early days were marred by persecution, most notably under Nero (r 54–68), but it slowly caught on, thanks to its popular message of heavenly reward and the evangelising efforts of Sts Peter and Paul. However, it was the conversion of the emperor Constantine (r 306–37) that really set Christianity on the path to European domination. In 313 Constantine issued the Edict of Milan, officially legalising Christianity, and later, in 378, Theodosius (r 379–95) made it Rome's state religion. By this time, the Church had developed a sophisticated organisational structure based on five major sees: Rome, Constantinople, Alexandria, Antioch and Jerusalem. At the outset, each bishopric carried equal weight, but in subsequent years Rome emerged as the senior party. The reasons for this were partly political – Rome was the wealthy capital of the Roman Empire – and partly religious – early Christian doctrine held that St Peter, founder of the Roman Church, had been sanctioned by Christ to lead the universal Church.

Papal Control

But while Rome had control of Christianity, the Church had yet to conquer Rome. This it did in the dark days that followed the fall of the Roman Empire. And although no one person can take credit for this, Pope Gregory the Great (r 590–604) did more than most to lay the groundwork. A leader of considerable foresight, he won many friends by supplying free bread to Rome's starving citizens and restoring the city's water supply after it had been cut by barbarian invaders. He also stood up to the menacing Lombards, who presented a very real threat to the city.

It was this threat that pushed the papacy into an alliance with the Frankish kings, an alliance that resulted in the creation of the two great powers of medieval Europe: the Papal States and the Holy Roman Empire. In Rome, the battle between these two superpowers translated into endless feuding between the city's baronial families and frequent attempts by the French to claim the papacy for their own. This political and military fighting eventually culminated in the papacy transferring to the French city of Avignon between 1309 and 1377, and the Great Schism (1378–1417), a period in which the Catholic world was headed by two popes, one in Rome and one in Avignon.

Longest-Serving Popes

....

St Peter (r 30–67)

....

Pius XI (r 1846–78)

....

John Paul II (r 1978–2005)

....

Leo XIII (r 1878–1903)

....

Pius Vi (r 1775–99)

1540	1555	1626	1632
Pope Paul III officially recognises the Society of Jesus, aka the Jesuits. The order is founded by Ignatius de Loyola, who spends his last days in the Chiesa del Gesù.	As fear pervades Counter-Reformation Rome, Pope Paul IV confines the city's Jews to the area known as the Jewish Ghetto. Official intolerance continues on and off until the 20th century.	After more than 150 years of construction, St Peter's Basilica is consecrated. The hulking basilica remains the largest church in the world until well into the 20th century.	Galileo Galilei is summoned to appear before the Inquisition. He is forced to renounce his belief that the earth revolves around the sun and is exiled to Florence.

As both religious and temporal leaders, Rome's popes wielded influence well beyond their military capacity. For much of the medieval period, the Church held a virtual monopoly on Europe's reading material (mostly religious scripts written in Latin) and was the authority on virtually every aspect of human knowledge. All innovations in science, philosophy and literature had to be cleared by the Church's hawkish scholars, who were constantly on the lookout for heresy.

Modern Influence

Almost a thousand years on and the Church is still a major influence on modern Italian life. Its rigid stance on social and ethical issues such as birth control, abortion, same-sex marriage and euthanasia informs much public debate, often with highly divisive results.

The relationship between the Church and Italy's modern political establishment has been a fact of life since the founding of the Italian Republic in 1946. For much of the First Republic (1946–94), the Vatican was closely associated with the Christian Democrat party (Democrazia Cristiana; DC), Italy's most powerful party and an ardent opponent of communism. At the same time, the Church, keen to weed communism out of the political landscape, played its part by threatening to excommunicate anyone who voted for Italy's Communist Party (Partito Comunista Italiano; PCI).

Today, no one political party has a monopoly on Church favour, and politicians across the spectrum tread warily around Catholic sensibilities. But this reverence isn't limited to the purely political sphere; it also informs much press reporting and even law enforcement. In September 2008 Rome's public prosecutor threatened to prosecute a comedian for comments made against the pope, invoking the 1929 Lateran Treaty under which it is a criminal offence to 'offend the honour' of the pope and Italian president. The charge, which ignited a heated debate on censorship and the right to free speech, was eventually dropped by the Italian justice minister.

New Beginnings, Protest & Persecution

Bridging the gap between the Middle Ages and the modern era, the Renaissance (*Rinascimento* in Italian) was a far-reaching intellectual, artistic and cultural movement. It emerged in 14th-century Florence but quickly spread to Rome, where it gave rise to one of the greatest makeovers the city had ever seen. Not everyone was impressed though, and in the early 16th century the Protestant Reformation burst into life. This, in turn, provoked a furious response by the Catholic Church, the Counter-Reformation.

You'll see the letters SPQR everywhere in Rome. They were adopted during the Roman Republic and stand for Senatus Populusque Romanus (the Senate and People of Rome).

The Borgias, led by family patriarch Rodrigo, aka Pope Alexander VI (r 1492–1503), were one of Renaissance Rome's most notorious families. Machiavelli supposedly modelled *Il Principe* (The Prince) on Rodrigo's son, Cesare, while his daughter, Lucrezia, earned notoriety as a femme fatale with a penchant for poisoning her enemies.

1656–67	1798	1870	1885
Gian Lorenzo Bernini lays out St Peter's Square for Pope Alexander VII. Bernini, along with his great rival Francesco Borromini, are the leading exponents of Roman baroque architecture.	Napoleon marches into Rome, forcing Pope Pius VI to flee. A republic is announced, but it doesn't last long and in 1801 Pius VI's successor Pius VII returns to Rome.	Nine years after Italian unification, Rome's city walls are breached at Porta Pia and Pope Pius IX is forced to cede the city to Italy. Rome becomes the Italian capital.	To celebrate Italian unification and honour Italy's first king, Vittorio Emanuele II, construction work begins on Il Vittoriano, the mountainous monument dominating Piazza Venezia.

Humanism & Rebuilding

The movement's intellectual cornerstone was humanism, a philosophy that focused on the central role of humanity within the universe, a major break from the medieval world view, which had placed God at the centre of everything. It was not anti-religious, though. Many humanist scholars were priests and most of Rome's great works of Renaissance art were commissioned by the Church. In fact, it was one of the most celebrated humanist scholars of the 15th century, Pope Nicholas V (r 1447–84), who is generally considered the harbinger of the Roman Renaissance.

When Nicholas became pope in 1447, Rome was not in good shape. Centuries of medieval feuding had reduced the city to a semi-deserted battleground, and its bedraggled population lived in constant fear of plague, famine and flooding (the Tiber regularly broke its banks). In political terms, the papacy was recovering from the trauma of the Great Schism and attempting to face down Muslim encroachment in the east.

It was against this background that Nicholas decided to rebuild Rome as a showcase for Church power. To finance his plans, he declared 1450 a Jubilee year, a tried and tested way of raising funds by attracting hundreds of thousands of pilgrims to the city (in a Jubilee year anyone who comes to Rome and confesses receives a full papal pardon).

Over the course of the next 80 years or so, Rome underwent a complete overhaul. Pope Sixtus IV (r 1471–84) had the Sistine Chapel built and, in 1471, gave the people of Rome a selection of bronzes that became the first exhibits of the Capitoline Museums. Julius II (r 1503–13) laid Via del Corso and Via Giulia, and ordered Bramante to rebuild St Peter's Basilica. Michelangelo frescoed the Sistine Chapel and designed the dome of St Peter's, while Raphael inspired a whole generation of painters with his masterful grasp of perspective.

The Sack of Rome & Protestant Protest

Rome's Renaissance rebuild wasn't all plain sailing. By the early 16th century, the long-standing conflict between the Holy Roman Empire, led by the Spanish Charles V, and the Italian city states remained the main source of trouble. This simmering tension came to a head in 1527 when Rome was invaded by Charles' marauding army and ransacked while Pope Clement VII (r 1523–34) hid in Castel Sant'Angelo. The sack of Rome, regarded by most historians as the nail in the coffin of the Roman Renaissance, was a hugely traumatic event. It left the papacy reeling and gave rise to the view that the Church had been greatly weakened by its own moral shortcomings. That the Church was corrupt was well known, and it was with considerable public support that Martin Luther

---

Historical Reads

SPQR: A History of Ancient Rome (Mary Beard; 2015)

Rome: The Biography of a City (Christopher Hibbert; 1985)

Absolute Monarchs (John Julius Norwich; 2011)

The pope's personal fiefdom, the Papal States were established in the 8th century after the Frankish King Pepin drove the Lombards out of northern Italy and donated large tracts of territory to Pope Stephen II. At the height of their reach, the States encompassed Rome and much of central Italy.

1922	**1929**	**1944**	**1946**
Some 40,000 fascists march on Rome. King Vittorio Emanuele III, worried about the possibility of civil war, invites the 39-year-old Mussolini to form a government.	Keen to appease the Church, Mussolini signs the Lateran Treaty, creating the state of the Vatican City. To celebrate, Via della Conciliazione is bulldozed through the medieval Borgo.	On 24 March, 335 Romans are shot by Nazi troops in an unused quarry on Via Ardeatina. The massacre is a reprisal for a partisan bomb attack in Via Rasella.	The Italian republic is born after a vote to abolish the monarchy. Two years later, on 1 January 1948, the Italian constitution becomes law.

pinned his 95 Theses to a church door in Wittenberg in 1517, thus sparking off the Protestant Reformation.

The Counter-Reformation

The Counter-Reformation, the Catholic response to the Protestant Reformation, was marked by a second wave of artistic and architectural activity as the Church once again turned to bricks and mortar to restore its authority. But in contrast to the Renaissance, the Counter-Reformation was also a period of persecution and official intolerance. With the full blessing of Pope Paul III, Ignatius Loyola founded the Jesuits in 1540, and two years later the Holy Office was set up as the Church's final appeals court for trials prosecuted by the Inquisition. In 1559 the Church published the *Index Librorum Prohibitorum* (Index of Prohibited Books) and began to persecute intellectuals and freethinkers. Galileo Galilei (1564–1642) was forced to renounce his assertion of the Copernican astronomical system, which held that the earth moved around the sun. He was summoned by the Inquisition to Rome in 1632 and exiled to Florence for the rest of his life. Giordano Bruno (1548–1600), a freethinking Dominican monk, fared worse. Arrested in Venice in 1592, he was burned at the stake eight years later in Campo de' Fiori.

Despite, or perhaps because of, the Church's policy of zero tolerance, the Counter-Reformation was largely successful in re-establishing papal prestige. And in this sense it can be seen as the natural finale to the Renaissance that Nicholas V had kicked off in 1450. From being a rural backwater with a population of around 20,000 in the mid-15th century, Rome had grown to become one of Europe's great 17th-century cities.

Power & Corruption

The exercise of power has long gone hand in hand with corruption. And no one enjoyed greater power than Rome's ancient emperors and Renaissance popes.

Imperial Follies & Papal Foibles

Of all ancient Rome's cruel, despotic leaders, few are as notorious as Caligula. A byword for depravity, he was initially hailed as a saviour when he inherited the empire from his hated great-uncle Tiberius in AD 37. But this optimism was soon to prove ill-founded, and after a bout of serious illness, Caligula began showing disturbing signs of mental instability. He made his senators worship him and infamously tried to make his horse a senator. By AD 41 everyone had had enough of him, and on 24 January the leader of his own Praetorian Guard stabbed him to death.

Political Reads

....

Good Italy: Bad Italy (Bill Emmott; 2012)

....

The Dark Heart of Italy (Tobias Jones; 2003)

....

Modern Italy: A Political History (Denis Mack Smith; 1959)

HISTORY POWER & CORRUPTION

Gladiatorial combat was part of the public games *(ludi)* put on at the Colosseum. Gladiators were prisoners of war, condemned criminals or volunteers who would fight in bouts of 10 to 15 minutes. Surprisingly, these rarely ended in death.

1957	1960	1968	1978
Leaders of Italy, France, West Germany, Belgium, Holland and Luxembourg meet in the Capitoline Museums to sign the Treaty of Rome and establish the European Economic Community.	Rome stages the Olympic Games while Federico Fellini films *La Dolce Vita* at Cinecittà studios. Three years later, Elizabeth Taylor falls for Richard Burton while filming *Cleopatra* there.	Widespread student unrest results in mass protests across Italy. In Rome, students clash with police at La Sapienza's architecture faculty, an event remembered as the Battle of Valle Giulia.	Former PM Aldo Moro is kidnapped and shot by a cell of the extreme left-wing Brigate Rosse (Red Brigades) during Italy's *anni di piombo* (years of lead).

Debauchery on such a scale was rare in the Renaissance papacy, but corruption was no stranger to the corridors of ecclesiastical power. It was not uncommon for popes to father illegitimate children and nepotism was rife. The Borgia pope Alexander VI (r 1492–1503) had two illegitimate children with the first of his two high-profile mistresses. The second, Giulia Farnese, was the sister of the cardinal who was later to become Pope Paul III (r 1534–59), himself no stranger to earthly pleasures. When not persecuting heretics during the Counter-Reformation, the Farnese pontiff managed to father four children.

Tangentopoli

The early 1990s was a traumatic time for Italy's political establishment which was virtually brought to its knees during the so-called *Tangentopoli* (Kickback City) scandal. Against a backdrop of steady economic growth, the controversy broke in Milan in 1992 when a routine corruption case – accepting bribes in exchange for contracts – blew up into a nationwide crusade against corruption.

Led by magistrate Antonio di Pietro, the Mani Pulite (Clean Hands) investigations exposed a political and business system riddled with corruption. Politicians, public officials and business people were investigated and for once no one was spared, not even the powerful Bettino Craxi (prime minister between 1983 and 1989), who rather than face trial fled Rome in 1993. He was subsequently convicted in absentia on corruption charges and died in self-imposed exile in Tunisia.

Contemporary Controversy

Controversy and lurid gossip were a recurring feature of Silvio Berlusconi's three terms as prime minister (1994, 2000–06, and 2008–11). Berlusconi himself faced a series of trials on charges ranging from abuse of power to paying for sex with an underage prostitute. To date, he has only been convicted once, for tax fraud in 2012, but in 2017 it was announced he would be facing yet another trial for bribing witnesses in one of his earlier cases.

Rome's City Hall has also been embroiled in scandal. In 2014, the so-called Mafia Capitale case broke as allegations surfaced that the city's municipal council had been colluding with a criminal gang to cream off public funds. The subsequent investigation, the largest anti-corruption operation since the Mani Pulite campaign of the 1990s, resulted in hundreds of arrests. Former mayor Gianni Alamenno is one of many currently facing charges.

The Rubygate affair centred on Silvio Berlusconi's trial for paying for sex with an underage dancer called Ruby the Heartstealer. He was found guilty, but his conviction was later overturned on appeal. In 2017, it was announced he was to be tried for bribing witnesses in the case.

1992–93	2000	2001	2005
A nationwide anti-corruption crusade, Mani Puliti (Clean Hands), shakes the political and business establishment. Many high-profile figures are arrested and former PM Bettino Craxi flees the country.	Pilgrims pour into Rome from all over the world to celebrate the Catholic Church's Jubilee year. A highpoint is a mass attended by two million people at Tor Vergata university.	Colourful media tycoon Silvio Berlusconi becomes prime minister for the second time. His first term in 1994 was a short-lived affair; his second lasts the full five-year course.	Pope John Paul II dies after 27 years on the papal throne. He is replaced by his long-standing ally Josef Ratzinger, who takes the name Benedict XVI.

The First Tourists

Pilgrims have been pouring into Rome for centuries but it was the classically minded travellers of the 18th and 19th centuries who established the city's reputation as a holiday hotspot.

Religious Pilgrimages

As seat of the Catholic Church, Rome was already one of the main pilgrim destinations in the Middle Ages, when, in 1300, Pope Boniface VIII proclaimed the first ever Holy Year (Jubilee). Promising full forgiveness for anyone who made the pilgrimage to St Peter's Basilica and the Basilica di San Giovanni in Laterano, his appeal to the faithful proved a resounding success. Hundreds of thousands answered his call and the Church basked in popular glory.

Some 700 years later and the Holy Year tradition is still going strong. Up to 24 million visitors descended on the city for Pope John Paul II's Jubilee, while it's estimated around 21 million pilgrims passed through the holy doors of St Peter's Basilica during Pope Francis' 2016 Holy Year.

The Grand Tour

While Rome has a long past as a pilgrimage site, its history as a modern tourist destination can be traced back to the late 1700s and the fashion for the Grand Tour. The 18th-century version of a gap year, the Tour was considered an educational rite of passage for wealthy young men from northern Europe, and Britain in particular.

The overland journey through France and into Italy followed the medieval pilgrim route, entering Italy via the St Bernard Pass and descending the west coast before cutting in to Florence and then down to Rome. After a sojourn in the capital, tourists would venture down to Naples, where the newly discovered ruins of Pompeii and Herculaneum were causing much excitement, before heading up to Venice.

Rome, enjoying a rare period of peace, was perfectly set up for this English invasion. The city was basking in the aftermath of the 17th-century baroque building boom, and a craze for all things classical was sweeping Europe. Rome's papal authorities were also crying out for money after their excesses had left the city coffers bare, reducing much of the population to abject poverty.

Thousands came, including Goethe, who stopped off to write his travelogue *Italian Journey* (1817), as well as Byron, Shelley and Keats, who all fuelled their romantic sensibilities in the city's vibrant streets. So many English people stayed around Piazza di Spagna that locals christened the area *er ghetto de l'inglesi* (the English ghetto).

In his 1818 work *Childe Harold's Pilgrimage*, the English poet Lord Byron quotes the words of the 8th-century monk Bede: 'While stands the Coliseum, Rome shall stand; When falls the Coliseum, Rome shall fall! And when Rome falls – the World.'

Romantic poet John Keats lived the last months of his short life in a house by the Spanish Steps. He died aged 25 in February 1821 and, along with fellow poet Percy Bysshe Shelley, was buried in Rome's Cimitero Acattolico per gli Stranieri.

HISTORY THE FIRST TOURISTS

2008	2013	2013	2014
Gianni Alemanno, a former member of the neo-fascist MSI (Movimento Sociale Italiano), sweeps to victory in Rome's mayoral elections. The news makes headlines across the world.	The anti-establishment Movimento 5 Stelle (Five Star Movement), led by charismatic rabble rouser, blogger and former comedian Beppe Grillo, takes a quarter of the vote in Italy's general election.	Pope Benedict XVI becomes the first pope to resign since Gregory XII in 1415. He is replaced by the Argentinian cardinal Jorge Mario Bergoglio who is elected Pope Francis.	Ex-mayor Gianni Alemanno and up to 100 politicians and public officials are placed under police investigation as the so-called *Mafia Capitale* scandal rocks Rome.

Artistically, rococo was the rage of the moment. The Spanish Steps, built between 1723 and 1726, proved a major hit with tourists, as did the exuberant Trevi Fountain.

The Ghosts of Fascism

Rome's fascist history is a highly charged subject. Historians on both sides of the political spectrum have accused each other of recasting the past to suit their views: left-wing historians have criticised their right-wing counterparts for glossing over the more unpleasant aspects of Mussolini's regime, while right-wingers have attacked their left-wing colleagues for whitewashing the facts to perpetuate an overly simplistic anti-fascist narrative.

Mussolini

Benito Mussolini was born in 1883 in Forlì, a small town in Emilia-Romagna, a region of northern Italy. As a young man he was a member of the Italian Socialist Party, but service in WWI and Italy's subsequent descent into chaos led to a change of heart, and in 1919 he founded the Italian Fascist Party. Calling for rights for war veterans, law and order, and a strong nation, the party won support from disillusioned soldiers, many of whom joined the squads of Blackshirts that Mussolini used to intimidate his political enemies.

In 1921 Mussolini was elected to the Chamber of Deputies. His parliamentary support was limited but on 28 October 1922 he marched on Rome with 40,000 black-shirted followers. Fearful of civil war between the fascists and socialists, King Vittorio Emanuele III responded by inviting Mussolini to form a government. His first government was a coalition of fascists, nationalists and liberals, but victory in the 1924 elections left him better placed to consolidate his power, and by the end of 1925 he had seized complete control of Italy. In order to silence the Church he signed the Lateran Treaty in 1929, which made Catholicism the state religion and recognised the sovereignty of the Vatican State.

On the home front, Mussolini embarked on a huge building program in Rome: Via dei Fori Imperiali and Via della Conciliazione were laid out; parks were opened on the Oppio Hill and at Villa Celimontana; the Imperial Forums and the temples at Largo di Torre Argentina were excavated; and the monumental Foro Italico sports complex and EUR were built.

Nowhere more vividly displays the fascist obsession with sport and the male ideal than the Foro Italico sports complex. The entrance is marked by an obelisk marked Dux Mussolini, while inside 59 giant marble nudes strike muscular poses at the Stadio dei Marmi (Stadium of the Marbles).

2016	2016	2016	2017
Onlookers applaud the Colosseum's polished new look after completion of an extensive three-year clean-up, the first in its 2000-year history. The makeover comes as part of a €25 million restoration project.	Virginia Raggi, a 37-year-old lawyer from the anti-establishment Five Star Movement, becomes Rome's first woman, and the youngest, mayor. She promises to take on corruption in City Hall.	Just two years after becoming PM, Matteo Renzi resigns after failing to win a referendum on constitutional reform. Foreign Minister Paolo Gentiloni succeeds him.	As Brexit shockwaves continue to rock Europe, 27 EU leaders gather on the Capitoline Hill to celebrate the EU's 60th anniversary. The 1957 Treaty of Rome paved the way for the birth of the union.

Abroad, Mussolini invaded Abyssinia (now Ethiopia) in 1935 and sided with Hitler in 1936. In 1940, standing on the balcony of Rome's Palazzo Venezia, he announced Italy's entry into WWII to a vast, cheering crowd. The good humour didn't last, as Rome suffered, first at the hands of its own fascist regime, then, after Mussolini was ousted in 1943, at the hands of the Nazis. Rome was liberated from German occupation on 4 June 1944.

Post-War Period

Defeat in WWII didn't kill off Italian fascism, and in 1946 hardline Mussolini supporters founded the Movimento Sociale Italiano (MSI; Italian Social Movement). For close on 50 years this overtly fascist party participated in mainstream Italian politics, while on the other side of the spectrum the Partito Comunista Italiano (PCI; Italian Communist Party) grew into Western Europe's largest communist party. The MSI was finally dissolved in 1994, when Gianfranco Fini rebranded it as the post-fascist Alleanza Nazionale (AN; National Alliance). AN remained an important political player until it was incorporated into Silvio Berlusconi's Popolo della Libertà (PdL; People of Freedom) party in 2009.

Outside the political mainstream, fascism (along with communism) was a driving force of the domestic terrorism that rocked Rome and Italy during the *anni di piombo* (years of lead), between the late 1960s and early '80s. Terrorist groups emerged on both sides of the ideological spectrum, giving rise to a spate of politically inspired violence. In one of the era's most notorious episodes, the communist Brigate Rosse (Red Brigades) kidnapped and killed former prime minister Aldo Moro in 1978, leaving his bullet-ridden body in the boot of a car on Via Michelangelo Caetani near the Jewish Ghetto.

The Arts

Rome's turbulent history and magical cityscape have long provided inspiration for painters, sculptors, film-makers, writers and musicians. The great classical works of Roman antiquity fuelled the imagination of Renaissance artists; Counter-Reformation persecution led to baroque art and popular street satire; the trauma of Mussolini and WWII found expression in neo-realist cinema. More recently, urban art has flourished and film-making has returned to the streets of Rome.

Painting & Sculpture

Home to some of the Western world's most recognisable art, Rome is a visual feast. Its churches alone contain more masterpieces than many small countries, and the city's galleries are laden with works by world-famous artists.

Etruscan Groundwork

Laying the groundwork for much later Roman art, the Etruscans placed great importance on their funerary rites and developed sepulchral decoration into a highly sophisticated art form. Elaborate stone sarcophagi were often embellished with a reclining figure or a couple, typically depicted with a haunting, enigmatic smile. A stunning example is the *Sarcofago degli Sposi* (Sarcophagus of the Betrothed) in the Museo Nazionale Etrusco di Villa Giulia.

The Etruscans were also noted for their bronze work and filigree jewellery. Bronze ore was abundant and was used to craft everything from chariots to candelabras, bowls and polished mirrors. One of Rome's most iconic sculptures, the 5th-century-BC *Lupa Capitolina* (Capitoline Wolf), is, in fact, an Etruscan bronze. Etruscan jewellery was unrivalled throughout the Mediterranean and goldsmiths produced elaborate pieces using sophisticated filigree and granulation techniques.

For Italy's best collection of Etruscan art, head to the Museo Nazionale Etrusco di Villa Giulia (p182); to see Etruscan treasures in situ head up to Cerveteri and Tarquinia.

Roman Developments

In art, as in architecture, the ancient Romans borrowed heavily from the Etruscans and Greeks. In terms of decorative art, the Roman use of mosaics and wall paintings was derived from Etruscan funerary decoration. By the 1st century BC, floor mosaics were a popular form of home decor. Typical themes included landscapes, still lifes, geometric patterns and depictions of gods. Later, as production and artistic techniques improved, mosaics were displayed on walls and in public buildings. In the Museo Nazionale Romano: Palazzo Massimo alle Terme (p138), you'll find some spectacular wall mosaics from Nero's villa in Anzio, as well as a series of superb 1st-century-BC frescoes from Villa Livia, one of the homes of Livia Drusilla, Augustus' wife.

The best-surviving examples of Etruscan frescoes are found in Tarquinia, where up to 6000 tombs have been discovered. Particularly impressive are the illustrations in the Tomba delle Leonesse (*Tomb of the Lionesses*).

One of Rome's great medieval artists was Pietro Cavallini (c 1240–1330). Little is known about this Roman-born painter, but his most famous work is the *Giudizio universale* (Last Judgment) fresco in the Chiesa di Santa Cecilia in Trastevere.

Sculpture

Sculpture was an important element of Roman art, and was largely influenced by Greek styles. In fact, early Roman sculptures were often made by Greek artists. They were largely concerned with the male physique and generally depicted visions of male beauty in mythical settings – the *Apollo Belvedere* and *Laocoön* in the Vatican Museums' Museo Pio-Clementino are classic examples.

However, over time Roman sculpture began to lose its obsession with form and to focus on accurate representation, mainly in the form of sculptural portraits. Browse the collections of the Capitoline Museums or the Museo Nazionale Romano: Palazzo Massimo alle Terme and you'll be struck by how lifelike so many of the marble faces are.

In terms of function, Roman art was highly propagandistic. From the time of Augustus (r 27 BC–AD 14), art was increasingly used to serve the state, and artists came to be regarded as little more than state functionaries. This new narrative art often took the form of relief decoration illustrating great military victories – the Colonna Traiana (p64) and Ara Pacis (p101) are stunning examples of the genre.

Early Christian Art

The earliest Christian art in Rome are the traces of biblical frescoes in the Catacombe di Priscilla (p182) and the Catacombe di San Sebastiano (p191). These, and other early works, are full of stock images: Lazarus being raised from the dead, Jesus as the good shepherd, the first Christian saints. Symbols also abound: the dove representing peace and happiness; the anchor or trident symbolising the cross.

Mosaics

With the legalisation of Christianity in the 4th century, these images began to move into the public arena, appearing in mosaics across the city. Mosaic work was the principal artistic endeavour of early Christian Rome and mosaics adorn many of the churches built in this period, including the **Chiesa di Santa Pudenziana** (Map p312; ☎06 474 25 29; www.stpudenziana.org; Via Urbana 160; ☺9am noon & 3-6pm; ⓂCavour), the Mausoleo di Santa Costanza (p184), and the Basilica di Santa Maria Maggiore (p139).

Eastern influences became much more pronounced between the 7th and 9th centuries, when Byzantine styles swept in from the East, leading to a brighter, golden look. The best examples in Rome are in the Basilica di Santa Maria in Trastevere (p154) and the 9th-century Basilica di Santa Prassede (p140).

The Renaissance

Originating in late-14th-century Florence, the Renaissance had already made its mark in Tuscany and Venice before it arrived in Rome in the latter half of the 15th century. But over the next few decades it was to have a profound impact on the city as the top artists of the day were summoned to decorate the many new buildings going up around town.

Michelangelo & the Sistine Chapel

Rome's most celebrated works of Renaissance art are Michelangelo's paintings in the Sistine Chapel (p126) – his cinematic ceiling frescoes, painted between 1508 and 1512, and the *Giudizio universale* (Last Judgment), painted between 1536 and 1541.

Michelangelo Buanarroti (1475–1564), born near Arrezzo in Tuscany, was the embodiment of the Renaissance spirit. A painter, sculptor, architect and occasional poet, he, more than any other artist of the era, left

---

THE ARTS PAINTING & SCULPTURE

Dramatically ensconced in a Richard Meier–designed pavilion, the Ara Pacis is a key work of ancient Roman sculpture. The vast marble altar is covered with detailed reliefs, including one showing Augustus at the head of a procession, followed by the entire imperial family.

Key Renaissance Works

Pietà (St Peter's Basilica)

La Scuola di Atene (Vatican Museums)

Deposizione di Cristo (Galleria e Museo Borghese)

Handing over of the Keys (Sistine Chapel)

TOP ART CHURCHES

St Peter's Basilica (p118) Michelangelo's divine *Pietà* is just one of the many masterpieces on display at the Vatican's showcase basilica.

Basilica di San Pietro in Vincoli (p140) Moses stands as the muscular centrepiece of Michelangelo's unfinished tomb of Pope Julius II.

Chiesa di San Luigi dei Francesi (p76) Frescoes by Domenichino are outshone by three Caravaggio canvases depicting the life and death of St Matthew.

Basilica di Santa Maria del Popolo (p99) A veritable gallery with frescoes by Pinturicchio, a Raphael-designed chapel, and two paintings by Caravaggio.

Chiesa di Santa Maria della Vittoria (p105) The church's innocuous exterior gives no clues that this is home to Bernini's extraordinary *Santa Teresa traffita dall'amore di Dio* (Ecstasy of St Teresa).

Basilica di Santa Prassede (p140) The Cappella di San Zenone features some of Rome's most brilliant Byzantine mosaics.

an indelible mark on the Eternal City. The Sistine Chapel, his *Pietà* in St Peter's Basilica, sculptures in the city's churches – his masterpieces are legion and they remain city highlights to this day.

Raphael, Master of Perspective

Renaissance art, inspired by humanism, which held man to be central to the God-created universe and beauty to represent a deep inner virtue, focused heavily on the human form. This, in turn, led artists to develop a far greater appreciation of perspective. Early Renaissance painters made great strides in formulating rules of perspective but they still struggled to paint harmonious arrangements of people. And it was this that Raffaello Sanzio (Raphael; 1483–1520) tackled in his great masterpiece *La scuola di Atene* (The School of Athens; 1510–11) in the Vatican Museums.

Originally from Urbino, Raphael arrived in Rome in 1508 and went on to become the most influential painter of his generation. A paid-up advocate of the Renaissance exaltation of beauty, he painted many versions of the Madonna and Child, all of which epitomise the Western model of 'ideal beauty' that perseveres to this day.

Big-Name Baroque Artists

Annibale Carracci (1560–1609)
....
Caravaggio (1573–1610)
....
Domenichino (1581–1641)
....
Pietro da Cortona (1596–1669)
....
Gian Lorenzo Bernini (1598–1680)

Counter-Reformation & The Baroque

The baroque burst onto Rome's art scene in the early 17th century in a swirl of emotional energy. Combining an urgent sense of dynamism with highly charged emotion, it was enthusiastically appropriated by the Catholic Church, which used it as a propaganda tool in its persecution of Counter-Reformation heresy. The powerful popes and cardinals of the day eagerly championed the likes of Caravaggio, Gian Lorenzo Bernini, Domenichino, Pietro da Cortona and Alessandro Algardi.

Not surprisingly, much baroque art has a religious theme and you'll often find depictions of martyrdoms, ecstasies and miracles.

Caravaggio

One of the key painters of the period was Michelangelo Merisi (1573–1610), the *enfant terrible* of the Roman art world better known as Caravaggio. A controversial and often violent character, he arrived in Rome from Milan around 1590 and immediately set about rewriting the artistic rule books. While his peers and Catholic patrons sought to glorify and overwhelm, he painted subjects as he saw them. He had no time for 'ideal beauty' and caused uproar with his lifelike portrayal of hitherto sacrosanct subjects – his *Madonna dei pellegrini* (Madonna of the Pilgrims) in the Chiesa di Sant'Agostino is typical of his audacious approach.

Gian Lorenzo Bernini

While Caravaggio shocked his patrons, Gian Lorenzo Bernini (1598–1680) delighted them with his stunning sculptures. More than anyone else before or since, Bernini was able to capture a moment, freezing emotions and conveying a sense of dramatic action. His depiction of *Santa Teresa traffita dall'amore di Dio* (Ecstasy of St Teresa) in the Chiesa di Santa Maria della Vittoria (p105) does just that, blending realism, eroticism and theatrical spirituality in a work that is widely considered one of the greatest of the baroque period. Further evidence of his genius is his series of mythical sculptures at the Museo e Galleria Borghese (p178).

Frescoes

Fresco painting continued to provide work for artists well into the 17th century. Important exponents include Domenichino (1581–1641), whose decorative works adorn the Chiesa di San Luigi dei Francesi and the Chiesa di Sant'Andrea della Valle; Pietro da Cortona (1596–1669), author of the extraordinary *Trionfo della divina provvidenza* (Triumph of Divine Providence) in Palazzo Barberini; and Annibale Carracci (1560–1609), the genius behind the frescoes in Palazzo Farnese, reckoned by some to equal those of the Sistine Chapel.

Twentieth-Century Futurism

Often associated with fascism, Italian futurism was an ambitious wide-ranging movement, embracing not only the visual arts but also architecture, music, fashion and theatre. The futurists, who first met in 1906 in a studio on Via Margutta, were evangelical advocates of modernism and their works highlighted dynamism, speed, machinery and technology.

One of the movement's founding fathers, Giacomo Balla (1871–1958) encapsulated the futurist ideals in works such as *Espansione dinamica velocità* (Dynamic Expansion and Speed) and *Forme grido Viva l'Italia* (The Shout Viva l'Italia), an abstract work inspired by the futurists' desire for Italy to enter WWI. Both are on show at La Galleria Nazionale (p181).

Contemporary Scene

Rome's contemporary art scene is centred on the capital's two flagship galleries: the Museo Nazionale delle Arti del XXI Secolo (p181), better known as MAXXI, and the Museo d'Arte Contemporanea di Roma (p182), aka MACRO.

Increasingly, though, you don't have to go to a gallery to see thought-provoking paintings. A recent trend for street art has taken the city by storm and many suburbs boast colourful wall displays. These range from a William Kentridge frieze on the Tiber embankment to a Ron English mural in the outlying Quadraro neighbourhood.

Emerging about 1520, mannerism bridged the gap between the Renaissance and baroque era. Signature traits include the use of artificial colours, and figures with elongated limbs posed in florid settings.

THE ARTS PAINTING & SCULPTURE

Top Galleries & Museums
....
Vatican Museums *(Vatican City, Borgo & Prati)*
....
Museo e Galleria Borghese *(Villa Borghese & Northern Rome)*
....
Capitoline Museums *(Ancient Rome)*

NEOCLASSICISM
....

Emerging in the late 18th and early 19th centuries, neoclassicism signalled a departure from the emotional abandon of the baroque and a return to the clean, sober lines of classical art. Its major exponent was the sculptor Antonio Canova (1757–1822), whose study of Paolina Bonaparte Borghese as *Venere Vincitrice* (Venus Victrix) in the Museo e Galleria Borghese is typical of the mildly erotic style for which he became known.

Literature

A history of authoritarian rule has given rise to a rich literary tradition, encompassing everything from ancient satires to dialect poetry and anti-fascist prose. As a backdrop, Rome has inspired authors as diverse as Goethe and Dan Brown.

The Classics

Famous for his blistering oratory, Marcus Tullius Cicero (106–43 BC) was the Roman Republic's pre-eminent author. A brilliant barrister, he became consul in 63 BC and subsequently published many philosophical works and speeches. Fancying himself as the senior statesman, he took the young Octavian under his wing and attacked Mark Antony in a series of 14 speeches, the *Philippics*. But these proved fatal, for when Octavian changed sides and joined Mark Antony, he demanded, and got, Cicero's head.

Virgil gave us some of our most famous expressions: 'Fortune favours the bold', 'Love conquers all' and 'Time flies'. However, it was Juvenal who issued the classic warning: *quis custodiet ipsos custodes?* (who guards the guards?)

Poetry & Satire

A contemporary of Cicero, Catullus (c 84–54 BC) cut a very different figure. A passionate and influential poet, he is best known for his epigrams and erotic verse.

On becoming emperor, Augustus (aka Octavian) encouraged the arts, and Virgil (70–19 BC), Ovid, Horace and Tibullus all enjoyed freedom to write. Of the works produced in this period, it's Virgil's rollicking *Aeneid* that stands out. A glorified mix of legend, history and moral instruction, it tells how Aeneas escapes from Troy and after years of mythical mishaps ends up landing in Italy where his descendants Romulus and Remus eventually found Rome.

Little is known of Decimus Iunius Iuvenalis, better known as Juvenal, but his 16 satires have survived as classics of the genre. Writing in the 1st century AD, he combined an acute mind with a cutting pen, famously scorning the masses as being interested in nothing but 'bread and circuses'.

PIER PAOLO PASOLINI, MASTER OF CONTROVERSY

Poet, novelist and film-maker, Pier Paolo Pasolini (1922–75) was one of Italy's most important and controversial 20th-century intellectuals. His works, which are complex, unsentimental and provocative, provide a scathing portrait of Italy's postwar social transformation.

Politically, he was a communist, but he never played a part in Italy's left-wing establishment. In 1949 he was expelled from the *Partito Comunista Italiano* (PCI; Italian Communist Party) after a gay sex scandal and for the rest of his career he remained a sharp critic of the party. His most famous outburst came in the poem *Il PCI ai giovani,* in which he dismisses left-wing students as bourgeois and sympathises with the police, whom he describes as *'figli di poveri'* (sons of the poor). In the context of Italy in 1968, a year marked by widespread student agitation, this was a highly incendiary position to take.

Pasolini was no stranger to controversy. His first novel *Ragazzi di Vita* (The Ragazzi), set in the squalor of Rome's forgotten suburbs, earned him success and a court case for obscenity. Similarly, his early films – *Accattone* (1961) and *Mamma Roma* (1962) – provoked righteous outrage because of their relentlessly bleak depiction of life in the Roman underbelly.

True to the scandalous nature of his art, Pasolini was murdered in 1975. A young hustler, Pino Pelosi, was convicted of the crime, but recent revelations have raised doubts that he acted alone, and question marks still hang over the case.

Ancient Histories

The two major historians of the period were Livy (59 BC–AD 17) and Tacitus (c 56–116). Although both wrote in the early days of the empire they displayed very different styles. Livy, whose history of the Roman Republic was probably used as a school textbook, cheerfully mixed myth with fact to produce an entertaining and popular tome. Tacitus, on the other hand, took a decidedly colder approach. His *Annals* and *Histories,* which cover the early years of the Roman Empire, are cutting and often witty, although imbued with an underlying pessimism.

Street Writing & Popular Poetry

Rome's tradition of street writing goes back to the dark days of the 17th century Counter-Reformation. With the Church systematically suppressing criticism, disgruntled Romans began posting *pasquinades* (anonymous messages; named after the first person who wrote one) on the city's so-called speaking statues. These messages, often archly critical of the authorities, were sensibly posted in the dead of night and then gleefully circulated around town the following day. The most famous speaking statue stands in Piazza Pasquino near Piazza Navona.

Dialect Verse

Poking savage fun at the rich and powerful was one of the favourite themes of Gioacchino Belli (1791–1863), one of a trio of poets who made their names writing poetry in Roman dialect. Born poor, Belli started his career with conventional and undistinguished verse, but found the crude and colourful dialect of the Roman streets better suited to his outspoken attacks on the chattering classes.

Carlo Alberto Salustri (1871–1950), aka Trilussa, is the best known of the trio. He also wrote social and political satire, although not exclusively so, and many of his poems are melancholy reflections on life, love and solitude. One of his most famous works, the anti-fascist poem *All' ombra* (In the Shadow), is etched onto a plaque in Piazza Trilussa, the Trastevere square named in his honour.

The poems of Cesare Pescarella (1858–1940) present a vivid portrait of turn-of-the-century Rome. Gritty and realistic, they pull no punches in their description of the everyday life of Rome's forgotten poor.

Rome as Inspiration

With its magical cityscape and historic atmosphere, Rome has provided inspiration for legions of foreign authors.

Romantic Visions

In the 18th century the city was a hotbed of literary activity as historians and Grand Tourists poured in from northern Europe. The German author Johann Wolfgang von Goethe captures the elation of discovering ancient Rome and the colours of the modern city in his celebrated travelogue *Italian Journey* (1817).

Rome was also a magnet for the English Romantic poets. John Keats, Lord Byron, Percy Bysshe Shelley, Mary Shelley and other writers all spent time in the city.

Later, in the 19th century, American author Nathaniel Hawthorne took inspiration from a sculpture in the Capitoline Museums to pen his classic *The Marble Faun* (1860).

Rome's most influential contribution to literature was the Vulgate Bible. This dates to the 4th century when Pope Damasus (r 366–384) had his secretary Eusebius Hieronymous, aka St Jerome, translate the bible into accessible Latin. His version is the basis for the bible currently used by the Catholic Church.

In 1559 Pope Paul IV published the *Index Librorum Prohibitorum* (Index of Prohibited Books), a list of books forbidden by the Catholic Church. Over the next 400 years it was revised 20 times, the last edition appearing in 1948. It was officially abolished in 1966.

Rome as Backdrop

In the first decade of the 2000s it became fashionable for novelists to use Rome as a backdrop. Most notably, Dan Brown's thriller *Angels and Demons* (2001) is set in Rome, as is Jeanne Kalogridis sumptuous historical novel *The Borgia Bride* (2006).

Robert Harris's accomplished fictional biographies of Cicero, *Imperium* (2006) and *Lustrum* (*Conspirata* in the US; 2010), are just two of many books set in ancient Rome. Other popular books in the genre include Lindsey Davis' Falco series of ancient murder mysteries.

Literature & Fascism

Roman Reads
....
*Roman Tales
(Alberto Moravia)*
....
*That Awful Mess on Via Merulana
(Carlo Emilio Gadda)*
....
*The Secrets of Rome, Love & Death in the Eternal City
(Corrado Augias)*

A controversial figure, Gabriele D'Annunzio (1863–1938) was the most flamboyant Italian writer of the early 20th century. A WWI fighter pilot and ardent nationalist, he was born in Pescara and settled in Rome in 1881. Forever associated with fascism, he wrote prolifically, both poetry and novels.

The Anti-Fascists

Roman-born Alberto Moravia (1907–90) was banned from writing by Mussolini and, together with his wife, Elsa Morante (1912–85), was forced into hiding for a year. The alienated individual and the emptiness of fascist and bourgeois society are common themes in his writing. In *La Romana* (The Woman of Rome; 1947) he explores the broken dreams of a country girl, Adriana, as she slips into prostitution and theft.

The novels of Elsa Morante are characterised by a subtle psychological appraisal of her characters and can be seen as a personal cry of pity for the sufferings of individuals and society. Her 1974 masterpiece, *La Storia* (History), is a tough tale of a half-Jewish woman's desperate struggle for dignity in the poverty of occupied Rome.

Taking a similarly anti-fascist line, Carlo Emilio Gadda (1893–1973) combines murder and black humour in his classic whodunnit, *Quer pasticciaccio brutto de Via Merulana* (That Awful Mess on Via Merulana; 1957). The book's brilliant portrayal of the pomposity and corruption that thrived in Mussolini's Rome.

Writing Today

Niccolò Ammaniti's 2009 novel *Che la festa cominci* (Let the Games Begin) offers debauchery, laughs, and Satanic sects as it gleefully satires the bizarre excesses of modern society.

Rome-born Niccolò Ammaniti is one of Italy's best-selling authors. In 2007 he won the Premio Strega, Italy's top literary prize, for his novel, *Come Dio comanda* (As God Commands), although he's best known internationally for *Io non ho paura* (I'm Not Scared; 2001), a soulful study of a young boy's realisation that his father is involved in a child kidnapping.

Another Strega winner is Melania Mazzucco, whose acclaimed 2003 novel *Vita* tells of two boys from Campania who emigrate to the US in the early 20th century. A later book, *Sei come sei* (2013) caused controversy when right-wing students protested at its gay subject matter.

Also of note is Andrea Bajani (b 1975), the award-winning author of *Ogni promessa* (Every Promise; 2010), a beautifully written novel exploring themes of relationships and vulnerability.

Cinema

Rome has a long cinematic tradition, spanning the works of the postwar neo-realists and film-makers as diverse as Federico Fellini, Sergio Leone and Paolo Sorrentino, the Oscar-winning director of *La grande belleza* (The Great Beauty).

The Golden Age

For the golden age of Roman film-making you have to turn the clocks back to the 1940s, when Roberto Rossellini (1906–77) produced a trio of neo-realist masterpieces. The first and most famous was *Roma città aperta* (Rome Open City; 1945), filmed with brutal honesty in the Prenestina district east of the city centre.

Federico Fellini (1920–94) took the creative baton from the neo-realists and carried it into the following decades. His disquieting style demands more of audiences, abandoning realistic shots for pointed images at once laden with humour, pathos and double meaning. Fellini's greatest international hit was *La Dolce Vita* (1960), starring Marcello Mastroianni and Anita Ekberg.

The films of Pier Paolo Pasolini (1922–75) are similarly demanding. A communist Catholic homosexual, he made films such as *Accattone* (The Scrounger; 1961) that not only reflect his ideological and sexual tendencies but also offer a unique portrayal of Rome's urban wasteland.

Contemporary Directors

Born in Naples but Roman by adoption, Paolo Sorrentino (b 1970) is the big name in Italian cinema. Since winning an Oscar for his 2013 hit *La grande bellezza* (The Great Beauty), he has gone on to direct Michael Caine and Harvey Keitel in *Youth* (2015) and Jude Law in the HBO–Atlantic Sky series *The Young Pope* (2016).

In contrast to Sorrentino, a Neapolitan best known for a film about Rome, Matteo Garrone (b 1968) is a Roman famous for a film about Naples. *Gomorra* (Gomorrah; 2008), his hard-hitting exposé of the Neapolitan *camorra* (mafia), enjoyed widespread acclaim.

More recently, Emanuele Crialese (b 1965) impressed with *Terraferma* (Dry Land; 2011), a thought-provoking study of immigration, and Lamberto Sanfelice won applause at the 2015 Sundance Film Festival for *Cloro* (Chlorine), a slow-burning drama about a teenage girl's struggles to keep her dreams alive in the face of family tragedy.

Gabriele Muccino (b 1967), director of the 2001 smash *L'ultimo bacio* (The Last Kiss), has by now established himself in Hollywood where he's worked with the likes of Russell Crowe and Will Smith, star of his 2006 hit *The Pursuit of Happyness* (2006).

THE ARTS CINEMA

Since its inception in 2006 the Festa del Cinema di Roma has established itself on the European circuit. But years of austerity have seen it pare back its ambitions and it now strives to champion home-grown talent.

ROME IN THE MOVIES

Rome's monuments, piazzas and atmospheric streets provide the backdrop to many classic, and some not so classic, films.

Roma città aperta (Rome Open City; 1945) Neo-realist masterpiece shot on the streets of Prenestina.

Roman Holiday (1953) Gregory Peck and Audrey Hepburn scoot around Rome's headline sights.

La Dolce Vita (1960) The Trevi Fountain stars in Fellini's great Roman masterpiece.

The Talented Mr Ripley (1999) Rome sets the stage for this chilling psychological thriller.

Angels & Demons (2009) Characters bounce between locations in this glossy Dan Brown adaption.

To Rome with Love (2012) Rome gets the Woody Allen treatment in this cliché-ridden comedy.

La grande belleza (The Great Beauty; 2013) Rome's beauty masks cynicism and moral decadence in Sorrentino's Oscar-winner.

SERGIO LEONE, MR SPAGHETTI WESTERN

Best known for virtually single-handedly creating the spaghetti western, Sergio Leone (1929–89) is a hero to many. Astonishingly, though, he only ever directed seven films. He made his directorial debut on *Il colosso di Rodi* (The Colossus of Rhodes; 1961), but it was with his famous dollar trilogy – *Per un pugno di dollari* (A Fistful of Dollars; 1964), *Per qualche dollari in piu* (For a Few Dollars More; 1965) and *Il buono, il brutto, il cattivo* (The Good, the Bad and the Ugly; 1966) – that he really hit the big time. The first, filmed in Spain and based on the 1961 samurai flick *Yojimbo,* set the style for the genre. No longer were clean-cut, morally upright heroes pitted against cartoon-style villains, but characters were complex, often morally ambiguous and driven by self-interest.

Stylistically, Leone introduced a series of innovations that were later to become trademarks. Chief among these was his use of musical themes to identify his characters. And in this he was brilliantly supported by his old schoolmate, Ennio Morricone (b 1928). One of Hollywood's most prolific composers, Morricone has worked on more than 500 films.

Going back a generation, Carlo Verdone (b 1950) and Nanni Moretti (b 1953) are two veterans of the Rome scene. Verdone, a comedian in the Roman tradition, specialises in satirising his fellow citizens in bittersweet comedies such as *Viaggi di nozze* (Honeymoons; 1995).

Moretti, on the other hand, falls into no mainstream tradition. A politically active writer, actor and director, his films are often whimsical and self-indulgent. Arguably his best work, *Caro diario* (Dear Diary; 1994) earned him the Best Director prize at Cannes in 1994 – an award he topped in 2001 when he won the Palme d'Or for *La stanza del figlio (The Son's Room).*

Inaugurated in 1937, Rome's Cinecittà studios are part of cinematic folklore. *Ben-Hur, Cleopatra, La Dolce Vita* and Martin Scorsese's 2002 epic *Gangs of New York* are among the classics that have been shot on the studios' vast 40-hectare site.

On Location in Rome

Rome itself has featured in a number of recent productions. Villa Borghese and the Terme di Caracalla were among the locations for Ben Stiller's camp fashion romp *Zoolander 2* (2016), while the Tiber riverside and Via della Conciliazione both appeared in the last James Bond outing, *Spectre* (2015). Down in the city's southern reaches, a remake of *Ben-Hur* was filmed at the Cinecittà film studios, the very same place where the original sword-and-sandal epic was shot in 1959.

Music

Despite austerity-led cutbacks, Rome's music scene is bearing up well. International orchestras perform to sell-out audiences, jazz greats jam in steamy clubs and rappers rage in underground venues.

Choral & Sacred Music

In a city of churches, it's little wonder that choral music has deep roots in Rome. In the 16th and 17th centuries, Rome's great Renaissance popes summoned the top musicians of the day to tutor the papal choir. Two of the most famous were Giovanni Pierluigi da Palestrina (c 1525–94), one of Italy's foremost Renaissance composers, and the Naples-born Domenico Scarlatti (1685–1757).

The papal choirs were originally closed to women and the high parts were taken by *castrati,* boys who had been surgically castrated to preserve their high voices. The use of *castrati* lasted until the early 20th century, when in 1913 Alessandro Moreschi (1858–1922), the last known *castrato,* retired from the Sistine Chapel choir.

To support the pope's musicians, Sixtus V established the Accademia di Santa Cecilia in 1585. Originally this was involved in the publication of sacred music, but it later developed a teaching function, and in 1839 it completely reinvented itself as an academy with wider cultural and academic goals. Today it is a highly respected conservatory with its own world-class orchestra.

Opera

Rome is often snubbed by serious opera buffs, who prefer their Puccini in Milan, Venice or Naples. Exacerbating the situation, the city opera house, the Teatro dell'Opera (p150), has been plagued by financial crises and labour disputes in recent years. But things took a decided turn for the better in May 2016 when Hollywood director Sofia Coppola's lavish production of *La Traviata* proved to be box-office gold.

The Romans have long been keen opera-goers and in the 19th century a number of important operas were premiered in Rome, including Rossini's *Il barbiere di Siviglia* (The Barber of Seville; 1816), Verdi's *Il trovatore* (The Troubadour; 1853) and Giacomo Puccini's *Tosca* (1900).

Tosca not only premiered in Rome but is also set in the city. The first act takes place in the Chiesa di Sant'Andrea della Valle, the second in Palazzo Farnese, and the final act in Castel Sant'Angelo, the castle from which Tosca jumps to her death.

Jazz, Rap & Hip Hop

Jazz has long been a mainstay of Rome's music scene. Introduced by US troops during WWII, it grew in popularity during the postwar period and took off in the 1960s. Since then, it has gone from strength to strength and the city now boasts some fabulous jazz clubs, including Alexanderplatz, Big Mama, and the Casa del Jazz. Big names to look out for include Enrico Pieranunzi, a Roman-born pianist and composer, and the acclaimed trio performing as Doctor 3.

Rome also has a vibrant underground scene. Rap and hip hop arrived in the city in the late 1980s and spread via the *centro sociale* (organised squat) network. Originally the scene was highly politicised and many early exponents associated themselves with Rome's alternative left-wing. Since then, exposure and commercialisation has diluted, though not entirely extinguished, this political element. Names to look out for include Colle der Fomento, Cor Veleno, Jesto, Assalti Frontali, and the ragamuffin outfit Villa Ada Posse.

Theatre & Dance

Surprisingly for a city in which art has always been appreciated, Rome has no great theatrical tradition. That said, theatres such as Teatro Vascello (p162) and Teatro India (p91) stage wide-ranging programs offering everything from avant-garde dance to cutting-edge street theatre.

Although not strictly speaking a Roman, Dacia Maraini (b 1936) has produced her best work while living in Rome. Considered one of Italy's most important feminist writers, she has more than 30 plays to her name, many of which continue to be translated and performed around the world.

Dance is a major highlight of Rome's big autumn festival, Romaeuropa (p23). But while popular, performances rarely showcase homegrown talent, which remains thin on the ground.

Major ballet performances are staged at the Teatro dell'Opera, home to Rome's principal ballet company, the Balletto del Teatro dell'Opera.

Focused on a world-weary habitué of Rome's dolce vita society, Paolo Sorrentino's 2013 film *La grande belleza* (The Great Beauty) presents Italy's ancient capital as a complex, suffocating city whose lavish beauty masks a decadent, morally bankrupt heart.

Architecture

From ancient ruins and Renaissance basilicas to baroque churches and hulking fascist *palazzi* (mansions), Rome's architectural legacy is unparalleled. Michelangelo, Bramante, Borromini and Bernini are among the architects who have stamped their genius on the city's remarkable cityscape, which features some of the Western world's most celebrated buildings. In more recent times a number of high-profile building projects have drawn the world's top architects to Rome, their futuristic designs provoking discussion, debate and soul-searching among the city's passionate critics.

The Ancients

Architecture was central to the success of the ancient Romans. In building their great capital, they were among the first people to use architecture to tackle problems of infrastructure, urban management and communication. For the first time, architects and engineers designed houses, roads, aqueducts and shopping centres alongside temples, tombs and imperial palaces. To do this, the Romans advanced methods devised by the Etruscans and Greeks, developing construction techniques and building materials that allowed them to build on a massive and hitherto unseen scale.

Etruscan Roots

By the 7th century BC the Etruscans were the dominant force on the Italian peninsula, with important centres at Tarquinia, Caere (Cerveteri) and Veii (Veio). These city-states were fortified with defensive walls, and although little actually remains – the Etruscans generally built with wood and brick, which don't age well – archaeologists have found evidence of aqueducts, bridges and sewers, as well as sophisticated temples. In Rome, you can still see foundations of an Etruscan temple on the Campidoglio (Capitoline Hill).

Much of what we now know about the Etruscans derives from findings unearthed in their elaborate tombs. Like many ancient peoples, the Etruscans placed great emphasis on their treatment of the dead and they built impressive cemeteries. These were constructed outside the city walls and harboured richly decorated stone vaults covered by mounds of earth. The best examples are to be found in Cerveteri, north of Rome.

OBELISKS

More readily associated with ancient Egypt than Rome, obelisks are a distinctive feature of the Roman cityscape. Many were brought over from Egypt after it was conquered by Augustus in AD 31 and used to decorate the *spina* (central spine) of the city's circuses (chariot-racing arenas). Later the Romans began to make their own for their elaborate mausoleums.

The tallest – and one of the oldest, dating to the 15th century BC – towers 46m (32m without the base) over Piazza San Giovanni in Laterano. The most curious sits atop Bernini's famous Elefantino statue outside the Chiesa di Santa Maria Sopra Minerva.

Roman Developments

When Rome was founded sometime around the 8th century BC, the Etruscans were at the height of their power and Greeks colonists were establishing control over southern Italy. In subsequent centuries a three-way battle for domination ensued, with the Romans emerging victorious. Against this background, Roman architects borrowed heavily from Greek and Etruscan traditions.

Ancient Roman architecture was monumental in form and often propagandistic in nature. Huge amphitheatres, aqueducts and temples joined muscular and awe-inspiring basilicas, arches and thermal baths in trumpeting the skill and vision of the city's early rulers and the nameless architects who worked for them.

Temples

Early republican-era temples were based on Etruscan designs, but over time the Romans turned to the Greeks for their inspiration. But whereas Greek temples had steps and colonnades on all sides, the classic Roman temple had a high podium with steps leading up to a deep porch. Good examples include the Tempio di Portunus near Piazza della Bocca della Verità, and, though they're not so well preserved, the temples in the Largo di Torre Argentina (p75). These temples also illustrate another important feature of Roman architectural thinking. While Greek temples were designed to stand apart and be viewed from all sides, Roman temples were built into the city's urban fabric, set in busy central locations and positioned to be approached from the front.

The Roman use of columns was also Greek in origin, even if the Romans preferred the more slender Ionic and Corinthian columns to the plain Doric pillars. To see how the columns differ, study the exterior of the Colosseum, which incorporates all three styles.

Aqueducts & Sewers

One of the Romans' crowning architectural achievements was the development of a water supply infrastructure, based on a network of aqueducts and underground sewers. In the early days, Rome got its water from the Tiber and natural underground springs, but as its population, demand exceeded supply. To meet this demand, the Romans constructed a complex system of aqueducts to bring water in from the hills of central Italy and distribute it around town.

The first aqueduct to serve Rome was the 16.5km Aqua Appia, which became fully operational in 312 BC. Over the next 700 years or so,

MAIN ARCHITECTURAL PERIODS

c 8th–3rd centuries BC

The Etruscans in central Italy and the Greeks in their southern Italian colony, Magna Graecia, lay the groundwork for later Roman developments. Particularly influential are Greek temple designs.

c 4th century BC–AD 5th century

The ancient Romans make huge advances in engineering techniques, constructing monumental public buildings, bridges, aqueducts, housing blocks and an underground sewerage system.

4th–12th centuries

Church building is the focus of architectural activity in the Middle Ages as Rome's early Christian leaders seek to stamp their authority on the city.

15th–16th centuries

Based on humanism and a reappraisal of classical precepts, the Renaissance hits an all-time high in the first two decades of the 16th century, a period known as the High Renaissance.

17th century

Developing out of the Counter-Reformation, the baroque flourishes in Rome, fuelled by Church money and the genius of Gian Lorenzo Bernini and his hated rival Francesco Borromini.

18th century

A short-lived but theatrical style born out of the baroque, the florid rococo gifts Rome some of its most popular sights.

late 18th–19th centuries

Piazza del Popolo takes on its current form and Villa Torlonia gets a facelift courtesy of Rome's top neoclassical architect, Giuseppe Valadier.

up to 800km of aqueducts were built in the city, a network capable of supplying up to one million cubic metres of water a day.

This was no mean feat for a system that depended entirely on gravity. All aqueducts, whether underground pipes, as most were, or vast overland viaducts, were built at a slight gradient to allow the water to flow. There were no pumps to force the water along so this gradient was key to maintaining a continuous and efficient flow.

At the other end of the water cycle, waste water was drained away via an underground sewerage system – the Cloaca Maxima (Great Sewer) – and emptied downstream into the river Tiber. The Cloaca was commissioned by Rome's last king, Tarquin the Proud (r 535–509 BC), as part of a project to drain the valley where the Roman Forum now stands. It was originally an open ditch, but from the beginning of the 2nd century BC it was gradually built over.

The Romans used a variety of building materials. Wood and tufa, a soft volcanic rock, were used initially but travertine, a limestone quarried in Tivoli, later took over as the favoured stone. Marble, imported from across the empire, was used mainly as decorative panelling, attached to brick or concrete walls.

Residential Housing

While Rome's emperors and aristocrats lived in luxurious palaces on the Palatino (Palatine Hill), the city's poor huddled together in large residential blocks called *insulae*. These were huge, poorly built structures, sometimes up to six or seven storeys high, that accommodated hundreds of people in dark, unhealthy conditions. Little remains of these early *palazzi* but near the foot of the Aracoeli staircase – the steps that lead up to the Chiesa di Santa Maria in Aracoeli – you can see a section of what was once a typical city-centre *insula*.

Concrete & Monumental Architecture

Most of the ruins that litter modern Rome are the remains of the ancient city's big, show-stopping monuments – the Colosseum, the Pantheon, the Terme di Caracalla, the Forums. These grandiose constructions are not only reminders of the sophistication and intimidatory scale of ancient Rome – just as they were originally designed to be – they are also monuments to the vision and bravura of the city's ancient architects.

One of the key breakthroughs the Romans made, and one that allowed them to build on an ever-increasing scale, was the invention of concrete in the 1st century BC. Made by mixing volcanic ash with lime and an aggregate, often tufa rock or brick rubble, concrete was quick to make, easy to use, and cheap. Furthermore, it freed architects from their dependence on skilled masonry labour – up to that point construction techniques required stone blocks to be specially cut to fit into each other. Concrete allowed the Romans to develop vaulted roofing, which

ALL ROADS LEAD TO ROME

The Romans were the great road builders of the ancient world. Approximately 80,000km of surfaced highways spanned the Roman Empire, providing vital military and communication links. Many of Rome's modern roads retain the names of their ancient forebears and follow almost identical routes.

Via Appia (p189) The 'queen of roads' ran down to Brindisi on the southern Adriatic coast.

Via Aurelia Connected Rome with France by way of Pisa and Genoa.

Via Cassia Led north to Viterbo, Siena and Tuscany.

Via Flaminia Traversed the Apennines to Rimini on the east coast.

Via Salaria The old salt road linked with the Adriatic port of Castrum Truentinum, south of modern-day Ancona.

they used to span the Pantheon's ceiling and the huge vaults at the Terme di Caracalla.

Concrete wasn't particularly attractive, though, and while it was used for heavy-duty structural work it was usually lined with travertine and coloured marble, imported from Greece and North Africa. Brick was also an important material, used both as a veneer and for construction.

Early Christian

The history of early Christianity is one of persecution and martyrdom. Introduced in the 1st century AD, it was legalised by the emperor Constantine in 313 AD and became Rome's state religion in 378. The most startling reminders of early Christian activity are the catacombs, a series of underground burial grounds built under Rome's ancient roads. Christian belief in the resurrection meant that the Christians could not cremate their dead, as was the custom in Roman times, and with burial forbidden inside the city walls they were forced to go outside the city.

Church Building

The Christians began to abandon the catacombs in the 4th century and increasingly opted to be buried in the churches the emperor Constantine was building in the city. Although Constantine was actually based in Byzantium, which he renamed Constantinople in his own honour, he nevertheless financed an ambitious building program in Rome. The most notable of the many churches he commissioned is the Basilica di San Giovanni in Laterano (p168). Built between 315 and 324 and re-worked into its present shape in the 5th century, it was the model on which many subsequent basilicas were based. Other period showstoppers include the Basilica di Santa Maria in Trastevere (p154) and the Basilica di Santa Maria Maggiore (p139).

A second wave of church-building hit Rome in the period between the 8th and 12th centuries. As the early papacy battled for survival against the threatening Lombards, its leaders took to construction to leave some sort of historical imprint, resulting in the Basilica di Santa Sabina (p171), the Basilica di Santa Prassede (p140) and the 8th-century Chiesa di Santa Maria in Cosmedin, home of the Bocca della Verità (p67; Mouth of Truth).

The 13th and 14th centuries were dark days for Rome as internecine fighting raged between the city's noble families. While much of northern Europe and even parts of Italy were revelling in Gothic arches and towering vaults, little of lasting value was being built in Rome. The one great exception is the city's only Gothic church, the Basilica di Santa Maria Sopra Minerva (p75).

Basilica Style

In design terms, these early Christian churches were modelled on, and built over, Rome's great basilicas. In ancient times, a basilica was a large rectangular hall used for public functions, but as Christianity took hold they were increasingly appropriated by the city's church-builders. The main reason for this was that they lent themselves perfectly to the new

---

late 19th century
Rome gets a major post-unification makeover – roads are built, piazzas are laid, and residential quarters spring up to house government bureaucrats.

early 20th century
Muscular and modern, Italian rationalism plays to Mussolini's vision of a fearless, futuristic Rome, a 20th-century *caput mundi* (world capital).

1990s–
Rome provides the historic stage upon which some of the world's top contemporary architects experiment. Criticism and praise are meted out in almost equal measure.

Rome's ancient ruins are revealing in many ways, but the one thing they lack is colour. Ancient Rome would have been a vivid, brightly coloured place with buildings clad in coloured marble, gaudily painted temples and multicoloured statues.

Early Basilicas

....

Basilica di San Giovanni in Laterano (San Giovanni & Testaccio)

....

Basilica di Santa Sabina (San Giovanni & Testaccio)

Basilica di Santa Maria Maggiore (Monti, Esquilino & San Lorenzo)

style of religious ceremonies that the Christians were introducing, rites that required space for worshippers and a central focus for the altar. Rome's pagan temples, in contrast, had been designed as symbolic cult centres and were not set up to house the faithful – in fact, most pagan ceremonies were held outside, in front of the temple, not inside as the Christian services required.

Over time, basilica design became increasingly standardised. A principal entrance would open onto an atrium, a courtyard surrounded by colonnaded porticoes, which, in turn, would lead to the porch. The interior would be rectangular and divided by rows of columns into a central nave and smaller, side aisles. At the far end, the main altar and bishop's throne (cathedra) would sit in a semicircular apse. In some churches a transept would bisect the central nave to form a Latin cross.

The Renaissance

Florence, rather than Rome, is generally regarded as Italy's great Renaissance city. But while many of the movement's early architects hailed from Tuscany, the city they turned to for inspiration was Rome. The Eternal City might have been in pretty poor nick in the late 15th century, but as the centre of classical antiquity it was much revered by budding architects and a trip to study the Colosseum and the Pantheon was considered a fundamental part of an architect's training.

One of the key aspects they studied, and which informs much Renaissance architecture, is the concept of harmony. This was achieved through the application of symmetry, order and proportion. To this end many Renaissance buildings incorporated structural features copied from the ancients – columns, pilasters, arches and, most dramatically, domes. The Pantheon's dome, in particular, proved immensely influential, serving as a blueprint for many later works.

Early Years

Giuseppe Valadier (1762–1839) was the Pope's go-to architect in the early 19th century. He is best known for his neoclassical revamp of Piazza del Popolo and the Pincio Hill, but also worked on important restorations of Ponte Milvio and the Arco di Tito.

It's impossible to pinpoint the exact year the Renaissance arrived in Rome, but many claim it was the election of Pope Nicholas V in 1447 that sparked off the artistic and architectural furore that was to sweep through the city in the next century or so. Nicholas believed that as head of the Christian world Rome had a duty to impress, a theory that was eagerly taken up by his successors, and it was at the behest of the great papal dynasties – the Barberini, Farnese and Pamphilj – that the leading artists of the day were summoned to Rome.

BRAMANTE, THE ARCHITECT'S ARCHITECT

One of the most influential architects of his day, Donato Bramante (1444–1514) was the godfather of Renaissance architecture. His peers, Michelangelo, Raphael and Leonardo da Vinci, considered him the only architect of their era equal to the ancients.

Born near Urbino, he originally trained as a painter before taking up architecture in his mid-30s in Milan. However, it was in Rome that he enjoyed his greatest success. Working for Pope Julius II, he developed a monumental style that while classical in origin was pure Renaissance in its expression of harmony and perspective. The most perfect representation of this is his Tempietto, a small but much-copied temple on Gianicolo Hill. His original designs for St Peter's Basilica also revealed a classically inspired symmetry with a Pantheon-like dome envisaged atop a Greek-cross structure.

Rich and influential, Bramante was an adept political operator who was not above badmouthing his competitors. It's said, for example, that he talked Pope Julius II into giving Michelangelo the contract for the Sistine Chapel ceiling in the hope that it would prove the undoing of his young Tuscan rival.

The Venetian Pope Paul II (r 1464–71) commissioned many works, including Palazzo Venezia (p67), Rome's first great Renaissance *palazzo*. His successor, Sixtus IV (r 1471–84), had the Sistine Chapel built, and enlarged the Chiesa di Santa Maria del Popolo.

High Renaissance

It was under Pope Julius II (1503–13) that the Roman Renaissance reached its peak, thanks largely to a classically minded architect from Milan, Donato Bramante (1444–1514).

Considered the high priest of Renaissance architecture, Bramante arrived in Rome in 1499. Here, inspired by the ancient ruins, he developed a refined classical style that was to prove hugely influential. His 1502 Tempietto (p157), for example, perfectly illustrates his innate understanding of proportion. Similarly harmonious is his 1504 cloister at the Chiesa di Santa Maria della Pace (p77) near Piazza Navona.

In 1506 Julius commissioned Bramante to start work on the job that would eventually finish him off – the rebuilding of St Peter's Basilica. The fall of Constantinople's Aya Sofya (Church of the Hagia Sofia) to Islam in the mid-14th century had pricked Nicholas V into ordering an earlier revamp, but the work had never been completed and it wasn't until Julius took the bull by the horns that progress was made. However, Bramante died in 1514 and he never got to see how his original Greek-cross design was developed.

St Peter's Basilica (p118) occupied most of the other notable architects of the High Renaissance, including Giuliano da Sangallo (1445–1516), Baldassarre Peruzzi (1481–1536) and Antonio da Sangallo the Younger (1484–1546). Michelangelo (1475–1564) eventually took over in 1547, modifying the layout and creating the basilica's crowning dome. Modelled on Brunelleschi's cupola for the Duomo in Florence, this is considered the artist's finest architectural achievement and one of the most important works of the Roman Renaissance.

Mannerism

As Rome's architects strove to build a new Jerusalem, the city's leaders struggled to deal with the political tensions arising outside the city walls. These came to a head in 1527 when the city was invaded and savagely routed by the troops of the Holy Roman Emperor, Charles V. This traumatic event forced many of the artists working in Rome to flee the city and ushered in a new style of artistic and architectural expression. Mannerism was a relatively short-lived form but in its emphasis on complexity and decoration, in contrast to the sharp, clean lines of traditional Renaissance styles, it hinted at the more ebullient designs that would arrive with the advent of the 17th-century baroque.

One of mannerism's leading exponents was Baldassarre Peruzzi, whose Palazzo Massimo alle Colonne on Corso Vittorio Emanuele II reveals a number of mannerist elements – a pronounced facade, decorative window mouldings, showy imitation stonework.

The Baroque

As the principal motor of the Roman Renaissance, the Catholic Church became increasingly powerful in the 16th century. But with power came corruption and calls for reform. These culminated in Martin Luther's 95 Theses and the far-reaching Protestant Reformation. This hit the Church hard and prompted the Counter-Reformation (1560–1648), a vicious and sustained campaign to get people back into the Catholic fold. In the midst of this great offensive, baroque art and architecture

---

ARCHITECTURE THE BAROQUE

Architecture Reads

Rome: An Oxford Archaeological Guide (Amanda Claridge; 2010)

The Genius in the Design: Bernini, Borromini and the Rivalry that Transformed Rome (Jake Morrissey; 2005)

Rome and Environs: An Archaeological Guide (Filippo Coarelli; 2008)

Forget the Colosseum, Rome's largest ancient monument is the 3rd century Aurelian Wall. Started by the emperor Aurelian (r 270–275) and completed by his successor Probus (r 276–282), the wall circled the city for a length of 19km, of which some 12.5km survives intact.

ROME'S SIGNATURE BUILDINGS

Rome's cityscape is a magical mix of ruins, monuments, palaces, piazzas and churches. Here are some of the city's most significant buildings.

Colosseum (p52) Rome's iconic arena bears the hallmarks of ancient Roman architecture: arches, the use of various building materials, unprecedented scale.

Pantheon (p72) The dome, one of the Romans' most important architectural innovations, finds perfect form atop this revolutionary structure.

Basilica di Santa Maria Maggiore (p139) Although much modified over the centuries, this hulking cathedral exemplifies the Christian basilicas being built in the early Middle Ages.

Castel Sant'Angelo (p130) Rome's landmark castle started life as a monumental mausoleum before taking on its current form after medieval and Renaissance revamps.

Tempietto di Bramante (p157) A masterpiece of harmonious design, Bramante's 1502 temple beautifully encapsulates High Renaissance ideals.

St Peter's Basilica (p118) Michelangelo's dome and Carlo Maderno's facade are the key architectural features of this, the greatest of Rome's Renaissance churches.

Chiesa del Gesù (p80) One of Rome's finest Counter-Reformation churches with a much-copied facade by Giacomo della Porta and an ornate baroque interior.

Chiesa di San Carlo alle Quattro Fontane A prized example of baroque architecture, Francesco Borromini's church boasts convex and concave surfaces, hidden windows and a complex elliptical plan.

Palazzo della Civiltà del Lavoro Nicknamed the 'Square Colosseum', this EUR landmark is a masterpiece of 1930s Italian rationalism.

Auditorium Parco della Musica (p181) Renzo Piano's audacious arts complex is the most influential contemporary building in Rome.

MAXXI (p181) Zaha Hadid's award-winning 2010 building provides a suitably striking setting for Rome's flagship contemporary arts museum.

emerged as a highly effective form of propaganda. Stylistically, baroque architecture aims for a dramatic sense of dynamism, an effect that it often achieves by combining spatial complexity with clever lighting and the use of flamboyant decorative painting and sculpture.

One of the first great Counter-Reformation churches was the Jesuit Chiesa del Gesù (p80), designed by the leading architect of the day, Giacomo della Porta (1533–1602). In a move away from the style of earlier Renaissance churches, the facade has pronounced architectural elements that create a contrast between surfaces and a play of light and shade.

The end of the 16th century and the papacy of Sixtus V (1585–90) marked the beginning of major urban-planning schemes. Domenico Fontana (1543–1607) and other architects created a network of major thoroughfares to connect previously disparate parts of the sprawling city and obelisks were erected at vantage points across town. Fontana also designed the main facade of Palazzo del Quirinale, the immense palace that served as the pope's summer residence for almost three centuries. His nephew, Carlo Maderno (1556–1629), also worked on the *palazzo* when not amending Bramante's designs for St Peter's Basilica.

Bernini versus Borromini

No two people did more to fashion the face of Rome than the two great figures of the Roman baroque – Gian Lorenzo Bernini (1598–1680) and Francesco Borromini (1599–1667). Two starkly different characters – Naples-born Bernini was suave, self-confident and politically adept; Borromini, from Lombardy, was solitary and peculiar – they led the transition from Counter-Reformation rigour to baroque exuberance.

Bernini is perhaps best known for his work in the Vatican. He designed St Peter's Square (p130), famously styling the colonnade as 'the motherly arms of the Church', and was chief architect at St Peter's Basilica (p118) from 1629. While working on the basilica, he created the baldachin (canopy) over the main altar, using bronze stripped from the Pantheon.

Under the patronage of the Barberini pope Urban VIII, Bernini was given free rein to transform the city, and his churches, *palazzi*, piazzas and fountains remain landmarks to this day. However, his fortunes nose-dived when the pope died in 1644. Urban's successor, Innocent X, wanted as little contact as possible with the favourites of his hated predecessor, and instead turned to Borromini, Alessandro Algardi (1595–1654) and Girolamo and Carlo Rainaldi (1570–1655 and 1611–91, respectively). Bernini later came back into favour with his 1651 Fontana dei Quattro Fiumi in the centre of Piazza Navona, opposite Borromini's Chiesa di Sant'Agnese in Agone.

Borromini, the son of an architect and well versed in stonemasonry and construction techniques, created buildings involving complex shapes and exotic geometry. A recurring feature of his designs was the skilful manipulation of light, often obtained by the clever placement of small oval-shaped windows. His most memorable works are the Chiesa di San Carlo alle Quattro Fontane, which has an oval-shaped interior, and the **Chiesa di Sant'Ivo alla Sapienza** (Map p296; Corso del Rinascimento 40; Corso del Rinascimento), which combines a complex arrangement of convex and concave surfaces with an innovative spiral tower.

Throughout their careers, the two geniuses were often at each other's throats. Borromini was deeply envious of Bernini's early successes, and Bernini was scathing of Borromini's complex geometrical style.

Post-Unification & the 20th Century

Rome's nomination as capital of Italy in 1870 unleashed a wave of urban development that was later to be continued by Mussolini and his fascist regime. Post-war, the focus was on practical concerns as the city worked to house its burgeoning population.

A Capital Makeover

Rome entered the 20th century in good shape. During the last 30 years of the 19th century it had been treated to one of its periodic makeovers – this time after being made capital of the Kingdom of Italy in 1870. Piazzas were built – Piazza Vittorio Emanuele II, at the centre of a new upmarket residential district, and neoclassical Piazza della Repubblica, over Diocletian's bath complex – and roads were laid. Via Nazionale and Via Cavour were constructed to link the city centre with the new railway station, Stazione Termini, and Corso Vittorio Emanuele II was built to connect Piazza Venezia with the Vatican.

Key Borromini Works

··············

Chiesa di San Carlo alle Quattro Fontane (Tridente, Trevi & the Quirinale)

··············

Chiesa di Sant'Agnese in Agone (Centro Storico)

Chiesa di Sant'Ivo alla Sapienza (Centro Storico)

Key Bernini Works

··············

St Peter's Square (Vatican City, Borgo & Prati)

··············

Chiesa di Sant'Andrea al Quirinale (Tridente, Trevi & the Quirinale)

··············

Fontana dei Quattro Fiumi (Centro Storico)

ROCOCO FRILLS

In the early days of the 18th century, as baroque fashions began to fade and neoclassicism waited to make its 19th-century entrance, the rococo burst into theatrical life. Drawing on the excesses of the baroque, it was a short-lived fad but one that left a memorable mark.

The **Spanish Steps** (p98), built between 1723 and 1726 by Francesco de Sanctis, provided a focal point for the many Grand Tourists who were pouring into town in the late 18th century. A short walk to the southwest, Piazza Sant'Ignazio was designed by Filippo Raguzzini (1680–1771) to provide a suitably melodramatic setting for the **Chiesa di Sant'Ignazio di Loyola** (p82), Rome's second most important Jesuit church.

Most spectacular of all, however, was the **Trevi Fountain** (p100), one of the city's most exuberant and enduringly popular monuments. It was designed in 1732 by Nicola Salvi (1697–1751) and completed three decades later.

Rationalism & Rebuilding

Influenced by the German Bauhaus movement, architectural rationalism was all the rage in 1920s Europe. In its international form it advocated an emphasis on sharply defined linear forms, but in Italy it took on a slightly different look, thanks to the influence of the Gruppo Sette, its main Italian promoters, and Benito Mussolini, Italy's fascist dictator. Basically, the Gruppo Sette acknowledged the debt Italian architecture owed to its classical past and incorporated elements of that tradition into their modernistic designs. Aesthetically and politically, this tied in perfectly with Mussolini's vision of fascism as the modern bearer of ancient Rome's imperialist ambitions.

Mussolini, a shrewd manipulator of imagery, embarked on a series of grandiose building projects in the 1920s and '30s, including the 1928–31 Foro Italico sports centre, Via dei Foro Imperiali, and the residential quarter of Garbatella. Now a colourful neighbourhood in southern Rome, Garbatella was originally planned as an English-style garden city to house city workers, but in the 1920s the project was hijacked by the fascist regime, which had its own designs. Central to these were innovative housing blocks, known as *alberghi suburbani* (suburban hotels), which were used to accommodate people displaced from the city centre. The most famous of these hotels, the Albergo Rosso, was designed by Innocenzo Sabbatini (1891–1983), the leading light of the Roman School of architecture.

The term *Scuola romana* (Roman School) is used to define a group of architects working in the 1920s and '30s, mainly on large-scale housing projects. Their designs sought to ally modern functionalism with a respect for tradition and a utopian vision of urban development.

Esposizione Universale Roma

Mussolini's most famous architectural legacy is the EUR district (p196) in the extreme south of the city. Built for the Esposizione Universale di Roma in 1942, this Orwellian quarter of wide boulevards and huge linear buildings owes its look to the vision of the *razionalisti* (rationalists). In practice, though, only one of their number, Adalberto Libera, actually worked on the project, as by this stage most of the Gruppo Sette had fallen out with the ruling Fascist junta. Libera's Palazzo dei Congressi is a masterpiece of rationalist architecture, but EUR's most iconic building is Palazzo della Civiltà del Lavoro (known as the Square Colosseum), designed by Giovanni Guerrini, Ernesto Bruno La Padula and Mario Romano.

Postwar Developments

For much of the postwar period, architects in Rome were limited to planning cheap housing for the city's ever-growing population. Swathes

Top: Interior of Basilica di Santa Maria Maggiore (p139)
Bottom: Visitors at the Colosseum (p52)

KAMIRA/SHUTTERSTOCK ©

of apartment blocks were built along the city's main arteries, and grim suburbs sprang up on land claimed from local farmers.

The 1960 Olympics heralded a spate of sporting construction, and both Stadio Flaminio and Stadio Olimpico date to this period. Pier Luigi Nervi, Italy's master of concrete and a hugely influential innovator, added his contribution in the form of the Palazzetto dello Sport.

Modern Rome

The 21st century has witnessed a flurry of architectural activity in Rome. A clutch of 'starchitects' have worked on projects in the city, including Renzo Piano, Italy's foremost architect; renowned American Richard Meier; Anglo-Iraqi Zaha Hadid; and Odile Decq, a major French architect.

Controversy & Acclaim

The foundations of this building boom date to the early 1990s, when the then mayor Francesco Rutelli launched a major clean-up of the historic centre. As part of the process, he commissioned Richard Meier to build a new pavilion for the 1st-century-AD Ara Pacis. Predictably, Meier's glass-and-steel Museo dell'Ara Pacis (p101) caused controversy when it was unveiled in 2006. Vittorio Sgarbi, an outspoken art critic and TV celebrity, claimed that the American's design was the first step to globalising Rome's unique classical heritage. The Roman public appreciated the idea of modern architecture in the city centre, but few were entirely convinced by Meier's design.

Meier won far more acclaim for a second project, his striking **Chiesa Dio Padre Misericordioso** (www.diopadremisericordioso.it; Piazza Largo Terzo Millennio 8; ⊙7.30am-12.30pm & 4-7.30pm; ⬚Via Francesco Tovaglieri) in Tor Tre Teste, a dreary suburb east of the city centre. This was one of a number of churches commissioned by the Vicariate of Rome for the 2000 Jubilee. Another, the Chiesa di Santa Maria della Presentazione, designed by the Rome-based Nemesi studio, sparked interest when it was inaugurated in the outlying Quartaccio neighbourhood in 2002.

Other headline buildings from this period include Renzo Piano's Auditorium Parco della Musica (p181; 2002), Zaha Hadid's MAXXI (p181; 2010) and Odile Decq's 2010 MACRO (p182) building.

Fuksas & Future Developments

Born in Rome in 1944, Massimiliano Fuksas is known for his futuristic vision, and while he has no signature building as such, his 55,000-sq-m Nuovo Centro Congressi (p196), aka the Nuvola, comes as close as any to embodying his style. A rectangular 40m-high glass shell containing a steel-and-Teflon cloud supported by steel ribs and suspended over a vast conference hall, its look is fearlessly modern. Yet it's not without its references to the past: in both scale and form it owes its inspiration to the 1930s rationalist architecture that surrounds it in EUR.

Construction started on the €239 million Nuvola in 2007 and was finally completed in 2016.

Elsewhere, work continues on a contemporary arts centre by award-winning French architect Jean Nouvel in the Forum Boarium area.

In the city's southern reaches, construction is set to start on a new 52,500-capacity stadium, the Stadio della Roma. The €400 million stadium will be the centrepiece of a vast development in the Tor di Valle neighbourhood, comprising a business park, training centre and public parkland.

Designed by Paolo Portoghesi, Rome's postmodernist mosque is one of Europe's largest. Its critically acclaimed design is centred on a beautiful, luminous interior capped by a cupola and 16 surrounding domes.

Rome's Eataly complex is a masterclass in urban regeneration, bringing life back to a derelict train station. Until the complex opened in 2012, the Air Terminal Ostiense, which had originally been designed to serve airport trains arriving for the 1990 football World Cup, had been an abandoned shell.

Architecture Glossary

apse	a semicircular or polygonal recess with a domed roof over a church's altar
architrave	a main beam set atop columns
baldachino (baldachin)	a permanent canopy over an altar or tomb; often supported by columns and freestanding
baroque	style of European art, architecture and music of the 17th and 18th centuries
basilica	an oblong hall with an apse at the end of the nave; used in ancient Rome for public assemblies and later adopted as a blueprint for medieval churches
cloister	enclosed court attached to a church or monastery; consists of a roofed ambulatory surrounding an open area
colonnade	a row of columns supporting a roof or other structure
cornice	a horizontal projection that crowns a building or wall; the upper part of an *entablature*
crypt	an underground room beneath a church used for services and burials
cupola	a rounded dome forming part of a ceiling or roof
entablature	the part of a classical facade that sits on top of the columns; it consists of an *architrave, frieze* and *cornice*
forum	in ancient Rome, a public space used for judicial business and commerce
frieze	a horizontal band, often with painted or sculptural decoration, that sits between the architrave and cornice
futurism	Italian early-20th-century artistic movement that embraced modern technology
loggia	a gallery or room with one side open, often facing a garden
nave	the central aisle in a church, often separated from parallel aisles by pillars
neoclassicism	dominant style of art and architecture in the late 18th and early 19th centuries; a return to ancient Roman styles
portico	a porch with a roof supported by columns
rationalism	international architectural style of the 1920s; its Italian form, often associated with fascism, incorporates linear styles and classical references
Renaissance	European revival of art and architecture based on classical precedents, between the 14th and 16th centuries
rococo	ornate 18th-century style of architecture
stucco	wall plaster used for decorative purposes
trompe l'oeil	a visual illusion tricking the viewer into seeing a painted object as a three-dimensional image
transept	in a cross-shaped church, the two parts that bisect the nave at right angles, forming the short arms of the cross

The Roman Way of Life

As a visitor, it's often difficult to see beyond Rome's spectacular veneer to the large, modern city that lies beneath: a living, breathing capital that's home to almost three million people. So how do the Romans live in their city? Where do they work? Who do they live with? How do they let their hair down?

A Day in the Life

Rome's average office worker lives in a small, two-bedroom apartment in the suburbs and works in a government ministry in the city centre. Their working day is typical of the many who crowd *i mezzi* ('the means'; public transport) in the morning rush hour.

The morning routine is the same as city dwellers the world over: a quick breakfast – usually nothing more than a sweet, black espresso – followed by a short bus ride to the nearest metro station. On the way they stop at an *edicola* (kiosk) to pick up their local paper *(Il Messaggero)* and share a joke with the kiosk owner. A quick scan of the headlines reveals few surprises – the usual political shenanigans in city hall; the Pope's latest utterances; Roma and Lazio match reports.

Rome's metro is not a particularly pleasant place to be in *l'ora di punta* (the rush hour), especially in summer when it gets unbearably hot, but the regulars are resigned to the discomfort and bear it cheerfully.

Their work, like many in the swollen state bureaucracy, is not the most interesting in the world, nor the best paid, but it's secure, and with a much sought-after *contratto a tempo indeterminato* (permanent contract) they don't have to worry about losing it. In contrast, their younger colleagues work in constant fear that their temporary contracts will not be renewed when they expire.

Lunch, which is typically taken around 1.30pm, is usually a snack or *pizza al taglio* (by the slice) from a nearby takeaway. Before heading back to the office for the afternoon session, there's time for a quick coffee in the usual bar.

Clocking off time in most ministries is typically from 5pm onwards and by about 7pm the evening rush hour is in full swing. Once home, there's time to catch the 8pm TV news before sitting down to a pasta supper at about 8.30pm.

Work

Employment in the capital is largely based on Italy's bloated state bureaucracy. Every morning armies of suited civil servants pour into town and disappear into vast ministerial buildings to keep the machinery of government ticking over. Other important employers include the tourist sector, finance, media and culture – Italy's state broadcaster RAI is based in Rome, as is much of the country's film industry, and there are hundreds of museums and galleries across town.

Rome is the most congested city in Italy, according to research carried out by traffic analysts Inrix. In 2016 the city's drivers spent an average of 35 hours stuck in traffic. Topping Europe's blacklist were Moscow (91 hours) and London (73 hours).

According to figures released in late 2016, the average salary in Rome was €30,685. This compared to €34,414 in Milan and €27,302 in Naples. Italy's national average was €29,176.

RELIGION IN ROMAN LIFE
....

Rome is a city of churches. From the great headline basilicas in the historic centre to the hundreds of parish churches dotted around the suburbs, the city is packed with places to worship. And with the Vatican in the centre of town, the Church is a constant presence in Roman life.

Yet the role of religion in modern Roman society is an ambiguous one. On the one hand, most people consider themselves Catholic, but on the other, church attendance is in freefall, particularly among the young, and atheism is growing.

But while Romans don't go to mass very often, the Church remains a point of reference for many people. The Vatican's line on ethical and social issues might not always meet with widespread support, but it's always given an airing in the largely sympathetic national press. Similarly, more than half of people who get married do so in church and first communions remain an important social occasion entailing gift-giving and lavish receptions.

Catholicism's hold on the Roman psyche is strong, but an increase in the city's immigrant population has led to a noticeable Muslim presence. This has largely been a pain-free process, but friction has flared on occasion and there were violent scenes in summer 2015 when far-right anti-immigration protestors clashed with police in the Casale San Nicola neighbourhood in north Rome.

But as Italy's economy continues to stagnate, it's tough for young people to get a foot on the career ladder. To land it lucky, it helps to know someone. Official figures are impossible to come by, but it's a widely held belief that personal or political connections are the best way of landing a job. This system of *raccomandazioni* (recommendations) is widespread and, while being tacitly accepted, regularly gives rise to scandal. In recent years controversies have centred on nepotistic appointments at Rome's La Sapienza University, at the city's public transport operator, and its waste disposal company.

Like everywhere in Italy, Rome's workplace remains predominantly male. Female unemployment is an ongoing issue and Italian women continue to earn less than their male counterparts. That said, recent signs have been positive. Half of PM Matteo Renzi's 2014 cabinet were women and in June 2016, Rome elected its first ever female mayor. Virginia Raggi, a 37-year old lawyer and city councillor, swept to a landslide victory in the city's 2016 municipal elections, thus becoming the first Roman able to call herself *sindaca,* as opposed to the more usual (and masculine) form, *sindaco*.

In 2017 the average price for a square metre of residential property was around €3200, with rates topping €8000 in the historic centre. In the suburbs, the going rate ranged from about €2500 to €4000 per square metre.

Home Life & the Family

Romans, like most Italians, live in apartments. These are often small – 75 to 100 sq m is typical – and expensive. House prices in Rome are among the highest in the country and many first-time buyers are forced to move out of town or to distant suburbs outside the GRA (the *grande raccordo anulare*), the busy ring road that marks the city's outer limit.

Almost all apartments are in self-managed *condomini* (blocks of individually owned flats), a fact which gives rise to no end of neighbourly squabbling. Regular *condominio* meetings are often fiery affairs as neighbours argue over everything from communal repairs to noisy dogs and parking spaces.

Rates of home ownership are relatively high in Rome and properties are commonly kept in the family, handed down from generation to generation. People do rent, but the rental market is largely targeted at Rome's huge student population.

FASHION & THE BELLA FIGURA

Making a good impression *(fare la bella figura)* is extremely important to Romans. For a style-conscious student that might mean wearing the latest street brands and having the right smartphone. For a middle-aged professional it will involve being impeccably groomed and dressed appropriately for every occasion. This slavish adherence to fashion isn't limited to clothes or accessories: it extends to all walks of life and trend-conscious Romans will frequent the same bars and restaurants, drink the same *aperitivi* and hang out on the same piazzas.

English journalist John Hooper examines the contradictions and insecurities that lie beneath the smooth veneer of Italian society in his entertaining 2015 book *The Italians*. Like Luigi Barzini's 1964 classic of the same name, it's an entertaining and informative read full of obscure details and quirky facts.

Italy's single most successful institution, and the only one in which the Romans continue to trust, is the family. It's still the rule rather the exception for young Romans to stay at home until they marry, which they typically do at around age 30. Figures report that virtually two thirds of Rome's 18-to-34-year olds still live at home with at least one parent. To foreign observers this seems strange, but there are mitigating factors: up to half of these stay-at-homes are out of work and property and rental prices are high. There's also the fact that young Romans are generally reluctant to downgrade and move to a cheaper neighbourhood. Seen from another perspective, it could just mean that Roman families like living together.

But while faith in the family remains, the family is shrinking. Italian women are giving birth later than ever and having fewer children – in 2016 the average number of children per woman was 1.34, a record low. Rome's army of *nonni* (grandparents) berate their children for this, as does Pope Francis, who has criticised married couples for not having children, claiming it's selfish. For their part, Italy's politicians worry that such a perilously low birth rate threatens the future tax returns necessary for funding the country's already over-burdened pension system.

Play

Despite perpetual economic and political crises, and all the trials and tribulations of living in Rome – dodgy public transport, iffy services and sky-high prices – few Romans would swap their city for anywhere else. They know theirs is one of the world's most beautiful cities and they enjoy it with gusto. You only have to look at the city's pizzerias, trattorias and restaurants to see that eating out is a much-loved local pastime. It's a cliché of Roman life but food really is central to social pleasure.

Drinking, in contrast, is not a traditional Roman activity. Recent times have seen trends for craft beer and cocktails sweep the city but the drinks are often little more than accessories to the main business of hanging out and looking cool. Romans are well practiced at this – just look at all those photos of dolce vita cafe society – and an evening out in Rome is as much about flirting and looking gorgeous as it is about consuming alcohol.

Rome's finest footballing hour came in 2000 and 2001. In 2000, the city turned sky-blue as Lazio fans celebrated their team's *scudetto* (championship). A year later it was the turn of Rome's red-and-yellow fans as their team ran out Serie A champions.

Clothes shopping is a popular Roman pastime, alongside cinema-going and football. Interest in Rome's two Serie A teams, Roma and Lazio, remains high and a trip to the Stadio Olimpico to watch the Sunday game is considered an afternoon well-spent. Depending on the result, of course.

Plenty of people play football as well, although sport isn't limited to *calcio* (soccer). The city's gyms and indoor pools are a hive of activity, while joggers take to the parks and groups of impeccably clad cyclists hit the roads out of town.

Romans are inveterate car-lovers and on hot summer weekends they will often drive out to the coast or surrounding countryside. Beach bums make for nearby Ostia or more upmarket Fregene, while those in search of a little greenery head to the Castelli Romani, a pocket of green hills just south of town famous for its Frascati wine and casual eateries.

Survival Guide

Transport

ARRIVING IN ROME

Most people arrive in Rome by plane, landing at one of its two airports: Leonardo da Vinci, better known as Fiumicino; or Ciampino, hub for European low-cost carrier Ryanair. Flights from New York take around nine hours, from London 2¾ hours, from Sydney at least 22 hours.

Domestic flights connect Rome with airports across Italy.

As an alternative to short-haul flights, trains serve Rome's main station, Stazione Termini, from a number of European destinations, including Paris (about 15 hours), as well as cities across Italy.

Long-distance domestic and international buses arrive at the Autostazione Tiburtina.

You can also get to Rome by boat. Ferries serve Civitavecchia, some 80km north of the city, from a number of Mediterranean ports.

Flights, cars and tours can be booked online at lonely planet.com/bookings.

Leonardo da Vinci Airport

Rome's main international airport, **Leonardo da Vinci** (Fiumicino; ☑06 6 59 51; www. adr.it/fiumicino), is 30km west of the city. It's divided into four terminals: Terminals 1,

2 and 3 are for domestic and international flights; Terminal 5 is for American and Israeli airlines flying to the US and Israel.

Terminals 1, 2 and 3 are within easy walking distance of each other in the main airport building; Terminal 5 is accessible by shuttle bus from Terminal 3.

The easiest way to get into town is by train, but there are also buses and private shuttle services.

Train

Leonardo Express (one-way €14) Runs to/from Stazione Termini. Departures from the airport every 30 minutes between 6.23am and 11.23pm, and from Termini between 5.35am and 10.35pm. Journey time is 30 minutes.

FL1 (one-way €8) Connects to Trastevere, Ostiense and Tiburtina stations, but not Termini. Departures from the airport every 15 minutes (half-hourly on Sundays and public holidays) between 5.57am and 10.42pm, from Tiburtina every 15 minutes between 5.01am and 7.31pm, then half-hourly to 10.01pm.

Bus

SIT Bus (☑06 591 68 26; www.sitbusshuttle.com; one-way/return €6/11) Regular departures to Stazione Termini (Via Marsala) from 8.30am to 12.30am, and from Termini

between 5am and 8.30pm. All buses stop near the Vatican (Via Crescenzio 2) en route. Tickets are available on the bus. Journey time is approximately one hour.

Cotral (☑800 174471; www. cotralspa.it; one-way €5, purchased on the bus €7) Runs between Fiumicino and Stazione Tiburtina via Termini. Three to six daily departures including night services from the airport at 1.15am, 2.15am, 3.30am and 5am, and from Tiburtina at 12.30am, 1.15am, 2.30am and 3.45am. Journey time is one hour.

Schiaffini Rome Airport Bus (☑06 713 05 31; www.rome airportbus.com; one-way/ return €5.90/7.90) Regular services run from the airport to Stazione Termini (**Via Giolitti**; Map p312) between 6.05am and 8.25pm, and from Termini between 5.10am and 9.30pm. Allow about an hour for the journey.

Private Shuttle

Airport Connection Services (☑06 2111 6248; www.airport connection.it) Transfers to/ from the city centre start at €22 per person.

Airport Shuttle (☑06 420 13 469; www.airportshuttle.it) Transfers to/from your hotel for €25 for one person, then €6 for each additional passenger up to a maximum of eight.

Taxi

The set fare to/from the city centre is €48, which is valid for up to four passengers including luggage. Note that taxis registered in Fiumicino charge more, so make sure you catch a Comune di Roma taxi – these are white with a taxi sign on the roof and Roma Capitale written on the door along with the taxi's licence number. Journey time is approximately 45 to 60 minutes depending on traffic.

Car

Follow signs for Roma out of the airport and onto the autostrada. Exit at EUR, following signs for the *centro*, to link up with Via Cristoforo Colombo, which will take you directly into the centre.

Ciampino Airport

Ciampino (☑06 6 59 51; www. adr.it/ciampino), 15km southeast of the city centre, is used by **Ryanair** (☑895 5895509; www.ryanair.com) for European and Italian destinations. It's not a big airport but there's a steady flow of traffic and at peak times it can get extremely busy.

To get into town, the best option is to take one of the dedicated bus services. You can also take a bus to Ciampino station and then pick up a train to Termini.

Bus

Schiaffini Rome Airport Bus (☑06 713 05 31; www.rome airportbus.com; Via Giolitti; one-way/return €4.90/7.90) Regular departures to/from Via Giolitti outside Stazione Termini. From the airport, services are between 4am and 10.50pm; from Via Giolitti, buses run from 4.50am to midnight. Buy tickets on board, online, at the airport, or at the bus stop. Journey time is approximately 40 minutes.

SIT Bus (☑06 591 68 26; www.sitbusshuttle.com; to/ from airport €6/5, return €9) Regular departures from the airport to **Via Marsala** (Map p312; Via Marsala 5) outside Stazione Termini between 7.45am and 11.15pm, and from Termini between 4.30am and 9.30pm. Get tickets on the bus. Journey time is 45 minutes.

Atral (www.atral-lazio.com) Runs buses between Ciampino Airport and Anagnina metro station (€1.20) and Ciampino train station (€1.20), where you can get a train to Termini (€1.50).

Private Shuttle

Airport Shuttle (☑06 420 13 469; www.airportshuttle.it) Transfers to/from your hotel for €25 for one person, then €6 for each additional passenger up to a maximum of eight.

Taxi

The set rate to/from the airport is €30. Journey time is approximately 30 minutes depending on traffic.

Car

Exit the station and follow Via Appia Nuova into the centre.

Termini Train Station

Rome's main station and principal transport hub is **Stazione Termini** (www. romatermini.com; Piazza dei Cinquecento; Ⓜ Termini). It has regular connections to other European countries, all major Italian cities and many smaller towns.

Train information is available from the Customer Service area on the main concourse to the left of the ticket desks. Alternatively, check www.trenitalia.com or phone ☑89 20 21.

From Termini, you can connect with the metro or take a bus from Piazza dei Cinquecento out front. Taxis are outside the main entrance/exit.

Left Luggage (Stazione Termini; 1st 5hr €6, 6-12hr per hour €0.90, 13hr & over per hour €0.40; ⊘6am-11pm; Ⓜ Termini) is available by platform 24 on the Via Giolitti side of the station.

CLIMATE CHANGE & TRAVEL

Every form of transport that relies on carbon-based fuel generates CO_2, the main cause of human-induced climate change. Modern travel is dependent on aeroplanes, which might use less fuel per kilometre per person than most cars but travel much greater distances. The altitude at which aircraft emit gases (including CO_2) and particles also contributes to their climate change impact. Many websites offer 'carbon calculators' that allow people to estimate the carbon emissions generated by their journey and, for those who wish to do so, to offset the impact of the greenhouse gases emitted with contributions to portfolios of climate-friendly initiatives throughout the world. Lonely Planet offsets the carbon footprint of all staff and author travel.

Tiburtina Bus Station

Long-distance national and international buses use **Autostazione Tiburtina** (Tibus; Largo Guido Mazzoni; MTiburtina). Get tickets at the bus station or at travel agencies.

From the bus station, cross under the overpass for the Tiburtina train station, where you can pick up metro line B and connect with Termini for onward buses, trains and metro line A.

Civitavecchia Port

The nearest port to Rome is at Civitavecchia, about 80km north of town. Ferries sail here from Barcelona and Tunis, as well as Sicily and Sardinia. Check www.traghettiweb.it for route details, prices, and to book.

Bookings can also be made at the Termini-based **Agenzie 365** (06 4782 5179; www.agenzie365.it; Stazione Termini, Via Giolitti 34; 8am-9pm; MTermini), at travel agents or directly at the port.

From Civitavecchia there are half-hourly trains to Stazione Termini (€5 to €16, 45 minutes to 1½ hours). Civitavecchia's station is about 700m from the entrance to the port.

GETTING AROUND ROME

Rome is a sprawling city, but the historic centre is relatively compact. Distances are not great and walking is often the best way of getting around. Public transport includes buses, trams, metro and a suburban train network. The main hub is Stazione Termini.

Metro

➡ Rome has two main metro lines, A (orange) and B (blue), which cross at Termini. A branch line, 'B1', serves the northern suburbs, and line C runs through the southeastern outskirts, but you're unlikely to need those.

➡ Trains run between 5.30am and 11.30pm (to 1.30am on Fridays and Saturdays).

➡ All stations on line B have wheelchair access and lifts except Circo Massimo, Colosseo and Cavour. On line A, Cipro and Termini are equipped with lifts.

➡ Take line A for the Trevi Fountain (Barberini), Spanish Steps (Spagna) and St Peter's (Ottaviano–San Pietro).

➡ Take line B for the Colosseum (Colosseo).

Bus & Tram

➡ Rome's bus and tram services are run by **ATAC** (06 5 70 03; www.atac.roma.it).

➡ The **main bus station** (Map p312; Piazza dei Cinquecento) is in front of Stazione Termini on Piazza dei Cinquecento, where there's an **information booth** (Map p312; Piazza dei Cinquecento; 8am-8pm; MTermini).

➡ Other important hubs are at Largo di Torre Argentina and Piazza Venezia.

➡ Buses generally run from about 5.30am until midnight, with limited services throughout the night.

➡ Rome's night bus service comprises more than 25 lines, many of which pass Termini and/or Piazza Venezia. Buses are marked with an 'n' before the number and bus stops have a blue owl symbol. Departures are usually every 15 to 30 minutes, but can be much slower. The most useful routes:

➡ **n1** Follows the route of metro line A.

➡ **n2** Follows the route of metro line B.

➡ **n7** Piazzale Clodio, Piazza Cavour, Via Zanardelli, Corso del Rinascimento, Corso Vittorio Emanuele II, Largo di Torre Argentina, Piazza Venezia, Via Nazionale and Stazione Termini.

Taxi

➡ Official licensed taxis are white with an ID number and *Roma Capitale* on the sides.

➡ Always go with the metered fare, never an arranged price (the set fares to and from the airports are exceptions).

➡ In town (within the ring road) flag fall is €3 between 6am and 10pm on weekdays, €4.50

BUSES FROM TERMINI

From Piazza dei Cinquecento outside Stazione Termini buses run to all corners of the city.

DESTINATION	BUS NO
St Peter's Square	40/64
Piazza Venezia	40/64
Piazza Navona	40/64
Campo de' Fiori	40/64
Pantheon	40/64
Colosseum	75
Terme di Caracalla	714
Villa Borghese	910
Trastevere	H

on Sundays and holidays, and €6.50 between 10pm and 6am. Then it's €1.10 per km. Official rates are posted in taxis and at https://romamobilita.it/it/servizi/taxi/tariffe.

➡ You can hail a taxi, but it's often easier to wait at a rank or phone for one. There are taxi ranks at the airports, Stazione Termini, Piazza della Repubblica, Piazza Barberini, Piazza di Spagna, Piazza Venezia, the Pantheon, the Colosseum, Largo di Torre Argentina, Piazza Belli, Piazza Pio XII, Piazza del Risorgimento.

➡ To book, call the automated **taxi line** (☏in Italian 06 06 09), which sends the nearest car available; a taxi company direct; or use the Chiama Taxi app.

➡ The website www.060608. it has a list of taxi companies – click on the transport tab, then 'getting around' and 'by taxi'.

➡ Note that when you call for a cab, the meter is switched on straight away and you pay for the cost of the journey from wherever the driver receives the call.

Pronto Taxi (☏06 66 45; www.6645.it)
Radiotaxi 3570 (☏06 35 70; www.3570.it)
Samarcanda (☏06 55 51; www.samarcanda.it)
Taxi Tevere (☏06 41 57; www. taxitevere.it)

Train

Apart from connections to Fiumicino airport, you'll probably only need the overground rail network if you head out of town.

TRANSPORT GETTING AROUND ROME

USEFUL BUS & TRAM ROUTES

BUS NO	ROUTE	OPERATING HOURS	FREQUENCY (HOURLY)
H	Termini, Via Nazionale, Piazza Venezia, Viale Trastevere	5.30am–midnight	up to 5
3 (tram)	Trastevere, Testaccio, Viale Aventino, Circo Massimo, Colosseo, San Giovanni, Porta Maggiore, San Lorenzo, Villa Borghese	5.30am–10pm	up to 7
8 (tram)	Piazza Venezia, Via Arenula, Trastevere	5.35am–12.30am	up to 14
23	Piazzale Clodio, Piazza del Risorgimento, Lungotevere, Testaccio, Ostiense, Basilica di San Paolo	5.15am–midnight	up to 6
40	Termini, Via Nazionale, Piazza Venezia, Largo di Torre Argentina, Borgo Sant'Angelo	6am–midnight	up to 12
64	Similar route to 40 but slower and with more stops	5.30am–12.30am	up to 12
170	Termini, Via Nazionale, Piazza Venezia, Via del Teatro Marcello, Piazza Bocca della Verità, Testaccio, EUR	5.30am–midnight	up to 7
492	Stazione Tiburtina, San Lorenzo, Piazza Barberini, Largo di Torre Argentina, Corso del Rinascimento, Piazza del Risorgimento, Cipro–Vatican Museums	5.30am–midnight	up to 6
660	Largo Colli Albani to Via Appia Antica	7.25am–9pm	2
714	Termini, Piazza Santa Maria Maggiore, Piazza San Giovanni in Laterano, Viale delle Terme di Caracalla, EUR	5.30am–midnight	up to 7
910	Termini, Piazza della Repubblica, Villa Borghese, Auditorium Parco della Musica, Piazza Mancini	5.30am–midnight	up to 6

TICKETS & PASSES

Public-transport tickets are valid on all of Rome's bus, tram and metro lines, except for routes to Fiumicino airport. They come in various forms:

➡ **BIT** (*biglietto integrato a tempo*, a single ticket valid for 100 minutes; in that time it can be used on all forms of transport but only once on the metro) €1.50

➡ **Roma 24h** (valid for 24 hours) €7

➡ **Roma 48h** (valid for 48 hours) €12.50

➡ **Roma 72h** (valid for 72 hours) €18

➡ **CIS** (*carta integrata settimanale*, a weekly ticket) €24

➡ **Abbonamento mensile** (a monthly pass) a pass restricted to a single user €35; a pass that can be used by anyone €53

➡ Children under 10 travel free.

Buy tickets at *tabacchi* (tobacconist's shops), newsstands and from vending machines at main bus stops and metro stations. They must be purchased before you start your journey and validated in the machines on buses, at the entrance gates to the metro, or at train stations. Ticketless riders risk a fine of at least €50.

The Roma Pass (p17) (two/three days €28/38.50) comes with a two/three-day travel pass valid within the city boundaries.

Travelling Out of Town

For destinations in the surrounding Lazio region, **Cotral** (📞800 174471, from a mobile 06 7205 7205; www.cotralspa.it) buses depart from numerous points throughout the city. The company is linked with Rome's public transport system, which means that you can buy tickets that cover city buses, trams, metro, and train lines, as well as regional buses and trains.

There are a range of tickets but your best bet is a daily BIRG (*biglietto integrato regionale giornaliero*) ticket, which allows unlimited travel on all city and regional transport. It's priced according to zones; tickets range from €3.30 to €14.

Get tickets from *tabacchi* and authorised ATAC sellers.

➡ Train information is available from the Customer Service area on the main concourse in **Stazione Termini** (www.romatermini.com; Piazza dei Cinquecento; Ⓜ Termini). Alternatively, check www.trenitalia.com or phone 📞89 20 21.

➡ Buy tickets on the main station concourse, from automated ticket machines, or from an authorised travel agency – look for an FS or *biglietti treni* sign in the window.

➡ Rome's second train station is **Stazione Tiburtina**, four stops from Termini on metro line B. Of the capital's eight other train stations, the most important are **Stazione Roma-Ostiense** and **Stazione Trastevere**.

Bicycle

➡ The centre of Rome doesn't lend itself to cycling: there are steep hills, treacherous cobbled roads and the traffic is terrible.

➡ Bikes can be transported on certain specified bus and tram routes, and on the metro at weekends and on weekdays from 5.30am to 7am, from 10am to noon, and from 8pm until the end of service.

➡ Bikes can be carried on the Lido di Ostia train on Saturday and Sunday and on weekdays from the beginning of service to 12.30pm and from 8pm until the end of service. You have to buy a separate ticket for the bike.

➡ On regional trains marked with a bike icon on the time-table, you can carry a bike if you pay a €3.50 supplement.

Car & Motorcycle

➡ Driving around Rome is not recommended. Riding a scooter or motorbike is faster and makes parking easier, but Rome is no place for learners, so if you're not an experienced rider, give it a miss. Hiring a car for a day trip out of town is worth considering.

➡ Most of Rome's historic centre is closed to unauthorised traffic from 6.30am to 6pm Monday to Friday, from 2pm to 6pm (10am to 7pm in some places) Saturday, and from 11pm to 3am Friday and Saturday. Evening restrictions also apply in Trastevere, San

Lorenzo, Monti and Testaccio, typically from 9.30pm or 11pm to 3am on Fridays and Saturdays (also Wednesdays and Thursdays in summer).

➡ All streets accessing the Limited Traffic Zone (ZTL) are monitored by electronic-access detection devices. If you're staying in this zone, contact your hotel. For further information, check www.agenzia mobilita.roma.it.

Driving Licence & Road Rules

All EU driving licences are recognised in Italy. Holders of non-EU licences should get an International Driving Permit (IDP) to accompany their national licence. Apply to your national motoring association.

A licence is required to ride a scooter – a car licence will do for bikes up to 125cc; for anything over 125cc you'll need a motorcycle licence.

Other rules:

➡ Drive on the right, overtake on the left.

➡ It's obligatory to wear seat belts, to drive with your headlights on outside built-up areas, and to carry a warning triangle and fluorescent waistcoat in case of breakdown.

➡ Wearing a helmet is compulsory on all two-wheeled vehicles.

➡ The blood alcohol limit is 0.05%; for drivers under 21 years and those who have had their licence for less than three years it's zero.

Unless otherwise indicated, speed limits are as follows:

➡ 130km/h on autostradas

➡ 110km/h on all main, non-urban roads

➡ 90km/h on secondary, non-urban roads

➡ 50km/h in built-up areas

A good source of information is the **Automobile Club d'Italia** (ACI; ✆roadside assistance from Italian mobile 803

116, roadside assistance from foreign mobile 800 116.800; www.aci.it), Italy's national motoring organisation.

Hire

To hire a car you'll require a driving licence (plus IDP if necessary) and credit card. Age restrictions vary but generally you'll need to be 21 or over.

Car hire is available at both Rome's airports and Stazione Termini. Reckon on at least €40 per day for a small car. Note also that most Italian hire cars have manual gear transmission.

Avis (✆06 45210 8391; www. avisautonoleggio.it)

Europcar (✆199 307030; www.europcar.it)

Hertz (✆Stazione Termini office 06 488 39 67; www. hertz.it)

Maggiore National (✆Termini office 06 488 00 49, central reservations 199 151120; www. maggiore.it; Via Giolitti 34, Stazione Termini; Ⓜ Termini)

To hire a scooter, prices range from about €30 to €120 depending on the size of the vehicle. Reliable operators:

Eco Move Rent (✆06 4470 4518; www.ecomoverent. com; Via Varese 48-50; bike/ scooter/Vespa hire per day from €8/40/110; ◷8.30am-7.30pm; Ⓜ Termini)

Treno e Scooter (✆06 4890 5823; www.trenoescooter.com; Piazza dei Cinquecento; per day €28; ◷9am-2pm & 4-7pm)

On Road (✆06 481 56 69; www.scooterhire.it; Via Cavour 80a; bicycle & scooter rental per day from €12/45; ◷10am-2pm & 2.30-6.30pm; Ⓜ Termini)

Parking

➡ Blue lines denote pay-and-display parking – get tickets from meters (coins only) and *tabacchi* (tobacconists).

➡ Expect to pay up to €1.20 per hour between 8am and 8pm (11pm in some places). After 8pm (or 11pm) parking is free until 8am the next morning.

➡ Traffic wardens are vigilant and fines are not uncommon. If your car gets towed away, call the **traffic police** (✆06 67691).

➡ There's a comprehensive list of car parks on www.060608. it – click on the 'transport' tab and then 'car parks'.

TOURS

Guided Tours

A Friend in Rome (✆340 501 92 01; www.afriendinrome. it) Silvia Prosperi and her team offer a range of private tours covering the Vatican and main historic centre as well as areas outside the capital. They can also organise kid-friendly tours, food and wine itineraries, vintage car drives and horse rides along Via Appia Antica. Rates start at €165 for a basic three-hour tour for up to eight people; add €55 for every additional hour.

Roman Guy (https://the romanguy.com) A professional setup that organises a wide range of group and private tours. Packages, led by English-speaking experts, include skip-the-line visits to the Vatican Museums (US$89), foodie tours of Trastevere and the Jewish Ghetto (US$84), and an evening bar hop through the historic centre's cocktail bars (US$225).

Through Eternity Cultural Association (✆06 700 93 36; www.through eternity.com) A reliable operator offering private and group tours led by English-speaking experts. Popular packages include a twilight tour of Rome's piazzas and fountains

(€39, 2½ hours), a night visit to the Vatican Museums (€69, 3½ hours), and a foodie tour of Testaccio (€79, four hours).

Arcult (339 650 31 72; www.arcult.it) Run by architects, Arcult offers excellent customisable group tours focusing on Rome's contemporary architecture. Prices depend on the itinerary but range from €250 to €370 for two to 10 people.

Dark Rome (City Wonders; 06 8336 0561; www. darkrome.com) Runs a range of themed tours, costing from €25 to €599, including skip-the-line visits to the Colosseum and Vatican Museums, and semiprivate visits to the Sistine Chapel. Other popular choices include a 'crypts and catacombs' tour, which takes in Rome's buried treasures, and a day trip to Pompeii.

Bus

Open Bus Cristiana (06 69 89 61; www.operaromana pellegrinaggi.org; single tour €12, 24/48hr ticket €25/28) The Vatican-sponsored Opera Romana Pellegrinaggi runs a hop-on, hop-off bus departing from Piazza Pia and Termini. Stops are situated near to main

sights including St Peter's Basilica, Piazza Navona, the Trevi Fountain and the Colosseum. Tickets are available on board, online, or at the info point just off St Peter's Square.

Bike & Scooter

Bici & Baci (Map p312; 06 482 84 43; www.bicibaci. com; Via del Viminale 5; bike tours from €30, Vespa tours from €145; 8am-7pm; Repubblica) Bici & Baci runs a range of daily bike tours, taking in the main historical sites and Via Appia Antica, as well as tours on vintage Vespas, in classic Fiat 500 cars or funky three-wheeled Ape Calessino. Its sparkling new flagship branch is near Stazione Termini (Map p312; 06 481 40 64; www.bicibaci.com; Via Rosmini 26; bike tours from €30, Vespa tours from €145; 8am-7pm Mon-Sat; Termini).

Vespa Style Roma (Map p312; 06 446 62 68; www. vespastyleroma.it; Via Milazzo 3a; Vespa rental per hour/ day €15/69, e-bikes per day €25; 9am-7pm; Termini) Wannabe Audrey Hepburns can rent a Vespa to scoot around town from Vespa Style Roma, across the road from Stazione

Termini. It also rents e-bikes and organises guided Vespa/ e-bike tours (from €70/40).

TopBike Rental & Tours (Map p306; 06 488 28 93; www.topbikerental.com; Via Labicana 49; 10am-7pm; Via Labicana) Offers a series of bike tours throughout the city, including a four-hour 16km exploration of the city centre (€45) and an all-day 30km ride through Via Appia Antica and environs (€79). Out-of-town tours take in Castel Gandolfo, Civita di Bagnoregio and Orvieto. Also offers bike hire from €15 per day.

Boat

Rome Boat Experience (Map p296; 06 8956 7745; www.romeboatexperience.com; adult/reduced €18/12) From April to October, this outfit runs hop-on, hop-off cruises along the Tiber. From May to October there are also dinner cruises (€65, two hours) every Friday and Saturday, and a daily wine bar cruise (€30, 1½ hours) from Monday to Thursday. The main embarkation point is Molo Sant'Angelo, over the river from Castel Sant'Angelo.

Directory A–Z

Customs Regulations

Entering Italy from another EU country you can bring, duty-free: 10L spirits, 90L wine and 800 cigarettes.

If arriving from a non-EU country, the limits are 1L spirits (or 2L fortified wine), 4L still wine, 60ml perfume, 16L beer, 200 cigarettes and other goods up to a value of €300/430 (travelling by land/sea); anything over this must be declared on arrival and the duty paid.

On leaving the EU, non-EU residents can reclaim value-added tax (VAT) on expensive purchases.

Dangers & Annoyances

Rome is a safe city but petty theft can be a problem.

➡ Pickpockets are active in touristy areas such as the Colosseum, Piazza di Spagna and St Peter's Square.

➡ Be alert around Stazione Termini and on crowded public transport – the 64 Vatican bus is notorious.

➡ Never drape your bag over an empty chair at a streetside cafe or put it where you can't see it.

➡ Beware of gangs of kids demanding attention. If you notice that you've been targeted, either take evasive action or shout 'Va via!' ('Go away!').

➡ Always check your change to see you haven't been shortchanged.

➡ In case of theft or loss, always report the incident to the police within 24 hours and ask for a statement.

Electricity

Type F
230V/50Hz

Type L
220V/50Hz

Emergency

Ambulance	118
Fire	115
Police	112, 113

Gay & Lesbian Travellers

Homosexuality is legal (over the age of 16) and even widely accepted, but Rome is fairly conservative in its attitudes and discretion is still wise.

The city has a thriving, if low-key, gay scene. There are relatively few queer-only venues but the Colosseum end of Via di San Giovanni in Laterano is a favourite hang out and many clubs host regular gay and lesbian nights. There is also a popular gay beach, Settimo Cielo, outside Rome at Capocotta, accessible via bus 61 from Ostia Lido.

The big annual event is **Gay Village** (www.gayvillage.it; Parco del Ninfeo; MEUR Magliana), held between June and September in EUR.

Resources include the following:

Arcigay (☑06 6450 1102; www.arcigayroma.it; Via Nicola Zabaglia 14) The Roman branch of Arcigay, Italy's national organisation for the LGBT community.

Circolo Mario Mieli di Cultura Omosessuale (Map p318;☑06 541 39 85; www.mariomieli.org; Via Efeso 2a; ◷9am-6pm Mon-Fri; MBasilica San Paolo) Organises debates, cultural events and social functions.

Coordinamento Lesbiche Italiano (www.clrbp.it; Via San Francesco di Sales 1b;

🖵Lungotevere della Farnesina) The national organisation for lesbians holds regular conferences and literary evenings at the Casa Internazionale delle Donne in Trastevere.

Internet Access

➡ Free wi-fi is widely available in hostels, B&Bs and hotels, though with signals of varying quality. Some also provide laptops/computers.

➡ Many bars and cafes offer wi-fi.

➡ There are many public wi-fi hotspots across town run by **Roma Wireless** (https://captivik.uni.it/romawireless) and **WiFimetropolitano** (www.cittametropolitanaroma.gov.it/wifimetropolitano). To use these

you'll need to register online using a credit card or an Italian mobile phone.

Legal Matters

The most likely reason for a brush with the law is to report a theft. If you have something stolen and you want to claim it on insurance, you must make a statement to the police. Insurance companies won't pay up without official proof of a crime.

The Italian police is divided into three main bodies: the *polizia*, who wear navy-blue jackets; the *carabinieri*, in a black uniform with a red stripe; and the grey-clad *guardia di finanza* (fiscal police), responsible for fighting tax evasion and drug smuggling. If you run into trouble, you're most likely to end up

DISCOUNT CARDS

DISCOUNT CARD	PRICE ADULT/ REDUCED (€)	VALIDITY	FEATURES
Archaeologia Card	25/15	7 days	Entrance to the Colosseum, Palatino, Roman Forum, Museo Nazionale Romano (Palazzo Altemps, Palazzo Massimo alle Terme, Terme di Diocleziano, Crypta Balbi), Terme di Caracalla, Mausoleo di Cecilia Metella and Villa dei Quintili. Available at participating sites or by calling ☑06 3996 7700.
Omnia Card	115	72 hours	Fast-track entry to the Vatican Museums and other major sites; audio guides for St. Peter's Basilica and Basilica di San Giovanni. Free travel on the Roma Cristiana Open Bus and unlimited public transport within Rome. Free entry to two sites, then 50% discount to extra sites. A 24-hour version is also available (€55). Details at www.omniakit.org.
Roma Pass	38.50	72 hours	Includes free admission to two museums or sites, as well as reduced entry to extra sites, unlimited city transport, and discounted entry to other exhibitions and events. The 48-hour Roma Pass (€28) is a more limited version. Further information at www.roma pass.it.

EU citizens aged between 18 and 25 qualify for discounts at state-run museums; under 18s get in free. City-run museums are free for children under six years and discounted for six to 25-year-olds. In all cases you'll need proof of age, ideally a passport or ID card.

dealing with the *polizia* or *carabinieri*.

If you're caught with what the police deem to be a dealable quantity of hard or soft drugs, you risk prison sentences of between two and 20 years. Possession for personal use is punishable by administrative sanctions, although first-time offenders might get away with a warning.

Medical Services

Italy has a public health system that is legally bound to provide emergency care to everyone. EU nationals are entitled to reduced-cost, sometimes free, medical care with a European Health Insurance Card (EHIC), available from your home health authority; non-EU citizens should take out medical insurance.

For emergency treatment, you can go to the *pronto soccorso* (casualty) section of an *ospedale* (public hospital). For less serious ailments call the **Guardia Medica Turistica** (☑06 7730 6650; Via Emilio Morosini 30; ☺8am–8pm Mon-Fri; ⬚Viale di Trastevere, ⬚Viale di Trastevere).

To arrange a (paid) home visit by a private doctor call the **International Medical Centre** (☑06 488 23 71; www.imc84.com/roma; Via Firenze 47; GP call-out & treatment fee €140, 8pm-9am & weekends €200; ☺24hr; MRepubblica).

If you need an ambulance, call ☑118.

Pharmacies

Marked by a green cross, *farmacie* (pharmacies) open from 8.30am to 1pm and 4pm to 7.30pm Monday to Friday and on Saturday mornings. Outside these hours they open on a rotational basis, and all are legally required to post a list of places open in the vicinity.

If you think you'll need a prescription while in Rome, make sure you know the drug's generic name rather than the brand name. Regular medications available over the counter – such as antihistamines or paracetamol – tend to be expensive in Italy.

Money

Italy's currency is the euro. The seven euro notes come in denominations of €500, €200, €100, €50, €20, €10 and €5. The eight euro coins are in denominations of €2 and €1, and 50, 20, 10, five, two and one cents.

ATMs

➡ ATMs (known in Italy as *bancomat*) are widely available in Rome and most will accept cards tied into the Visa, MasterCard, Cirrus and Maestro systems.

➡ The daily limit for cash withdrawal is €250.

➡ Always let your bank know when you are going abroad, in case they block your card when payments from unusual locations appear.

➡ Beware of transaction fees. Every time you withdraw cash, you'll be hit by charges – typically your home bank will charge a foreign exchange fee (usually around 1%) as well as a transaction fee of around 1% to 3%. Check details with your bank.

➡ If an ATM rejects your card, try another one before assuming the problem is with your card.

Changing Money

➡ You can change your money in banks, at post offices or at a *cambio* (exchange office). There are exchange booths at Stazione Termini and at Fiumicino and Ciampino airports.

➡ Take your passport or photo ID when exchanging money.

Credit Cards

➡ Virtually all midrange and top-end hotels accept credit cards, as do most restaurants and large shops. Some cheaper *pensioni* (pensions), trattorias and pizzerias only accept cash. Don't rely on credit cards at museums or galleries.

➡ Major cards such as Visa, MasterCard, Eurocard, Cirrus and Eurocheques are widely accepted. Amex is also recognised, although it's less common than Visa or MasterCard.

➡ Note that using your credit card in ATMs can be costly. On every transaction there's a fee, which can reach US$10 with some credit-card issuers, as well as interest per withdrawal. Check with your issuer before leaving home.

➡ If your card is lost, stolen or swallowed by an ATM, telephone to have an immediate stop put on its use.

Opening Hours

Banks 8.30am–1.30pm and 2.45–4.30pm Monday to Friday

Bars & cafes 7.30am–8pm, sometimes until 1am or 2am

Shops 9am–7.30pm or 10am–8pm Monday to Saturday, some 11am–7pm Sunday; smaller shops 9am–1pm and 3.30–7.30pm (or 4pm to 8pm) Monday to Saturday; some shops are closed Monday morning

Clubs 10pm–4am or 5am

Restaurants noon–3pm and 7.30–11pm (later in summer)

Post

Italy's postal system, **Poste Italiane** (☑803 160; www.poste.it), is reasonably reliable, though parcels do occasionally go missing.

Stamps (*francobolli*) are available at post offices and authorised tobacconists (look for the official *tabacchi* sign: a big 'T', usually white on black).

Opening hours vary but are typically 8.30am to

6pm Monday to Friday and 8.30am to 1pm on Saturday. All post offices close two hours earlier than normal on the last business day of each month.

Main Post Office (Map p300; ☑06 6973 7205; Piazza di San Silvestro 19; ☺8.20am-7pm Mon-Fri, to 12.35pm Sat; ☐Via del Tritone)

Vatican Post Office (Map p304; ☑06 6989 0400; St Peter's Square; ☺8.30am-6.45pm Mon-Fri, 8am-1.45pm Sat Sep-Jun, 8am-1.45pm Jul & Aug) Letters can be posted in yellow Vatican post boxes only if they carry Vatican stamps.

Postal Rates

Letters up to 20g cost €0.95 to destinations in Italy, €1 to Zone 1 (Europe and the Mediterranean basin), €2.20 to Zone 2 (other countries in Africa, Asia and the Americas) and €2.90 to Zone 3 (Australia and New Zealand). For more important items, use registered mail *(raccomandata)*, which costs €5 to Italian addresses, €6.60 to Zone 1, €7.80 to Zone 2 and €8.40 to Zone 3.

Public Holidays

Most Romans take their annual holiday in August. This means that many businesses and shops close for at least part of the month, particularly around Ferragosto (Feast of the Assumption) on 15 August.

Public holidays include the following:

Capodanno (New Year's Day) 1 January

Epifania (Epiphany) 6 January

Pasquetta (Easter Monday) March/April

Giorno della Liberazione (Liberation Day) 25 April

Festa del Lavoro (Labour Day) 1 May

Festa della Repubblica (Republic Day) 2 June

Festa dei Santi Pietro e Paolo (Feast of Sts Peter & Paul) 29 June

Ferragosto (Feast of the Assumption) 15 August

Festa di Ognisanti (All Saints' Day) 1 November

Festa dell'Immacolata Concezione (Feast of the Immaculate Conception) 8 December

Natale (Christmas Day) 25 December

Festa di Santo Stefano (Boxing Day) 26 December

Safe Travel

The greatest risk visitors face in Rome is from pickpockets and thieves. There's no reason for paranoia, but you need to be aware that the problem exists and to protect your valuables with this in mind.

Pickpockets go where the tourists go, so watch out around the most touristed and crowded areas, such as the Colosseum, Piazza di Spagna, St Peter's Square and Stazione Termini. Note that thieves prey on disoriented travellers at the bus stops around Termini, fresh in from airports. Crowded public transport is another hot spot. If travelling on the metro, try to use the end carriages, which are usually less busy.

In case of theft or loss, always report the incident to the police within 24 hours and ask for a statement.

Main Police Station (Questura; ☑06 4 68 61; http://questure.poliziadistato.it; Via San Vitale 15; ☺8.30am-1.30pm Mon-Sat & 3.30-7pm Mon-Fri; ☐Via Nazionale) Rome's Questura is just off Via Nazionale.

Taxes & Refunds

A 22% value-added tax known as IVA *(Imposta sul Valore Aggiunta)* is included in the price of most goods and services. Tax-free shopping is available at some shops.

Non-EU residents who spend more than €155 at one shop at a single time can claim a refund when leaving the EU. The refund only applies to purchases from stores that display a 'Tax Free' sign. When making the purchase, ask for a tax-refund voucher, to be filled in with the date of the purchase and its value. When leaving the EU, get this voucher stamped at customs and take it to the nearest tax-refund counter where you'll get an immediate refund, either in cash or charged to your credit card.

Telephone

Domestic Calls

➔ Rome's area code is ☑06. Area codes are an integral part of all Italian phone numbers and must be dialled even when calling locally.

➔ Mobile-phone numbers begin with a three-digit prefix starting with a ☑3.

➔ Toll-free numbers are known as *numeri verdi* and usually start with ☑800.

➔ Some six-digit national-rate numbers are also in use (such as those for Alitalia and Trenitalia).

International Calls

➔ To call Rome from abroad, dial your country's international access code, then Italy's country code (☑39) followed by ☑06 and the telephone number.

➔ To call abroad from Italy dial ☑00, then the country and area codes, followed by the full number.

➔ Avoid making international calls from a hotel, as rates are high.

➔ The cheapest way to call is to use an app such as Skype or Viber, connecting through the wi-fi at your hotel/B&B etc.

➔ Another cheap option is to use an international calling card. Note, however, that there are very few public payphones left in Rome, so consider a prepaid card that allows you to call from any phone. Cards are available at newsstands and tobacconists.

Mobile Phones

➔ Italian mobile phones operate on the GSM 900/1800 network, which is compatible with the rest of Europe and Australia but not always with the North American GSM or CDMA systems – check with your service provider.

➔ The cheapest way of using your mobile is to buy a prepaid *(prepagato)* Italian SIM card. TIM (Telecom Italia Mobile; www.tim.it), Wind (www.wind. it), Vodafone (www.vodafone. it) and Tre (www.tre.it) all offer SIM cards and have retail outlets across town.

➔ Note that by Italian law all SIM cards must be registered in Italy, so make sure you have a passport or ID card with you when you buy one.

Public Phones

There are very few payphones left in Rome. Those that are still working take telephone cards *(schede telefoniche)*, available from tobacconists and newsstands.

Time

Italy is in a single time zone, one hour ahead of GMT. Daylight-saving time, when clocks move forward one hour, starts on the last Sunday in March. Clocks are put back an hour on the last Sunday in October.

Italy operates on a 24-hour clock, so 6pm is written as 18:00.

Toilets

Public toilets are not widespread but you'll find them at St Peter's Square and Stazione Termini (€1). If you're caught short, the best thing to do is to nip into a cafe or bar.

Tourist Information

There are tourist information points at **Fiumicino** (Fiumicino Airport; International Arrivals, Terminal 3; ☺8am-8.45pm) and **Ciampino** (Arrivals Hall; ☺8.30am-6pm) airports, and locations across the city:

➔ **Piazza delle Cinque Lune** (Map p296; Piazza delle Cinque Lune; ☺9.30am-7pm; ☑Corso del Rinascimento) Near Piazza Navona.

➔ **Stazione Termini** (Map p312; ☑06 06 08; www. turismoroma.it; Via Giovanni Giolitti 34; ☺9am-5pm; ⓜTermini) In the hall adjacent to platform 24.

➔ **Fori Imperiali** (Map p292; Via dei Fori Imperiali; ☺9.30am-7pm; ☑Via dei Fori Imperiali)

➔ **Via Marco Minghetti** (Map p300; ☑06 06 08; www. turismoroma.it; Via Marco Minghetti; ☺9.30am-7pm; ☑Via del Corso) Between Via del Corso and the Trevi fountain.

➔ **Via Nazionale** (Map p312; ☑06 06 08; www.turismoroma. it; Via Nazionale 184; ☺9.30am-7pm; ☑Via Nazionale) In front of the Palazzo delle Esposizioni.

➔ **Castel Sant'Angelo** (Map p304; Piazza Pia; ☺9.30am-7pm; ☑Piazza Pia)

For information about the Vatican, contact the **Ufficio Pellegrini e Turisti** (Map p304; ☑06 6988 1662; St

Peter's Square; ⊗8.30am-6.30pm Mon-Sat; ⬛Piazza del Risorgimento, ⓂOttaviano-San Pietro).

The **Comune di Roma** (☑06 06 08; www.060608.it; ⊗9am-9pm) runs a free multilingual tourist information phone line providing info on culture, shows, hotels, transport etc. Its website is also an excellent source of information.

More practical information, for example, the nearest hospital, car park, etc can be answerd by phoning the Comune di Roma's **ChiamaRoma** (☑06 06 06; ⊗24hr) call centre.

Travellers with Disabilities

➡ Rome isn't an easy city for travellers with disabilities. Cobbled streets, paving stones, blocked pavements and tiny lifts are difficult for the wheelchair-bound, while the relentless traffic can be disorienting for partially sighted travellers or those with hearing difficulties.

➡ Getting around on public transport is difficult. All stations on metro line B have wheelchair access and lifts except for Circo Massimo, Colosseo and Cavour. On line A, Cipro and Termini are equipped with lifts. Note, however, that just because a station has a lift doesn't mean it will necessarily be working.

➡ Bus 590 covers the same route as metro line A and is one of 19 bus and tram services with wheelchair access. Routes with disabled access are indicated on bus stops.

➡ If travelling by train, ring the national helpline ☑199 30 30 60 to arrange assistance. At Stazione Termini, the **Sala Blu Assistenza Disabili** (Map p312; ☑800 90 60 60; Stazione Termini; ⊗6.45am-9.30pm; ⓂTermini) next to platform 1 can provide information on wheelchair-accessible

trains and help with transport in the station. Contact the office 24 hours ahead if you know you're going to need assistance. There are similar offices at Tiburtina and Ostiense stations.

➡ Airline companies should be able to arrange assistance at airports if you notify them of your needs in advance. Alternatively, contact ADR Assistance (www.adrassistance.it) for assistance at Fiumicino or Ciampino airports.

➡ Some taxis are equipped to carry passengers in wheelchairs; ask for a taxi for a *sedia a rotelle* (wheelchair).

➡ Download Lonely Planet's free Accessible Travel guide from http://lptravel.to/AccessibleTravel.

Organisations

Presidio del Lazio (☑800 271027; www.presidiolazio.it; ⊗call centre 9am-1pm) is a regional service centre that can provide useful local information.

Sage Traveling (www.sagetraveling.com) is a US-based agency started by wheelchair user John Sage, who has visited over 70 countries in Europe. It offers practical advice and tailor-made tours for disabled travellers.

Visas

➡ Italy is one of the 26 European countries to make up the Schengen area. There are no customs controls when travelling between Schengen countries, so the visa rules that apply to Italy apply to all Schengen countries.

➡ EU citizens do not need a visa to enter Italy – a valid ID card or passport is sufficient.

➡ Nationals of some other countries, including Australia, Canada, Israel, Japan, New Zealand, Switzerland and the USA,

do not need a visa for stays of up to 90 days.

➡ Nationals of other countries will need a Schengen tourist visa – to check requirements see www.schengenvisainfo.com/tourist-schengen-visa.

➡ All non-EU and non-Schengen nationals entering Italy for more than 90 days or for any reason other than tourism (such as study or work) may need a specific visa. Check http://visto peritalia.esteri.it for details.

Permesso di Soggiorno

➡ A *permesso di soggiorno* (permit to stay, also referred to as a residence permit) is required by all non-EU nationals who stay in Italy longer than three months. In theory, you should apply for one within eight days of arriving in Italy.

➡ EU citizens do not require a *permesso di soggiorno* but are required to register with the local registry office (*ufficio anagrafe*) if they stay for more than three months.

➡ Check exact requirements on www.poliziadistato.it – click on the English tab and then follow the links.

➡ The main office dealing with permits is the **Ufficio Immigrazione** (☑06 4686 3911; http://questure.poliziadistato.it/it/Roma; Via Teofilo Patini; ⊗8.30-noon Mon-Fri & 3-5pm Tue & Thu; ⬛Via Salviati).

Women Travellers

Sexual harrassment can be an issue in Rome. If you feel yourself being groped on a crowded bus or metro, a loud '*che schifo!*' (how disgusting!) will draw attention to the incident. Otherwise take all the usual precautions you would in any large city and, as in most places, avoid wandering around alone late at night, especially in the area around Termini station.

Language

When in Rome, you'll find that locals appreciate you trying their language, no matter how muddled you may think you sound. Italian is not difficult to pronounce as the sounds used in spoken Italian can all be found in English.

Note that, in our pronunciation guides, ai is pronounced as in 'aisle', ay as in 'say', ow as in 'how', dz as the 'ds' in 'lids', and that r is a strong and rolled sound. Keep in mind too that Italian consonants can have a stronger, emphatic pronunciation – if the consonant is written as a double letter, it should be pronounced a little stronger. This difference in the pronunciation of single and double consonants can mean a difference in meaning, eg *sonno* *son·no* (sleep) versus *sono* *so·no* (I am). The Italian ch is usually pronounced as a hard c, so, for example, 'chiesa' is 'key-esa'.

If you read our coloured pronunciation guides as if they were English, you'll be understood. The stressed syllables are indicated with italics.

BASICS

Italian has two words for 'you' – use the polite form *Lei* lay if you're talking to strangers, officials or people older than you. With people familiar to you or younger than you, you can use the informal form *tu* too.

In Italian, all nouns and adjectives are either masculine or feminine, and so are the articles *il/la* eel/la (the) and *un/una* oon/oo·na (a) that go with the nouns.

In this chapter the polite/informal and masculine/feminine options are included where necessary, separated with a slash and indicated with 'pol/inf' and 'm/f'.

WANT MORE?

For in-depth language information and handy phrases, check out Lonely Planet's *Italian phrasebook*. You'll find it at **shop. lonelyplanet.com**, or you can buy Lonely Planet's iPhone phrasebooks at the Apple App Store.

Hello.	*Buongiorno.*	bwon·*jor*·no
Goodbye.	*Arrivederci.*	a·ree·ve·*der*·chee
Yes.	*Sì.*	see
No.	*No.*	no
Excuse me.	*Mi scusi.* (pol)	mee *skoo*·zee
	Scusami. (inf)	*skoo*·za·mee
Sorry.	*Mi dispiace.*	mee dees·*pya*·che
Please.	*Per favore.*	per fa·*vo*·re
Thank you.	*Grazie.*	*gra*·tsye
You're welcome.	*Prego.*	*pre*·go

How are you?
Come sta/stai? (pol/inf)   *ko*·me sta/stai

Fine. And you?
Bene. E Lei/tu? (pol/inf)   *be*·ne e lay/too

What's your name?
Come si chiama? pol   *ko*·me see *kya*·ma
Come ti chiami? inf   *ko*·me tee *kya*·mee

My name is ...
Mi chiamo ...   mee *kya*·mo ...

Do you speak English?
Parla/Parli   *par*·la/*par*·lee
inglese? (pol/inf)   een·*gle*·ze

I don't understand.
Non capisco.   non ka·*pee*·sko

ACCOMMODATION

Do you have a ... room?	*Avete una camera ...?*	a·*ve*·te oo·na *ka*·me·ra ...
double	*doppia con letto matrimoniale*	*do*·pya kon *le*·to ma·tree·mo·*nya*·le
single	*singola*	*seen*·go·la
How much is it per ...?	*Quanto costa per ...?*	*kwan*·to *kos*·ta per ...
night	*una notte*	oo·na *no*·te
person	*persona*	per·*so*·na

LANGUAGE DIRECTIONS

Is breakfast included?
La colazione è compresa?
la ko·la·tsyo·ne e kom·pre·sa

air-con	*aria condizionata*	a·rya kon·dee·tsyo·na·ta
bathroom	*bagno*	ba·nyo
campsite	*campeggio*	kam·pe·jo
guesthouse	*pensione*	pen·syo·ne
hotel	*albergo*	al·ber·go
youth hostel	*ostello della gioventù*	os·te·lo de·la jo·ven·too
window	*finestra*	fee·nes·tra

DIRECTIONS

Where's ...?
Dov'è ...?
do·ve ...

What's the address?
Qual'è l'indirizzo?
kwa·le leen·dee·ree·tso

Could you please write it down?
Può scriverlo, per favore?
pwo skree·ver·lo per fa·vo·re

Can you show me (on the map)?
Può mostrarmi (sulla pianta)?
pwo mos·trar·mee (soo·la pyan·ta)

at the corner	*all'angolo*	a·lan·go·lo
at the traffic lights	*al semaforo*	al se·ma·fo·ro
behind	*dietro*	dye·tro
far	*lontano*	lon·ta·no
in front of	*davanti a*	da·van·tee a
near	*vicino*	vee·chee·no
next to	*accanto a*	a·kan·to a
opposite	*di fronte a*	dee fron·te a
straight ahead	*sempre diritto*	sem·pre dee·ree·to
to the left	*a sinistra*	a see·nee·stra
to the right	*a destra*	a de·stra

EATING & DRINKING

What would you recommend?
Cosa mi consiglia?
ko·za mee kon·see·lya

What's in that dish?
Quali ingredienti ci sono in questo piatto?
kwa·li een·gre·dyen·tee chee so·no een kwe·sto pya·to

What's the local speciality?
Qual'è la specialità di questa regione?
kwa·le la spe·cha·lee·ta dee kwe·sta re·jo·ne

That was delicious!
Era squisito!
e·ra skwee·zee·to

Cheers!
Salute!
sa·loo·te

KEY PATTERNS

To get by in Italian, mix and match these simple patterns with words of your choice:

When's (the next flight)?
A che ora è (il prossimo volo)?
a ke o·ra e (eel pro·see·mo vo·lo)

Where's (the station)?
Dov'è (la stazione)?
do·ve (la sta·tsyo·ne)

I'm looking for (a hotel).
Sto cercando (un albergo).
sto cher·kan·do (oon al·ber·go)

Do you have (a map)?
Ha (una pianta)?
a (oo·na pyan·ta)

Is there (a toilet)?
C'è (un gabinetto)?
che (oon ga·bee·ne·to)

I'd like (a coffee).
Vorrei (un caffè).
vo·ray (oon ka·fe)

I'd like to (hire a car).
Vorrei (noleggiare una macchina).
vo·ray (no·le·ja·re oo·na ma·kee·na)

Can I (enter)?
Posso (entrare)?
po·so (en·tra·re)

Could you please (help me)?
Può (aiutarmi), per favore?
pwo (a·yoo·tar·mee) per fa·vo·re

Do I have to (book a seat)?
Devo (prenotare un posto)?
de·vo (pre·no·ta·re oon po·sto)

Please bring the bill.
Mi porta il conto, per favore?
mee por·ta eel kon·to per fa·vo·re

I'd like to reserve a table for ...	*Vorrei prenotare un tavolo per ...*	vo·ray pre·no·ta·re oon ta·vo·lo per ...
(two) people	*(due) persone*	*(doo·e)* per·so·ne
(eight) o'clock	*le (otto)*	le (o·to)

I don't eat ...	*Non mangio ...*	non man·jo ...
eggs	*uova*	wo·va
fish	*pesce*	pe·she
nuts	*noci*	no·chee
(red) meat	*carne (rossa)*	kar·ne (ro·sa)

Key Words

bar	*locale*	lo·ka·le
bottle	*bottiglia*	bo·tee·lya
breakfast	*prima colazione*	pree·ma ko·la·tsyo·ne

Signs

Entrata/Ingresso	Entrance
Uscita	Exit
Aperto	Open
Chiuso	Closed
Informazioni	Information
Proibito/Vietato	Prohibited
Gabinetti/Servizi	Toilets
Uomini	Men
Donne	Women

cafe	bar	bar
cold	freddo	fre·do
dinner	cena	che·na
drink list	lista delle bevande	lee·sta de·le be·van·de
fork	forchetta	for·ke·ta
glass	bicchiere	bee·kye·re
grocery store	alimentari	a·lee·men·ta·ree
hot	caldo	kal·do
knife	coltello	kol·te·lo
lunch	pranzo	pran·dzo
market	mercato	mer·ka·to
menu	menù	me·noo
plate	piatto	pya·to
restaurant	ristorante	ree·sto·ran·te
spicy	piccante	pee·kan·te
spoon	cucchiaio	koo·kya·yo
vegetarian (food)	vegetariano	ve·je·ta·rya·no
with	con	kon
without	senza	sen·tsa

Meat & Fish

beef	manzo	man·dzo
chicken	pollo	po·lo
clams	vongole	vong·o·lay
duck	anatra	a·na·tra
fish	pesce	pe·she
herring	aringa	a·reen·ga
lamb	agnello	a·nye·lo
lobster	aragosta	a·ra·gos·ta
meat	carne	kar·ne
mussels	cozze	ko·tse
oysters	ostriche	o·stree·ke
pork	maiale	ma·ya·le
prawn	gambero	gam·be·ro
salmon	salmone	sal·mo·ne
scallops	capasante	ka·pa·san·te
seafood	frutti di mare	froo·tee dee ma·re
shrimp	gambero	gam·be·ro
squid	calamari	ka·la·ma·ree
trout	trota	tro·ta
tuna	tonno	to·no
turkey	tacchino	ta·kee·no
veal	vitello	vee·te·lo

Fruit & Vegetables

apple	mela	me·la
beans	fagioli	fa·jo·lee
cabbage	cavolo	ka·vo·lo
capsicum	peperone	pe·pe·ro·ne
carrot	carota	ka·ro·ta
cauliflower	cavolfiore	ka·vol·fyo·re
cucumber	cetriolo	che·tree·o·lo
fruit	frutta	froo·ta
grapes	uva	oo·va
lemon	limone	lee·mo·ne
lentils	lenticchie	len·tee·kye
mushroom	funghi	foon·gee
nuts	noci	no·chee
onions	cipolle	chee·po·le
orange	arancia	a·ran·cha
peach	pesca	pe·ska
peas	piselli	pee·ze·lee
pineapple	ananas	a·na·nas
plum	prugna	proo·nya
potatoes	patate	pa·ta·te
spinach	spinaci	spee·na·chee
tomatoes	pomodori	po·mo·do·ree
vegetables	verdura	ver·doo·ra

Question Words

How?	Come?	ko·me
What?	Che cosa?	ke ko·za
When?	Quando?	kwan·do
Where?	Dove?	do·ve
Who?	Chi?	kee
Why?	Perché?	per·ke

Other

bread	*pane*	*pa*·ne
butter	*burro*	*boo*·ro
cheese	*formaggio*	for·*ma*·jo
eggs	*uova*	*wo*·va
honey	*miele*	*mye*·le
ice	*ghiaccio*	*gya*·cho
jam	*marmellata*	mar·me·*la*·ta
noodles	*pasta*	*pas*·ta
oil	*olio*	*o*·lyo
pepper	*pepe*	*pe*·pe
rice	*riso*	*ree*·zo
salt	*sale*	*sa*·le
soup	*minestra*	mee·*nes*·tra
soy sauce	*salsa di soia*	*sal*·sa dee *so*·ya
sugar	*zucchero*	*tsoo*·ke·ro
vinegar	*aceto*	a·*che*·to

Drinks

beer	*birra*	*bee*·ra
coffee	*caffè*	ka·*fe*
(orange) juice	*succo (d'arancia)*	*soo*·ko (da·*ran*·cha)
milk	*latte*	*la*·te
red wine	*vino rosso*	*vee*·no *ro*·so
soft drink	*bibita*	*bee*·bee·ta
tea	*tè*	te
(mineral) water	*acqua (minerale)*	*a*·kwa (mee·ne·*ra*·le)
white wine	*vino bianco*	*vee*·no *byan*·ko

EMERGENCIES

Help!
Aiuto! a·*yoo*·to

Leave me alone!
Lasciami in pace! la·*sha*·mee een *pa*·che

I'm lost.
Mi sono perso/a. (m/f) mee *so*·no *per*·so/a

There's been an accident.
C'è stato un incidente. che *sta*·to oon een·chee·*den*·te

Call the police!
Chiami la polizia! *kya*·mee la po·lee·*tsee*·a

Call a doctor!
Chiami un medico! *kya*·mee oon *me*·dee·ko

Where are the toilets?
Dove sono i gabinetti? *do*·ve *so*·no ee ga·bee·*ne*·tee

I'm sick.
Mi sento male. mee *sen*·to *ma*·le

It hurts here.
Mi fa male qui. mee fa *ma*·le kwee

I'm allergic to ...
Sono allergico/a a ... (m/f) *so*·no a·*ler*·jee·ko/a a ...

SHOPPING & SERVICES

I'd like to buy ...
Vorrei comprare ... vo·*ray* kom·*pra*·re ...

I'm just looking.
Sto solo guardando. sto *so*·lo gwar·*dan*·do

Can I look at it?
Posso dare un'occhiata? *po*·so *da*·re oo·no·*kya*·ta

How much is this?
Quanto costa questo? *kwan*·to *kos*·ta *kwe*·sto

It's too expensive.
È troppo caro/a. (m/f) e *tro*·po *ka*·ro/a

Can you lower the price?
Può farmi lo sconto? pwo *far*·mee lo *skon*·to

There's a mistake in the bill.
C'è un errore nel conto. che oo·ne·*ro*·re nel *kon*·to

ATM	*Bancomat*	ban·ko·mat
post office	*ufficio postale*	oo·*fee*·cho pos·*ta*·le
tourist office	*ufficio del turismo*	oo·*fee*·cho del too·*reez*·mo

TIME & DATES

What time is it?	*Che ora è?*	ke *o*·ra e
It's one o'clock.	*È l'una.*	e *loo*·na
It's (two) o'clock.	*Sono le (due).*	*so*·no le (*doo*·e)
Half past (one).	*(L'una) e mezza.*	(*loo*·na) e *me*·dza

in the morning	*di mattina*	dee ma·*tee*·na
in the afternoon	*di pomeriggio*	dee po·me·*ree*·jo
in the evening	*di sera*	dee *se*·ra

yesterday	*ieri*	*ye*·ree
today	*oggi*	*o*·jee
tomorrow	*domani*	do·*ma*·nee

Monday	*lunedì*	loo·ne·*dee*
Tuesday	*martedì*	mar·te·*dee*
Wednesday	*mercoledì*	mer·ko·le·*dee*
Thursday	*giovedì*	jo·ve·*dee*
Friday	*venerdì*	ve·ner·*dee*
Saturday	*sabato*	*sa*·ba·to
Sunday	*domenica*	do·*me*·nee·ka

January	gennaio	je·na·yo
February	febbraio	fe·bra·yo
March	marzo	mar·tso
April	aprile	a·pree·le
May	maggio	ma·jo
June	giugno	joo·nyo
July	luglio	loo·lyo
August	agosto	a·gos·to
September	settembre	se·tem·bre
October	ottobre	o·to·bre
November	novembre	no·vem·bre
December	dicembre	dee·chem·bre

NUMBERS

1	uno	oo·no
2	due	doo·e
3	tre	tre
4	quattro	kwa·tro
5	cinque	cheen·kwe
6	sei	say
7	sette	se·te
8	otto	o·to
9	nove	no·ve
10	dieci	dye·chee
20	venti	ven·tee
30	trenta	tren·ta
40	quaranta	kwa·ran·ta
50	cinquanta	cheen·kwan·ta
60	sessanta	se·san·ta
70	settanta	se·tan·ta
80	ottanta	o·tan·ta
90	novanta	no·van·ta
100	cento	chen·to
1000	mille	mee·lel

TRANSPORT

At what time does the ... leave/arrive?
A che ora parte/arriva ...? — a ke o·ra par·te/a·ree·va ...

boat	la nave	la na·ve
bus	l'autobus	low·to·boos
ferry	il traghetto	eel tra·ge·to
metro	la metropolitana	la me·tropo·lee·ta·na
plane	l'aereo	la·e·re·o
train	il treno	eel tre·no

... ticket	un biglietto ...	oon bee·lye·to
one-way	di sola andata	dee so·la an·da·ta
return	di andata e ritorno	dee an·da·ta e ree·tor·no

bus stop	fermata dell'autobus	fer·ma·ta del ow·to·boos
platform	binario	bee·na·ryo
ticket office	biglietteria	bee·lye·te·ree·a
timetable	orario	o·ra·ryo
train station	stazione ferroviaria	sta·tsyo·ne fe·ro·vyar·ya

Does it stop at ...?
Si ferma a ...? — see fer·ma a ...

Please tell me when we get to ...
Mi dica per favore quando arriviamo a ... — mee dee·ka per fa·vo·re kwan·do a·ree·vya·mo a ...

I want to get off here.
Voglio scendere qui. — vo·lyo shen·de·re kwee

I'd like to hire a bicycle.
Vorrei noleggiare una bicicletta. — vo·ray no·le·ja·re oo·na bee·chee·kle·ta

I have a flat tyre.
Ho una gomma bucata. — o oo·na go·ma boo·ka·ta

I'd like to have my bicycle repaired.
Vorrei fare riparare la mia bicicletta. — vo·ray fa·re ree·pa·ra·re la mee·a bee·chee·kle·ta

Glossary

abbazia – abbey

(pizza) al taglio – (pizza) by the slice

albergo – hotel

alimentari – grocery shop; delicatessen

anfiteatro – amphitheatre

aperitivo – pre-evening meal drink and snack

arco – arch

autostrada – motorway; highway

battistero – baptistry

biblioteca – library

biglietto – ticket

borgo – archaic name for a small town, village or town sector (often dating to Middle Ages)

camera – room

campo – field

cappella – chapel

Cappella Sistina – Sistine Chapel

carabinieri – police with military and civil duties

Carnevale – carnival period between Epiphany and Lent

casa – house

castello – castle

cattedrale – cathedral

catacomba – catacomb

centro sociale –social centre; often a venue for concerts, club nights, cultural events

centro storico – historic centre

chiesa – church

chiostro – cloister; covered walkway, usually enclosed by columns, around a quadrangle

città – town; city

colonna – column

comune – equivalent to a municipality or county; a town or city council; historically, a self–governing town or city

corso – boulevard

duomo – cathedral

enoteca – wine bar

espresso – short black coffee

EUR (Esposizione Universale di Roma) – outlying district in south Rome known for its rationalist architecture

ferrovia – railway

festa – feast day; holiday

fontana – fountain

foro – forum

fiume – river

gelateria – ice-cream shop

giardino – garden

grattachecca – ice drink flavoured with fruit and syrup

grotta – cave

isola – island

lago – lake

largo – small square

locanda – inn; small hotel

mar, mare – sea

mausoleo – mausoleum; stately and magnificent tomb

mercato – market

necropoli – ancient name for cemetery or burial site

nord – north

osteria – casual tavern or eatery presided over by a host

palazzo – mansion; palace; large building of any type, including an apartment block

palio – contest

Papa – Pope

passeggiata – traditional evening stroll

pasticceria – cake/pastry shop

pensione – guesthouse

piazza – square

piazzale – large open square

pietà – literally 'pity' or 'compassion'; sculpture, drawing or painting of the dead Christ supported by the Madonna

pinacoteca – art gallery

PIT (Punto Informativo Turistico) – Tourist Information Point

ponte – bridge

porta – gate; door

porto – port

prenotare – to book or reserve

reale – royal

ristorante – restaurant

rocca – fortress

sala – room; hall

salumeria – delicatessen

santuario – sanctuary; 1. the part of a church above the altar; 2. an especially holy place in a temple (antiquity)

scalinata – staircase

scavi – excavations

spiaggia – beach

stadio – stadium

stazione – station

stazione marittima – ferry terminal

strada – street; road

sud – south

superstrada – expressway; highway with divided lanes

tartufo – truffle

tavola calda – literally 'hot table'; pre-prepared meat, pasta and vegetable selection, often self-service

teatro – theatre

tempietto – small temple

tempio – temple

terme – thermal baths

tesoro – treasury

Tevere – Tiber

torre – tower

trattoria – simple restaurant

Trenitalia – Italian State Railways; also known as Ferrovie dello Stato (FS)

via – street; road

Via Appia Antica – Appian Way

viale – avenue

vico – alley; alleyway

villa – town house; country house; also the park surrounding the house

---

Food Glossary

abbacchio al forno – lamb roasted with rosemary and garlic; usually accompanied by rosemary-roasted potatoes

agnello alla cacciatora – lamb 'hunter-style' with onion and fresh tomatoes

baccalà – salt cod, often served deepfried in the Roman–Jewish tradition

bresaola – wind-dried beef, a feature of Roman-Jewish cuisine; served as a replacement for *prosciutto* (ham)

bruschette – grilled bread rubbed with garlic, splashed with olive oil and sprinkled with salt, most commonly then topped by tomatoes.

bucatini all'amatriciana – thick spaghetti with tomato sauce, onions, pancetta, cheese and chilli; originated in Amatrice, a town east of Rome, as an adaptation of *spaghetti alla gricia*

cacio e pepe – pasta mixed with freshly grated *pecorino romano*, ground black pepper and a dash of olive oil

carciofi alla giudia – deepfried 'Jewish-style' artichokes; the heart is soft and succulent, the leaves taste like delicious crisps

carciofi alla romana – artichokes boiled with oil, garlic and mint

coda alla vaccinara – beef tail stewed with garlic, parsley, onion, carrots, celery and spices

fiori di zucca – courgette flowers, usually stuffed with mozzarella and anchovies and fried

frutti di mare – seafood; usually served as a sauce with pasta, comprising tomatoes, clams, mussels, and perhaps prawns and calamari

gnocchi alla romana – semolina-based mini-dumplings baked with ragù or tomato sugo; traditionally served on Thursdays

involtini – thin slices of veal or beef,rolled up with sage or sometimes vegetables and mozzarella.

minestra di arzilla con pasta e broccoli – skate soup with pasta and broccoli; Roman-Jewish dish served only at the most traditional restaurants

pasta con lenticchie – popular local dish of pasta with lentils

pasta e ceci – pasta with chickpeas; warms the cockles in winter

pizza bianca – 'white pizza' unique to Rome; a plain pizza brushed with salt, olive oil and often rosemary; can split and fill to make a sandwich

pollo alla romana – chicken cooked in butter, marjoram, garlic, white wine and tomatoes or peppers

polpette al sugo – meatballs with traditional tomato sauce

porchetta – a hog roasted on a spit with herbs and an abundance of finocchio *selvatico* (wild fennel)

ragù– classic Italian meat sauce traditionally made by slowly stewing cuts of meat, or mince, in a rich tomato sugo

rigatoni alla pajata – thick ridged pasta tubes with the small intestine of a milk-fed calf or lamb

saltimbocca alla romana – the deliciously named 'leap in the mouth'; a veal cutlet jazzed up with sparing amounts of prosciutto and sage

spaghetti alla carbonara – sauce of egg, cheese and *guanciale* (cured pig's cheek); the egg is added raw, and stirred into the hot pasta to cook it

spaghetti alla gricia – pasta with pecorino cheese, black pepper and pancetta;

spaghetti con le vongole – spaghetti with clams and a dash of red chilli to pep things up; sometimes served with tomatoes, sometimes without

stracciatella – humble chicken broth given a lift by the addition of Parmesan and whisked egg

sugo – all-purpose tomato sauce served in many dishes; it's traditionally combined with *basilico* (basil)

supplì – rice balls, like large croquettes; if they contain mozzarella, they're called *supplì a telefono* because when you break one open, the cheese forms a string like a telephone wire between the two halves

trippa alla romana – tripe cooked with potatoes, tomato and mint and sprinkled with pecorino cheese; a typical Saturday-in-Rome dish

Behind the Scenes

SEND US YOUR FEEDBACK

We love to hear from travellers – your comments keep us on our toes and help make our books better. Our well-travelled team reads every word on what you loved or loathed about this book. Although we cannot reply individually to your submissions, we always guarantee that your feedback goes straight to the appropriate authors, in time for the next edition. Each person who sends us information is thanked in the next edition – the most useful submissions are rewarded with a selection of digital PDF chapters.

Visit **lonelyplanet.com/contact** to submit your updates and suggestions or to ask for help. Our award-winning website also features inspirational travel stories, news and discussions.

Note: We may edit, reproduce and incorporate your comments in Lonely Planet products such as guidebooks, websites and digital products, so let us know if you don't want your comments reproduced or your name acknowledged. For a copy of our privacy policy visit lonelyplanet.com/privacy.

WRITER THANKS

Duncan Garwood

A big thank you to fellow author Nicola Williams for her suggestions and great work, and to Anna Tyler at LP for all her support. In Rome, *grazie* to Silvia Prosperi for all her useful insights and Richard McKenna for his entertaining lunch company. As always, a big, heartfelt hug to Lidia and the boys, Ben and Nick.

Nicola Williams

Grazie mille to those who shared their Roman love and insider knowledge: Linda Martinez (The Beehive), Daniela and Lorenza (Arco del Lauro), Elyssa Bernard (smart dining tips around Trevi Fountain), Fiona Brewer (food tour guide), Sian Lloyd and Lorna Davidson (superb clubbing recommendations and Trastevere drinking tips), Gina Tringali and Eleonora Baldwin (professional foodies at Casa Mia), passionate art historians Molly McIllWrath and Daisy de Plume. Finally, kudos to my highly skilled, enthusiastic, trilingual, family-travel research team: Niko, Mischa and Kaya.

ACKNOWLEDGEMENTS

Cover photograph: View of St Peter's Basilica from Castel Sant'Angelo, Giuseppe Greco/4Corners ©
Illustration on pp58–9 by Javier Zarracina.

THIS BOOK

This 10th edition of Lonely Planet's *Rome* guidebook was researched and written by Duncan Garwood and Nicola Williams. The previous edition was written by Duncan Garwood and Abigail Blasi. This guidebook was produced by the following:

Curator Saralinda Turner
Destination Editor Anna Tyler
Product Editors Jenna Myers, Sandie Kestell
Senior Cartographer Anthony Phelan
Book Designer Clara Monitto
Assisting Editors Katie Connolly, Victoria Harrison, Gabrielle Innes, Monique Perrin, Gabbi Stefanos, Fionn Twomey
Cover Researcher Naomi Parker
Thanks to Will Allen, Liz Heynes, Chris Martin, Norma Postin, Lukasz Sokolowski, Tony Wheeler

Index

✕ EATING

INDEX DRINKING & NIGHTLIFE

Rome Maps

Sights
- Beach
- Bird Sanctuary
- Buddhist
- Castle/Palace
- Christian
- Confucian
- Hindu
- Islamic
- Jain
- Jewish
- Monument
- Museum/Gallery/Historic Building
- Ruin
- Shinto
- Sikh
- Taoist
- Winery/Vineyard
- Zoo/Wildlife Sanctuary
- Other Sight

Activities, Courses & Tours
- Bodysurfing
- Diving
- Canoeing/Kayaking
- Course/Tour
- Sento Hot Baths/Onsen
- Skiing
- Snorkelling
- Surfing
- Swimming/Pool
- Walking
- Windsurfing
- Other Activity

Sleeping
- Sleeping
- Camping
- Hut/Shelter

Eating
- Eating

Drinking & Nightlife
- Drinking & Nightlife
- Cafe

Entertainment
- Entertainment

Shopping
- Shopping

Information
- Bank
- Embassy/Consulate
- Hospital/Medical
- Internet
- Police
- Post Office
- Telephone
- Toilet
- Tourist Information
- Other Information

Geographic
- Beach
- Gate
- Hut/Shelter
- Lighthouse
- Lookout
- Mountain/Volcano
- Oasis
- Park
- Pass
- Picnic Area
- Waterfall

Population
- Capital (National)
- Capital (State/Province)
- City/Large Town
- Town/Village

Transport
- Airport
- Border crossing
- Bus
- Cable car/Funicular
- Cycling
- Ferry
- Metro station
- Monorail
- Parking
- Petrol station
- S-Bahn/Subway station
- Taxi
- T-bane/Tunnelbana station
- Train station/Railway
- Tram
- Tube station
- U-Bahn/Underground station
- Other Transport

Routes
- Tollway
- Freeway
- Primary
- Secondary
- Tertiary
- Lane
- Unsealed road
- Road under construction
- Plaza/Mall
- Steps
- Tunnel
- Pedestrian overpass
- Walking Tour
- Walking Tour detour
- Path/Walking Trail

Boundaries
- International
- State/Province
- Disputed
- Regional/Suburb
- Marine Park
- Cliff
- Wall

Hydrography
- River, Creek
- Intermittent River
- Canal
- Water
- Dry/Salt/Intermittent Lake
- Reef

Areas
- Airport/Runway
- Beach/Desert
- Cemetery (Christian)
- Cemetery (Other)
- Glacier
- Mudflat
- Park/Forest
- Sight (Building)
- Sportsground
- Swamp/Mangrove

Note: Not all symbols displayed above appear on the maps in this book

Tiber River

PARIOLI

FLAMINIO
PINCIANO

TRIESTE

NOMENTANO

VILLA
BORGHESE

SALARIO

TRIONFALE

4

PRATI

CAMPO
MARZIO

SALLUSTIANO

LUDOVISI

10

TIBURTINO

VATICAN CITY
(CITTÀ DEL
VATICANO)

BORGO

CASTRO
PRETORIO

COLONNA

2

5

PONTE

SANT'
EUSTACHIO

TREVI

SAN
LORENZO

PARIONE

PIGNA

MONTI

REGOLA

ESQUILINO

GIANICOLO

3

SANT'
ANGELO

PIGNETO

9

8

TRASTEVERE

CAMPITELLI

1

SAN
GIOVANNI

TUSCOLANO

RIPA

7

AVENTINO

CELIO

11

MONTEVERDE

TESTACCIO

6

APPIO-
LATINO

Tiber River

GARBATELLA

GIANCOLENSE

Marrana della Caffarella

PORTUENSE

OSTIENSE

N

0 — 2 km
0 — 1 mile

SAN
PAOLO

MAP INDEX

ANCIENT ROME Map on p292

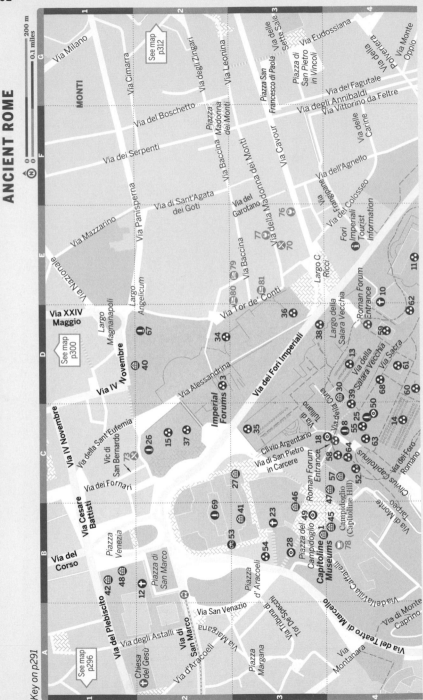

ANCIENT ROME

Key on p291

See map p296

See map p300

See map p312

MONTI

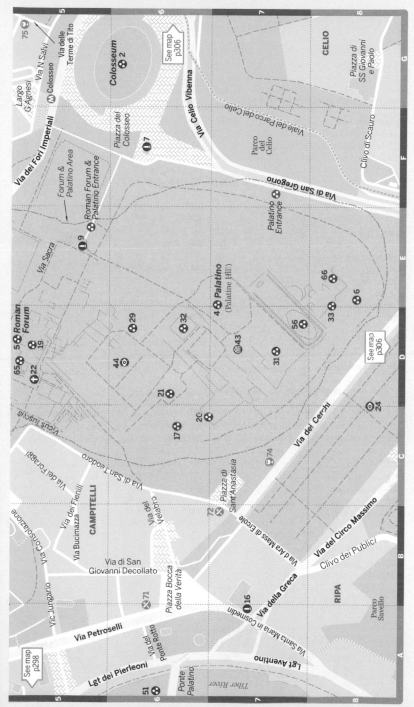

See map p306

Via N Salvi

Via delle Terme di Tito

75

Largo G Agnesi

Via dei Fori Imperiali

Colosseo M

Colosseum
2

Piazza del Colosseo

7

Via Celio Vibenna

CELIO

Piazza di SS Giovanni e Paolo

Clivo di Scauro

Viale del Parco del Celio

Forum & Palatino Area

Roman Forum & Palatino Entrance

9

Via Sacra

Via di San Gregorio

Palatino Entrance

Parco del Celio

Roman Forum
5

65

19

22

44

29

32

4 Palatino (Palatine Hill)

43

56

66

6

33

31

See map p306

21

20

17

Vicus Tuscus

Via dei Cerchi

24

74

Via del Foraggi

Via di San Teodoro

CAMPITELLI

Via dei Fienili

Via Bucimazza

Via del Velabro

Piazza di Sant'Anastasia

72

Via d Ara Mass di Ercole

Via del Circo Massimo

Clivo dei Publici

Vic Jungario

Via Consolazione

Via di San Giovanni Decollato

Piazza Bocca della Verità

71

Via della Greca

16

Via Santa Maria in Cosmedin

RIPA

Parco Savello

Via Petroselli

Via del Ponte Rotto

See map p298

Lgt dei Pierleoni

51

Ponte Palatino

Tiber River

Lgt Aventino

CENTRO STORICO NORTH *Map on p296*

Key on p294

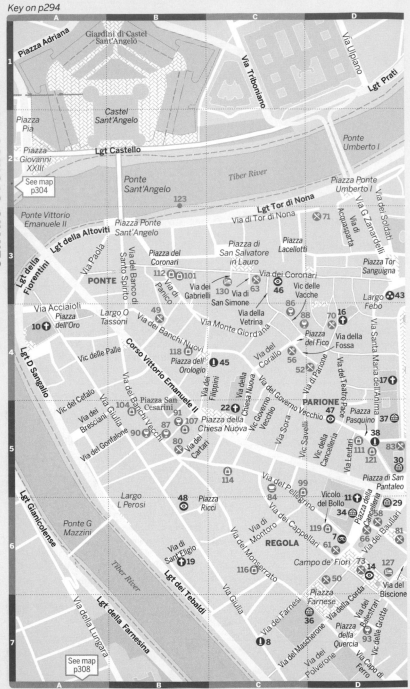

CENTRO STORICO SOUTH

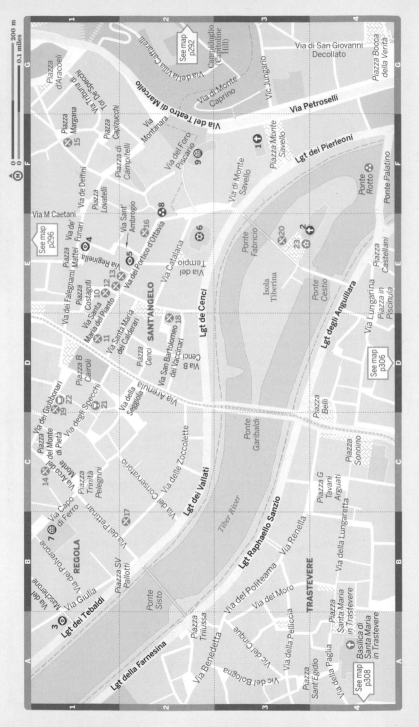

See map p292
See map p296
See map p306
See map p308

200 m
0.1 miles

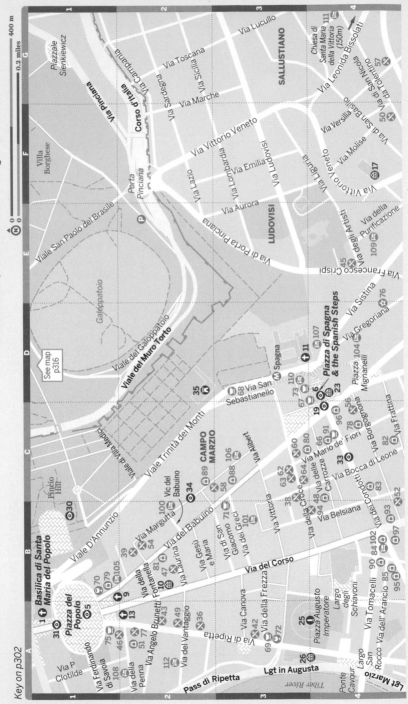

0   400 m
0   0.2 miles

Piazzale
Sienkiewicz

Via Campania

Via Toscana

Via Lucullo

Chiesa di
Santa Maria
della Vittoria
(150m)

111

SALLUSTIANO

Corso d'Italia

Villa
Borghese

Viale Pinciana

Via Sardegna

Via Sicilia

Via Marche

Via Leonida Bissolati

57

Via di San Basilio

50

Porta
Pinciana

Via Vittorio Veneto

Via Lazio

Via Lombardia

Via Emilia

Via Ludovisi

Via Versilia

Via di Porta Pinciana

Via Aurora

LUDOVISI

Via Liguria

Via Molise

Via Vittorio Veneto

17

Galoppatoio

Viale San Paolo del Brasile

Via della
Purificazione

109

Viale del Galoppatoio

45

Via Francesco Crispi

Via degli Artisti

Viale del Muro Torto

Via Sistina

Via Gregoriana

76

See map
p316

35

11

Piazza di Spagna
& the Spanish Steps

104

107

Piazza
Mignanelli

Viale di Villa Medici

Via San
Sebastianello

68

M Spagna

73

110

6

23

Via Frattina

Viale Trinità dei Monti

CAMPO
MARZIO

89

34

Via Albert

60

80

66

91

96

78

56

82

Via Borgognona

Via del Babuino

Vic del
Babuino

106

88

58

62

63

64

Via Mario de' Fiori

33

Via Bocca di Leone

Via Margutta

100

54

71

Via delle
Carrozze

94

48

38

83

52

Via Gesù
e Maria

Via di San
Giacomo

Via dei Greci

101

Via della Croce

Via Vittoria

Via Belsiana

93

Pincio
Hill

30

Viale D'Annunzio

39

81

47

Via Laurina

Via del Corso

Via Canova

97

90

84 102

Basilica di Santa
Maria del Popolo

70

79

105

10

9

13

36

Via della Frezzetta

Via Canova

25

Piazza Augusto
Imperatore

Largo
degli
Schiavoni

Via del Condotti

Via Tomacelli

85

95

Piazza del
Popolo

31

5

43

49

42

72

69

Via di Ripetta

26

Largo
San
Rocco

Via dell'Arancio

Via P
Clotilde

Via Ferdinando
di Savoia

75

46

51 77

112

Via del Vantaggio

Pass di Ripetta

Lgt in Augusta

Ponte
Cavour

Lgt Marzio

Via della
Penna

108

Via Angelo Brunetti

Tiber River

Via della Fontanella

37

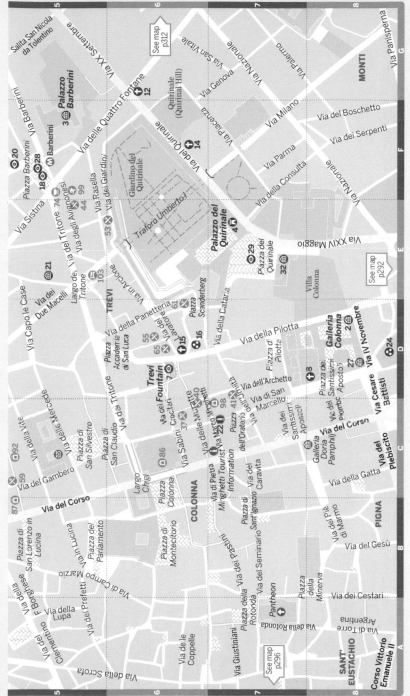

TRIDENTE, TREVI & THE QUIRINALE Map on p300

TRIDENTE, TREVI & THE QUIRINALE

VATICAN CITY, BORGO & PRATI

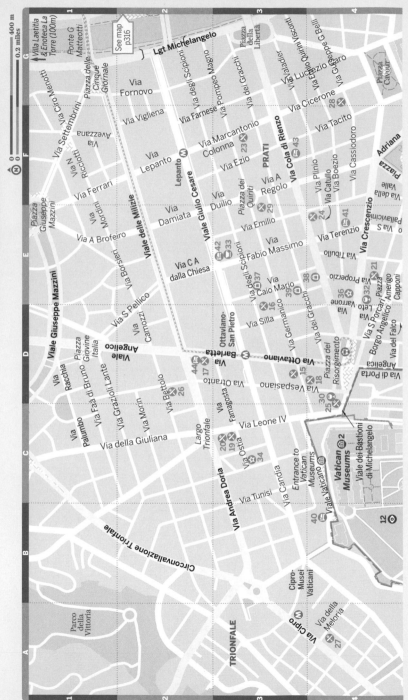

See map p316

◎ Top Sights p118

1 St Peter's Basilica...............C5
2 Vatican Museums................C4

◎ Sights p130

3 Castel Sant'Angelo..............F5
4 Museo Storico Artistico...C6
5 Necropoli Via
   Triumphalis....................C5
6 Ponte Sant'Angelo...........F5
7 Sistine Chapel...................C5
8 St Peter's Basilica
   Dome...............................C5

9 St Peter's Square................D5
10 Stanze di Raffaello.............C5
11 Tomb of St Peter................C5
12 Vatican Gardens.................B4
13 Vatican Grottoes................C5

◎ Eating p131

14 Cotto Crudo........................E5
15 Dal Toscano........................D3
16 Del Frate.............................D3
17 Dolce Maniera.....................D2
18 Fa-Bìo..................................D4
19 Fatamorgana.......................C3

20 Hostaria Dino e Toni........C3
21 Il Sorpasso...........................E4
22 La Veranda..........................E5
23 Mondo Arancina.................F3
24 Mo's Gelaterie....................C5
25 Old Bridge...........................D4
26 Oster a dell'Angelo............D2
27 Pizzarium............................A4
28 Ristorante
   L'Arcangelo......................G4
29 Velavevodeto Ai
   Quiriti...............................E3

◉ Drinking & Nightlife p133

30 Be.re...................................C3
31 Makasar Bistrot.................E4
32 Passaguai...........................E5
33 Sciascia Caffè.....................E3

◉ Entertainment p133

34 Alexanderplatz...................C3
35 Auditorium
   Conciliazione...................E5
36 Fonclea................................E4

◉ Shopping p133

37 Il Sellaio.............................E3
38 Piazza dell' Unità..............E4
39 Rechicle...............................E3

◎ Sleeping p213

40 Casa di Accoglienza
   Paolo VI...........................B4
41 Colors Hotel........................E4
42 Fabio Massimo Design
   Hotel................................E3
43 Le Stanze di Orazio...........F3
44 Quod Libet...........................D2

SAN GIOVANNI & TESTACCIO

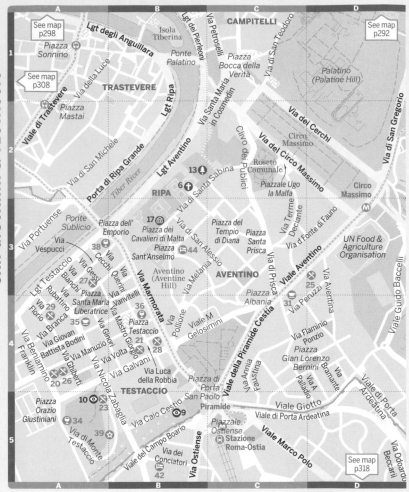

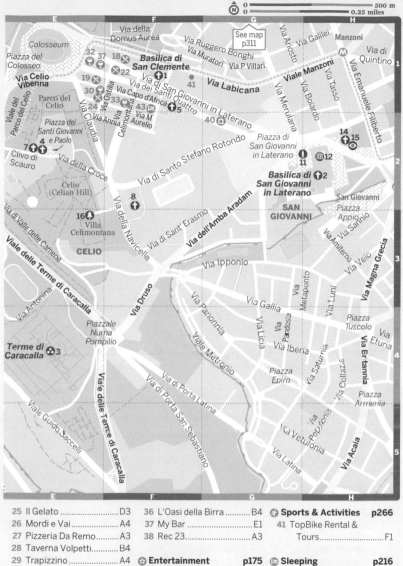

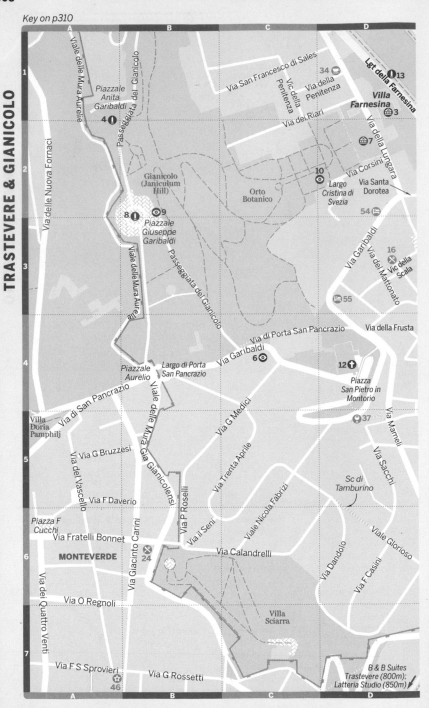

Key on p310

Viale delle Mura Aurelie

Passeggiata del Gianicolo

Piazzale Anita Garibaldi

4

Via San Francesco di Sales

34

13

Lgt della Farnesina

Villa Farnesina

3

Vic della Penitenza

Via della Penitenza

Via dei Riari

Via della Lungara

7

Via delle Nuova Fornaci

Gianicolo (Janiculum Hill)

Orto Botanico

10

Largo Cristina di Svezia

Via Corsini

Via Santa Dorotea

54

8 9

Piazzale Giuseppe Garibaldi

Via Garibaldi

16

Vic della Scala

Via del Mattonato

Passeggiata del Gianicolo

55

Via della Frusta

Viale delle Mura Aurelia

Via di Porta San Pancrazio

Via Garibaldi

6

12

Piazza San Pietro in Montorio

Piazzale Aurelio

Largo di Porta San Pancrazio

Via G Medici

Via Mameli

Villa Doria Pamphilj

Via di San Pancrazio

Viale delle Mura Gia Gianicolensi

37

Via Sacchi

Via G Bruzzesi

Via Trenta Aprile

Sc di Tamburino

Via del Vascello

Via F Daverio

Via P Roselli

Via il Seni

Viale Nicola Fabrizi

Viale Glorioso

Piazza F Cucchi

Via Fratelli Bonnet

Via Giacinto Carini

MONTEVERDE

24

Via Calandrelli

Via Dandolo

Via F Casini

Via O Regnoli

Villa Sciarra

Via dei Quattro Venti

Via F S Sprovieri

46

Via G Rossetti

B & B Suites Trastevere (800m); Latteria Studio (850m)

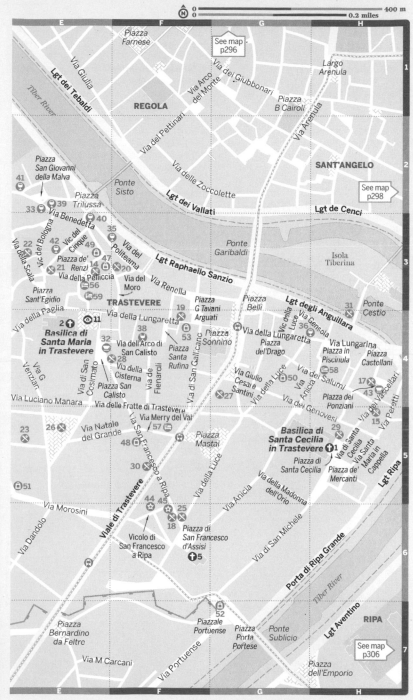

TRASTEVERE & GIANICOLO *Map on p308*

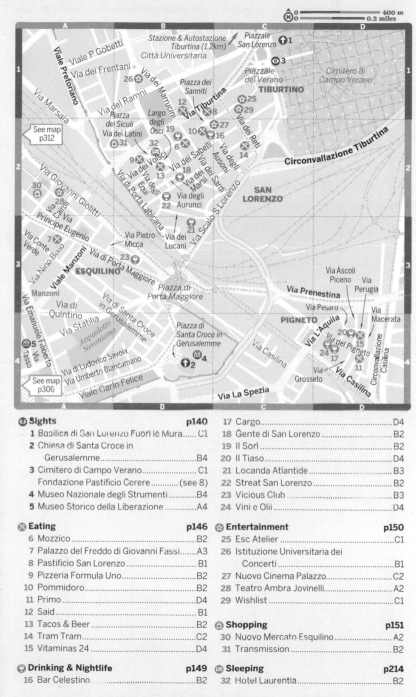

Key on p314

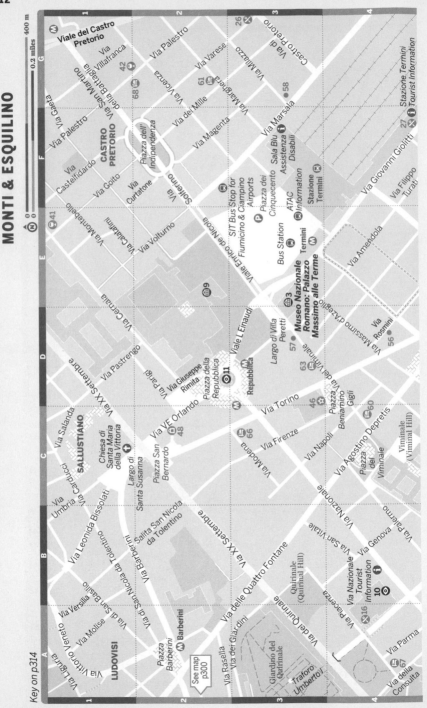

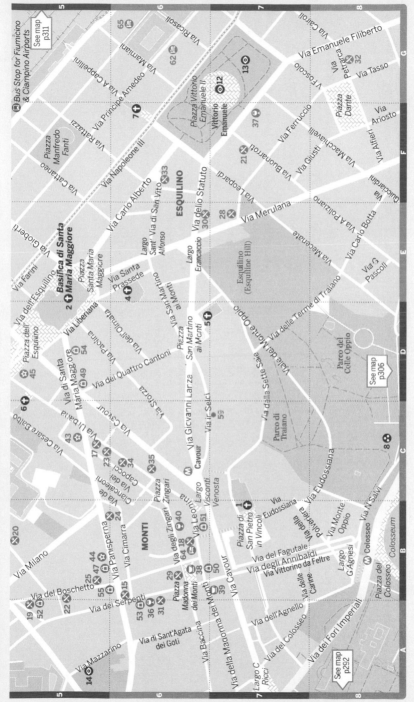

MONTI & ESQUILINO

Bus Stop for Fiumicino & Ciampino Airports

See map p311

Via A Cappellini

Via Mamiani

65

Via Ricasoli

62

Via Principe Amedeo

Via Emanuele Filiberto

Via Petrarca

32

Via Tasso

V Foscolo

7

Piazza Vittorio Emanuele II

13

Piazza Dante

Via Ariosto

Via Alfieri

Via Ratazzi

Via Napoleone III

Vittorio Emanuele

12

37

Via Ferruccio

Piazza Manfredo Fanti

Via Cattaneo

Via Carlo Alberto

33

ESQUILINO

Via dello Statuto

21

Via Buonarroti

Via Giusti

Via Machiavelli

Via Buonarroti

Via Giotberti

Via Farini

Basilica di Santa Maria Maggiore

2

Piazza Santa Maria Maggiore

Largo Sant' Via di San Vito Alfonso

Largo Brancaccio

30

28

Via Merulana

Via A Poliziano

Via Carlo Botta

Via G Pascoli

Via Libertana

Via Santa Prassede

4

Via San Martino ai Monti

Esquilino (Esquiline Hill)

Via dell'Olmata

5

Piazza San Martino ai Monti

Piazza dell' Esquilino

45

Via di Santa Maria Maggiore

54

Via dei Quattro Cantoni

Via Paolina

Via Urbana

Via Panisperna

Via Sforza

Via Giovanni Larza

Viale del Monte Oppio

Via delle Terme di Traiano

6

43

17

23

34

35

Via Cavour

Via ir Selci

59

Parco di Traiano

See map p306

Parco del Colle Oppio

Via Cesare Balbo

Via dei Cianfaleoni

Via de Capocci

Piazza Zingari

Via degli Zingari

M Cavour

Largo Visconti Venosta

Via delle Sette Sale

8

20

MONTI

24

Via Cimarra

64

18

40

Via Leonina

51

Piazza di San Pietro in Vincoli

1

Via Eudossiana

Via della Polveriera

Via Eudossiana

44

29

38

50

Via del Fagutale

Via degli Annibaldi

Via Monte Oppio

Via N Salvi

Colosseo M

25

47

55

15

39

Madonna dei Monti

Via Vittorino da Feltre

Largo G Agnesi

Piazza del Colosseo

Via del Boschetto

22

Piazza Madonna dei Monti

Via delle Carine

Colosseo

19

52

53

36

31

Via dei Serpenti

Via Cavour

Via del Colosseo

Colosseum

Via Milano

Via Baccina

Via di Sant'Agata dei Goti

Via della Madonna dei Monti

Via dell'Agnello

14

Via Mazzarino

Largo C Ricci

Via del Colosseo

Via dei Fori Imperiali

See map p292

VILLA BORGHESE & NORTHERN ROME *Map on p316*

VILLA BORGHESE & NORTHERN ROME

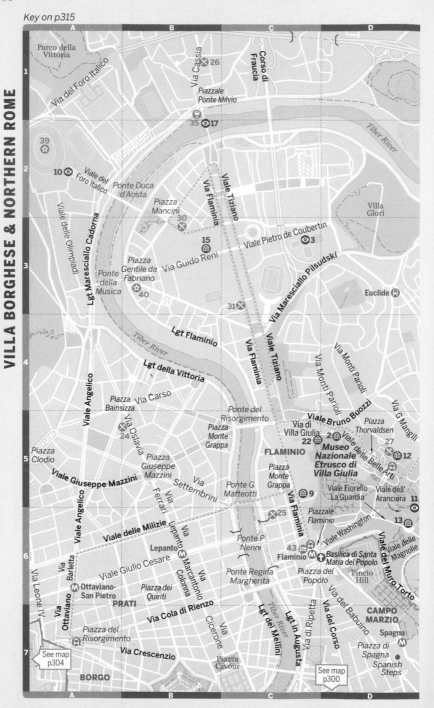

VILLA BORGHESE & NORTHERN ROME

Parco della Vittoria

Via del Foro Italico

Via Cassia **26**

Piazzale Ponte Milvio

Corso di Fraucia

Tiber River

35 **17**

39

10

Viale del Foro Italico

Ponte Duca d'Aosta

Piazza Mancini

30

Via Flaminia

Via Tiziano

Villa Glori

Viale delle Olimpiadi

Lgt Maresciallo Cadorna

Viale Pietro de Coubertin **3**

15

Via Guido Reni

Piazza Gentile da Fabriano

Ponte della Musica

40

Via Maresciallo Pilsudski

Euclide

31

Lgt Flaminio

Via Flaminia

Via Tiziano

Lgt della Vittoria

Via Flaminia

Viale Angelico

Piazza Bainsizza

Via Carso

Ponte del Risorgimento

Via Monti Parioli

Viale Bruno Buozzi

Via G Mangili

Piazza Thorvaldsen

Via Oslavia

24

Piazza Giuseppe Mazzini

Via Settembrini

Piazza Monte Grappa

Via di Villa Giulia

22 **2**

27

Viale delle Belle Arti

12

FLAMINIO

Museo Nazionale Etrusco di Villa Giulia

Piazza Clodio

Viale Giuseppe Mazzini

Via Ferrari

Via Lepanto

Ponte G Matteotti

Piazza Monte Grappa

9

Viale Fiorello La Guardia

Viale dell' Aranciera

11

Viale delle Milizie

Lepanto

Via Marcantonio Colonna

Ponte P Nenni

Via Flaminia

25

Piazzale Flaminio

13

Viale Angelico

Viale Giulio Cesare

Piazza dei Quiriti

Ponte Regina Margherita

Viale Washington

43

Flaminio

Basilica di Santa Maria del Popolo

Piazza del Popolo

Pincio Hill

Viale del Muro Torto

Viale delle Magnolie

Via Barletta

Via Leone IV

Ottaviano-San Pietro

PRATI

Via Cola di Rienzo

Via Cicerone

Lgt del Mellini

Lgt in Augusta

Tiber River

Via di Ripetta

Via del Babuino

Via del Corso

CAMPO MARZIO

Spagna

Via Ottaviano

Piazza del Risorgimento

Via Crescenzio

Piazza Cavour

Piazza di Spagna

Spanish Steps

See map p304

BORGO

See map p300

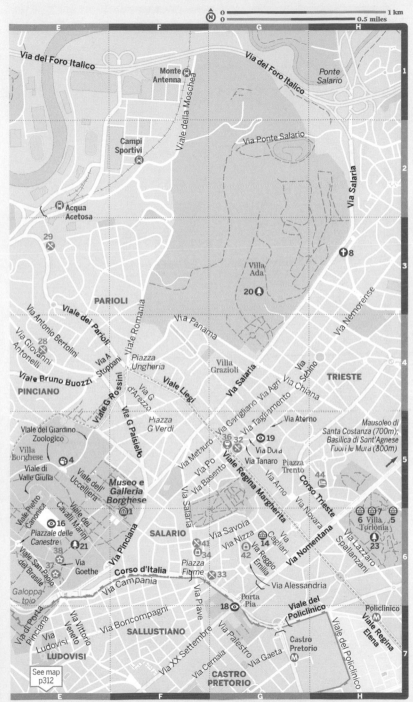

0 | 1 km
0 | 0.5 miles

Via del Foro Italico
Monte Antenna
Ponte Salario
Via del Foro Italico
Viale della Moschea
Campi Sportivi
Via Salaria
Via Ponte Salario
Acqua Acetosa
29
8
Villa Ada
20
PARIOLI
Via Panama
Via Antonio Bertolini
Viale dei Parioli
Via Nemorense
Via Giovanni Antonelli
28
Via A. Stoppani
Viale Romania
Piazza Ungheria
Villa Grazioli
Viale Bruno Buozzi
Viale G. Rossini
Via G. d'Arezzo
Viale Liegi
Via Salaria
Via Chiana
Via Sebino
TRIESTE
PINCIANO
Piazza G Verdi
Via Gariglano
Via Agri
Via Tagliamento
Via Aterno
Mausoleo di Santa Costanza (700m); Basilica di Sant'Agnese Fuori le Mura (800m)
Viale del Giardino Zoologico
Via G Paisiello
Via Metauro
36 32
19
Via Dora
Villa Borghese
4
Via Po
Viale Regina Margherita
Via Tanaro
Piazza Trento
Via Arno
Corso Trieste
44
Viale di Valle Giulia
Viale dell'Uccelliera
Via Basento
Via Salaria
Via Novara
Museo e Galleria Borghese
1
SALARIO
Via Savoia
Via Nizza
Cagliari
Via Nomentana
Via Lazzaro Spallanzani
6 Villa Torlonia 5
7
Via Pietro Canonica
16
Viale dei Cavalli Marini
Piazzale delle Canestre
21
Via Pinciana
41
34
14
42
Via Reggio Emilia
23
38
37
Via Goethe
Corso d'Italia
Piazza Fiume
33
Via Alessandria
Viale San Paolo del Brasile
Galoppa-toio
Via Campania
Via Plave
18
Porta Pia
Viale del Policlinico
Policlinico
Via di Porta Pinciana
Via Vittorio Veneto
Via Boncompagni
Castro Pretorio
Viale Regina Elena
Ludovisi
LUDOVISI
SALLUSTIANO
Via XX Settembre
Via Palestro
Via Gaeta
CASTRO PRETORIO
Via Cernaia
Viale del Policlinico

See map p312

SOUTHERN ROME

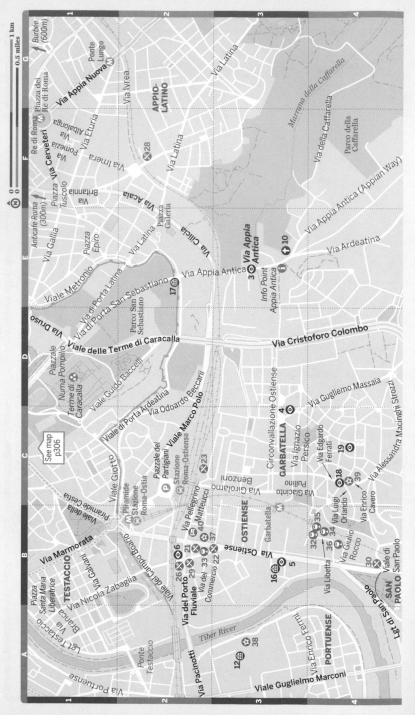

Burbée (600m)

Anticafe Roma (300m)

See map p306

Ponte Lungo

Piazza dei Re di Roma

Re di Roma

Via Appia Nuova

Via Albalonga

Via Pomezia

Via Cerveteri

Via Eturia

Via Imera

Via Britannia

Via Tuscolo

APPIO-LATINO

Via Latina

Via Latina

Via Latina

Marrana della Caffarella

Via della Caffarella

Parco della Caffarella

Piazza Galeria

Via Acaia

Via Cilicia

Via Latina

Via Appia Antica (Appian Way)

Via Ardeatina

Via Appia Antica

Info Point Appia Antica

Via Gallia

Piazza Tuscolo

Piazza Epiro

Via Metronio

Viale Metronio

Piazzale Numa Pompilio

Terme di Caracalla

Viale delle Terme di Caracalla

Via Druso

Via di Porta Latina

Via di Porta San Sebastiano

Parco San Sebastiano

Viale Guido Baccelli

Viale di Porta Ardeatina

Via Odoardo Beccarii

Viale Marco Polo

Via Cristoforo Colombo

Circonvallazione Ostiense

Via Guglielmo Massaia

Via Alessandra Macinghi Strozzi

GARBATELLA

Via Ignazio Persico

Via Edgardo Ferrati

Via Giacinto Pullino

Via Girolamo Benzoni

Via Enrico Cavero

Via Luigi Orlando

Via Giulio Rocco

Viale della Piramide Cestia

Viale Giotto

Piramide

Stazione Roma-Ostia

Stazione Roma-Ostia

Piazzale dei Partigiani

Via Marmorata

TESTACCIO

Piazza Santa Maria Liberatrice

Via Nicola Zabaglia

Via Galvani

Via Branca

Lgt Testaccio

Ponte Testaccio

Via del Campo Boario

Viale del Porto Fluviale

Via del Commercio

Via Pellegrino Matteucci

OSTIENSE

Via Ostiense

Garbatella

PORTUENSE

Tiber River

Via Pacinotti

Via Enrico Fermi

Viale Guglielmo Marconi

Via Portuense

SAN PAOLO

Viale di San Paolo

Lgt di San Paolo

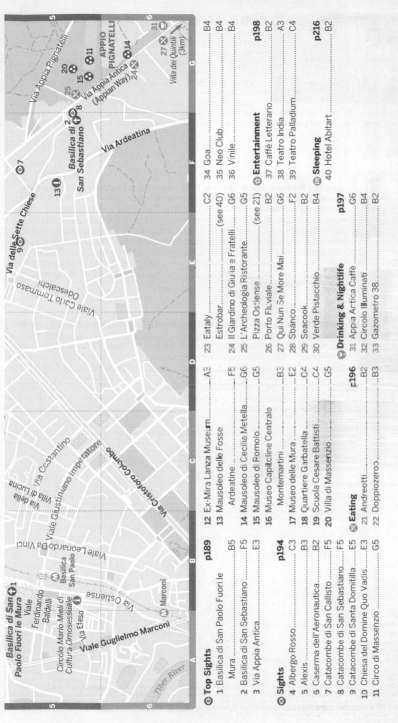

Our Story

A beat-up old car, a few dollars in the pocket and a sense of adventure. In 1972 that's all Tony and Maureen Wheeler needed for the trip of a lifetime – across Europe and Asia overland to Australia. It took several months, and at the end – broke but inspired – they sat at their kitchen table writing and stapling together their first travel guide, *Across Asia on the Cheap*. Within a week they'd sold 1500 copies. Lonely Planet was born.

Today, Lonely Planet has offices in Franklin, London, Melbourne, Oakland, Dublin, Beijing and Delhi, with more than 600 staff and writers. We share Tony's belief that 'a great guidebook should do three things: inform, educate and amuse'.

Our Writers

Duncan Garwood

Ancient Rome; Centro Storico; San Giovanni & Testaccio; Vatican City, Borgo & Prati; Villa Borghese & Northern Rome From facing fast bowlers in Barbados to sidestepping hungry pigs in Goa, Duncan's travels have thrown up many unique experiences. These days he largely dedicates himself to Italy, his adopted homeland where he's been living since 1997. From his base in the Castelli Romani hills outside Rome, he's clocked up endless kilometres exploring the country's well-known destinations and far-flung reaches, working on guides to Rome, Sardinia, Sicily, Piedmont, and Naples and the Amalfi Coast. His other LP titles include *Italy's Best Trips*, *Food Lover's Guide to the World*, and *Pocket Bilbao & San Sebastian*. He also writes on Italy for newspapers, websites and magazines.

Nicola Williams

Monti, Esquilino & San Lorenzo; Southern Rome; Trastevere & Gianicolo, Tridente, Trevi & the Quirinale Border-hopping is way of life for British writer, runner, foodie, art aficionado and mum-of-three Nicola Williams. She has lived in a French village on the southern side of Lake Geneva for more than a decade. Nicola has authored more than 50 guidebooks on Paris, Provence, Rome, Tuscany, France, Italy and Switzerland for Lonely Planet, and covers France as a destination expert for the *Telegraph*. She also writes for the *Independent*, *Guardian*, lonelyplanet.com, *Lonely Planet Magazine*, *French Magazine*, *Cool Camping France* and others. Catch her on the road on Twitter and Instagram at @tripalong.

Published by Lonely Planet Global Limited
CRN 554153
10th edition – Jan 2018
ISBN 978 1 78657 259 2
© Lonely Planet 2018   Photographs © as indicated 2018
10 9 8 7 6 5 4 3 2 1
Printed in China